THE ECONOMIC ACCOMPLICES TO THE ARGENTINE DICTATORSHIP

Much has been written about the Argentine dictatorship and the transitional justice movement that brought its members to justice. However, there has been no study to date of the economic accomplices to this dictatorship and the recent advancements in Argentina toward holding these actors accountable. What was the role of banks, companies, and individuals in perpetuating a murderous regime? To what extent should they be held responsible?

As the first academic study on economic complicity in Argentina, this book attempts to answer these questions. Renowned human rights scholars investigate the role played by such actors as Ford, Mercedes Benz, the press, foreign banks, and even the Catholic Church. Across numerous case studies, the authors make a compelling argument for the legal responsibility of economic accomplices.

A groundbreaking interdisciplinary study, this book will be essential to anyone interested in transitional justice, business, and human rights.

Horacio Verbitsky is President of Argentina's Center for Legal and Social Studies (CELS) and a member of the International Consortium of Investigative Journalists and of the Board of Human Rights Watch Americas. Author of twenty-one books, he has been named the best journalistic anchorman on Argentine TV.

Juan Pablo Bohoslavsky is the United Nations Independent Expert on Foreign Debt and Human Rights. A doctor of law with wide experience in international relations and litigation, he is the author of numerous books and articles on sovereign financing, economic complicity, and human rights.

The Economic Accomplices to the Argentine Dictatorship

OUTSTANDING DEBTS

Edited by

HORACIO VERBITSKY

Center for Legal and Social Studies, Buenos Aires

JUAN PABLO BOHOSLAVSKY

UN Independent Expert on Foreign Debt and Human Rights

Translated into English by

LAURA PÉREZ CARRARA

CAMBRIDGE
UNIVERSITY PRESS

CAMBRIDGE
UNIVERSITY PRESS

32 Avenue of the Americas, New York, NY 10013-2473, USA

Cambridge University Press is part of the University of Cambridge.

It furthers the University's mission by disseminating knowledge in the pursuit of education, learning, and research at the highest international levels of excellence.

www.cambridge.org
Information on this title: www.cambridge.org/9781107114197

Originally published in Spanish as Cuentas pendientes: Los cómplices económicos de la dictadura by Siglo Veintiuno Editores, Buenos Aires 2013

Third Spanish edition 2014

First English edition 2016

A catalog record for this publication is available from the British Library.

Library of Congress Cataloging in Publication Data
Cuentas pendientes. English
The economic accomplices to the Argentine dictatorship : outstanding debts / [edited by] Horacio Verbitsky, Juan Pablo Bohoslavsky.
pages cm
Includes bibliographical references and index.
ISBN 978-1-107-11419-7 (hardback)
1. Argentina – Economic policy. 2. Argentina – Economic conditions – 1945–1983. 3. Argentina – History – Dirty War, 1976–1983 – Economic aspects. 4. Business people – Argentina – Attitudes – History – 20th century. I. Verbitsky, Horacio. II. Bohoslavsky, Juan Pablo. III. Title.
HC175.C79513 2015
330.982′064–dc23 2015017086

ISBN 978-1-107-11419-7 Hardback

Contents

Contributors

Eduardo M. Basualdo holds a BA in Economics from the Pontifical Catholic University of Argentina (UCA) and a PhD in history from the School of Philosophy and Letters of the University of Buenos Aires (UBA). He is a senior researcher at the National Science and Technology Research Council (CONICET) and researcher and coordinator of the Economy and Technology area and the Master's Degree Program in Political Economy at the Latin American School of Social Sciences (FLACSO). He is also a member of the board at the Center for Legal and Social Studies (CELS) and coordinator of the Research and Training Center of the Republic of Argentina (CIFRA) of the Federation of Workers of Argentina (CTA).

Victoria Basualdo holds a PhD in history from Columbia University. She is a researcher at the CONICET based in FLACSO-Argentina and a professor in the Political Economy Master's Degree Program (FLACSO). She specializes in economic and labor history and has published books and several chapters and peer-reviewed journal articles on the subject.

Juan Pablo Bohoslavsky is Independent Expert on Foreign Debt and Human Rights of the United Nations. He previously worked at the United Nations Conference on Trade and Development (UNCTAD) and as a consultant for the United Nations Economic Commission for Latin America and the Caribbean (ECLAC). He has earned a doctoral degree in law, and his published works include books and articles on public debt, direct foreign investment, and human rights.

Alfredo Fernando Calcagno is an economist with a PhD from University Paris I. He is head of the Macroeconomics and Development Policies Branch at UNCTAD in Geneva. From 1984 to 1989, he held positions at the Secretariat of Planning, the National Economy Ministry, the Central Bank of the Republic of Argentina, and the International Economy Center. From 1989 to 2003, he worked as economist at ECLAC. He coauthored the book *El universo neoliberal* (2006), with Alfredo Eric Calcagno.

Agustín Cavana, a lawyer with a degree from the UBA, is an assistant legal and reporting counsel of the Court of Cassation in Criminal Matters of the Province of Buenos Aires. He was advisor to the National House of Representatives of Argentina. He is an undergraduate teaching assistant in the Criminal Law and Criminology Department, School of Law, UBA.

Alejandra Dandan holds a degree in social communications from the UBA and is currently pursuing a master's degree in anthropology (IDES-IDAES, National San Martín University). She is a journalist for *Página/12* and has coauthored the books *Los Juárez* (2004), *Joe Baxter: la historia secreta de un guerrillero* (2006), and *Nunca más y los crímenes de la dictadura* (2007).

Federico Delgado is a lawyer (UBA) and holds a bachelor's degree in political science (UBA). He is currently a lecturer at the University of Palermo and has taught in the past at the UBA and the Judicial School of the Association of Magistrates and Employees of the National Justice System. He is first instance prosecutor in the Criminal and Federal Correctional Courts of the City of Buenos Aires. He has published works on political philosophy, law, and sociology. He has completed a postgraduate course on corruption (UCA).

Leonardo Filippini is a lawyer (UBA) with a master's degree in law (University of Palermo and Yale University). He is a professor of undergraduate and graduate courses in the Universities of Buenos Aires and Palermo, and a parliamentary advisor. He has been a researcher at the International Center for Transitional Justice (ICTJ) and a consultant for organizations such as the German Technical Cooperation Agency (GTZ), the United Nations Development Program (UNDP), the ICTJ, and CELS.

Hannah Franzki holds a bachelor's degree in political science and a master's degree in international law, having studied in Marburg (Germany), Montevideo (Uruguay), and Warwick (United Kingdom). She is a doctoral candidate at the School of Law, Birkbeck College, University of London, with a scholarship from the Heinrich Böll Foundation. Her current project is concerned with the legal construction of the economic dimensions of state crimes. Her academic interests include critical theory of law, international criminal law, postcolonial studies, and philosophy of history. She is a member of the research team of the "Transnational Corporations and State Terrorism" DeCyt Project (UBA).

Andrea Gualde is a lawyer (UBA) with a master's degree in administrative law and a visiting researcher at Yale Law School. She served as National Director for Legal Affairs at the Human Rights Secretariat and is currently a professor at the Torcuato Di Tella University and in the Master's Degree Program on Human Rights at ECAE-UNTREF (School for Lawyers Employed by the State, Tres de Febrero

National University). She was an instructor at the Raphael Lemkin Seminar for Genocide Prevention, Auschwitz Institute (AIPR), Poland. In the past, she has chaired the Memorials and Museums Working Group of the International Holocaust Remembrance Alliance.

Mariana Heredia is a sociologist (UBA) and holds a PhD in sociology from École des Hautes Études en Sciences Sociales (EHESS) in Paris. She is a researcher at CONICET, a lecturer and researcher at the Institute of Higher Social Studies (IDAES) of the University of San Martín, a lecturer at the UBA, and an associate researcher at Institut des Recherche Interdisciplinaire sur les Enjeux Sociaux (IRIS-EHESS). She specializes in sociology of the elites and recent historical sociology of Argentina. She has published several articles in national and foreign journals, as well as the book *A quoi sert un économiste* (Paris: La découverte).

The International Commission of Jurists, composed of 60 eminent judges and lawyers from all regions of the world, promotes and protects human rights through the Rule of Law, by using its unique legal expertise to develop and strengthen national and international justice systems. Established in 1952 and active on the five continents, the ICJ aims to ensure the progressive development and effective implementation of international human rights and international humanitarian law.

Damián Loreti is a lawyer and holds a PhD in information sciences. He is CELS secretary and professor of information law at the School of Social Sciences of the UBA. He specializes in freedom of expression and the right to communication, and his published works include *América Latina y la libertad de expresión* (2005) and *Derecho a la información: relación entre medios, público y periodistas* (1995).

Victorio Paulón is a member of the action committee that organized the 1975 strike in the metalworks industry. He was arrested in 1975 and imprisoned until 1981. After his release he lived in exile in France until 1984, when he was reinstated in his job at the Villber factory, where he was elected for the position of press secretary of the UOM-Villa Constitución trade union with 88 percent of the votes. From 2000 to 2008 he served as general secretary of this organization. He is currently an international affairs secretary of the CTA.

Leigh A. Payne is Professor of Sociology and Latin America at the University of Oxford. Together with Tricia D. Olsen she has created the Corporate Human Rights Database. She has written extensively in books and journals on how societies reckon with past violence in authoritarian and civil conflict situations.

Gabriel Pereira is a postdoctoral researcher at the Department of Sociology of the University of Oxford. He completed his PhD in politics at the same institution. He writes in journals and books on fields including transitional justice, human rights, and judicial politics. He teaches political science at the University of San Pablo-T (Argentina). He is also Deputy Director of the human rights organization ANDHES.

Tomás Ojea Quintana is a lawyer specializing in human rights. He worked at the Inter-American Commission on Human Rights (IACHR) and was a coordinator of the OHCHR Program for Protection and Promotion of Human Rights in Bolivia. He represented the Grandmothers of Plaza de Mayo Association and was litigating counsel in cases of crimes against humanity, including the criminal action brought against Ford Argentina executives. He is currently UN Special Rapporteur on the situation of human rights in Myanmar.

Mario Rapoport holds a bachelor's degree in political economy (UBA), a PhD in history (University of Paris I / Pantheon-Sorbonne), and a Doctor Honoris Causa degree from the National University of San Juan. He is a consultant professor at the School of Economic Sciences and the School of Social Sciences, UBA, and a senior researcher at CONICET. His leading books include *Historia económica, política y social de la Argentina, 1880–2003* (2012, fifth ed.) and *Las crisis económicas del capitalismo contemporáneo* (2010). He was awarded the Bernardo Houssay prize for scientific research (CONICET) in 1987.

Héctor Recalde is a lawyer (UBA) specializing in labor law. He is a university professor, a national representative, chairman of the Labor Law Committee of the national House of Representatives, and a member of the National Council of the Judiciary. He has written various books and articles published in newspapers, magazines, and specialized journals.

Naomi Roht-Arriaza is Distinguished Professor of Law at the University of California, Hastings College of the Law. She is the author of *Impunity and Human Rights in International Law and Practice* (1995) and *The Pinochet Effect* (2005), coeditor of *Transitional Justice in the Twenty-First Century* (2006), and coauthor of *The International Legal System* (2010, sixth ed.). She is president of the Board of the Due Process of Law Foundation and member of the Advisory Council of the Center for Justice and Accountability.

Martín Schorr holds a PhD in social sciences from FLACSO. He is a member of the Scientific Researcher Course program at CONICET, a researcher at the Economy and Technology area of FLACSO, and a lecturer in undergraduate and graduate programs at the UBA, FLACSO, and the National San Martín University (UNSAM). His research focuses on Argentine economy in the period beginning in 1976.

Jorge E. Taiana is a sociologist (UBA), an elected representative in the Legislature of the Autonomous City of Buenos Aires, and Director of the International

Center for Political Studies at the National San Martín University (UNSAM). He has held public office as Ambassador and as Minister of Foreign Affairs of Argentina (2005–2010), among other high-ranking positions. At the international level, he served as Executive Secretary of the Inter-American Commission on Human Rights of the Organization of American States (1996–2001). He frequently lectures at universities and other institutions around the world and publishes articles on international relations and human rights. He has been decorated by several states in Latin America and other regions.

Claudio Tognonato holds a PhD in sociology and philosophy (Sapienza University of Rome) and teaches Economic Sociology and Development and History of Sociological Thought at Roma Tre University. A Jean Paul Sartre scholar, he founded a group for Sartrean studies in Italy. His publications include *Affari nostri. Diritti umani e rapporti Italia Argentina, 1976–1983* (2012), *Economia senza società. Oltre i limiti del mercato globale* (2014), and *Le corps du social. Esquisse pour une sociologie existentielle* (2014).

Carolina Varsky is a lawyer (UBA) and Assistant Secretary in Legal Matters at the Public Prosecutor's Office. She has worked at CELS since 1998, where she headed the Memory and Struggle against State Terrorism Impunity program, and later the Litigation and Legal Defense program. She has taught Human Rights and Constitutional Law and Information Law at the UBA. She has written numerous articles published in books and specialized journals.

Horacio Verbitsky is a writer and journalist. He is the author of twenty-one books on political, military, economic, ecclesiastic, and human rights issues. He is head of CELS and is member of the board of Human Rights Watch (Advisory Committee – Americas Division) and of the International Consortium of Investigative Journalists. He was a member of the steering council of Fundación del Nuevo Periodismo Iberoamericano since it was founded by Gabriel García Márquez.

Alfredo Zaiat is a journalist and economist. He is a feature writer at *Página/12* and chief of the Economy section. He works in radio and television as host and columnist. Among his published works are the books *Economistas o astrólogos* (2004), *Historia de la economía argentina del siglo XX* (2007), coauthored with Mario Rapoport, and *Economía a contramano* (2012). He is a lecturer in the Amartya Sen Program of the Economic Sciences School at the UBA. He served as an advisor for the "Economía y política. 200 años de historia" exhibit at Casa Nacional del Bicentenario (2011).

Acknowledgments

We would like to thank Laura Pérez Carrara for her work translating the book, Cambridge University Press for embarking on this project, Leigh Payne for encouraging us and helping us publish this version in English, Ricardo Julio de Titto for preparing the index, and Siglo Veintiuno Editores for authorizing this publication.

Abbreviations

ACDE	Asociación Cristiana de Dirigentes de Empresa (Christian Association of Business Leaders)
ACHR	American Convention on Human Rights
ADEBA	Asociación de Bancos Argentinos (Association of Argentine Banks)
ADEPA	Asociación de Entidades Periodísticas Argentinas (Association of Argentine News Bodies)
AECL	Atomic Energy of Canada Limited
AICA	Agencia Informativa Católica Argentina (Argentine Catholic Information Agency)
ANCLA	Agencia de Noticias Clandestina (Clandestine News Agency)
APCEA	Asamblea Plenaria de la Conferencia Episcopal Argentina (Plenary Assembly of the Argentine Episcopal Conference)
APEGE	Asamblea Permanente de Entidades Gremiales Empresarias (Permanent Assembly of Business Associations)
ATCA	Alien Tort Claims Act
ATE	Asociación Trabajadores del Estado (Association of State Workers)
ATS	Alien Tort Statute
BAC	Banco de Análisis y Computación (Analysis and Computing Bank)
BADECEL	Base de Datos Estadísticos de Comercio Exterior (Foreign Commerce Statistical Database)
BANADE	Banco Nacional de Desarrollo (National Development Bank)
BCRA	Banco Central de la República Argentina (Central Bank of the Republic of Argentina)
BEABA	Boletín Eclesiástico del Arzobispado de Buenos Aires (Ecclesiastic Bulletin of the Archbishopric of Buenos Aires)

BIT	Bilateral Investment Treaty
CACBA	Colegio de Abogados de la Ciudad de Buenos Aires (Bar Association of the City of Buenos Aires)
CADHU	Comisión Argentina de Derechos Humanos (Argentine Human Rights Commission)
CAL	Comisión de Asuntos Legislativos (Legislative Affairs Commission)
CARBAP	Confederaciones de Asociaciones Rurales de Buenos Aires y La Pampa (Confederation of Rural Associations of Buenos Aires and La Pampa)
CAFRA	Comitato Antifascista contro la Repressione in Argentina
CEA	Consejo Empresario Argentino (Argentine Business Council)
CEA	Conferencia Episcopal Argentina (Argentine Episcopal Conference)
CELS	Centro de Estudios Legales y Sociales (Center for Legal and Social Studies)
CEMA	Centro de Estudios Macroeconómicos de Argentina (Center for Macroeconomic Studies of Argentina)
CEPED	Centro de Estudios de Población, Empleo y Desarrollo (Center for Population, Employment, and Development Studies)
CGE	Confederación General Económica (General Economic Confederation)
CGT	Confederación General del Trabajo (General Confederation of Labor)
CGTA	CGT de los Argentinos (Argentines' CGT)
CIAE	Compañía Ítalo Argentina de Electricidad
CIA	Central Intelligence Agency
CIFRA	Research and Training Center of the Republic of Argentina
CISH	Centro de Investigaciones Socio Históricas (Socio-Historical Research Center)
CNV	Comisión Nacional de Valores (National Securities Commission)
COMFER	Comité Federal de Radiodifusión (Federal Broadcasting Committee)
CONADE	Consejo Nacional de Desarrollo (National Development Council)
CONADEP	Comisión Nacional sobre la Desaparición de Personas (National Commission on the Disappearance of Persons)

CONAE	Convocatoria Nacional Empresaria (National Business Call)
CONAREPA	Comisión Nacional de Responsabilidad Patrimonial (National Commission for Asset Responsibility)
CONICET	National Science and Technology Research Council
CONINAGRO	Confederación Intercooperativa Agropecuaria Limitada (Agricultural Inter-Cooperative Confederation Limited)
CONINTES	Conmoción Interna del Estado (State Internal Unrest)
CPI	Consumer Price Index
CPM	Comisión Provincial por la Memoria (Provincial Commission for Memory)
CPVR	Comisión Peruana de la Verdad y Reconciliación (Peruvian Truth and Reconciliation Commission)
CRA	Confederaciones Rurales Argentinas (Rural Confederations of Argentina)
CRM	Cuenta de Regulación Monetaria (Monetary Regulation Account)
CSJN	Corte Suprema de Justicia de la Nación (National Supreme Court)
CTA	Central de Trabajadores de la Argentina (Federation of Workers of Argentina)
DFID	Department for International Development
DIPBA	Dirección de Inteligencia de la Policía de la Provincia de Buenos Aires (Intelligence Division of the Buenos Aires Province Police)
ECLAC	Economic Commission for Latin America and the Caribbean
EHESS	École des Hautes Études en Sciences Sociales
ENI	Ente Nazionale Idrocarburi
ERP	Ejército Revolucionario del Pueblo (People's Revolutionary Army)
ESC rights	Economic, social, and cultural rights
ESMA	Escuela de Mecánica de la Armada (Naval Mechanics School)
FAA	Federación Agraria Argentina (Argentine Agrarian Federation)
FACA	Federación Argentina de Colegios de Abogados (Argentine Federation of Bar Associations)
FETIA	Federación de Trabajadores de la Industria y Afines (Federation of Industry and Related Workers)
FIEL	Fundación de Investigaciones Económicas Latinoamericanas (Foundation for Latin American Economic Research)

FLACSO	Facultad Latinoamericana de Ciencias Sociales (Latin American School of Social Sciences)
FNIA	Fiscalía Nacional de Investigaciones Administrativas (National Prosecutor's Office for Administrative Investigations)
FONAVI	Fondo Nacional de la Vivienda (National Housing Fund)
FORES	Foro de Estudios sobre la Administración de Justicia (Forum for Justice Administration Studies)
FOTIA	Federación Obrera Tucumana de la Industria del Azúcar (Tucumán Sugar Industry Workers' Federation)
GATT	General Agreement on Tariffs and Trade
GDP	Gross Domestic Product
GTZ	German Technical Cooperation Agency
IACHR	Inter-American Commission on Human Rights
I/A Court HR	Inter-American Court of Human Rights
IADE	Instituto Argentino para el Desarrollo Económico (Argentine Institute for Economic Development)
IAPA	Inter-American Press Association
IATRA	Inter-American Treaty of Reciprocal Assistance
IBRD	International Bank for Reconstruction and Development
ICC	International Chamber of Commerce
ICE	Istituto del Commercio Estero
ICJ	International Commission of Jurists
ICSID	International Center for Settlement of Investment Disputes
ICTJ	International Center for Transitional Justice
IDAES	Instituto de Altos Estudios Sociales (Institute of Higher Social Studies)
IDEP	Instituto de Estudios sobre Estado y Participación – CTA (Institute for Studies on State and Participation)
IDES	Instituto para el Desarrollo Económico y Social (Economic and Social Development Institute)
IEERAL-FM	Instituto de Estudios Económicos de la Realidad Argentina y Latinoamericana de la Fundación Mediterránea (Institute for Economic Studies on Argentine and Latin American Reality of the Mediterranean Foundation)
IMF	International Monetary Fund
INDEC	Instituto Nacional de Estadística y Censos (National Statistics and Census Institute)
INGO	International nongovernmental organization
JTP	Juventud Trabajadora Peronista (Peronist Working Youth)
LCT	Ley de Contrato de Trabajo (Employment Contract Act)

LIA	Liga Independiente Antiimperialista (Anti-Imperialist Independent League)
Merval	Mercado de Valores de Buenos Aires (Buenos Aires Stock Market)
NAM	Non-Aligned Movement
NATO	North Atlantic Treaty Organization
NGO	Nongovernmental Organization
OAS	Organization of American States
OPEC	Organization of Petroleum Exporting Countries
OPIC	Overseas Private Investment Corporation
PCR	Partido Comunista Revolucionario (Revolutionary Communist Party)
PFA	Policía Federal Argentina (Federal Police of Argentina)
PLANARA	Plan Nacional de Radiodifusión (National Broadcasting Plan)
SCBA	Suprema Corte de Justicia de la Provincia de Buenos Aires (Supreme Court of Justice of the Province of Buenos Aires)
SIPRI	Stockholm International Peace Research Institute
SMATA	Sindicato de Mecánicos y Afines del Transporte Automotor (Union of Automotive Transport Mechanics and Related Workers)
SOEAIL	Sindicato de Obreros y Empleados del Azúcar del Ingenio Ledesma (Union of Sugar Workers and Employees of Ingenio Ledesma)
SOMISA	Sociedad Mixta Siderúrgica Argentina
SRA	Sociedad Rural Argentina (Argentine Rural Society)
SWIID	Standardized World Income Inequality Database
TRC	Truth and Reconciliation Commission (South Africa)
UBA	University of Buenos Aires
UCA	Pontifical Catholic University of Argentina
UCR	Unión Cívica Radical (Radical Civic Union Party)
UCRI	Unión Cívica Radical Intransigente (Intransigent Radical Civic Union Party)
UNCITRAL	United Nations Commission on International Trade Law
UNCTAD	United Nations Conference on Trade and Development
UNDP	United Nations Development Program
UNGS	Universidad Nacional de General Sarmiento
UNITA	União Nacional para a Independência Total de Angola
UNSAM	Universidad Nacional de San Martín
UNTS	United Nations Treaty Series
UOM	Unión Obrera Metalúrgica (Metalworkers' Union)

UTA	Unión Tranviarios Automotor (Automotive Tramway Workers' Union)
VAT	Value Added Tax
YPF	Yacimientos Petrolíferos Fiscales (State Oil Company)

Introduction

State Terrorism and the Economy: From Nuremberg to Buenos Aires

Horacio Verbitsky and Juan Pablo Bohoslavsky

The year 2015 marks thirty-two consecutive years without a coup d'état interrupting Argentina's democratic institutional process. This had not happened before in two centuries of republican existence. Thus, more than recovering democracy, as was the preferred formula in 1983, what is commemorated today is its foundational experience. The demand for memory, truth, and justice was one of the common threads running through that process, which experienced advances and setbacks until, in 2001, the impunity laws and decrees were declared null by the courts and the proceedings that had been interrupted from 1987 to 1990 after the military uprisings were resumed.

As of August 2014, 506 convictions and 90 acquittals or dismissals had been handed down in the trials conducted throughout the country, according to the figures from the Center for Legal and Social Studies. This proportion reveals them to be true acts of justice in which nobody has been convicted without proof. In all these cases the defendants were either direct perpetrators of crimes against humanity committed in the 1970s and 1980s or they were armchair perpetrators of such crimes. Among those convicted are military officers, policemen, agents of other security forces, a civilian minister of the terrorist state, and a Catholic priest.

Although the structural economic causes of the dictatorship, the repression of workers, and the consequences of the economic policies implemented during that period have all been subject of attention and study since the return to democracy, it has only been in recent years that the focus has been placed also on the role and possible responsibility (whether political, criminal, or civil) of the individuals, bodies, and companies that supplied goods and/or services to the dictatorship or obtained benefits from it while they provided political support in return, thus consolidating the regime and facilitating the execution of its criminal plan.

The views and conclusions presented in this introduction are solely those of the authors and are in no way intended to reflect those of the institutions with which they are affiliated.

The term "military dictatorship" is being increasingly abandoned in favor of other more complex terms that more closely reflect the reality of a bloc that was formed by civilian, military, business, and Church elements. Businesspersons who are criminally prosecuted for contributing to the disappearance of their workers,[1] victims who sue the banks that financed the dictatorship,[2] economic actions filed in labor courts for detentions in the workplace that resulted in disappearances and are declared not subject to statutory limitations,[3] sentences that call for investigating the editorial complicity of newspapers,[4] effective prosecution requests against media entrepreneurs for having carried out information manipulation campaigns in connivance with the government's repressive plans,[5] prosecutions for extortion of businesspersons and the seizing of their property,[6] the state investigation into the Papel Prensa case,[7] and the establishment under the National Secretariat of Human Rights of a special unit for the investigation of crimes against humanity motivated by economic interests[8] and an office for the coordination of human rights, memory, truth, and justice policies within the National Securities Commission (Comisión Nacional de Valores, CNV)[9] are some of the signs of this new tendency.[10]

What changed in Argentina to explain this recent and astonishing growth in interest and efforts in holding economic accomplices accountable? The answer contains both global and domestic factors.

At the international level, the jurisprudence of the Nuremberg International Military Tribunal was clear with respect to the responsibility of the entrepreneurs who had provided goods and services to the Nazi state machinery:

> [T]hose who execute the plan do not avoid responsibility by showing that they acted under the direction of the man who conceived it.... [That person] had

1 See the cases of Blaquier (Ingenio Ledesma) in Chapter 13 and Ford and Mercedes Benz in Chapter 11 in this book.

2 On this action, see Chapter 7.

3 On the Ingegnieros ruling, see Chapter 12.

4 For example, these sentences ordered the investigation of the role played by *La Nueva Provincia* in featuring information on alleged military clashes with supposed subversive elements during the dictatorship. Tribunal Oral Federal de Bahía Blanca, "Bayón, Juan Manuel y otros s. privación ilegal de la libertad agravada," sentence of September 12, 2012.

5 On the directors of the newspaper *La Nueva Provincia*, see Diego Martínez, "Un engranaje más dentro del plan criminal," *Página/12* (Buenos Aires), May 11, 2013, and "Hechos que muestran complicidad con la dictadura," *Página/12* (Buenos Aires), May 12, 2013.

6 See Chapters 18, 19, and 20.

7 Secretaría de Comercio Interior, Resolution 126/10.

8 Decree 3216/10.

9 Comisión Nacional de Valores, Resolution 594/11.

10 Between August and October 2012, the School of Economic Sciences of the University of Buenos Aires held a conference on economic power and state terrorism ("Poder económico y terrorismo de Estado") that examined the consolidation of that same tendency.

> to have the co-operation of statesmen, military leaders, diplomats, and business men. When they, with knowledge of his aims, gave him their cooperation, they made themselves parties to the plan he had initiated. They are not to be deemed innocent ... if they knew what they were doing.[11]

However, after the trials of the immediate postwar, issues associated with the responsibility of non-state individuals in human rights violations entered a cone of silence in international law. The reason for this silence was the prevailing paradigm that the beast of human rights was in the state itself, not outside it. Another influencing factor in this was the start of the cold war, with its call to forget the responsibilities of significant sectors in the new alliances.

The end of the cold war and the beginning of what is known as the process of globalization, shaped by the growth of transnational corporations, highlighted the power and immense capacity for harming human rights that lay outside the state. That explains, to a great extent, why in the past ten years the international community has moved forward in gradual agreements for the application of human rights standards to companies. The adoption in 2011 of the Guiding Principles on Business and Human Rights (Ruggie Report) by the United Nations Human Rights Council marked the formal crystallization of that process.

Also, the more recent truth commissions have begun to consider both the economic problems that underlie armed conflicts and authoritarian regimes and the behavior adopted by businesspersons during those periods. This is the case of the commissions in Kenya, Liberia, Sierra Leone, South Africa, and Timor-Leste.

This trend in international law was furthered by the hundreds of judicial actions brought in dozens of countries with the aim of holding companies accountable for their involvement in or facilitation of human rights abuses.[12] U.S. jurisprudence, in application of the Alien Tort Claims Act (ATCA),[13] has played a reference role in this subject, having found companies guilty for violating human rights abroad. Academia has also done its part, with business and human rights becoming one of the major issues of contemporary debate in international law.[14]

[11] The Nuremberg Trial (*United States v. Goering*), 6 F.R.D. 69, 112 (Int'l Mil. Trib. at Nuremberg, 1946). See, more extensively, F. Nicosia and J. Huener (eds.), *Business and Industry in Nazi Germany* (New York and Oxford: Berghahn Books, 2004).

[12] C. Hutto and A. Jenkins, "Report on Corporate Complicity Litigation in the Americas: Leading Doctrines, Relevant Cases, and Analysis of Trends," in *Human Rights Clinic* (Texas: University of Texas, 2010).

[13] On this U.S. law, see Chapter 9.

[14] See, for example, A. Clapham, *Human Rights Obligations of Non-State Actors* (Oxford: Oxford University Press, 2006); and, more specifically in the field of transitional justice, S. Michalowski (ed.), *Corporate Accountability in the Context of Transitional Justice* (London: Routledge, 2013); D. Sharp (ed.), *Justice and Economic Violence in Transition* (New York: Springer Publications, 2013).

In the past few years, the tailwind of international law has shifted the course toward non-state actors, thus encouraging the widening of the rings of responsibility to include economic accomplices, and that tendency has reached Argentina.

At the national level, the establishment of the National Commission on the Disappearance of Persons (CONADEP) in 1983 (which was the world's first truth commission) produced a double "process of osmosis between Argentina and the international human rights system," which intensified after the resumption of trials in the first decade of the twenty-first century. On the one hand, Argentina's political processes and domestic judicial production "influenced the evolution of the international human rights system." On the other hand, the country has developed a great receptivity to approaches originating from other parts of the world.[15]

The trials against military and police perpetrators are a consolidated reality. As the president of the Supreme Court of Justice, Ricardo Lorenzetti, said: they are part of the social contract of Argentines,[16] so that it is difficult to imagine new scenarios of amnesty and impunity. In this way, the fact that the most severe and cruel behaviors have found their way to justice makes it possible to expand the scope and analyze the context in which those crimes were committed, focusing on civilian, economic, and Church accomplices, whose contributions *enabled, facilitated, or improved the efficiency in* the commission of such crimes.[17]

At the same time, the gradual – but insufficient – systematization of information and investigations on the role played by numerous companies has led to the development of novel ideas and perspectives regarding economic complicity.

Are economic actors relevant in the framework of authoritarian regimes? In a context in which fundamental human rights are systematically violated, democratic deliberations are, by definition, silenced. In a sense, there are some certainties, from the perspective of rational choice, about how such a regime will behave: it will try to stay in power by guaranteeing privileges for the elites and/or the military.[18] For that purpose it has two instruments available, and its success will depend on the interaction and balance between the two.

On the one hand, authoritarian governments can assign civil and political freedoms, yielding to the demands of greater democratization, or denying them by repressing. On the other hand, they can also assign – or deny – economic resources

[15] See P. de Stefani, "La contribución de Argentina al afianzamiento internacional de los derechos humanos," conference delivered at University of Padua, April 22, 2012.

[16] R. Lorenzetti and A. Kraut, *Derechos humanos: justicia y reparación* (Buenos Aires: Sudamericana, 2011), pp. 9–10.

[17] International Commission of Jurists, *Corporate Complicity & Legal Accountability*, Geneva, vol. I, 2008, pp. 8 and ff.

[18] G. O'Donnell, "Reflections on the Patterns of Change in the Bureaucratic-Authoritarian State" (1978) 13 *Latin American Research Review*, 6.

with the aim of purchasing loyalties in key economic and political sectors. Using these instruments – effective repression and the purchasing of loyalties – requires means.[19]

Contributing to the regular and efficient operation of a regime that commits systematic human rights abuses entails helping that regime attain its main objective: perpetrating the crimes in line with the political and economic purposes of the organization. In this sense, with the argument that a shortage of resources hinders and limits the criminal action that is sought to be prevented, the United Nations Security Council applies economic sanctions. In fact, the government of the United States, during the Jimmy Carter administration, repeatedly denied the granting of financial aid to Argentina's military junta because of the systematic human rights abuses that were being committed in the country.[20]

The explanation of the role of economic actors in authoritarian contexts from the theory of rational choice must be complemented with an interdisciplinary historical and analytical narrative – as is developed in numerous chapters in this book – of the link between the criminal state and the economy during the Argentine dictatorship. The nature of that link was determined by the (imposed) supremacy of the armed forces over the constitutional order and their will to remain in power and seize the resources that such an enterprise required, but that did not prevent sectors of the economy from forging the scenario of the coup and its economic plan, from treating the military as their equals or ordering them at times, or even from co-participating in coercive state power to repress and commit criminal acts, as is shown in Part V of this book.

In 2012, in the criminal trial that investigates the complicity of the owners and executives of the sugar mill Ingenio Ledesma in the disappearance of numerous workers, the judge clearly explained that

> the jailing, torturing, murdering, and disappearing of individuals by the security forces during the last civilian-military dictatorship were, thus, not only motivated by the desire to preserve a given ideology, but rather the purpose of the illegal repression was to establish and defend an economic model with neoliberal overtones that would be free of threats from labor demands and claims.[21]

This statement by a court reveals the intricate relationship that existed between the activities and interests of the state and those of certain economic sectors. This poses the need to develop and apply a political, economic, and legal theory that is

19 See B. Bueno de Mesquita et al., *The Logic of Political Survival* (Massachusetts: MIT Press, 2003), and R. Wintrobe, *The Political Economy of Dictatorship* (Cambridge: Cambridge University Press, 1998).

20 M. Griesgraber, "Implementation by the Carter Administration of Human Rights Legislation Affecting Latin America," PhD thesis, Georgetown, Georgetown University (1983), pp. 227–241.

21 Juzgado Federal de Jujuy no. 2, November 15, 2012, order initiating criminal proceedings, p. 92.

sophisticated enough to capture the nuances presented by the various relationships established between businesspersons and state officials. Mounting a criminal organization to kidnap businesspersons and seize their property, instigating and implementing social exclusion policies, requesting and facilitating the disappearance of employees, granting loans to the regime, and benefiting from the government's exchange policy are not the same thing. Co-perpetrators, partners, instigators, conspirators, direct perpetrators, accomplices, and beneficiaries are some of the possible forms that can embody such material relationships, and which in this book are included under the generic term "economic accomplices," but only for the sake of expository simplicity.

Identifying and exposing the true and specific role played by economic actors poses a challenge that exceeds the legal sphere. It involves questioning the static and monolithic notion of state[22] toward capturing the public-private interrelations and interdependencies woven together during the authoritarian period, so that the meaning of the expression "state terrorism" properly reflects that public-private web.

In any case, even in international criminal law, a holistic approach is applied in the prosecuting of authoritarian regimes and their legacies. As noted by the recently appointed International Criminal Court Prosecutor Fatou Bensouda:

> When prosecuting crimes against humanity, we must consider all elements and focus on all the actors involved: political and military leaders, perpetrators, and even those who financed such crimes. In principle, they too are responsible and must be held accountable for the civilian victims they contributed to create with their support to systematic plans against civilian populations.[23]

Moreover, transitional justice in Argentina has evolved to a point that it is possible to recognize that not taking into account the economic factors that contributed to maintain a dictatorship poses a certain danger of historical blindness that can result in an amnesia that compromises the promise of *never again*. Addressing only the political factors of a period of repression and omitting the economic dimension promotes the risk that – because they have not received any kind of penalizing signal from the law, and very especially when the activity has been profitable – those same economic factors will again facilitate the emergence and maintenance of a similar regime in the future.

[22] On this discussion on the very notion of the state with respect to the Nazi regime and the role of businesspersons, see D. Lustig, "The Nature of the Nazi State and the Question of International Criminal Responsibility of Corporate Officials at Nuremberg: Revisiting Franz Neumann's Concept of Behemoth at the Industrialist Trials," (2011) 43(4) *New York University Journal of International Law and Politics*, 965.

[23] "Aquellos que financiaron crímenes de lesa humanidad deben rendir cuentas," *Perfil*, July 22, 2012, available at www.perfil.com/ediciones/internacionales/-20127-696-0077.html.

This book intends to contribute to a more complete historical narrative about what happened under state terrorism in Argentina, countering the idea that it was a plan of a handful of senior and junior officers of the armed and security forces who carried out a mass murder campaign on their own. State terrorism rested on a political and economic plan that had its winners and losers, as noted by Eduardo Basualdo in Chapter 5. This end result was a reflection of a web of economic relations that is explained in detail by the authors and which converged in the abrupt and antidemocratic interruption of the import substitution model. The government obtained economic support (and political support connected with the economy) precisely from those who benefited both from economic advantages granted by the dictatorial state (subsidies, tax exemptions, elimination – even physical – of business competitors, corrupt business deals, privatizations, etc.) and from the market conditions generated by the repression of certain sectors of society.[24]

This scheme of reciprocal supports and benefits was acknowledged by Alfredo Martínez de Hoz himself, the man who served as economy minister from 1976 to 1981, who openly explained:

> The Armed Forces are the pillar and mainstay of the current process. I can say that my administration has received all sorts of support from the Armed Forces, as is to be expected because this economic program was approved by the Armed Forces before they assumed power, and I am carrying out a program approved by the Armed Forces.[25]

The profound regressive redistribution of income implemented to the detriment of the working class (with the participation of wage-earners dropping from 43 percent in 1975 to 22 percent in 1982)[26] and the reshaping, downsizing, and concentration of the industrial sector that occurred under the dictatorship were made possible through the effective repression of the labor movement. The workers who survived had to perform their tasks for a meager wage, literally with guns to their heads. The militarization of Argentina's large industries and the ensuing systematic repression applied with the aim of disciplining workers and their representatives entailed not just collusion but an active involvement from the companies, which, in turn, benefited enormously from the curtailment of labor rights. The goal was not merely to eliminate the *internal enemy*, but also to refound a model of production based on

[24] On the corporate liberalism that characterized the Argentine dictatorship, see A. Pucciarelli (coord.), *Empresarios, tecnócratas y militares. La trama corporativa de la última dictadura* (Buenos Aires: Siglo XXI, 2004); on the privileged spaces of accumulation during the dictatorship, see A. Castellani, *Estado, empresas y empresarios. La construcción de ámbitos privilegiados de acumulación entre 1966 y 1989* (Buenos Aires: Prometeo, 2009).

[25] Ministerio de Economía, *Memoria 29-3-1976/29-3-1981*, vol. 1, Buenos Aires, 1982, p. 95.

[26] E. Basualdo, *Estudios de historia económica argentina. Desde mediados del siglo XX a la actualidad* (Buenos Aires. Siglo XXI, 2006), p. 122.

the violent dispossession of workers. Economic think tanks and business associations attempted a technical, political, and institutional defense of that economic and criminal machinery, whose social, economic, legal, and political repercussions are still vividly felt today.

Although there is an increasingly stronger tendency in the transitional justice agenda toward picking up economic accomplices on its radar, there is a heated debate among academics over whether violations of economic, social, and cultural rights should be incorporated into the processes of transitional justice, and if so, how. These are two delicate questions, as they exceed the issue of holding non-sate accomplices responsible and the economic contextualization of such behaviors. In fact, both questions may demand legal definitions regarding what the best political and economic system is for preventing and repairing economic, social, and cultural rights violations (economic violence).

While it is unacceptable for the mechanisms of transitional justice to be blindly determined by the supposed "spillover effect" of the economic measures of liberalization, it is no less true that the discussion regarding economic, social, and cultural rights must not be resolved exclusively with arguments of legality and efficiency, because that reduces the political and democratic debate around the economy to its minimum expression.[27]

The approach proposed in this book emphasizes the legal responsibility of economic actors that contribute to authoritarian governments and considers the socioeconomic dimension of that same period toward:

(1) fully understanding the relationship that existed between corporate behavior, the regime's economic policy and its consequences, the consolidation of the regime, and the crimes committed by the regime;
(2) identifying the socioeconomic problems and tensions that fueled the conflict and which can be reproduced even under democratic rule;
(3) designing proper instruments for holding economic accomplices responsible; and
(4) ensuring any current institutional conditions that may facilitate discussion in the framework of a democratic government capable of responding and delivering effective solutions to today's structural socioeconomic problems, which may be a legacy of – and an explanation for – the authoritarian period.

[27] Similarly, it could be argued that the liberal notion of rule of law that informs the modern paradigm of transitional justice could condition, at times, the self-determination of the country in question. On this subject, see extensively H. Franzki and M. C. Olarte, "Understanding the Political Economy of Transitional Justice: A Critical Theory Perspective," in S. Zistel et al. (eds.), *Transitional Justice Theories* (London: Routledge, 2013).

In addition to this Introduction, the book is divided into eight parts. In Part I, Naomi Roht-Arriaza explores, in Chapter 1, the reason for the marginalization of considerations regarding distributive justice, economic, social, and cultural rights, economic complicity in the conceptualization of transitional justice, and why this has been changing in recent years.

The reasons for that marginalization are to be found in the fact that in its origins transitional justice was limited to the protection of civil and political rights. There was also a strategic decision to use the international mechanisms for the protection of human rights available at that time, to focus on criminal trials against the state perpetrators of the crimes, to break the silence surrounding the crimes, and to not antagonize the liberal economic policies of the 1990s. However, as Roht-Arriaza explains, the persistence of the socioeconomic problems underlying authoritarian periods, the growing economic, social, and cultural rights demands, the greater human rights focus on non-state subjects, and the convergence of agendas leading to look for the roots of current economic struggles in the failure to adequately confront the past are all factors that explain transitional justice's increasing attention to the economic dimension.

In Chapter 2, Leigh Payne and Gabriel Pereira take a comparative perspective to analyze the innovative advances on the subject of responsibility for corporate complicity that are currently observed in Argentina with the aim of determining if that model could be used in other countries in transition. With this in mind, they seek to build a theoretical framework that will connect the field of corporate responsibility for human rights violations with the more general field of transitional justice. To that effect, they ask why and how corporate responsibility became a new focus of transitional justice, and where and how that same transformation is happening, using to that end an extensive database on which they have been working along with other researchers for some years. They conclude that the most novel factor observed in Argentina is the creation, involvement, and synergy of a series of state agencies that traditionally do not participate, at least not so actively, in this kind of cases. They note, however, that this is a preliminary conclusion and that further research is necessary to develop firmer conclusions with respect to how the Argentine model could be used by other countries.

Part II presents the intellectual framework and the international geopolitical dimension of economic complicity. In Chapter 3, Mariana Heredia analyzes the responsibility of economic ideas and those who produce them, and concludes that numerous liberal intellectuals – in particular economists – and the research centers that gathered them formed the symbolic columns of the regime, first instigating the coup d'état and then supporting the dictatorial government. By contributing economic ideas – even conflicting ideas – to the public debate and for government action, they sought to legitimize a social exclusion plan that benefited only a small sector of the economy, based on the repression of the majority of the population.

In Chapter 4, Jorge Taiana explains how the international geopolitical scenario determined the foreign military, political, economic, and financial aid received by the dictatorship. The evolution of world economy, the cold war, and the National Security Doctrine, in line with the dictatorship's economic and military strategy, contribute to unravel the reasons, the complexities, and even the contradictions of the external supports – and rejections – received by the Argentine dictatorship.

Part III seeks to prove two points. First, the rational connection that existed between the means used by state terrorism (economic policy and repression) and the economic model planned and imposed during that period. Second, the fact that micro-behaviors (both economic and criminal) had their quantitative and macroeconomic correlate. In Chapter 5, Eduardo Basualdo describes the economic and social tensions that preceded the coup and the way in which the new model imposed a pattern of capital accumulation based on financial valorization, deindustrialization, economic liberalization, and displacement of workers.

In Chapter 6, Alfredo Calcagno explains the handling of public finances during the dictatorship, and concludes that these were intrinsically tied to the imposed country project: regressive tendencies were introduced in the structure of both spending and income, after reshaping Argentina's economy and society, pushing back the integrating role of the state to consolidate the predominance of the (national and foreign) financial sector and large economic groups.

In Chapter 7, Juan Pablo Bohoslavsky studies the role of foreign financing in the consolidation of the regime, which facilitated both the purchasing of loyalties of key national political and economic sectors and the funding of increasing military spending used primarily for repression.

Part IV analyzes in depth the legal implications entailed by economic contributions to the commission of gross human rights abuses. Chapter 8 provides a summary of the report on "corporate complicity and legal accountability" produced and issued in 2008 by the International Commission of Jurists (ICJ), which crystallized international standards on this subject.

In Chapter 9, Juan Pablo Bohoslavsky examines whether contributing to human rights abuses is considered unlawful from the perspectives of international law and domestic law. He also looks at the factual and legal conditions under which economic accomplices can be held responsible in civil courts and suggests that the real and foreseeable effects of corporate contributions – rather than the intrinsic nature of the service provided – must be the guiding criterion for prosecuting complicit behavior.

In Chapter 10, Juan Pablo Bohoslavsky, Agustín Cavana, and Leonardo Filippini examine the effects of the passage of time on the possibility of bringing civil actions (statutory limitation) on grounds of responsibility for complicity with state terrorism. The chapter analyzes national, comparative, and international jurisprudence on the subject and suggests that the arguments that justify the application of statutory limitations to ordinary civil actions do not apply to the special case of crimes against humanity, which demands taking into account truth, justice, and reparations as complementary aspirations.

In Part V, the authors present and explain in detail various cases in which large local and foreign companies were active accomplices of the military with the aim of repressing and disciplining workers and their representatives. In Chapter 11, Victoria Basualdo, Tomás Ojea Quintana, and Carolina Varsky study the cases of the automotive companies Ford and Mercedes Benz. First they give an account of the logistic, intelligence, and material aid given by these two companies to the repressive forces so that they could commit crimes against workers and their union representatives with the ultimate aim of disciplining them and blocking their labor demands. Then they describe and analyze both the progress attained and the obstacles encountered in the trials for complicity that are being held against these companies' executives in Argentina and abroad.

In Chapter 12, Victorio Paulón looks at the cases of the steel companies Acindar and Techint, showing the involvement of these companies in the planning and execution of the kidnapping and disappearance of workers, in particular in Villa Constitución. Moreover, he explains how these companies' economic consolidation during the dictatorship determined their economic and political role in Argentina over the following two decades.

The third case, addressed in depth by Alejandra Dandan and Hannah Franzki in Chapter 13, is the case of Ingenio Ledesma and the disappearance of numerous workers of that sugar mill. The authors set out to explain corporate complicity (intelligence work on employees, provision of company facilities and transportation to carry out the kidnappings, etc.) through the *confusion/overlapping* that existed between Ingenio Ledesma and the state apparatus. At the same time, the authors use a case file of a pending criminal proceeding against Carlos Pedro Blaquier and other company executives for complicity as a source for forging memory and as a factor for raising political issues in today's social struggles.

Although the companies mentioned here are representative of the universe of corporate complicity and the murdering of workers by request, it is not a comprehensive sample. Other cases involve the companies Astilleros Astarsa, Astilleros Río Santiago, Propulsora Siderúrgica, Dalmine-Siderca, Molinos Río de la Plata, Loma Negra, and La Veloz del Norte,[28] among others.

[28] On these cases, see L. Filippini and A. Cavana, "Responsabilidade empresarial e terrorismo de estado na Argentina," (2012) 6 *Revista Anistia Política e Justiça de Transição*, in particular 321–338; and

As if the workers who were victims of state terrorism had not suffered enough under the brutality of the armed forces and the greed of their complicit employers, in Chapter 14 Victoria Basualdo also shows how orthodox unionism (focusing on the case of the SMATA labor union) contributed deliberately to make all that happen. Certain sectors of orthodox labor leadership supported, legitimized, and collaborated in the repression against combative and rank-and-file groups both in the years prior to the coup and after, during the dictatorship. This analysis is made against the general backdrop of the tensions and conflicts at the heart of the working class and the fundamental contradiction between capital and labor.

Lastly, in Chapter 15, Héctor Recalde describes in detail and from a legal perspective the scope and implications of the labor law reforms carried out during the dictatorship, which had negative direct effects on workers. The massive and systematic curtailment of individual and collective rights of workers resulted in an overall loss of worker participation in the national product and in the deterioration of working conditions.

Part VI describes the political support provided to the regime by industrial and agricultural chambers, as well as by the country's large industries and landholders, a support that explains the direct economic benefits that those same actors received from the economic policies of the dictatorship. In Chapter 16, Martín Schorr describes the participation of industrial entrepreneurs in government executive positions, the generalized and swift process of deindustrialization, the selective industrial development that favored a concentrated group of national and transnational corporations that *re-primarized* the country's industry, the financial speculation to the detriment of the state, the subsidies granted by the state, and the drop in the real wages of industrial workers, and how it all led to greater political power for that concentrated industrial group that enabled it to condition the course of the national economy.

Agricultural chambers, for their part, as early as 1974 assumed an attitude of open confrontation against the democratic government and its constitutional bases, as explained by Mario Rapoport and Alfredo Zaiat in Chapter 17. These same bodies were unsurprised by the news of the 1976 coup and welcomed it. Even when there were differences – founded on economic motives – among the various bodies, they all gave their explicit support to the policies of the military junta, as numerous members of the economic cabinet, the liberalization and deregulation plan, and the political ideology of the government were all in line with the thinking and needs of these agricultural bodies.

D. Cieza, *La muerte por cuenta ajena. Terrorismo de Estado, gran empresa y trabajadores en conflicto en Argentina* (La Plata: De la Campana, 2012).

Part VII begins with Chapter 18 in which, based on judicial investigations, Federico Delgado describes the administrative and criminal system of the National Commission for Asset Responsibility (Comisión Nacional de Responsabilidad Patrimonial, CONAREPA) through which government officials carried out a deliberate plan to appropriate a number of financial and industrial companies, such as Chavanne, Oddone, Defranco Fantin, Gutheim, and Saiegh. This plan included the kidnapping and torturing of businesspersons to force them to sign agreements or conduct corporate or administrative operations that made it possible to divest them of their corporate assets, all of which was done under the cloak of the apparent administrative legality that CONAREPA offered and which was covered under the Economic Subversion Act (Law 20,840). In two words: organized pillaging.

In Chapter 19, Alejandra Dandan presents the report published in 2013 by the CNV on its own conduct during the dictatorship. This document reveals how the CNV was a decisive part of a bureaucratic criminal machinery used to persecute, extort, kidnap, torture, and disappear more than 130 businesspersons, with the declared aims of finding funds of guerrilla organizations and combating economic subversion, when what was actually sought was benefiting certain economic groups to the detriment of others, while civilian and military groups seized the opportunity to pillage the targeted companies, which were acquired from their owners under torture. The criminal efforts of the CNV focused on financial companies, evidencing the exacerbation of the prevailing predatory financial logic of the time.

Lastly, in Chapter 20, Andrea Gualde describes in detail the Papel Prensa case. This company was snatched from its original owners, the Graiver family, through a sophisticated and planned contractual, corporate, regulatory, and criminal ploy, as it included the commission of abhorrent crimes against the members of that family and other executives of the company, with the aim of forcing them to transfer ownership to the newspapers *La Nación*, *Clarín*, and *La Razón*. This case of illegal appropriation of a company is framed by the plan for the extermination of dissidents, the propaganda needs of the dictatorship and of a pro-regime written press, the strategic importance of newsprint for printed media, and the advantages that having a monopolistic control over this input entailed for the major newspapers.

The final part includes four chapters that show the diversity and wide scope of the economic complicity that supported the dictatorship. In Chapter 21, Damián Loreti describes the editorial complicity of the country's leading media outlets, as well as the economic benefits that they received in exchange. In that context, the authors discuss the Broadcasting Act, the Papel Prensa case, the coverage of the Malvinas/Falklands war, and the (pro-regime) editorial line of large media in both political and economic matters.

In Chapter 22, Horacio Verbitsky reveals a new facet of the role of the Catholic Church during the dictatorship: the economic benefits granted by the Argentine state to that religious institution and its authorities in exchange for silence, and even its general blessing, with respect to the crimes.

In Chapter 23, Claudio Tognonato presents the political and economic history of the ties between Italy and Argentina in the years before and after 1976. These relations, involving government officials of both countries, were furthered by the Propaganda Due Masonic lodge, a support that was translated into disregard for the authoritarian context and its utilization for economic gain, through a range of illegal business deals that included banks, energy resources, weapons, and publishing houses.

In Chapter 24, Horacio Verbitsky analyzes the complicit role played by numerous lawyers of the Bar Association of the City of Buenos Aires (Colegio de Abogados de la Ciudad de Buenos Aires, CACBA) and the Forum for Justice Administration Studies (Foro de Estudios sobre la Administración de Justicia, FORES) during the dictatorship, their defense of foreign capital, and the central role they currently play in the way the system of international arbitration works to the detriment of the Argentine state, and, with that, in the reproduction of socioeconomic tensions and international relations that condition the enjoyment of economic, social, and cultural rights in Argentina.

Lastly, in their conclusion, the editors propose a number of concrete instruments to implement the ideas developed by the authors throughout the book, with the aim of attaining the goals of truth, justice, memory, reparations, and institutional reforms, which require effort and commitment from the three branches of the state, from civil society, and from companies themselves.

The authors of this book come from a wide range of scientific disciplines, which guarantee an interdisciplinary approach to state terrorism, as proposed in this introduction. They include economists, social communicators, historians, lawyers, sociologists, and philosophers, as well as professors, researchers, human rights activists, journalists, and officials from the three branches of national government and from international bodies. Their own experiences enhance the analysis of economic complicity. In addition, the diversity of ages of the book's contributors guarantees an intergenerational perspective on state terrorism that interlinks, addresses, and updates agendas and approaches regarding the atrocities of the past, social justice, and the strengthening of democracy.

POSTSCRIPT UPDATE

This book was originally published in Spanish by the publishing house Siglo XXI Editores in October 2013, in Buenos Aires. This English version includes an additional chapter, written by Leigh Payne and Gabriel Pereira. Since its publication in late 2013, there have been numerous developments in connection with the agenda of responsibility for economic complicity in Argentina.

In 2014, the national Congress passed a law with a provision that is unique in the world: the new Civil and Commercial Code that stipulates (under section 2, 561) the non-applicability of statutory limitations to civil actions arising from crimes against humanity, including actions for economic complicity in this kind of crimes. This means that actions for damages can be brought against economic accomplices toward obtaining compensations, acknowledgments, apologies, or other forms of reparation recognized under international law.

In April 2014, the governing party presented a bill in the national Congress creating a National Commission of Truth on Economic Complicity. The relevant committees in the lower house (the Petitions, Powers, and Regulations; Budget and Finances; and Human Rights and Guarantees Committees) approved the opinion issued in favor of that bill, which will be submitted to parliamentary discussion in 2015.

In December 2014, the Central Bank of the Republic of Argentina created a human rights unit. This new office is mandated with, among other tasks, systematizing all the documentation produced and kept by the bank during the last dictatorship. The task will include an analysis of board minutes, files, internal newsletters, and annual reports, and an exchange with external document sources with the aim of learning the extent of the responsibility that the bank or its executives may have had in crimes against humanity during the dictatorship. This initiative is similar to what was done in the NSC, whose first report – published in 2013 – is analyzed in this book (see Chapter 19).

There are also a number of investigative parliamentary initiatives active at the provincial level. In March 2014, the legislature of the Province of Río Negro (in the Argentine Patagonia) passed a law creating a provincial committee for investigating the economic dimension of the Argentine dictatorship. In September 2014, the Human Rights Committee of the lower chamber of the Province of Buenos Aires voted to establish a bicameral body mandated with investigating "civilian complicity with state terrorism." In November 2014, a bill for the establishment of a bicameral investigative committee on economic complicity was approved by one of the chambers of the legislature of the Province of Santa Fe and is pending approval by the other.

In October 2014, federal prosecutor Federico Delgado – one of the book's contributors – promoted an investigation to determine the responsibility of the International Monetary Fund (IMF) for its complicity with the economic policies that accompanied state terrorism in Argentina from 1976 to 1983.

The legal proceedings referred to in this book are still underway despite resistances and dilatory tactics, as occurs in the Ingenio Ledesma case (see the chapter by

Alejandra Dandan and Hannah Franski). Nonetheless, significant judicial progress was achieved in 2014. Two federal prosecutors requested preliminary investigations concerning two former Mercedes Benz executives for supplying information to the military on workers who were later kidnapped, including where they could be found. In addition, there are an increasing number of criminal proceedings that were not analyzed in detail in this book and under which businesspersons are being investigated or in which there is an order to investigate businesspersons who are believed to have facilitated and/or requested the kidnapping and disappearance of their own workers and their labor representatives. Among these are the cases of Minera Aguilar (mining company), the shipbuilders Astarsa and Mestrina (maritime navigation), the ceramics manufacturers Cattáneo and Lozadur (construction materials), Molinos Río de La Plata (food products), Las Marías (yerba company), and Loma Negra (cement company).

PART I

Past and Present of Economic Complicity

1

Why Was the Economic Dimension Missing for So Long in Transitional Justice? An Exploratory Essay

Naomi Roht-Arriaza

The question that titles this essay requires us to first define our terms. The economic dimension has several intertwined aspects to it. First, patterns of economic inequality and exclusion, and lack of economic, social, and cultural rights, lie behind many conflicts; governments choose repression as a response to demands for greater social justice, or disaffected groups, who feel excluded and with little left to lose, take up arms against the regime. Second, once a government has embarked on a path that will lead to massive and/or systematic rights violations, it is often armed, financed, informed, or otherwise supported by powerful economic actors. Thus, for example, in Argentina as elsewhere, allegations abound that executives of private companies used the security apparatus to rid themselves of bothersome union or peasant activists. Mining interests in the Democratic Republic of Congo and elsewhere have been accused of fomenting, profiting from, and underwriting wars that kill thousands. Third, the economic aspect could refer to massive and systematic corruption, as both a cause and a consequence of conflict.

These three different meanings require different responses in a post-conflict or post-transition environment: a greater attention to distributive justice and to economic, social, and cultural rights; an effort to expose and hold responsible those powerful economic actors who were complicit (or worse) in the violence; and an attack on the causes and means of corruption. I focus on the first and second meanings and leave the discussion of the third to other authors in this volume.

EARLY TJ EFFORTS AND THE FOCUS ON BASIC INTEGRITY RIGHTS

In its first decade or two, the transitional justice agenda focused largely on violations of basic physical integrity rights. Advocates pushed to overturn amnesties and statutes of limitations in cases involving forced disappearances, executions, and torture. The first generation of truth commissions likewise focused on bringing forth evidence of death squads and secret arrests and killings by security forces; only in the last ten years or so has a new generation of truth-seeking exercises gone beyond this same narrow band of violations and violators. Reparations, both through courts and through government administrative programs, were generally limited, where provided at all, to monetary compensation for wrongful death, disappearance, torture, or arbitrary detention or exile, and to health and education services for the survivors and families of victims of those violations.

This focus on a narrow set of crimes attributed to security forces and government leaders goes back to the origins of transitional justice as a field. Although war crimes trials have existed for centuries, and Nuremberg and other post–World War II trials and reparations programs set some of the basic norms and standards for international justice, the field as we know it today largely originated with the end of the military regimes in Latin America, the fall of Eastern Europe's pro-Soviet regimes, and later the transition to majority rule in South Africa. As Paige Arthur has discussed,[1] the human rights movements' turn to dealing with the past in the wake of a change from dictatorship to elected governments reflected the politics of the moment. In particular, it reflected the failure of both right- and left-wing projects aimed at changing the economic or structural bases of society in "developing" countries. On the right, the theories of economic takeoff of Rostow and others, reflected in the Alliance for Progress, had been unsuccessful. On the left, the revolutionary project of social justice through renegotiating terms of trade and redistributing land and wealth, with its intellectual underpinnings in Marxism and dependency theory, was similarly unsuccessful, with limited exceptions. Combined with this, in most countries of Latin America, the Left had been defeated, often violently. Its remnants were exhausted and, after 1989, it had no clear alternative economic reform project. There was a turn from a politics of redistribution to a politics of participation, democracy, and rule of law. This was true in South Africa and Eastern Europe as well. In this context, human rights became synonymous with basic physical integrity and civil rights.

Part of what drove the legal form that many efforts at TJ assumed was the predominance of lawyers, rather than economists, in these early efforts. Lawyers particularly wanted to take advantage of increasingly robust international human rights mechanisms. The early fact-finding mission of the United Nations Human Rights Commission to Chile in 1975 was the first use of the Commission's fact-finding powers outside the sui generis issues of South Africa and Palestine, and it strengthened the Commission's ability to react to violations.[2] The Inter-American

[1] Paige Arthur, "How 'Transitions' Reshaped Human Rights: A Conceptual History of Transitional Justice" (2009) 31 *Human Rights Quarterly*, 321.

[2] Ingrid Nifosi, *The UN Special Procedures in the Field of Human Rights* (Intersentia, 2005), p. 16.

Human Rights Commission's 1979 visit to Argentina, combined with the entering into force of the American Convention (Pacto de San José) a year earlier, increased the visibility and perceived legitimacy of the regional human rights system.[3] The Torture Convention was being drafted during these years, and opened for signature in 1984.

But even as the international human rights machinery was gearing up and becoming more effective, it was marginalizing economic, social, and cultural rights. The UN mechanisms required a showing of a consistent pattern of gross violations,[4] which were interpreted to mean violations of physical integrity and extreme discrimination. The American Convention does not contain ESC rights, and the subsequent Protocol of San Salvador makes very few such rights justiciable before the Inter-American Court.[5] By 1993, the Vienna Conference on Human Rights had declared all rights to be interdependent and indivisible, but this declaration was not followed up by consistent action. It was not until 2013 that individual complaints about violations of economic, social, and cultural rights could be brought to a UN treaty body.[6]

Soft law on transitional justice was also skewed in favor of seeking truth and justice about government and insurgent or militia forces, but not necessarily about their private-sector backers or collaborators. When the UN then–Human Rights Commission initially took up the subject of impunity, for example, it divided the subject into two studies: one on civil and political rights, with Louis Joinet as rapporteur; and one on economic, social, and cultural rights, with El Hadji Gisse as rapporteur. M. Gisse's report[7] recommended, among other things, criminalization of corruption-related crimes, debt relief for poor countries, and compensation in

3 Kathryn Sikkink and Carrie Walling, "Argentina's Contribution to Global Trends in Transitional Justice," in Naomi Roht-Arriaza and Javier Mariezcurrena (eds.), *Transitional Justice in the Twenty-First Century, Beyond Truth versus Justice* (Cambridge, New York: Cambridge University Press, 2006), pp. 301–324.

4 See the language of UNGA Resolutions 1235 and 1503.

5 The Inter-American Commission and Court have addressed ESC issues, but largely through the lenses of discrimination, equal protection, protection of property, family life, or others. The San Salvador Protocol only allows cases involving education and labor rights to be taken to the Court. Organization of American States, *Additional Protocol to the American Convention on Human Rights in the Area of Economic, Social and Cultural Rights ("Protocol of San Salvador")*, November 16 1999, OAS Treaty Series No. 69; 28 ILM 156 (1989). The Commission also supervises the implementation of the American Declaration of the Rights and Duties of Man, which contains extensive provisions on ESC rights, but it has not often invoked those provisions.

6 The Optional Protocol of the UN International Covenant on Economic, Social and Cultural Rights, which provides for an individual complaint mechanism to the expert Committee on ESC Rights, entered into force in 2013, and to date has seventeen state parties.

7 United Nations Sub-Commission on the Promotion and Protection of Human Rights, *Final Report on the Question of the Impunity of Perpetrators of Human Rights Violations (Economic, Social and Cultural Rights)*, 1997 (E/CN.4/Sub.2/1997/8).

cases of violations. While Joinet's report was followed up on and eventually updated,[8] there was no follow-up on Gisse's report, and eventually the concerns he raised were transferred to other rapporteurs and taken out of the anti-impunity context, to become part of a development- and debt-related discourse.

Part of the hesitation regarding opening up the discourse and practice of transitional justice to include a broader range of actors and of violations was the emphasis on "transition." The paradigm was that of a relatively short period of changeover from one reality to another, accompanied by specific, manageable actions like a (short-term) truth commission or reparations program. Given the pacted or negotiated nature of most transitions and the long-standing and complex issues of structural inequality in Latin America (and South Africa), there was a sense that these larger issues would bog down any specific TJ initiatives, and that the moment in which past-focused initiatives could prosper would quickly pass. In practice, of course, most TJ initiatives have taken far longer than their proponents initially envisioned: reparations programs and trials continue some twenty to thirty years after the events at issue.[9] But concern for speed, manageability, and the politics of coalition dictated a narrow choice of objectives.

The weight of the Inter-American Court and its jurisprudence on ensuring rights and on amnesties also affected the conceptualization of transitional strategies in the region. As a human rights body, the focus of the system was (and is) necessarily on states and state actors. Admittedly, from its earliest days the Inter-American Court of Human Rights recognized that non-state actors could commit violations, but the focus was on the responsibility of the state to prevent the violations, and, if it failed, to investigate, prosecute, and provide redress.[10] The rules of international humanitarian law, which bind both state and non-state actors, were little used in Latin America because neither side was much interested in using them. States did not want these characterized as "internal armed conflicts" because of the fear that their opponents would be considered legitimate belligerents, while human rights advocates thought that it was wrong to speak of a state of war in cases where a state repressed its (mostly) unarmed civilian population.[11] The emphasis on state actors, especially political and military leaders and security forces, also derived from an

8 UN Human Rights Council, *Report of Diane Orentlicher, independent expert to update the Set of principles to combat impunity – Updated Set of principles for the protection and promotion of human rights through action to combat impunity*, August 2, 2005, E/CN.4/2005/102/Add.1.

9 See, e.g., Cath Collins, *Post-Transitional Justice: Human Rights Trials in Chile and El Salvador* (University Park: Penn State University Press, 2010).

10 Velasquez Rodriguez Case, Judgment of July 29, 1988, Inter-Am.Ct.H.R. (Ser. C) No. 4 (1988); Barrios Altos Case, Judgment of November 30, 2001, Inter-Am Ct. H.R. (Ser. C) No. 87 (2001).

11 Chile was something of an exception. Courts found that whether or not there actually was a state of war, the military regime had declared that such a state existed in September 1973 and so was bound to respect the laws of war, including Common Article 3 of the Geneva Conventions.

insistence by advocates and family members of victims on the special role of the state as guarantor of rights. Recognition of this special role counteracted the "theory of the two devils" under which both sides committed equivalent violations. It was politically as well as legally necessary to keep the focus on the state – which meant that other actors, especially economic actors, were largely ignored.

The limitations imposed by a focus on prosecutions also explain why the initial focus of transitional justice was not on economic actors. Criminal prosecutions, which generally require guilt beyond a reasonable doubt for a narrowly defined band of acts, do not deal well with shades of culpability. Passive acquiescence, moral complicity, acceptance of benefit, being a far link in a long causal chain may all be wrongs, but they are generally not criminal acts. Bystanders are not easily reached by the criminal law, which means that the focus turns to the small group of people who gave the orders (or refrained from suppressing the crimes) and who acted on them.[12] So to the extent advocates focused on criminal prosecution as the centerpiece and ultimate goal of their efforts, attention to broader patterns of complicity were abandoned.

Legal doctrines also tend to shield economic actors from criminal liability. The Rome Statute of the International Criminal Court only extends to natural, not corporate, persons. Its definition of aiding and abetting requires that the aider or abettor share the purpose of the principal in committing the crime. This is difficult to prove and a departure from earlier jurisprudence of international tribunals, which required merely that he (or she) have knowledge of the crime.[13] In most cases, economic actors were supremely indifferent to the specific purposes of the military, so long as order was maintained, troublemakers were removed and profit making continued.

With respect to truth-telling, the imperative of breaking the silence dominated demands for truth commissions in Latin America, South Africa, and Eastern Europe. This demand for respect of the "right to truth" centered around the denial of the security forces that they had engaged in forced disappearances, use of death

[12] L. Fletcher and H. Weinstein, "Violence and Social Repair: Rethinking the Contribution of Justice to Reconciliation" (2002) 24 *Human Rights Quarterly*, 573.

[13] Rome Statute, Article 25(c). Some commentators have said that purpose can be secondary or nonexclusive. For example, Cassel, "Corporate Aiding and Abetting of Human Rights Violations: Confusion in the Courts" (2008) 6 *Northwest Journal of International Human Rights*, 315, writes that "one who knowingly sells gas to the gas chamber operator for the primary purpose of profit may be inferred to have a secondary purpose of killing people, so that he can keep selling more gas to kill more people." See also Doe v. Nestle, Case No. 10-56739, U.S. Ninth Circuit Court of Appeals, Sept. 4, 2014 ("Driven by the goal to reduce costs in any way possible, the defendants [chocolate producers] allegedly supported the use of child slavery, the cheapest form of labor available… the use of child slavery benefitted the defendants and furthered their operational goals in the Ivory Coast, and therefore, the allegations support the inference that the defendants acted with the purpose to facilitate child slavery.")

squads, and use of widespread secret informers and surveillance. While the Peruvian and Guatemalan official truth commission reports discussed structural factors to a greater or lesser extent as background conditions for violence, the focus was on the actions of armed groups.[14] Similarly, the South African Truth and Reconciliation Commission (TRC) recognized the structural nature of apartheid and held a thematic hearing on the role of business, but its mandate and focus were on those acts that were illegal at the time under South African law, including murder, torture, forced disappearance, and arbitrary detention.

The social networks involved in the fight against impunity and the fight for economic justice have also been separate until recently. The participants, funders, and institutional forums – national and international – have had few points of intersection, and both networks are small and under-resourced, which means little time has been available to work on issues, however worthy, that fall outside each group's stated mandate. Human rights, in part due to the visibility of networks of family members, victims, and advocates, came to be defined largely in terms of civil and political rights in the public space. Those activists, often from a younger generation, working on socioeconomic justice did not frame their demands in terms of rights. It is only quite recently, with the increased visibility of resource-related struggles around indigenous peoples, climate justice, and questionable "development" projects, that the human rights, environment, women's, and development communities have (partially) converged.

Finally, the governments that replaced repressive regimes or that followed peace deals, and their international supporters, were for the most part content to follow the economic orthodoxy of the time. Transitional justice was seen as important to reestablish the rule of law. But the rule of law included respect for property rights and existing economic arrangements, and was part of a global paradigm that aligned liberal democracy with open markets and the free flow of capital. This was especially true in the 1990s, and in South Africa and Eastern Europe, but it was also the case in Latin America during the period of the Washington Consensus. Under these conditions, new governments were reluctant to antagonize the business community by inquiring into their role in support of repression, or demanding any kind of reparations or anything, for that matter, that might scare off foreign investment. The few initiatives along these lines were largely unsuccessful. South Africa's TRC proposed a one-time surcharge or "wealth tax" on South African business and industry,[15] but the government at the time rejected the idea.

[14] See, e.g., Volume 8 of the Peruvian Truth and Reconciliation Commission final report ("Factors that made the violence possible"); Guatemalan Commission for Historical Clarification, Memory of Silence, Conclusions.

[15] TRC Final Report, Vol. 6, Section 5. Former Archbishop Desmond Tutu revived the idea of a wealth tax in 2011.

IS THE PANORAMA CHANGING, AND IF SO, WHY?

Starting in the mid-2000s, the reluctance to tackle the economic dimensions of dealing with the past began to change slowly. In part this is due to the continuing fragility of post-conflict/post-dictatorship countries, where economic and social marginalization drives continuing violence and dampens enthusiasm for democratic reform. The early hopes that trials and truth commissions focused on core crimes and civil and political rights violations would usher in robust, inclusive democracies have, not surprisingly, proven difficult to fulfill. Critics, including many from countries that have implemented one or more transitional justice measures, began to note that despite a wealth of transitional justice measures, the everyday lives of the majority had changed little or even gotten worse. At the same time, the elites who had, by all accounts, been complicit in the violations were enjoying most of the fruits of the new dispensation. Obviously, there was something missing.

The critique of transitional justice as too "top-down," too elite-driven, and too responsive to donor rather than local priorities merged with a sense that transitions were not generally a neat, short-term, one-dimensional package but a messy, unpredictable, and longer-term affair. This critique, in turn, coincided with one that found that the emphasis on civil and political rights in transitional justice unnecessarily reflects the – unjustified – privilege those rights receive in Western rights discourse.

There is now greater recognition among academics and policy makers that justice is broader than just criminal justice, and a look at root causes of conflict is a key component of truth-seeking.[16] Moreover, the prevailing view today insists that socioeconomic rights must have their due in considering both the violations and their remedy, although how exactly to do so remains quite uncertain.

The new attention to root causes is reflected in the findings, and mandate, of some recent truth commissions. The Sierra Leone Truth Commission, for example, placed "the central cause of the war" as "endemic greed, corruption, and nepotism that deprived the nation of its dignity and that reduced most people to a state of poverty."[17] The Commission traced how the actions of elites, including but not limited to the extraction and exploitation of diamonds, had set the stage and

[16] *Louise Arbour*, "Economic and Social Justice for Societies in Transition," in Annual Lecture (New York University School of Law, 2006); Zinaida Miller, "Effects of Invisibility: In Search of the 'Economic' in Transitional Justice" (2008) 2 (3) *International Journal of Transitional Justice*, 266; Ismael Muvingi, "Sitting on Powder Kegs: Socioeconomic Rights in Transitional Societies," (2009) 3 (2) *International Journal of Transitional Justice*, 180; James Cavallaro and Sebastián Albuja, "The Lost Agenda: Economic Crimes and Truth Commissions in Latin America and Beyond," in Kieran McEvoy and Lorna McGregor (eds.), *Transitional Justice from Below, Grassroots Activism and the Struggle for Change* (Oxford and Portland, OR: Hart Publishing, 2008), p. 122.

[17] *Witness to Truth, Report of the Sierra Leone Truth and Reconciliation Commission* (2004), Vol. II, 27.

contributed to the conflict. Its recommendations were broad-ranging, including land reform, better service delivery, and combating corruption. However, most of the recommendations dealing with ESC rights were not made mandatory.[18] The Liberian Truth Commission also focused on economic root causes, denouncing an "entrenched political and social system founded on privilege, patronage … and endemic corruption which created limited access to education, and justice, economic and social opportunities," as well as recognizing the centrality of "historical disputes over land acquisition, distribution and accessibility."[19] The Kenyan Truth Commission's report has a chapter on Land and Conflict detailing injustices regarding land acquisition, forced eviction, and displacement by colonial authorities, postindependence political and economic elites, and multinational companies.[20]

Broadening the transitional justice agenda to consider economic violence corresponds to a new attention to ESC rights as both justiciable and necessary, one that emerged with the end of the cold war. Thus, courts in South Africa, the Philippines, and elsewhere have found that such rights may be claimed in court.[21] As mentioned, the UN Optional Protocol on ESC Rights went into force in 2013. The UN Human Rights Council has paid increasing attention to ESC rights, appointing Special Rapporteurs or Representatives on food, water, environment, housing, extreme poverty, and other ESC issues.

Alongside the attention to these rights is a new focus on the inequalities driven by globalization. These have been broadly reflected in social movements from those opposing trade and investment agreements deemed to undermine national regulatory protections to the "Occupy" and related movements protesting increasing concentrations of wealth in ever-fewer hands. In this contest, private actors, especially corporations and banks, have come under increasing scrutiny for their roles as both economic and social/political actors. Companies and states have responded with a plethora of voluntary and mandatory initiatives. Major private banks have signed

[18] William Shabas, "The Sierra Leone Truth and Reconciliation Commission," in Roht-Arriaza and Mariezcurrena, *Transitional Justice*.

[19] *Liberia Truth and Reconciliation Commission, Consolidated Final Report* (2009), Vol. II, 16–17.

[20] *The Truth, Justice and Reconciliation Commission of Kenya, "The Final Report of the TJRC" (2013)*, available at www.tjrckenya.org/index.php?option=com_content&view=article&id=573&Itemid=238. The Report, like the Commission itself, was controversial: three non-Kenyan members protested in an unofficial dissenting opinion, charging that the president's staff had forced the Kenyan commissioners to alter the Land Chapter to diminish allegations of illegal conduct against former President Jomo Kenyatta (father of the current president) and his family. Christopher Gitari Ndungú, Lessons to Be Learned: An Analysis of the Final Report of Kenya's Truth, Justice and Reconciliation Commission (ICTJ, May 2014).

[21] Government of the Republic of South Africa & Others v. Grootboom & Others 2000 (11) BCLR 1169. (Constitutional Court); Oposa et al. v. Fulgencio S. Factoran, Jr. et al (G.R. No. 101083, Supreme Court of the Philippines), July 30, 1993.

on to the Equator Principles committing them to socially responsible finance, while multilateral development banks have put in place safeguards and created investigation mechanisms for complaints about their lending.[22] In a number of countries, national legislation requires attention to trade in conflict minerals; an example is the provision in the U.S. Dodd-Frank Act requiring disclosures about the sourcing of such minerals, or the "Kimberley process," which attempts to restrict the sale of "conflict diamonds."[23] Tort suits in the United States and elsewhere have attacked corporate aiding and abetting of core human rights violations.[24] Disclosure regimes, national and international, attempt to trace the use and abuse of corporate funds.[25]

In the UN human rights framework, the work of UN Special Rapporteur John Ruggie to create a framework[26] and Guidelines[27] on Business and Human Rights led to the formation of a Working Group on Corporate Responsibility at the Human Rights Council and to efforts to create national implementation plans. In June 2014, two resolutions moved forward the process of studying, and possibly drafting, a legally binding instrument on corporations and human rights. While most host countries of large multinational corporations opposed the idea, and any such process would be long, contested, and uncertain, the issue is once more on the table after decades of failed efforts.[28]

[22] See, e.g., safeguards on indigenous people and on forced displacement. The World Bank has created an Inspection Panel and other banks use similar mechanisms to deal with complaints. This is not to suggest that such measures are sufficient or even effective, simply that they have assumed more salience in the last decade or so. These safeguards are now under review by the Bank; initial drafts indicate an attempt to weaken a number of the safeguards. For the Equator Principles, see www.equatorprinciples.org. See also Chapter 9.

[23] See, e.g., Reuters, "Financial Regulation Hits Congo Mineral Trade," at www.reuters.com/article/2010/07/15/financial-regulation-congo-idAFN1545972220100715?pageNumber=1&virtualBrandChannel=0. On the Kimberley Process, see www.kimberleyprocess.org.

[24] The most prominent, although not the only, example are suits under the U.S. Alien Tort Statute. See Chapter 9. These suits have been curtailed by the U.S. Supreme Court's decision in Kiobel v. Royal Dutch Petroleum Co., 133 S. Ct. 1659 (2013), but they have not been eliminated. See, e.g., Doe v. Nestle, note 14 in this chapter.

[25] See, e.g., the Extractive Industries Transparency Initiative, at www.eiti.org.

[26] His "respect, protect, remedy" framework can be found at www.reports-and-materials.org/Ruggie-report-7-Apr-2008.pdf. See Chapter 9.

[27] The Guidelines can be found at www.ohchr.org/Documents/Publications/GuidingPrinciplesBusinessHR_EN.pdf.

[28] The 26th session of the UN Human Rights Council in Geneva considered two resolutions. The first, led by Ecuador and South Africa, directs the Council "to establish an open-ended intergovernmental working group with the mandate to elaborate an international legally binding instrument on Transnational Corporations and Other Business Enterprises with respect to human rights." The second, less controversial, requests that the UN Working Group prepare a report considering, among other things, the benefits and limitations of legally binding instruments. For a skeptical view on a binding treaty, see John Ruggie, "The Past as Prologue? A Moment of Truth for UN Business and Human Rights Treaty," July 8, 2014, available at www.ihrb.org/commentary/past-as-prologue.html.

The new attention to private actors is reflected in transitional justice initiatives. Here, in addition to the work of truth commissions, there have been calls to extend criminal investigations to the financiers of repression and the buyers of conflict minerals. Several factors contribute to the increased willingness to look beyond a narrow group of state agents as perpetrators. First, the very success in some (but not all) countries in overcoming the obstacles and bringing the military and security forces to trial has established that democracy can coexist with trials, that the sky will not fall, the military will not stage a new coup d'état, and the economy will not disintegrate if individuals are held to account. This confidence allows for thinking about establishing a more fulsome and complete story about what happened during the years of repression and armed conflict, one that includes the role of actors like the church or the economic elite.

Second, the distance between groups focused on justice for the crimes of the past on the one hand and those involved in current struggles for justice on the other has decreased. Both groups now find that their issues are interrelated, and that the failure of justice for past crimes creates the conditions for continuing impunity, criminalization of social protest, and mistreatment and violence against protesters. Thus, for example, many of the disputes around control of natural resources, mining and oil exploration, protection of indigenous and rural communities, and the like bring together the human rights, environmental, and development communities in new ways. This convergence, in turn, creates new civil society coalitions around a broader narrative of the past, one that explores the roots of today's struggles in a failure to adequately confront the past. It also reflects a generational passing of the torch, to a new generation unencumbered by the defeats of the past and conscious of the increasing inequality and impoverishment of many globalized societies.

2

Accountability for Corporate Complicity in Human Rights Violations: Argentina's Transitional Justice Innovation?

Leigh A. Payne and Gabriel Pereira

"Democracy or Corporations" were the words that appeared on posters and in graffiti on the March 26, 2014 commemoration of the 1976 coup in Argentina. Those words capture the efforts that the country has begun in holding businesses accountable for their role in the military regime's repressive apparatus. It might not be surprising that Argentina, as the world leader in transitional justice innovations,[1] might add corporate accountability to its set of accomplishments. The puzzle underlying this chapter, however, is whether other countries will follow Argentina's lead or if the factors shaping the corporate accountability processes in Argentina are unique and nontransferable to other contexts. We thus explore Argentina's efforts in a comparative framework and also attempt to build a theoretical link connecting accountability for business complicity with the broader transitional justice field.

To fulfill these objectives we raise and address the following questions: *Why* and *when* should corporate accountability become a new focus within transitional justice? *Where* and *how* are these transitional justice innovations occurring? We conclude with some reflections on the question of what factors contribute to success in achieving transitional justice goals through accountability for corporate complicity. Our responses to these questions draw on our cross-national research on accountability for corporate complicity, with a particular focus on Argentina in a comparative context.[2]

[1] Francesca Lessa, Leigh A Payne, and Gabriel Pereira, "Overcoming Barriers to Justice in the Age of Human Rights Accountability," *Human Rights Quarterly*, 2015.

[2] Our cross-national research on accountability for corporate complicity is part of two larger projects: the "Alternative Accountabilities for Past Human Rights Abuses" project led by Professor Leigh Payne and Professor Kathryn Sikkink, and the "Corporations and Human Rights Database" project led by Professor Leigh Payne and Dr. Tricia Olsen. Dr. Gabriel Pereira is a team member of both projects. We have received generous support from a number of sources that we wish to acknowledge. The National Science Foundation (Grant No. 1228519) and the Arts and Humanities Research Council (Grant No. AH/K502856/1) supported our project "Alternative Accountabilities for Past Human Rights Abuses." The British Academy and the Leverhulme Trust, as well as the John Fell OUP Research

TRANSITIONAL JUSTICE AND CORPORATE COMPLICITY: WHY AND WHEN

Traditionally, transitional justice (hereafter TJ) has focused on the behavior of states and their direct associates in perpetrating human rights violations. The definition of TJ and its practice, however, have not excluded non-state actors as targets for accountability. TJ could thus be extended to include corporate accountability for complicity in past dictatorships and civil conflict, as we argue in this chapter.

TJ has been defined as a response to "systematic or widespread violations of human rights ... [in] recognition for the victims and to promote possibilities for peace, reconciliation, and democracy."[3] Nothing in the definition and purpose of TJ precludes the inclusion of businesses as long as they have participated in the *systematic or widespread* use of repression and if the aim of corporate accountability advances TJ goals.

In practice, moreover, non-state actors have been included in TJ mechanisms. Truth commissions and trials have focused on state forces and their civilian allies in death squads or paramilitary groups, as in Peru and El Salvador. They have also held accountable rebel or revolutionary forces fighting against the state, as in Guatemala and South Africa. The domestic prosecution of a priest in Argentina and a doctor in Uruguay for their involvement in torture provide two additional examples of the incorporation of non-state and civil society actors within TJ's scope. The South African Truth and Reconciliation Commission (TRC) investigated religious organizations as well as businesses for their complicity in the apartheid era. In other words, TJ implicitly includes non-state forces engaged in the systematic and widespread violation of human rights. Including corporate complicity in TJ thus signifies the recognition of businesses involvement in the systematic and widespread human rights violations carried out by states and quasi states under dictatorships and in civil conflict.

The *why* of including corporate complicity in TJ is the importance of holding businesses accountable for their past involvement in human rights violations, thereby advancing the TJ goals of peace, reconciliation, and democracy. Peace depends on the guarantee of non-repetition; raising the reputational or financial

Fund No. 121/482, provided funds for a pilot study on Latin American business and human rights and to create the "Corporations and Human Rights Database." The University of Denver's PROF, Faculty Research Fund, and Internationalization Grants were also instrumental in the data collection efforts for Latin America. We are also indebted to Kathryn Babineau and Laura Bernal-Bermúdez for their research for this project. In addition, we thank Juan Pablo Bohoslavsky, Tricia D. Olsen, and Horacio Verbitsky for their comments on an earlier version of this chapter.

3 International Center for Transitional Justice (ICTJ). 2009. "What Is Transitional Justice?" www.ictj.org/about/transitional-justice (accessed July 16, 2009).

costs to businesses of directly or indirectly participating in human rights violations increases the possibility of deterring future complicity. Reconciliation depends on knowledge and acknowledgment of past violations or truth; the truth about business involvement in violence holds them accountable for remedy and repair of those past harms. Advancing democracy, finally, depends on respect for human rights, protection from violations, and remedy when they occur; the principles of respect, protect, and remedy are businesses' duties as much as states' responsibilities.[4] Thus corporate accountability is consistent with TJ goals of advancing justice, reparations, truth-telling, and guarantees of non-repetition.[5]

When to include corporate complicity as part of TJ depends on the direct or indirect involvement of state-, privately, or jointly-owned businesses to the authoritarian regime or civil conflict violence. Although conducting business with repressive authoritarian regimes or warring armies, and making profits from that business, might be considered immoral, illegal behavior is the focus of TJ. Maassarani usefully identifies four categories of business behavior that moves from immoral to illegal conduct: (1) joint criminal enterprises; (2) conspiracy to violence; (3) instigation of violence with knowledge of outcome; and (4) procurement, or profiting from sales or services knowing that it contributes to violence but without necessarily having criminal intent.[6] When corporations engage in one or more of these four types of activities, they should face accountability for past state violence and thus fall within TJ's remit.

Some contend that TJ, or a "special kind of justice" is not necessary for business complicity when domestic torts law is sufficient. TJ, however, is not an exceptional form of justice;[7] civil torts and criminal courts can form part of the TJ toolkit aimed at fulfilling victims' demands for justice, reparations, truth-telling, and guarantees of non-repetition.[8] Incorporating accountability for corporate complicity within TJ recognizes the unique role of businesses, not a unique form of justice. When past state violence, or the extent of violence, would not have been possible without

4 John Ruggie, Special Representative of the Secretary General on the issue of human rights and transnational corporations and other business enterprises. "Business and Human Rights: Further Steps Toward the Operationalization of the 'Protect, Respect and Remedy' Framework," in Human Rights Council, United Nations, 2010.

5 Clara Sandoval, Leonardo Filippini, and Roberto Vidal, "Linking Transitional Justice and Corporate Accountability," in Sabine Michalowski (ed.), *Corporate Accountability in the Context of Transitional Justice* (London: Routledge Press, 2013).

6 Tarek F. Maassarani, "Four Counts of Corporate Complicity: Alternative Forms of Accomplice Liability Under the Alien Tort Claims Act," (2005) 38 *New York University Journal of International Law & Politics*, 39–65.

7 Ruti G. Teitel, *Transitional Justice* (Oxford: Oxford University Press, 2000).

8 Youseph Farah, "Toward a Multi-Directional Approach to Corporate Accountability" in Sabine Michalowski (ed.), *Corporate Accountability in the Context of Transitional Justice* (London: Routledge Press, 2013).

corporate sponsorship, when businesses provided the legitimacy for violence and the capacity to carry out that violence, and when businesses knowingly contributed to that violence directly or indirectly, they moved beyond "dirty" business and into legal claims regarding corporate abuse increasingly recognized in international laws, as well as many states' domestic tort law.

Indeed, businesses themselves have begun to recognize their responsibility to uphold principles of respect, protect, and remedy. Norms of corporate conduct, underway and expanding via international voluntary agreements since the 1970s, embody these concepts, particularly in the UN Guiding Principles. Firms and industry sectors, in response, have increasingly addressed human rights in their bylaws or voluntary associations. These soft law agreements tend to act preemptively as guidelines to avoid costly lawsuits or campaigns; they do not constitute the conditions by which companies will be held accountable after they commit atrocities. The argument behind including corporate accountability in TJ is to acknowledge the universality of human rights; businesses are not above the law. It also provides victims and states with the tools to advance justice, truth, reparations, and guarantees of non-repetition. It is not solely about punishing firms for past behavior, but about building a democratic future on a solid terrain of respect for human rights, protection of those rights, and remedy when those rights are violated.

TRANSITIONAL JUSTICE AND CORPORATE COMPLICITY: WHERE AND HOW

Although corporate accountability is not new, we find that it is newly incorporated into the TJ toolkit. We further find that the way in which it is incorporated has involved innovations in the types of TJ mechanisms employed. Mechanisms traditionally associated with TJ – trials and truth commissions – have been used around the world to address corporate complicity; new kinds of civil trials have been added to the toolkit as a kind of "alternative accountability" mechanism.

We do not mean to exaggerate the claims about how far TJ has gone in including corporate complicity globally. Our preliminary study of TJ and corporate complicity in 116 countries that transitioned from civil conflict or authoritarian rule since 1970, reveals only a small fraction – 17 – that have addressed corporate complicity. These seventeen countries represent all of the regions of the world, suggesting that these innovations may be spreading. However, it is equally possible, as we discuss further in our concluding reflections, that these efforts will not expand and will remain a unique TJ phenomenon.

Our analysis of how TJ addressed corporate complicity in these cases, reveals a new trend. On one hand, nonjudicial mechanisms, particularly truth commissions, have been used in several countries, as other chapters in this book discuss. On the other hand, judicial mechanisms have also expanded. The use of trials as a TJ mechanism has tended to involve criminal prosecutions. In the case of corporate complicity, however, civil trials have outnumbered criminal trials.[9] In our preliminary global study of accountability for corporate complicity, we found a total of sixty-one trials, most of them ongoing. Of these, about two-thirds are civil (thirty-nine trials, or 64 percent) compared to one-third that are criminal cases (twenty-two trials, or 36 percent). This trend is represented in Table 2.1.

The use of this nontraditional TJ mechanism is observed in both transnational and domestic litigation.[10] The most common use has been in foreign civil trials against businesses.[11] Of these, nearly all (thirty-three of thirty-nine cases), were advanced under the Alien Torts Statute (ATS), a statute that allows foreign citizens to seek justice in U.S. courts for violations committed outside the United States. Indeed, more than half of all – criminal and civil – trials in our database (54 percent) involved ATS.

9 By "civil trials," we mean any prosecution in which individuals, groups, companies, and/or the state are held accountable for human rights violations by a *civil court*. We use the term "civil" as opposed to both criminal and military courts. Thus, we include in our definition lawsuits in which plaintiffs bring legal complaints seeking remedy for damages through acts committed by individuals, groups, companies, and/or the state. By "remedy for damages," we mean monetary compensation, reparation, and nonfinancial remedies.

10 Despite the creation of two UN ad hoc criminal tribunals in Yugoslavia and Rwanda, and the creation of the International Criminal Court with the Rome Statute of 1998, we found only one case of an international criminal trial. As expected, given the nature of the international human rights bodies, this is a criminal trial. The International Criminal Tribunal for Rwanda processed and convicted three businessmen in the well-known "media case" for their direct and public incitement to commit the 1994 genocide. In the *Prosecutor v. Nahimana, Barayagwiza and Ngeze* case, the defendants were accused of having been the masterminds behind a media campaign to desensitize the Hutu population and incite them to murder the Tutsi population in Rwanda in 1994. Ferdinand Nahimana and Jean-Bosco Barayagwiza were both influential members of the "Comité d'Initiative" (the Steering Committee) that founded *Radio Télévision Libre des Mille Collines* (RTLM), a radio station that from July 1993 to July 1994, broadcast virulent messages branding Tutsis as the enemy and Hutu opposition members as accomplices. Hassan Ngeze was the owner, founder, and editor of the *Kangura* newsletter, which was published from 1990 to 1995 and was widely read across Rwanda. *Kangura* produced hate-filled messages, characterizing Tutsis as enemies who wanted to subvert the democratic system and seize power for themselves. On November 28, 2007 an Appeals Chamber acquitted the defendants of a number of crimes but found them guilty of public incitement to commit genocide. See Sophia Kagan, "The 'Media Case' before the Rwanda Tribunal: The Nahimana et al. Appeal Judgment," *The Hague Justice Portal*, April 24, 2008, www.haguejusticeportal.net/index.php?id=9166 (accessed November 22, 2014).

11 By "foreign trials" or "foreign litigation," we mean judicial process that occurred or are occurring in a country different from where the violations of human rights took place.

TABLE 2.1. *TJ and corporate complicity: cross-national study*

Criminal trials			
REGION (countries)	Domestic	Foreign	International
AFRICA (3)	1 (DRC)	3 (DRC) 1 (Liberia)	1 (Rwanda)
AMERICAS (2)	14 (Argentina) 1 (Chile)		
ASIA (1)	1 (Myanmar)		
EUROPE			
MENA			
TOTAL (6)	17	4	1

Civil trials			
REGION (countries)	Domestic	Foreign-ATS	Foreign
AFRICA (4)	1 (DRC)	1 (DRC 1 (Morocco) 5 (Nigeria) 10 (South Africa)	
AMERICAS (1)	4 (Argentina)	1 (Argentina)	
ASIA (3)		2 (Indonesia) 2 (Myanmar) 1 (Papua NG)	1 (Myanmar)
EUROPE (1)		1 (Croatia)	
MENA (2)		8 (Iraq) 1 (Syria)	
TOTAL (11)	5	33	1

Source: Corporate Complicity Database (under construction by the authors) to be linked to the Corporate Human Rights Database (www.chrdproject.com).

These cases are concentrated in three countries: South Africa, Nigeria, and Iraq. Eight of the cases are in response to the South Africa apartheid era. For example, in one class-action suit, the plaintiffs argued that in selling cars and computers to the government, these companies aided and abetted violations of international law. The Khulumani victims' support group also used U.S. courts and ATS to address companies' apartheid-era crimes.

The Ogoni peoples of Nigeria brought a successful case against Shell Oil for collaborating with the authoritarian regime's military and police in the murder of political activists. Two U.S.-based human rights advocacy groups used ATS to bring cases against Shell and other defendants for abuses, including summary execution, crimes against humanity, torture, inhuman treatment, and arbitrary arrest and detention. Despite attempts by Shell to have the cases dismissed, a trial date was set. Right before the trial, the company settled for $15.5 million in what is recognized "as a milestone moment in the movement towards corporate accountability and human rights."[12] We discuss later in this chapter, as other chapters in this book explore, the subsequent Kiobel case brought against Shell and decided in the U.S. Supreme Court that has had a negative impact on the use of ATS to remedy victims of corporate abuse.

The eight cases related to corporate complicity and human rights abuse in Iraq also involve ATS. In one case, families of men working for a U.S. oil services company in Iraq claim that their passports were confiscated and they were trafficked to work at a U.S. air base and en route, they were killed. Most of the other cases involve Iraqi plaintiffs seeking justice for torture they endured or remedy for long periods of detention without trial.

Although corporate complicity in South Africa, Nigeria, and Iraq is reliant on the ATS, three of the four cases related to the atrocities in the Democratic Republic of Congo (DRC) are taking place not in the United States or the DRC, but in Germany, Switzerland, and Canada. Three employees of the Anvil Mining Company were acquitted for complicity in war crimes by a military court in the DRC. In Germany, Olof von Gagern, a senior manager of the Danzer Group, faces prosecution for being complicit in human rights abuses committed by Congolese police and military during an attack on the village of Bongulu in northern DRC in 2011. A criminal complaint in Switzerland is against Argor-Heraeus SA for benefiting from raw materials extracted through pillage and war crimes during an armed conflict between 2004 and 2005. Finally, a class action suit was brought in a Canadian court against Argor-Heraeus SA for being complicit in human rights abuses, by providing logistical support to the Congolese army who raped, murdered, and brutalized the people of the town of Kilwa in 2004.

Domestic litigation has been also used to address business complicity.[13] Nearly four in ten cases (36 percent) of the judicial cases that we found were heard in

[12] See Center for Constitutional Rights, "Factsheet: The Case Against Shell," June 16, 2009. See http://ccrjustice.org/learn-more/faqs/factsheet%3A-case-against-shell-0 (accessed November 22, 2014).

[13] By "domestic litigation" or "domestic trials," we mean judicial processes that took or are taking place in the same country where the violation of human rights occurred.

domestic courts. Argentina has been the leader in these cases. No other country has gone as far as Argentina in TJ or has innovated as much. It is perhaps, then, unsurprising that corporate complicity is a new innovation in Argentina's TJ toolkit. In our preliminary investigation into corporate complicity cases around the world, well more than half (64 percent) of all criminal cases and nearly a third of all criminal and civil cases (31 percent) are from Argentina. In addition, Argentina is using law creatively to find ways to hold businesses accountable for their complicity in past human rights abuses. In that regard, although most of the trials are criminal ones (fourteen out of nineteen), civil trials were introduced as an alternative mechanism to address business complicity. We found four trials of this kind.

In sum, this brief overview of where and how TJ was used in cases of corporate accountability suggest that no region is exempt from the efforts. It also shows that innovations in TJ – particularly the use of civil trials – have accompanied the advancement of corporate accountability. Nonetheless, the number of countries engaged, the number of cases included, and the few outcomes of these cases, suggest that accountability for corporate complicity could be considered an innovation, or an aberration in the advancement of TJ. An in-depth study of Argentina – the country that has gone the furthest in including corporate complicity in TJ – allows us to consider the factors that advance or thwart the process.

EXPLAINING TRANSITIONAL JUSTICE AND CORPORATE COMPLICITY

Argentina provides a good focus for the study of TJ and corporate complicity because it has used the largest set (four) of mechanisms to examine the largest number (nineteen) of cases. Nearly all of the other countries that have included corporate complicity in TJ used only one type of mechanism (thirteen out of seventeen countries). No other country included four types of mechanisms. In addition, Argentina has begun to examine twenty cases of corporate complicity, compared to the next highest country – Iraq – that is investigating eight cases and all in U.S. courts.

The comparison between Iraq and Argentina show that we cannot consider advancement in TJ as a good indicator of which countries will likely include corporate accountability in their TJ processes. Whereas Argentina has gone the furthest in TJ, Iraq has not initiated such a process. The list of countries included in our analysis range in terms of those that have a high level of accountability (Argentina, Chile, Rwanda) and those that have not had any accountability for past violations (Brazil, Cote D'Ivoire, Kenya, Liberia, Nigeria).

One of our arguments about "alternative accountabilities" could explain the Iraq phenomenon. We hypothesize that countries least able to advance criminal prosecutions, owing to legal or political obstacles, might adopt instead alternative accountability mechanisms, such as civil trials, customary justice, reparations processes, and vetting. As discussed previously, we seem to have a U-curve explanation, in which corporate accountability as the missing piece in TJ is introduced as an alternative to the traditional TJ mechanism of criminal prosecutions or as a culmination of that prosecutorial strategy to include civil society along with state violators.

The U-curve description further challenges the factors that we have used to explain why countries fall on one end of the impunity-accountability continuum or the other. We consider the importance of four factors – civil society demand, judicial leaderships, international pressure, and absence of veto players – to explain accountability.[14] As mentioned earlier, countries with a very high level of impunity with regard to state violations are some of the leaders in terms of corporate accountability. Yet some of the leaders in terms of accountability for state violations are also leaders in corporate accountability. Adding corporate accountability to our model challenges it.

Nonetheless, when we disaggregate the explanatory factors to look only at corporate accountability, some patterns emerge. We consider three main groups. First, those that benefit from international innovative processes. The use of foreign or international bodies in attempting to bring accountability explains fourteen of the seventeen country cases. Where international linkages find ways to bring cases outside the country, accountability efforts advance. International pressure takes the form of international nongovernmental organizations (INGOs) and their local linkages to try cases in international or foreign courts.

Left out of this group is the second category of explanations for innovations in Brazil, Cote D'Ivoire, and Kenya. These three countries are at the impunity end of the accountability spectrum. They do not have cases in international courts. In these cases, accountability for business abuses may be possible where accountability for state abuses is not. Here, corporate accountability provides the kind of alternative accountability that shares the responsibility for past abuses among a range of state and civil society actors.

Moreover, these international cases often do not deliver justice. The recent Kiobel decision in the U.S. Supreme Court has even further weakened the already questionable strength of the ATS. It is not clear, therefore, that countries whose

[14] Lessa et al., "Overcoming Barriers to Justice."

cases are brought within U.S. or other foreign civil courts benefit from these processes. Argentina provides an example. It has had only one case in U.S. courts, and the U.S. Supreme Court dismissed it in early 2014. The plaintiffs Bauman et al., a group of twenty-three Argentine citizens, accuse DaimlerChrysler AG (now known as Daimler) and its subsidiary, Mercedes Benz Argentina, of cooperating with authoritarian security forces to kidnap, torture, illegally detain eight workers and kill nine others that were employees of the company and thought to be labor organizers and union leaders. Following Kiobel, the Supreme Court dismissed the case on the grounds that there were insufficient ties between the violations and the U.S. branch of the company to prove the U.S. federal courts had jurisdiction to hear the suit and make a decision.

Thus reliance on linkages to bring cases in international or foreign courts is not too promising for advancing TJ and corporate accountability. Instead, we contend that the pathway may depend on innovators who have included corporate accountability as the missing piece of their TJ processes. In this set of countries, businesses are recognized as co-responsible for the violence and thus equally accountable to states in the truth and justice process. Rather than the first stage, or the foreign stage, of TJ, this is the last phase. It holds that the foundation of a sustainable peace, reconciliation, and democracy depends on the adoption of human rights practices in the state and civil society. The cry for "never again" targets not just armed groups but also those who sustained them in civil society.

In these situations, domestic judicial leaders already exist who have found ways around legal loopholes that block accountability. It is also likely that a propitious domestic political context may be necessary to get around the power of businesses in the economy, politics, and society.

This is the case of Argentina. We suggest that Argentina is worthy of analysis not because the factors that explain its advance can explain the diffusion of corporate accountability elsewhere. On the contrary, we contend that Argentina is unique in having found ways around past obstacles to accountability. Few countries have pursued the extensive set of TJ mechanisms used in the country. On the other hand, Argentina's innovations in TJ have shown what is possible in accountability. Similarly, examining its progress on accountability for corporate complicity, Argentina presents models – like its earlier advances on state accountability for past violations – that can be adapted elsewhere, in contexts in which corporate accountability is the first TJ step or where countries seek a domestic complement to the international efforts at corporate accountability.

Our preliminary analysis of the trials addressing business complicity in Argentina reveal four models that could be adapted elsewhere and that overlap with Maassarani's legal criteria, although not the same labels: (1) direct complicity in criminal violence; (2) violations of labor law; (3) financing repression; and (4) illegal business. We now discuss these categories and illustrate each with a few of the twenty cases underway in Argentine domestic courts.

Direct Complicity in Criminal Violence

A number of top officers from several companies face criminal prosecution for their alleged participation in human rights violations.[15] The emblematic case in this category involves the trial of the corporate leaders of the Ledesma sugar mill in 2012 in Jujuy. The company is accused of being complicit in the well-known "Noche del Apagón" ("Night of the Blackout") between July 20 and 27, 1976. An estimated 400 workers, students, and professionals were allegedly kidnapped, tortured, killed, and disappeared during this incident. Four policemen were detained for their involvement in the repression. From Ledesma's top management, Alberto Lemos and Carlos Pedro Blaquier were indicted for the firm's involvement in human rights violations, including providing the trucks used in kidnapping workers. In addition, the company is accused of having caused the blackout by cutting off electricity to facilitate the military operation. The company further allowed the armed forces to set up a clandestine detention center, Escuadrón 20, on its grounds. As a result of their involvement in these abuses, the firm's directors are now barred from traveling outside the country during the investigation.[16]

The top managers of two automobile manufacturers – Mercedes Benz and Ford Motor Company – have also faced investigation for direct human rights violations. The charges against Mercedes Benz involve the company's creation of a blacklist of workers who were subsequently kidnapped. These workers were members of the internal workers committee. A criminal action was opened in 2002 but there have been no indictments so far.[17] In October 2013, an Appeals Court confirmed the charges against three former Ford Motor Company executives (Pedro Müller, Guillermo Galarraga, and Héctor Francisco Jesús Sibilla) for their crimes against humanity of targeting union leaders for kidnapping and torture. They stand accused, and are under house arrest, for having helped the repressive security apparatus in the illegal kidnapping and torture by providing names, national identification numbers, photographs, and home addresses. The army forces seized two dozen union workers

15 In addition to Ledesma, Mercedes-Benz, and Ford Motor Company discussed here, top officers from the following companies are being prosecuted currently for direct involvement in human rights abuses: Techint; Atarsa; Minera Aguilar S.A.; Loma Negra; La Veloz del Norte; and Acindar.

16 See latest developments at http://tiempo.infonews.com/2012/11/16/argentina-91029-la-justicia-proceso-a-blaquier-por-29-casos-de-secuestro-en-1976.php.

17 See www.ambito.com/noticia.asp?id=724383. Accessed July 16, 2015.

off the Ford factory floor to be tortured and interrogated and sent to military prisons. Bail is set at $142,000.[18]

These cases illustrate situations in which the extent of violence would not have been possible without corporate involvement. The companies are alleged to have contributed to the violence directly and, thus, accountability for their wrongdoing is justified by the aim to provide victims with redress and remedy, to raise the cost of human rights abuses, and to advance justice norms and promote non-repetition. In addition, the use of criminal prosecution is consistent with one transitional justice view that the prosecutorial model is the most effective means to achieve these goals.

The possibility of holding the managers of these companies accountable seems to result from two main factors. First, they are large and visible companies that are associated with particularly egregious and well-known offenses. The Argentine case suggests that these types of cases may resonate more than others because there is more information in the public domain, the companies are recognizable, and the violations are particularly abhorrent. Their visibility is likely to send a message not only to other subsidiaries of the transnational company or the industrial sector, but to all firms, about the reputational, financial, and legal risks of becoming partners with authoritarian regimes and armed violent actors.

Labor Law Violations

The creative use of Argentine labor law is a model that could be replicated elsewhere. In these cases, companies have been charged with failing to protect their workers' safety. In February 2012 in the "Ingegnieros" case, an Appeals Labor Court dismissed the statute of limitations claims of a legal action brought to the court. María Gimena Ingegnieros, the daughter of Enrique Roberto Ingegnieros, brought the case. She requested financial compensation for her father's disappearance during the civil-military dictatorship. She claimed that Techint SA, owing to its coauthorship of the crime of disappearance on the company's grounds, should pay compensation. The company has denied the claim and further contends that the worker safety law, under which the case was brought, has a two-year statute of limitations that had long ago run out. The Appeals Court rejected that claim, declaring that statutes of limitation do not apply to compensation claims linked to crimes against humanity.[19]

[18] Whereas Müller is a Czech national, the other two accused are Argentine. See the latest development here www.cij.gov.ar/nota-11452-Lesa-humanidad–procesaron-a-ex-directivos-de-la-empresa-Ford.html. Accessed July 16, 2015.

[19] See latest developments here www.diariojudicial.com.ar/fuerolaboral/Se-le-vino-la-noche-a-empresas-donde-hubo-desaparecidos-20120215-0002.html. Accessed July 16, 2015.

The April 2007 SIDERCA case, brought by Ana María Cebrymsky, the wife of Oscar Orlando Bordisso, heard by the Supreme Court of the Province of Buenos Aires follows a similar logic. Bordisso disappeared shortly after he left work in 1977. In 1995, his wife claimed compensation from his employer – SIDERCA – under Argentine labor law, specifically that the country's work safety law obliged the company to protect her husband on entering and exiting the work site. The company rejected the claim and argued against legal action owing to the statute of limitations. The first instance tribunal accepted the claim against the company. On appeal, the company again lost in the Provincial Supreme Court. The Court ordered compensation for Bordisso's widow.

These cases illustrate an innovative use of labor law in TJ. They involve a blending of domestic law and international human rights law to recognize the company's duty to respect and protect human rights and remedy abuses. The importance of judicial leadership in linking domestic and international law is crucial to the success of the case, which might have been dismissed easily because of the normal application of statutes of limitations in worker safety cases. Families of employees could use this innovative linkage to crimes against humanity in other countries where union leaders and activists died or disappeared owing to the complicity of their employers and where criminal trials with particular evidentiary constraints may face obstacles. Although tried in civil courts, the use of international law recognizes the crime against humanity, the responsibility of the firm in committing such a crime, and providing some form of reparations for the victims' families.

Financing Repression

Argentina has also investigated cases in which businesses have financially collaborated with the dictatorship's repressive apparatus in illegal economic activity. In 2009, a group of victims of human rights violations brought the Ibañez case to a civil court to investigate the complicity of banks in crimes against humanity. The group alleged that the banks financed the de facto regime, facilitating the commission of grave human rights violations against the civilian population. In the Ibañez case, the large sums of the loans provided to the regime thus sustained, expanded, and intensified the military and its repressive apparatus.

A similar case was brought to courts in 2010. The Garragone case was filed by Martin Garragone, the son of one of Argentina's disappeared, against Citibank and the Bank of America. Garragone argued that the banks' loans to the dictatorship were crucial for its abuses of human rights and demanded the right to truth about the links between the companies and the disappearance of his father. Garragone cited a report prepared by Juan Pablo Bohoslavsky, an Argentine expert on financial complicity at the UN Human Rights Council, demonstrating that the banks were aware that the funds transferred to Argentina would be used to support the illegal and repressive infrastructure. The case is in its early stages; the court still needs to declare that it has jurisdiction to review the case under procedural law.[20]

Cases in this category deal with the crucial question of the financing of the illegal state apparatus. It goes beyond a company's investment opportunities and into knowledge of the use of those funds to finance illegal activities. State violence would not have been possible without corporate sponsorship. Additionally, accountability for financial complicity offers an opportunity to provide remedy for victims. And raising the cost of financing repression may deter future corporate complicity.

On the other hand, these cases are very difficult to win. Both cases are "frozen" because of a number of legal technicalities. They have nonetheless, brought attention to banking sector complicity in the civilian-military dictatorship that, at the very least, plays a truth-telling role and potentially raises the reputational costs for those banks involved.

Illegal Business

In an additional creative legal turn, Argentine courts have begun to investigate companies' involvement in illegal business transactions. The Papel Prensa case is illustrative. Some observers consider the case to be an example of the Kirchner government's political misuse of transitional justice to punish and weaken the government's current political opponents; others see it as an important case for correcting the wrongs of the previous regime and its corporate allies. After an initial flurry of activity around the case, it somewhat died down until the end of 2012 when files related to the case were discovered along with other military regime files in an air force headquarters.

The case involves events following the death in 1976 (in an airplane crash) of David Graiver, the owner of the Papel Prensa newsprint company. Graiver had alleged links to the left-wing urban guerrilla Montonero movement opposed to the dictatorship.[21] After his death, Graiver's wife, Lidia Papaleo, and some months later, his brother, Isidoro Graiver, the heirs to the company, were allegedly threatened and pressured into selling the company to FAPEL (Fábrica Argentina de Papel). FAPEL subsequently sold the company to the three biggest Argentine newspapers loyal to the military regime (La Nación, Clarín, and La Razón), securing their monopoly

[20] Link to the latest developments: http://tiempo.infonews.com/2013/09/09/argentina-109064-argentina-a-un-paso-de-investigar-a-bancos-por-creditos-a-la-dictadura.php. Accessed July 16, 2015.

[21] The Montoneros urban guerrilla movement was one of the most important clandestine and illegal leftist groups during the 1970s in Argentina.

over news production in the country during the dictatorship. The criminal trial is in its early stages, and the investigation is allegedly frozen.[22]

A second judicial case relates to the commission of human rights violations and money laundering. In the Vildoza case, several military officers and civilians are accused of the illegal procurement of property from detained individuals and the sale of the real estate to private individuals and companies connected to the military. The investigation was initiated by the public prosecutor and private partners and later included the Financial Information Unit (Unidad de Información Financiera), the state agency in charge of investigating money laundering activities. The controversy about the case is whether a money laundering law initiated in 2004 could be applied to a case from the 1970s. This has been resolved by showing that the profit from the sale of the real estate transaction continues to benefit the individuals who initially seized the property.

These cases of illegal transactions show the tight connections between the private sector and the authoritarian regime. Not only did the authoritarian regime fail to monitor business transactions, its repressive apparatus facilitated, participated in, and profited from the sale of stolen property and monopolistic practices. Drawing attention to illegal economic activity weakens the image of the regime and the businesses involved even among those who might otherwise support human rights violations under the guise of national security. No justification exists for these economic crimes. By tarnishing reputations, these cases raise the cost of violations, even if they do not end in criminal prosecutions.

CONCLUSION: ARGENTINA AS TJ AND CORPORATE COMPLICITY INNOVATOR OR LONER

The impact of these cases in terms of actual justice outcomes is limited. Whereas the labor law cases have delivered some remedy to the families of the victims, the other cases are stalled in courts and may never deliver accountability. One lesson to take away from the Argentine case is that civil cases are more likely to progress, with lower evidentiary standards, than criminal ones. The barriers to justice for corporate complicity, however, are high even in Argentina's propitious political and judicial environment.

Impact may not be measured only in holding trials. We have shown in our earlier work that trials do not necessarily deliver justice.[23] Scholars have also argued that guilty verdicts are not the only means to measure the impact of TJ. The truth-telling

[22] See latest developments at www.telam.com.ar/notas/201401/48677-para-fresneda-la-causa-de-papel-prensa-se-encuentra-cajoneada.html. Accessed July 16, 2015.

[23] Lessa et al., "Overcoming Barriers to Justice."

process that emerges from investigation delivers corporate accountability in the form of reputational costs. Targeting certain companies with name recognition – Ledesma, Ford, Mercedes, Volkswagen, Bank of America, Citibank, Techint, and so on – associates those companies with unscrupulous practices even without guilty verdicts. Although large companies may be able to absorb negative campaigns in local markets, the opening up of these cases may expose the company to global campaigns against them.

Argentina thus plays a pivotal role in TJ and corporate accountability. On one hand, it is a loner in pursuing so many cases through so many different types of TJ mechanisms. On the other hand, it has proved to be an innovator, shaping the sorts of models of corporate accountability, and creatively combining labor and business law with international human rights law, that could be used elsewhere. One step forward in this process is a blueprint for addressing economic crimes, including business involvement in the perpetration of crimes against humanity during the last dictatorship elaborated by the National Prosecutor's Office.[24] This blueprint, released in 2015, is a valuable resource for public prosecutors as it suggests the key judicial measures that should be taken to collect evidence proving businesses' involvement in human rights violations.

As an innovator, Argentina has faced particular challenges. First, it is advancing these cases in a void, without prior experience or models from elsewhere. In addition, as in other contexts, it faces corporate veto players. Most of the cases it has confronted involve companies that remain powerful in society. Some of them are transnational (e.g., Ford and Mercedes Benz), and others are large national companies (such as Grupo Clarín). Even a propitious Kirchner government political environment willing to take on these powerful actors may not prove capable of advancing these claims.

Where these cases have advanced, Argentina presents an interesting model of uniting agencies with different expertise. Traditional TJ practices have involved mainly the Public Prosecutor and Human Rights Secretariat offices. In corporate complicity cases, the Financial Information Unit became involved in the Papel Prensa and Vildoza cases mentioned earlier. Also, the state has provided valuable information for the development of prosecutorial investigations, such as in the Paper Prensa, in which the Financial Information Unit wrote a report accounting for the alleged involvement of the Grupo Clarín in the illegal sale of a paper mill company and the disappearance and torture of individuals. Tentatively, the involvement of a wide range of state agencies, judicial and nonjudicial ones, might be a factor facilitating the emergence of accountability process. However, this is only a tentative conclusion and further research should be conducted in this realm.

[24] Judith König and Carolina Varsky, Protocolo de Medidas Previas para la Investigación de la Responsabilidad Empresarial en Causas de Lesa Humanidad (Buenos Aires: Procuraduría de Crímenes contra la Humanidad y la Oficina de Investigación Económica y Análisis Financiero, 2014).

PART II

Theoretical Framework and International Dimension

3

Economic Ideas and Power during the Dictatorship

Mariana Heredia

The dictatorship marked a turning point in the way the socioeconomic order was conceived and organized in Argentina. As of the 1930s, and especially after 1943, under the ideal of economic independence, first, and of industrial development, later, the state was assigned the responsibility of leading social progress. Driven by those ideals, Argentina moved forward – albeit intermittently and not without conflict – expanding the state's functions, developing an increasingly complex production structure, and furthering the quality of life of the masses. With the dictatorship that began in 1976, these aspirations and their driving force were abandoned. In that way, it anticipated by fire and sword many of the policies that would later spread across the rest of the Western world. Questioning the possibility of a collective project led by public authorities, the conceptions that would become predominant justified the retreat of state intervention, the specialization of the economy, and the ensuing intensification of social inequalities. This was done by extolling – paradoxically under a dictatorship – the virtues of individual freedom and private enterprise.

What responsibility can be attributed, at that watershed moment, to ideas and the individuals who produced them? If we look at the concepts expressed publicly through the written and spoken word, it is undeniable that intellectuals were crucial symbolic pillars of the conspiracy that led to the coup d'état. In the context of the cold war, they encouraged and justified both the seizing of power and the need to resort to extraordinary means to restore order. These ideas, however, were not limited to the public space or to their thinkers and the heated essays they wrote; instead, their influence continued as their representatives accessed power and faced the dilemmas of governing. In critical moments, such as 1976, those same people who embraced and promoted certain conceptions not only produced discourses, but also participated in the development of government guidelines. The "emergency" regimes made it possible for certain principles – even the most radical – to be turned into decisions. Within more narrow and, in some cases, more ideologically cohesive circles, battles continue to be waged. These involve ways of translating ideas into decisions that enable the crystallization of certain values in the institutions that organize society.

As principles become involved in government decisions, they mutate. They tend to move away from an "ethics of conviction" to commit themselves to an "ethics of responsibility."[1] According to the virtuous formula by German sociologist Max Weber, those observing events from outside, guided only by their conscience, can believe in a virtuous link between means and ends toward achieving the transformations they desire. Those who, instead, take the reins of state power have more power and at the same time greater limitations. In their efforts to navigate and steer junctures, political decision-makers face a number of challenges that push them to employ questionable means to achieve ends they consider laudable. But, of course, government positions do not entail limitations only. As Weber himself said, politics open up the possibility of "put[ting one's] hand on the wheel of history," of leaving a mark that transcends – and by far – the mark imprinted in discourses and recorded in consciences.

Although the distinction between intellectuals and politicians applies equally to democratic and dictatorial governments, the analysis of ideas, in all their aspects and responsibilities, takes on greater relevance in the latter, and especially under the Process of National Reorganization (*Proceso de Reorganización Nacional*, commonly known as *el Proceso*, or the Process) implemented in Argentina from 1976 to 1983. It has been held that because of their illegitimate origins dictatorships are driven to conquer a measure of legitimacy in their exercise of power that will justify them in the eyes of at least a portion of society.[2] Intellectuals would thus have the mission of both instigating coups and afterwards promoting the government's virtues. This thesis has the advantage of underlining the need that any regime – even the most authoritarian – has of building consensus. Nonetheless, such an assertion merits certain qualifications.

The first is that Argentina's unique instability in a way exempted the 1976 militaries from having to justify the coup. In contrast to Chile and Uruguay, where the breakdown of the institutions in the 1970s was an extraordinary event, in Argentina military interventions had occurred regularly and were seen as natural. With the exception of some minority groups, a wide spectrum of actors encouraged the armed forces. Military intervention was seen as a necessary solution not only by

[1] M. Weber, *Politics as a Vocation* (1919), several editions, available at: http://anthropos-lab.net/wp/wp-content/uploads/2011/12/Weber-Politics-as-a-Vocation.pdf.

[2] H. Quiroga, *El tiempo del "Proceso." Conflictos y coincidencias entre políticos y militares, 1976–1983* (Rosario: Homo Sapiens, 2004).

business and industry associations and the Church, but also by political parties, even on the left, and members of the deposed government.

The second qualification is that the legitimizing discourses were not aimed exclusively at the middle classes or at the popular sectors that were most affected. Although the dictatorship responded to many of the demands made by the business sector, the size of the state apparatus and the guidelines of the anti-inflation policy were two issues that faced strong opposition and objections from the business community and from right-wing intellectuals. The "economic" discussion was far from settled in 1976 and some aspects triggered intense conflicts in the higher circles of power. Even when such confrontations were waged in an elitist and antipopular framework, where everyone agreed on the need for social disciplining and combating subversion, the consensus was not complete when it came to deciding on the best way to capitalize on the situation.

It is in this sense that the study of ideas and power is essential for understanding the dictatorship, as certain economic differences were both the subject of heated debates and an excuse to implement a number of novel initiatives that would have profound consequences. The involvement of intellectuals and experts was not limited to instigating and supporting the dictatorship as accomplices. In some cases they played a leading role, even against the wishes of many military officers, in the most regressive transformations left by the Process of National Reorganization.

This is what the history recounted here is about: about liberals and their ideas and how they were present from the dawning of the dictatorship and until its final hour. Two arguments will serve as thematic threads to develop it. First, that liberals and liberalism were agents of change, but at the same time they themselves underwent deep transformations. Second, that through a number of decisions inspired by (neo)liberal ideas, the continuity of some of the most destructive effects of the dictatorship was grounded on the new economic (dis)order's capacity to perpetuate its power under a democracy, without requiring the intervention of traditional intellectuals or their legitimizing discourses. With the advent of democracy, economists would accompany the process with their science, eventually replacing nineteenth-century liberal thinkers.

To understand this, McGann Blyth proposes a trilogy of the importance – and responsibility – of ideas.[3] Against adversaries, ideas can serve as "weapons" to question the rationality of governing institutions and mercilessly attack the fractures and weaknesses of the enemy. In a situation in which a motley group of allies presents a confused front, they can serve as "blueprints," scale models indicating alternatives and paths to be followed. And, once the workings of the previous order

3 M. McGann Blyth, "Great Transformations: Economic Ideas and Political Change in the Twentieth Century," PhD thesis, School of Arts and Sciences, Columbia University (1999).

have been overturned, they can become "conventions," more or less tacit agreements that guide and organize the everyday conduct of organizations and people. Ideas, in their three forms, structure this history.

PREHISTORY OF ARGENTINE LIBERALISM

The construction of the nation-state and the country's rapid insertion in the world market were closely connected with the consolidation of a group of leaders who adhered to the principles of liberalism. The peculiarity of Argentina's liberal tradition lies in its early coexistence with conservatism, a phenomenon that prevented it from achieving the degree of vitality and perdurability that characterized similar currents of thought in other nations of the continent.[4] The inheritors of the patrician generation of the late nineteenth and early twentieth centuries furthered the belief in a stratified and meritocratic society, and continuously expressed their disdain for "the masses." As of the 1930s, the main concern of Argentine liberals was the defense of private property and economic freedoms, which led them to repeatedly bypass the constitutional order and ignore civil and political rights.

Tracking the course of liberalism in Argentina is not easy, as since the first decades of the twentieth century the country lacked an electorally significant right-wing party.[5] There were, of course, right-wing nationalist or liberal-conservative groupings. These organizations, however, did not always have an explicitly political-party character and the ones that did venture into that arena were sporadic and inefficient.[6] With no solid political platforms available to them, other forums served liberal ideas as spaces for convergence and expression. On the one hand, intellectuals participated regularly in public debates by virtue of their privileged relationship with century-old newspapers (in particular *La Prensa* and *La Nación*).[7] On the other hand, even with the profound transformations that the Argentine economy underwent beginning in the 1930s, many

4 T. Halperin Donghi, *El espejo de la historia. Problemas argentinos y perspectivas latinoamericanas* (Buenos Aires: Sudamericana, 1987).

5 That is, at the national level. Owing to the subject addressed – namely, the relationship between liberalism and national economic policies – this text does not delve into the links between the Right, liberalism, and provincial governments. On that subject, see E. Gibson, "Democracy and the New Electoral Right in Argentina" (1990) 32(3) *Journal of Interamerican Studies and World Affairs*, 177–228.

6 L. Senkman, "The Right and Civilian Regimes, 1955–1976," in S. McGee Deutsch and R. Dolkart (eds.), *The Argentine Right. Its History and Intellectual Origins, 1970 to the Present* (Wilmington: SR Books, 1993), 119–145.

7 On the press and liberal ideas, see the notable works by R. Sidicaro, *La política mirada desde arriba. Las ideas del diario* La Nación, 1909–1989 (Buenos Aires: Sudamericana, 1993); and F. Ruiz, *El señor de los mercados.* Ámbito Financiero, *la City y el poder del periodismo económico de Martínez de Hoz a Cavallo* (Buenos Aires: El Ateneo, 2005).

businessmen from traditional families continued to steer the leading companies and monopolize the direction of the business associations.[8]

The inexistence of right-wing parties did not, however, mean that liberals were excluded from government. Without candidates of their own who could fill top executive positions, the military administrations turned to their civilian supporters to recruit their ministers. In several military governments or under control of the military, José Alfredo Martínez de Hoz, Roberto Alemann, and Álvaro Alsogaray, among others, had their first experiences in government. Does that mean that the armed forces were for liberals what political parties were for Radical, Peronist, or developmentalist government officials? Yes and no. Military pressures and coups were, in fact, the primary channel through which these groups accessed power. But the armed forces were not loyal to them. Once politicized, military institutions ultimately faced the same fractures that affected society. Whereas in some cases military governments recruited liberal ministers, in others they opted for specialists more connected with developmental theories. As aptly noted by Alain Rouquié, Argentina has experienced different kinds of military administrations.[9]

When they were called on, liberals usually filled economy ministry positions, and in doing so they grounded their legitimacy on technical knowledge. Nonetheless, at least until the 1960s, it would be hasty to assume an association between liberalism and economic science. Considering the different ministers who were appointed over time, it is evident that the military tended to highlight the university qualifications and specific knowledge of their candidates for these executive positions.[10] This does not mean that the officials they chose were more qualified than those of civilian administrations. It merely means that, in the absence of electoral support and in the face of the government's disregard for the Constitution, expertise was the only merit they could claim.

Moreover, the liberalism of that time was not considered a specialized knowledge and economic science was not defined as liberal. On the one hand, although the leading feature of Argentine conservative liberalism was the protection of economic freedoms more than political freedoms, even in the case of those who were recognized as "economy experts," their ideas were far from being defined as an "economic" doctrine. It was an integral philosophy, a country project that

[8] J. Schvarzer, "Estructura y comportamiento de las grandes corporaciones empresarias argentinas (1955–1983)," (Buenos Aires: CISEA, mimeograph, 1991).

[9] A. Rouquié, *Poder militar y sociedad política en la Argentina* (Buenos Aires: Emecé, 1994).

[10] For a systematic study of such appointments, see M. Heredia and M. Gené, "Atributos y legitimidades del gabinete nacional: sociohistoria de los ministerios de Economía e Interior en la prensa (1930–2009)," (2009) *Revista de Ciencia Política El Príncipe*, 109–135.

involved all spheres of social life.[11] On the other hand, as in most Latin American countries at the time, while the novel study centers and public agencies connected with economic science that had sprung up in Argentina expressed certain pluralism, they were in fact dominated by interventionist tendencies.[12]

Even when they succeeded in accessing power between 1930 and 1976, liberal circles saw their initiatives frustrated, just as much as other protagonists did during that period, which was marked by instability and the play of reciprocal obstructions. Any intentions liberal officials had of reducing the size of government and the corporate state always met with the intransigence of their military partners in government. The economic power and ideological strength of liberals and their position in business associations gave them certain veto power, but neither their programs nor their actions were able to successfully oppose, until 1976, the advancing interventionist state.

LIBERALISM AGAINST POWER: THE ROLE OF INTELLECTUAL WEAPONS IN INSTIGATING THE COUP

Liberal intellectuals were major actors in the political radicalization that Argentina experienced between the *Cordobazo* and the 1976 coup d'état. The control of production by business, the capacity of government officials to impose authority, and the monopoly held by the state over the use of legitimate violence were all put into question, evidencing the depth of a crisis that, in line with what was happening in other places, questioned the very foundations of capitalist society. In the context of these tensions, faced with social unrest, and with the subsequent return of Peronism to power, liberal intellectuals were called to interpret events, overcome their differences, and contribute to forge explanations and common strategies to address the threat.

An analysis of liberal discourses yields a surprising conclusion: the intellectuals of liberalism failed to reach an agreement on some key tactical issues right up to the very moment of the coup. Faced with the Córdoba uprising and the emergence of new radicalized actors, some analysts blamed the corporate nationalism of Juan Carlos Onganía, whereas others called for greater coordination with trade unions. In response to Lanusse's call for a Great National Agreement, some demanded the exclusion of Peronism, while others emphasized that Juan Domingo Perón was the only one capable of saving Argentina's republican – and capitalist – institutions.

[11] On this subject, see the books written by liberals of that time, as well as the controversy raised by Álvaro Alsogaray with "the" economists in J. C. de Pablo, *Los economistas y la economía argentina* (Buenos Aires: Macchi, 1977).

[12] In this sense, see the studies on Chile, Mexico, Brazil, Argentina, and the United States in V. Montecinos and J. Marcoff (eds.), *Economists in America* (Massachusetts: Edward Egard, 2009).

It was only with the death of Perón and his widow's confrontation with the labor movement that a certain consensus was achieved. Toward 1975, both intellectuals of *La Nación* and *La Prensa* and most of the business community considered that the threat was not so much in guerrilla groups – which they saw as very weakened in their military capacity – but in the very way society had been organized since the 1940s.[13]

With Peronism tearing itself apart in power, the liberals began calling for a coup and at the same time developing part of its ideas. While publicly they stressed the government's failure to straighten its course and guarantee order, in closer quarters they provided a diagnosis of the deviations caused by "three decades of collectivism." Intellectuals such as Alberto Benegas Lynch, Jaime Perriaux, and Ricardo Zinn contributed to form a common set of ideas for the liberal-conservative faction of the Process. As summarized by Morresi, these ideas identified the state and trade unions as the main causes of the country's problems, argued that reducing public intervention and breaking labor power were desirable goals toward restoring order, and posited that respect for property rights and free enterprise were the only means for achieving prosperity. The global revitalization of liberalism, with the founding and expansion of the Mont Pèlerin Society and the works by Ludwig von Mises, Friedrich von Hayek, Milton Friedman, and Gary Becker, was already inspiring these Argentine liberals.[14]

But these circles did not limit their involvement to instigating actions through thinking and writing. As shown by Morresi and Vicente, the Azcuénaga Group contributed to forge closer ties between intellectuals, the business community, and the military, and facilitated the coup by organizing business lockouts and campaigns in the press throughout 1975. Once the government had been overthrown, the group saw several of its members appointed to government positions, and those who remained outside the government continued to participate by drafting many of the initial documents of the regime.[15]

13 The reconstruction of the different positions mentioned is based on the systematic study of press editorials and public discourses by intellectuals and business leaders. See M. Heredia, "La ideología liberal conservadora frente a los conflictos sociales y políticos de los años 70" (2000) 8 *Sociohistórica-Cuadernos del CISH*, La Plata, 83–120.

14 For an international overview of the origins and the spread of neoliberalism, see P. Mirowski and D. Plehwe (dir.), *The Road from Mont Pèlerin: The Making of the Neoliberal Thought Collective* (Cambridge, MA: Harvard University Press, 2009). Among Morresi's studies on the subject in Argentina, see "Neoliberales antes del neoliberalismo. Consideraciones acerca del análisis del neoliberalismo desde un ángulo ético-político," in S. Frederic and G. Soprano (comps.), *Política y variaciones de escalas en el análisis de la Argentina* (Buenos Aires: Prometeo UNGS, 2009), 242, 321–350.

15 Morresi, "Neoliberales antes del neoliberalismo," and M. Vicente, "Los intelectuales liberal-conservadores argentinos y la última dictadura. El caso del Grupo Azcuénaga," (2012) 29 *KAIROS. Revista de Temas Sociales*, Year 16, 1–17.

LIBERALISM IN POWER: PROJECTS IN TENSION IN THE LABYRINTHS OF THE PROCESS

Although liberals shared these common core ideas, from the beginning there were certain aspects that brought them closer to and other aspects that distanced them from their new partners in power. Among the aspects that brought the leading actors of the Process together, and which would continue to unite them, was the conviction that in 1976 a "battle against subversion" was necessary and that no expenses or lives were to be spared in pursuing the goal of disciplining society. But even as the whole of the armed forces, the government, and a large part of their heterogeneous civilian supporters rallied around this goal and its methods, economic policy guidelines became the main focus of internal conflict, just as in previous military governments.[16]

Even before the coup, the dictatorships in Brazil and Chile were antagonistic sources of inspiration for pro-Process officials. Whereas some members of the military wished to replicate the "Brazilian miracle" by furthering the country's industrialization through authoritarian means, others admired Pinochet's radical approach to combating inflation and "statism." The appointment of Martínez de Hoz to head the economy ministry immediately after the coup seemed to echo the prevalence of liberals in that ministry. However, apart from the decision to freeze salaries, a measure that triggered a steep drop in the purchasing power of workers, during the initial months the minister showed clear signs of moving with caution and gradualism.

In the government, the internal differences in economic matters were aggravated. As Canelo shows, Commander Emilio Massera's attacks on the economic policy, the resistance of pro-statism officials who barricaded themselves in Fabricaciones Militares (the state's military manufacturing division), and the resentments of the "politicalist" faction of the government emerged as strong vectors of internal opposition to the economic team.[17] In contrast to Augusto Pinochet, who succeeded in subordinating the armed forces in a form of government described as a "sultanate," Jorge Videla was never able to overcome the relative "feudalism" of Argentina's armed forces. In Argentina's case, the military junta established itself as the "supreme state body" and concentrated all the prerogatives granted by the Constitution to the president and to Congress. The nation's territory and government positions were divided proportionately among the three branches of the armed forces. Thus, the adoption of the more controversial decisions became a slow process, at some points reaching a state of total paralysis.

16 M. Yannuzzi, *Política y dictadura. Los partidos políticos y el "Proceso de Reorganización Nacional", 1976–1982* (Rosario: Fundación Ross, 1996).

17 P. Canelo, *El Proceso en su laberinto: la interna militar de Videla a Bignone* (Buenos Aires, Prometeo, 2008).

Liberals, then, might be expected to have taken advantage of such disagreements to demonstrate their cohesion and unity of criteria. But this was not exactly the case, especially when it came to combating inflation. During 1978, most comments by business operators and analysts focused on the government's failure to bring the increase in prices down to less than an annual 150 percent. Despite sharing the same theoretical framework, liberals faced difficulties translating their ideas into projects and making them viable in the prevailing power scheme. This led to the surfacing of certain differences.

In the diagnosis made by liberal intellectuals, there was only one way of resolving the problem of the steady rise in prices: contracting the money supply through a reduction in public spending. This required rationalizing public administration, cutting investments in infrastructure, and privatizing state companies. But the military had veto power over the economic team and prevented it from moving forward in this sense.

While implementing in rapid succession a series of equally ineffective anti-inflationary policies, Martínez de Hoz approached a new generation of liberals: the technocrats. According to these young economists, external junctures could be exploited to their advantage to keep the military happy while at the same time addressing the issue of inflation. The availability of capital, the disciplinary power of international prices, and the monetarist theory for open economies – developed in the University of Chicago[18] – could present a solution to the dead end caused by the military's internal situation. As noted in an interview with a member of the Center for Macroeconomic Studies of Argentina (Centro de Estudios Macroeconómicos de Argentina, CEMA) conducted for this study, the technocrats had something to offer in response to the perplexity of the top officials of the Process.

THE NEOLIBERAL EXPERIMENT OF DECEMBER 1978: NEW CONVENTIONS FOR THE GREAT TRANSFORMATION

Shortly after taking office, the team headed by Martínez de Hoz became a space in which liberals of various profiles worked together. The more well-known among these came from the intellectual circles mentioned earlier. What was new here was that, along with the recruitment of some liberal technocrats, the Process favored the expansion of a new form of organization: think tanks. As in other countries,[19]

[18] On this subject, see G. Biglaiser, "The Internationalization of Chicago's Economics in Latin America," (January 2002) 50 (2), *Economic Development and Cultural Change*, 269–286.

[19] Neoliberals and neoconservatives formed the first think tanks in English-speaking countries. Having originated there, they were later replicated in other countries. D. Béland, "Idées, institutions politiques et production de l'expertise: une perspective comparative sur le rôle des *think tanks* au Canada et aux États-Unis," (Autumn 2009) 70 *Quaderni*, 39–48.

these spaces introduced a unique and lasting link between three spheres: academic, economic and social, and political. Through a process that unfolded simultaneously in government, political, and university settings, these new liberals and their centers elevated (neo)liberalism to the status of scientific theory, to then, years later, establish it as the only legitimate economic science.

In Argentina, the first think tanks were the result of the convergence of the training of economists in the United States (furthered by a U.S. diplomatic strategy),[20] the intention of the domestic business community of strengthening their representation and influence in the state, and a demand on the part of the dictatorship for ideas and executives to fill government positions. Of the three Argentine neoliberal centers, only one had been founded before the coup. In 1964, four traditional business associations and the Ford Foundation created the Foundation for Latin American Economic Research (Fundación de Investigaciones Económicas Latinoamericanas, FIEL). The financial support for this center did not come from the Argentine business associations. When the Ford Foundation funds for the center were exhausted, FIEL became a consultant that catered to the country's large private corporations. Led by intellectuals from a range of ideological backgrounds, it would be one of the bodies that contributed the most number of officials to the Process.

The Institute for Economic Studies on Argentine and Latin American Reality of the Mediterranean Foundation (Instituto de Estudios Económicos de la Realidad Argentina y Latinoamericana de la Fundación Mediterránea, IEERAL-FM) and CEMA were instead both established during the dictatorship. In both cases, its members (which included Domingo Cavallo, Pedro Pou, Carlos Rodríguez, and Roque Fernández) were economists who had just completed graduate studies in the United States and had garnered the support of a group of business operators to finance their activities. Their involvement in the Process was less organic, but that did not make it any less decisive.[21]

As Argentina lacked a long-standing cohesive group or a program like that of the Chicago Boys and their proposal summarized in the document *El ladrillo* (The Brick), these liberal technocrats participated individually and in specific decisions.[22]

[20] E. Berman, *The Influence of Carnegie, Ford, and Rockefeller Foundations on American Foreign Policy: The Ideology of Philanthropy* (New York: State University of New York Press, 1983); Y. Dezalay and B. Garth, *La mondialisation des guerres de palais* (Paris: Seuil, 2002).

[21] For a detailed account of how these centers were formed, their contributions to the dictatorship, and the argument among liberals over the issue of inflation, see M. Heredia, "El Proceso como bisagra. Emergencia y consolidación del liberalismo tecnocrático en la Argentina," in A. Pucciarelli (comp.), *Empresarios, tecnócratas y militares. La trama corporativa de la última dictadura militar* (Buenos Aires: Siglo XXI, 2004), 313–382.

[22] For a systematic comparison, see S. Boisard and M. Heredia, "Laboratoires de la mondialisation: les dictatures militaires argentine et chilienne et la pensée économique néo-classique," (January-March 2010) 105 *Vingtième siècle. Revue d'histoire*, 109–125.

Over the course of 1976, the market opened up more and more, with the reduction of tariffs that protected several goods. Because this measure was adopted with a devalued local currency, it did not trigger much opposition. This was followed in 1977 with the launching of a financial reform, which consisted in the liberalization of and ensuing rise in interest rates. This measure had been developed by Adolfo Diz, a Chicago graduate who had been appointed president of the Central Bank and who hoped to take advantage of international liquidity to attract capital to the country. Initially, the inflationary spiral prevented most actors from gauging the magnitude of these decisions. It was the exchange rate regime known as the *tablita*, or crawling peg, recommended by CEMA members among others, that, in late 1978, caused a great rupture. It was based on the argument that setting some key prices – the exchange rate for the dollar, public utilities, and basic wages – would first halt the inflationary spiral and later reduce it. The combination of these guidelines and the opening up of trade would ideally lead to increased competition and, therefore, a disciplining of prices. It was thus hoped that domestic inflation would gradually converge with international inflation.

These concrete decisions had profound effects. The persistence of inflation with a preset exchange rate had major consequences for the newly reformed financial system. At first, the increase in prices resulted in negative real rates and encouraged indebtedness. The Central Bank accumulated large reserves throughout 1979. At the end of that year, however, the exchange rate lag and price distortion fueled uncertainty and raised internal interest rates, which reached positive values in real terms. A chorus of business operators, unionists, political leaders, and even liberal intellectuals raised their voices to denounce the effects of the measures. But the economic team had a new ally: high liquidity investors, on whose expectations now rested not only the continuity of the program but also the functioning of the economy as a whole. The newspaper *Ámbito Financiero* was, in fact, founded during this time to inform and guide these new investors. Grounded on such volatile foundations, the economic policy focused on cultivating the trust of these investors: it reinstated the guaranteeing of deposits and used reserves to maintain the value of the dollar.

As Daniel Fridman notes, the main difference between classic liberalism and neoliberalism is that, whereas state institutions must secure and supervise behaviors among entrepreneurs for the former, for the latter, the government must create favorable conditions for that behavior without imposing limitations or penalties. According to this last perspective, economic agents must enjoy the greatest freedoms and these freedoms can only be coordinated by incentives that "from a distance" will lead to the pursuit of profit.[23] In the face of decentralized decisions, which the

[23] D. Fridman, "A New Mentality for a New Economy: Performing the Homo Economicus in Argentina (1976–1983)," (2010) 39(2) *Economy and Society*, 271–302.

government neither controls nor represses, but which have consequences for the community, "market signals" become crucial. That is precisely what happened with bank deposits and investor confidence in sustaining the exchange rate.

It goes without saying that even if draconian, these "signals" are often not enough. When in 1980, the first bank filed for bankruptcy and threatened to bring down the rest of the system with it, the Argentine state came to the rescue of banking institutions. After Martínez de Hoz was replaced and the currency was devaluated, the state implemented a number of mechanisms that led to the nationalization of private debts. Cavallo would make one of his great contributions as president of the Central Bank by saving those who had contracted debt, in many cases to take it out of the country.

A new convention was thus established between the authorities and "economic agents." As the "repressive" measures of price and salary controls and agreements were considered exhausted, they would give way to anti-inflationary strategies centered on "anchoring expectations." More than relying on a pact between business and workers, democratic governments would prefer to use the setting of exchange and interest rates as their leading anti-inflationary policies (the Austral Plan and the Convertibility Act).[24] This option entailed greater reliance on coordinating – as opposed to penalizing – risky behaviors as a means of attaining stability and growth. These complex technical innovations would not only accept and reward speculative behaviors, they would also have consequences that society would pay, over and over again.

CONCLUSION: IDEAS AND THE PARADOXES OF VICTORY

For intellectual history, the responsibility of ideas and intellectuals lies in their interpretations and their capacity to influence consciences. In critical episodes, such as the lead-up to the dictatorship, intellectuals can not only instigate but also, as was the case here, contribute to stage a military coup. Toward that end, they can also avail themselves of words to make the option of resorting to violence acceptable and even unavoidable. Although in their writings Argentine liberals did not explicitly refer to the methods used, they underlined that Argentina was one of the scenarios in which the third world war was being waged, and therefore it was necessary to militarily and culturally defeat anti-Western Marxism.[25]

24 L. Llach, "¿Dos décadas perdidas? Desafíos, respuestas y resultados de la política económica de la democracia," in M. Novaro and V. Palermo (comps.), *La historia reciente. Argentina en democracia* (Buenos Aires: Edhasa, 2004), 133–154.

25 In this respect, see the speeches by Ricardo Zinn, analyzed by Morresi in "Neoliberales antes del neoliberalismo," 115.

From the perspective of the analysis of public policies, ideas are prone to be turned into projects that are embodied in specific decisions and then succeed in taking root in institutions. The translation of doctrines into policies is not simple: supporters of the same ideas can reproach each other for betraying certain ideals in the construction of available options. It was the vetoes of nationalist militaries, their fractured power scheme, and the country's pervasive inflation that aggravated the differences and precipitated the change in the cast of liberal actors.

The critical voices raised have often been seen as limitations to the actions of the team headed by Martínez de Hoz, as objections to the "correct implementation" of the proposed models. However, these critical voices can also be interpreted as a sign that, as events were unfolding, there was an awareness of the risks faced and the consequences that could ensue. If the responsibility of government officials entails freedom and conscience, the economic team to a certain extent had both.

Lastly, seen from the perspective of the government, the devices implemented can contribute to distort the relation between benefits and responsibility. It is often said that whoever concentrates power also holds the greatest responsibilities. While this refers to public authorities, it may also apply to those who are in charge of steering the economy and who derive the greatest benefits from it. It is in this that neoliberal ideas made their great contribution.

While the dictatorship's economic policies left the state bankrupt and, therefore, weakened in its intervention capacities, they also strengthened a group of actors who benefited from public bankruptcy. With the independence of financial markets, indebtedness, and an entrenched instability, the military authorities exonerated those who most benefited from any accountability for the consequences of their actions. In other words, in contrast to postwar business operators who were tied to the fate of the country's domestic economy by a number of agreements and penalties, the new economic actors and their spokespersons acquired an unprecedented power for conditioning public authorities and were held free from any responsibility. On the one hand, as the state assumed the debt and the International Monetary Fund took on new roles,[26] the U.S. government, and the world financial community acquired veto power and the capacity to condition domestic affairs. These prerogatives were not derived from a democratic participation of the citizenry in the body's direction and could only be justified by the country's dependency on its financial aid. On the other hand, for the local and international agents who learned to speculate with the relation between exchange and interest rates, there was no penalty in sight other than the possibility that, as part of the risky game of their investments, they could be trapped by an unexpected political decision.

[26] S. Babb and A. Buira, "Mission Creep, Mission Push and Discretion: The Case of IMF Conditionality," in A. Buira (ed.), *The IMF and the World Bank at Sixty* (Malta: Anhem Press, 2005), 59–83.

As suggested by O'Donnell,[27] the post-dictatorship democratic governments were left at the mercy of groups from which they requested funds at high interest rates, instead of having the means to impose themselves and force those groups to act in a way that favored the general interest. In sum, the focus on investor confidence led, as of then, to a virtual monopolization of the economy ministry by non-partisan experts.[28] Thus, although endorsed by constitutional authorities, "economic" decisions were in substance developed by experts who did not participate in elections and were free from the accountability that applies to political authorities.

In this way, a fundamental continuity that links the dictatorship to the first three democratic governments is the split between economics and politics, to which numerous liberal economists and the think tanks that gathered them contributed decisively. This separation made it possible for economic decisions to be associated more to the management of things – which are by nature neutral – as opposed to the governing of individuals – who have conflicting and diverse values and interests. Not only was the economy to be left to operate autonomously and with the least possible intervention from political authorities, the rest of society, and particularly the sectors that were most affected, had to curb their demands and resign themselves to relinquishing past gains so that the dictates of the market could be heeded.

This disciplining process was possible because the new "economic" (dis)order succeeded, thanks to ideas, in crystallizing a new distribution of power. In evoking "market coups" in late 1989, *Ámbito Financiero* observed: "This democratic Argentina wants no more military coup d'états; it has succeeded in adopting a new strategy to defend itself from the demagogy of politicians."[29] Paradoxically, with the triumph of (neo)liberalism and the threat of new types of coups, the impersonal violence of the markets tended to exonerate the powerful from the imperative of justifying themselves. It no longer mattered if inequalities were acceptable or not (as the idea of legitimacy supposes): they had set themselves up as the only possible and imaginable reality (as is established by the idea of naturalization). With benefits naturalized and veto powers consolidated, traditional and technocratic liberals continued to move forward in the intensification of these changes, and to the virtues of words they added a recurring threat to the social order.

[27] G. O'Donnell, "Transitions, Continuities, and Paradoxes," in G. O'Donnell, S. Mainwaring, and J. Samiel Valenzuela (eds.), *Issues in Democratic Consolidation. The New South American Democracies in Comparative Perspective* (Notre Dame: Notre Dame University Press, 1992), 17–56.

[28] B. Ross Schneider, "The Material Bases of Technocracy: Investor Confidence and Neoliberalism in Latin America," in M. Centeno and P. Silva (eds.), *The Politics of Expertise in Latin America* (New York: St. Martin's Press, 1998), 77–95.

[29] *Ámbito Financiero* (Buenos Aires), December 15, 1989, 1–2.

4

Foreign Powers, Economic Support, and Geopolitics

Jorge E. Taiana

The military coup that was set in motion on March 24, 1976 – with its well-known and devastating human, social, and political costs – cannot be analyzed without taking into account the regional and international scenario in which it occurred. This scenario ensured a framework of political legitimation, economic cooperation, and security that in turn enabled the development and consolidation of the military dictatorship.

What follows is a series of reflections on the global and regional context that preceded and accompanied the coup d'état in Argentina, as well as on the role played by the United States and the dynamics of Argentine diplomacy and economic and military actors.

THE COLD WAR

To begin with, the context was the world of the cold war, built on the ruins left by World War II, based on the division of the world into areas of influence of the two great superpowers that emerged as victors of the conflict: the United States of America and the Soviet Union.

These two nations acted as heads of two poles of global power set against each other in a confrontation that extended to the spheres of politics (liberal democracy versus one-party system; civil and political rights versus economic and social rights), the economy (capitalism based on the market and great corporations versus socialism based on central planning and public property), and ideology (individualism versus socialism). As these two models were presented as mutually exclusive, antagonistic, and in permanent conflict, adherence and subordination to the interests and priorities of whichever power dominated their region would over time turn into a demand that greatly curtailed the autonomy of the countries of the periphery that were not central to the scheme of power, and it severely limited their possibilities of developing policies of their own.

Part of the agreement resulted in the creation of the United Nations, which came to replace the failed Society of Nations and became a political forum for channeling differences and consolidating the new global political reality. A system of power was crystallized in the 1945 San Francisco Conference, giving the "five great" powers the right to veto and virtual control over an organization whose main goals were to avoid a new world war, manage tensions between the central countries, and regulate the anti-colonialist struggle that was being waged in the so-called Third World and that over the following decades would bring the great colonial empires to an end.

It was not only the political order that was restructured after the global conflict, but the economic order as well. The reordering of the capitalist world was directed by the United States through the signing of the Bretton Woods Agreements in 1944. These agreements laid the foundations for the creation of the International Monetary Fund and the World Bank and set the rules of the game for the financial world, while at the same time giving a privileged role to the dollar. The General Agreement on Tariffs and Trade (GATT) came shortly after, in 1947. These structures, which are still operating today, tended to establish free trade and the free flow of capitals, with clear prerogatives for the production and expansion of developed countries, protecting their agricultural productions at the same time that they obtained favorable conditions to export their goods and services and to place their capital in the developing world.

This polarized world avoided a direct confrontation between the superpowers under the "nuclear deterrence" doctrine, based on an equilibrium of forces that guaranteed "mutually assured destruction" in the event of a nuclear war, which, precisely because of that, made such a possibility politically impossible.

The concept of "cold war" is actually equivocal, as it is often understood to mean the existence of a long period of political rivalry and tension between two blocs but with no open armed conflicts. There is nothing further from the truth. While a nuclear war between the superpowers was effectively avoided, the cold war decades were filled with a wide range of violent conflicts, which left millions dead, injured, and displaced, and in which each great power took sides with the aim of supporting an ally, gaining influence in the region, or, more restrictively, destabilizing their rival's area of influence.

From the war in the Korean Peninsula in the early 1950s, to the feat of the Vietnamese people (achieving independence and national reunification in 1975 after three decades of conflict, having defeated three world powers, and losing as many as two million lives), and with the Igbo secession war in Nigeria in the 1960s, the various wars in the Middle East, and the insurrections and revolutionary uprisings in Latin America in between, all of these conflicts, even the apparently local ones, contain elements that polarize, antagonize, and place them in the broader scenario of the great powers' search for dominance and influence.

Concurrently with the cold war, a process of decolonization took place, led by the United Nations. Concentrated first in Asia and moving later to Africa, to finally reach the Caribbean and Pacific islands, this decolonization in fact comprised very different processes and attained various degrees of agreement or confrontation between colonizer and colonized, ranging from the partition of India in 1947 to the independence of Zimbabwe in 1980. This enabled the emergence of new states, which in less than thirty years increased the number of UN member states threefold. In all of these processes, the interests and actions of the great powers were also present, as they sought to establish better relations with the new countries. Generally speaking, the Second World, headed by the Soviet Union, provided greater support to Third World independence and liberation struggles, confronting a First World that identified with the colonizer.

The division of the world into two great blocs – formed by capitalists and communists – pitted against each other in all spheres and "blocked together" in opposing military alliances (NATO, or the North Atlantic Treaty Organization, for the countries aligned under the leadership of the United States, and the Warsaw Pact for followers of the Soviet Union), together with the new states emerging from the decolonization process generated the conditions for the emergence of autonomous positions that refused to align themselves with either bloc and proposed equidistant stances; that is, a third position: non-alignment. In this sense, the independence of the Third Position raised early on by Juan Domingo Perón, which led him to exclude Argentina from the Bretton Woods Agreements, is well known, as are the actions of leaders such as Nasser, Tito, Nehru, and Sukarno, resulting in the forming of the Non-Aligned Movement (NAM) after the Bandung Conference, which became a major political representative of developing countries.

The core of non-alignment or the Third Position was, as its name indicates, the rejection of bloc politics. The aim was not, naturally, to deny the existence of these blocs, but to maintain that as bloc politics responded to the interests of the superpowers, if a country wished to be sovereign it should not align itself with either.

If politically the search for autonomy and an independent voice in the international scenario led to the creation of the NAM, the need to coordinate positions and make common diagnoses with respect to economic issues, international commerce, and the model of development led to the forming of the coalition known as the Group of 77. This body became the voice of the interests of developing and periphery countries to counter the positions of developed or central countries, as these normally provided support for the policies and interests of large companies, which around those years were beginning to be known as multinational corporations.

Coinciding with the cold war, the multiplicity of conflicts, and the process of decolonization, starting in the postwar period, the world experienced a sustained period of growth, which is considered a golden age of development and extends uninterruptedly over almost three decades. In a world in which the economy of the United States represented almost 50 percent of the gross world product, the lasting effects of the crisis of the 1930s appeared to have been left permanently behind, and the expansion of international commerce and the world economy seemed limitless.

This growth was enjoyed by the global economy as a whole and extended to different political and economic regimes, both Western capitalist economies and the socialist world, as well as the various models of the Third World. The widespread assumption of economic growth and development was thus such that the debate between models seemed to focus on which would be the fastest and least costly road to economic growth and development.

LATIN AMERICA AND THE UNITED STATES

In this bipolar world, Latin America fell under the influence of the United States, a fact that further consolidated and institutionalized the predominant role that the United States had already attained in the region. While its influence and interference in the region had seen numerous antecedents since the nineteenth century, it is during World War II that the countries of Latin America, with the exception of Argentina, agree to subordinate themselves to the hemispheric defense and security policy.

In the sphere of defense, the United States promoted the signing of a number of offensive and defensive treaties that were aimed at incorporating the other countries to its military containment strategy against the Soviet Union. In the region, the 1945 Act of Chapultepec was succeeded by the Inter-American Treaty of Reciprocal Assistance (IATRA), which was signed in 1947, in Rio de Janeiro, and whose bases had already been secured during the war. This process of institutionalization culminated in the creation of the Organization of American States (OAS) at the Bogotá Conference, held amid unrest over the murder of popular leader Eliécer Gaitán.

In that framework, ideological, political, and military subordination to the leadership of the United States was accompanied by a growing presence of large U.S. companies, which headed processes of modernization, concentration, and increasing foreign ownership in the region's economies. As the cold war advanced and social unrest grew, this process became more and more intolerant of autonomous national experiences that questioned subordination to the interests of the hegemonic power. The cases of the Guatemala of Arbenz, toppled in 1954 with the open intervention of the United States, and the overthrow of Perón in Argentina in 1955 exemplify the disciplining actions taken and the curtailment and stifling of national and popular experiences.

The great conflict that marked the region and whose effects continued beyond the end of the cold war was, of course, the Cuban Revolution, led by Fidel Castro, and the repeated and failed attempts by the United States to end a self-proclaimed socialist experience that was openly allied with and supported by the Soviet Union. Cuba's experience exposed the region's prevailing inequality and injustices, as well as the illegitimacy of regimes that based their existence on the support of one of the great powers and on a firm anticommunist alignment. As this experience tensed the global "order," it questioned the division of the world into areas of influence.

Regional politics took on a global dimension when the Cuban question marked an intensification of the cold war. The failed invasion of the island and the "missile crisis" put the two superpowers on the brink of a full-blown war. At the same time that in the region it called for sanctions against Cuba and for the breaking off of diplomatic relations with the revolutionary regime, in 1961 the United States launched the Alliance for Progress. Conceived as a global response to the regional challenge posed by the Cuban Revolution, in practice it was a financial aid program implemented by the United States to promote the modernization of economic and social structures, in the framework of the support for free enterprise and foreign investments. Its very meager results underscored the limitations of that policy in the region and the failure by the United States to support substantial changes for the democratization of productive structures and improved income distribution.

Even with all its limitations, the years of economic growth of that long postwar cycle entailed major changes in production, the modernization of archaic agrarian production models, the emergence of organized hubs of industrial workers, the expansion of the public sector and the role of the state, the forming of massive trade unions representing state and education workers, the strengthening of independent middle sectors, and, in general, a greater demand for participation in and democratization of the traditionally oligarchic political structures.

The consequence of these processes was a proliferation of social, political, and economic demands that, in the absence of true processes of development and structural democratization, the prevailing political system tended to repress rather than satisfy. Thus a period of great social unrest began, with frequent economic crises, democratic governments that were increasingly more restrictive and less legitimate, and a growing involvement of the armed forces in repressive activities, in crisis resolution, and in the political direction of the states.

The armed forces had a long history of political involvement in Latin America. What sets this stage apart from previous experiences is the institutional nature of this participation, and the fact that it acquired a more significant dimension, both locally and regionally, as it fell under the "National Security Doctrine," which provided a strategic framework for military action and gave the armed forces a prominent role in the fight against international communism in the scenario of the cold war.

THE NATIONAL SECURITY DOCTRINE

Developed in U.S. military academies and universities, the National Security Doctrine was the ideological basis and strategic thinking that enabled the structuring of all the actions aimed at consolidating the global hegemony of the United States, blocking the growth of the soviet area of influence and disciplining the demands in its own area of influence. Although it had its origins in the French strategy applied in the colonial wars of Indochina and Algeria, under the name "Counterrevolutionary War Doctrine," and was brought to Argentina by French instructors even before it reached the United States, it was widely disseminated in Latin America by U.S. institutions that adapted it to the context of the cold war. In this way, it became the official doctrine of the armies of the region, with two important political consequences. On the one hand, it completely changed the focus of attention of the training and actions of the armed forces. They no longer faced an exclusively external enemy, from which they had to defend their own population, but – on the contrary – the enemy was a *part* of that population, which in alliance with international communism sought to destroy the traditional values of society. The armed forces thus went from being the defenders of their own people to being its repressors. On the other hand, democracy and political participation became practices that needed to be subordinated to the main objective of fighting communism and wiping out the subversive elements that questioned the status quo. The political system not only had to prevent the triumph of communism, it also had to successfully remove communism from the societies of the region.

In the early 1970s, several situations converged to form the scenario that would turn the region, and in particular the Southern Cone, into the territory in which military dictatorships inspired by the National Security Doctrine toppled democratic governments, eliminated all forms of political participation and most civil liberties, and applied mass systematic repression policies that targeted broad sectors of the population.

The long cycle of economic growth that had begun with the postwar had come to an end. Heralded by the crisis prompted by Richard Nixon's decision to drop the gold standard in 1971, the so-called oil crisis that began in October 1973, when oil producing countries members of the Organization of Petroleum Exporting Countries (OPEC) quadrupled the price per barrel, sunk the economies of the developed world into a recession and put an end to cheap-fuel-based growth. The substantial resources generated by oil sales were recycled through Western banks and gave way to the indebtedness of Third World countries, a phenomenon that would have an enormous weight in the last quarter of the twentieth century. The effects on the world economy were long-lasting and would initiate an extended process of capitalist restructure, which had its greatest exponents in conservative leaders Ronald Reagan and Margaret Thatcher.

As the economic cycle began its downward turn at the global level, in the region the masses were increasingly mobilizing, demanding greater political participation, better income distribution, and profound changes in the systems of production and property. They also demanded a more active and controlling role for the state in directing economic growth and in productive activities themselves.

The political and social forces that converged in these demands had diverse origins but they all agreed on the need to introduce urgent and far-reaching changes. Different sectors of popular nationalism, the revolutionary Left, Christian movements committed to the poor, rank-and-file and class-based trade unionism, and factions of the more traditional parties all stepped up their social and political activism while at the same time radicalizing their critique of the status quo, influenced by the processes of deep transformation that were taking place across the Third World and as a reaction to the obvious political crisis that had been stirring Europe and the United States since the 1960s.

This boom of the masses, as it was referred to then, was expressed in various ways and affected the whole of the region, where it took on diverse forms of participation and struggle that went from different groups joining together in new electoral coalitions and forces to insurrectional union strikes and insurgent movements. Although there were governments in several countries that tried to implement measures that contemplated these demands for change, the two emblematic experiences in the region were the Unidad Popular government headed by Salvador Allende in Chile and the return of Peronism and Perón to the government in Argentina.

The democratic path to the construction of socialism proposed by Allende and the return of Perón after almost two decades in which popular nationalism had been banned represented great efforts to transform economically dependent societies dominated by oligarchic sectors and foreign capital into participatory democracies, in which key sectors of the economy would be controlled by the state, the power of multinational corporations would be limited, and income distribution would be significantly modified.

Despite their contradictions and internal conflicts, these processes met with open resistance from and destabilization efforts by the forces that opposed change, which saw their immediate interests affected and wanted to return to a scenario of greater social disciplining, dismantling of labor protection legislation,[1] limited control of the state over the economy, and enhanced privileges for the operation of large corporations.

[1] On the reforms of Argentine labor law carried out during the dictatorship, see Chapter 15 in this book.

The end of economic expansion in the international scenario and the recession faced by the global economy only served to further strengthen the determination of traditional exporters, large corporations, and the financial sector to quash popular experiences. Thus, with the active involvement of U.S. policy in the region during the Richard Nixon and Gerald Ford administrations, all pretense of democratic legitimacy was dropped in favor of resorting instead to the armed forces unified under the National Security Doctrines. The armed forces then set in motion actions to wipe out any form of popular organization and to radically transform the economic and social structures that had enabled the development of such powerful efforts to question the status quo.

THE 1976 COUP D'ÉTAT

The Gerald Ford administration offered its silent but consistent support to the actions that culminated in the 1976 coup. In part, that support reflected the conviction that the definition of the direction in Argentina's economic course that was most convenient for the United States could not be left in the hands of a civilian government.[2] The attitude of the U.S. Embassy in Buenos Aires was representative of the anticommunist and free market tendencies that had been typical of Nixon's policies with respect to Latin America. This is evident, for example, in its reporting of the coup as "probably the best executed and most civilized coup in Argentine history." According to its assessment of the situation, the best interests of both Argentina and the United States depended on the "success of the moderate gov[ernment] now led by Gen Videla."[3] Secretary of State Kissinger, for his part, sentenced in a memorandum:

> The three service commanders are known for their pro-U.S., anticommunist attitudes. ... Investment problems will be minimized by the junta's favorable attitude toward foreign capital, while the government's probable intention of seeking U.S. aid, tangible and/or moral, to overcome pressing economic problems will provide added insurance against openly anti-U.S. attitudes and policies.[4]

[2] The U.S. Embassy in Buenos Aires viewed "leftist terrorism" as a "threat to U.S. business interests." Department of State telegram, Buenos Aires, A-143, U.S. Embassy (Montllor) to secretary of state (Kissinger), June 16, 1975, subject: "Political Violence in Argentina," quoted in W. Schmidli, "Institutionalizing Human Rights in US Foreign Policy: US-Argentine Relations 1976–1980" (2011) 35 (2) *Diplomatic History*, 355.

[3] Department of State telegram, Buenos Aires, 2061, U.S. Embassy (Hill) to secretary of state (Kissinger), March 29, 1976, quoted in Schmidli, "Institutionalizing Human Rights," 359.

[4] Department of State telegram (Kissinger), Washington, to all diplomatic posts in the republics of the Americas, February 25, 1976, on the analysis of developments in Argentina, quoted in Schmidli, "Institutionalizing Human Rights," 360.

Kissinger had given the green light to Argentina: within forty-eight hours after the coup, the United States formally recognized the new government and the International Monetary Fund granted it a previously approved loan of US$127 million. Soon, however, the embassy would begin conveying its concern over the serious reports of human rights abuses perpetrated by members of the security forces.

On June 10, 1976, Kissinger met with then Minister of Foreign Affairs César Augusto Guzzetti to discuss bilateral relations. This private meeting was held during an OAS conference in Santiago de Chile. The affable tone of the exchange surprised the Argentine minister, who was half expecting to be reprimanded for the human rights abuses reported. Between comments regarding the upcoming world cup championship, Kissinger defined these reports as an obstacle that had no chance of interfering with the friendly support of the United States to Argentina in its challenge of solving as soon as possible the conflict faced by the country.[5] After this meeting, while on an official mission to the United States, Guzzetti was received by Vice President Nelson Rockefeller.[6]

Meanwhile, the junta took the initiative of strengthening foreign investments in the country and its participation in international commerce. Specifically, it invested enormous sums in a strategy to boost confidence in the Argentine state through the image portrayed in the press and its public relations with the U.S. business community and conservative politicians. This activity was carried out in coordination with the Council for the Americas, an association founded and at that time presided by David Rockefeller, which still gathers the leading U.S. companies with interests in Latin America. As explained in Chapter 3 in this book, neoliberal economic thinking deeply influenced Argentina's economic research centers and, transitorily, the policies of the national government.

Following Jimmy Carter's victory over Gerald Ford in the 1977 U.S. elections, the Department of State entered a new stage, with the establishment of an office for Human Rights Affairs under the coordination of Patricia Derian and the work by Tex Harris at the U.S. Embassy in Buenos Aires. Derian and Harris, along with members of U.S. Congress and human rights organizations based in Washington, DC, received information from their peers in Argentina and from exile groups and

5 U.S. Department of State, Memorandum of Conversation, Santiago, Chile, June 6 (sic), 1976, available at www2.gwu.edu/~nsarchiv/NSAEBB/NSAEBB133/19760610%20Memorandum%20of%20Conversation%20clean.pdf

6 U.S. Department of State, Electronic Telegram, 1976BUENOS06871_b, Buenos Aires, October 19, 1976, where Ambassador Hill reports on Minister Guzzetti's impressions upon his return to Washington, DC: "Guzzetti said his reception at the Department of State, by the Secretary … and the ceremonies dedicating the San Martin monument had gone far beyond his expectations. He expressed appreciation that high officials in our government 'understand the Argentina problem and stand with us in this difficult period.' He said he was 'satisfied that the State Department clearly understands the problem and that there would be no confrontation between the two governments over human rights.'" Available at www.wikileaks.org/plusd/cables/1976BUENOS06871_b.html.

played a key role in the process of documenting and reporting the human rights violations that were being perpetrated in the country, a process that determined a change in the U.S. government's policy toward the military regime in Argentina.

This change was implemented, in part, through economic rewards and penalties, such as the reduction in military aid from US$48 million to US$15 million and the withholding of over US$1 billion in nonmilitary imports, including bank transactions, pending an improvement in the human rights situation.[7] The approval of credits for the purchase of hydroelectric turbines was, in fact, conditioned to the Argentine government's acceptance of a mission to the country, which was finally carried out in 1979, headed by the Inter-American Commission on Human Rights.

After the Soviet Union's invasion of Afghanistan and the embargo on grain exports to that country, a paradoxical shift in Argentina-U.S. relations occurred when Argentina decided to sell millions of tons of grain to the USSR. Nonetheless, diplomatic ties between the two countries would be strengthened again with the election of Ronald Reagan in 1980.

CONCLUSIONS

The military regime inaugurated in April 1976 opened a new chapter in Argentina's international situation, in the context of the stagnation and recession of the global economy that prevailed after the energy crisis. The military regime implemented its foreign policy at the "economic diplomacy" level, headed by Economy Minister Martínez de Hoz, and at the "military diplomacy" level, under the direction of the juntas, in the framework of Argentina's active insertion in the East-West conflict, but not without some disagreements with the United States (the Argentine government's refusal to abandon its independent nuclear program, despite pressure from Carter, and its decision to continue with its grain exports to the Soviet Union, which during the U.S. ban became Argentina's top buyer). Relations between the two countries were not always smooth, as is reflected in the Malvinas/Falklands war.

The immediate result of Martínez de Hoz's economic diplomacy was the rapid improvement in the country's relations with the international banking system and the U.S. financial sector, in exchange for benefits derived from the new engineering of national economic programs and the growth of the country's external debt. The regime's explicit will to subordinate itself to the world economic order was, in turn, what it offered in consideration for "understanding" and tolerance of the repressive policies implemented in the country.

Military diplomacy, for its part, fed on the "vanguard" conviction that a nonconventional "third world war" was being waged against an enemy represented

7 On this change of policy that was reflected in the bilateral and multilateral aid that was (not) granted during the Carter administration, see Chapter 7 in this book.

by national subversive movements supported by the Soviet Union and its allies, and that the freedom of the West depended on the outcome of this war. Although the leadership of the United States was acknowledged, it was believed that repressive military actions at the national and transnational levels had to be free of moral and legal limitations, such as those represented by Jimmy Carter's human rights policy.

These two tracks of Argentina's foreign policy – military diplomacy and economic diplomacy – were the manifestation of the power of two actors whose alliance enabled the overtaking of the state: the armed forces and the economic groups connected with exporting and financial interests.

PART III

The Macroeconomics of the Dictatorship

5

The Legacy of the Dictatorship: The New Pattern of Capital Accumulation, Deindustrialization, and the Decline of the Working Class

Eduardo M. Basualdo

INTRODUCTION

This chapter analyzes the last military dictatorship, which – despite having ended thirty years ago – still enjoys a notable presence today. One of the reasons for its continued presence is the culmination of the trials of the perpetrators of repression, which only as of 2003 found an institutional course to move firmly forward. Another reason is that since 2008 the government of Cristina Fernández de Kirchner did not only have to stand up to international credit institutions and financial capital but also to local economic groups, which controlled politics during those tragic years.

The approach proposed in this chapter is based on an examination of the economic aspects of the dictatorship, linking them to certain political and social elements. Establishing such connections is inevitable as the main hypothesis of this study is that the military dictatorship set in motion a specific pattern of capital accumulation.[1] In other words, the dictatorship promoted an economic, political, and social process comparable in magnitude to the agro-export model of the early twentieth century headed by the Pampas-based oligarchy; or to the initial stage of the subsequent import substitution model, which came to a close during the early half of the 1950s with the first governments of President Perón; or the second stage of import substitution with the introduction of heavy industry in the country and its expansion as of 1958, in the framework of the transnational economic growth of the postwar.

This study focuses on two key issues. After introducing the subject, it provides a brief analysis of the second stage of import substitution. Analyzing this stage is

This study was conducted in the framework of a CONICET project (112-2008-0103153) on the behavior of big business in Argentina, in FLACSO's Economy and Technology Area.

[1] On this issue, see E. M. Basualdo, "Concepto de patrón o régimen de acumulación y conformación estructural de la economía," *Documento n° 1*, Master's Program in Argentine Political Economy; Economy and Technology Area, FLACSO, Buenos Aires (2007).

relevant because it was during that period that the context in which the March 1976 military coup and subsequent dictatorship took shape. The relation of forces between the working class and the sectors in power was altered and a new role was assumed by the armed forces, as they established themselves as a military party that expressed the interests of the ruling classes. During this stage two domestic military factions were also formed (known as the *Azules*, or Blues, and the *Colorados*, or Reds), which went up against each other in the framework of the popular resistance to the dictatorship.

Exploring this stage is also significant because of the belief that by the mid-1970s industrialization had been exhausted and the country's economic course had to be redirected, a view held by both conventional wisdom and certain academic conceptions.[2] According to this view, a radical change of direction in the country's economic policy was imperative, a change that would introduce structural changes toward recovering the growth that had been lost. This challenge had supposedly been taken up by the military dictatorship.

The second issue deals with the economic and social processes under the dictatorship, which gave way to a new pattern of capital accumulation. The genesis of the class-based revenge launched with the military coup, which eliminated by fire and sword the gains achieved by workers and imposed an unprecedented regressive redistribution that would become from then on a structural characteristic is, no doubt at all, one of the crucial elements of that analysis. Another is the central importance acquired by external debt and capital flight, as well as their relation with the power bloc that emerged under these new circumstances.

BACKGROUND: THE SECOND STAGE OF IMPORT SUBSTITUTION

The Peronist governments stretched light industrialization out unnecessarily, which is why one of the leading unsettled accounts of these governments is having failed

[2] The classic study by Juan Carlos Portantiero ("Clases dominantes y crisis política," *Pasado y Presente*, no. 1, Buenos Aires, 1973) is an eloquent example of academic analyses that posited the exhaustion of industrialization throughout the process of import substitution, as the basic assumption of his important theory of the existence of a "hegemonic tie" is that the process of industrialization had ended in the 1950s. The exhaustion theory acquired new strength with the military dictatorship, but as an underlying conclusion in the analysis of the limitations of that pattern of accumulation. An example of this is the study by Bernardo Kosacoff on industrial transformations ("Desarrollo industrial e inestabilidad macroeconómica. La experiencia argentina reciente," in B. Kosacoff and D. Azpiazu, *La industria argentina: desarrollo y cambios estructurales* (Buenos Aires: CEAL-CEPAL, 1989)). The exhaustion thesis reemerged during the 1989 hyperinflationary crisis, but this time focusing the problem on the substitution state. This appears to be the case of the following works, among others: T. Halperin Donghi, *La larga agonía de la Argentina peronista* (Buenos Aires: Ariel, 1994); V. Palermo and M. Novaro, *Política y poder en el gobierno de Menem* (Buenos Aires: Norma, 1996); and J. J. Llach, *Otro siglo, otra Argentina. Una estrategia para el desarrollo económico y social nacida de la convertibilidad y de su historia* (Buenos Aires, Ariel: 1997).

to take the country's industrialization to a higher level[3] – although they did try and even had some success in metallurgy, which expanded beyond the average growth of manufacture in the country.[4]

Heavy industry began to be implemented after the coup that interrupted Perón's second term, even though in very different conceptions and under very different circumstances, in the context of the transnationalization that prevailed in the postwar world. The second stage of import substitution began in that framework, supported by the inflow of foreign capital, which came to dominate the country's industry through the activities that were incorporated during those years (automobile, chemical and petrochemical, steel, etc.) and which were the most dynamic sectors in an industry that led the economy as a whole.[5]

Without going into detail here regarding that pattern of accumulation, on which there is a significant and extensive body of literature, it should be noted that between 1956 and 1974 the country's gross domestic product (GDP) grew considerably (at a cumulative annual growth rate of 4.2 percent) but without using all of its potential production capacity owing to periodic foreign exchange bottlenecks, which determined typical short-term cycles based on the stop-and-go pattern.

As some studies indicate, the second import substitution period was divided into two stages with differences that are critical for the issues analyzed here.[6] The first stage stretched from 1956 to 1963, a period in which GDP grew at an annual rate of 2.1 percent and production fell in absolute terms (negative rates) during the down phase of short-term cycles. The other stage extended from 1964 to 1974, with GDP growing at an annual 5.1 percent, resulting in a rapid expansion in the up-phase of short-term cycles and lower but still positive annual rates (slowdown) in the down-phase. The passage from an absolute drop to a slowdown in the down-phase is even more significant as it occurred in spite of an industry that works with "short

3 On this subject, see J. V. Sourrouille and J. Lucángeli, "Apuntes sobre la historia reciente de la industria argentina," *Boletín informativo Techint* n° 219, July–August–September 1980, Buenos Aires.

4 See J. F. Picabea, "Análisis de la trayectoria tecnoproductiva de la industria estatal argentina. El caso de IAME, 1952–1955," master's thesis, Master's Program in Political Economy, Economy and Technology Area, FLACSO (2011)), and E. Basualdo, *Los primeros gobiernos peronistas y la consolidación del país industrial: éxitos y fracasos* (Buenos Aires: Página/12-FLACSO, 2004).

5 See, among other works, D. Azpiazu, "Las empresas transnacionales de una economía en transición. La experiencia argentina en los años ochenta," *Estudios e informes de la CEPAL* no. 91, Santiago, Chile, 1989.

6 On this subject, see M. Brodersohn, "Política económica de corto plazo, crecimiento e inflación en la Argentina, 1950–1972," in *Problemas económicos argentinos* (Buenos Aires: Macchi, 1977), pp. 3–54; E. Basualdo, *Estudios de historia económica argentina. Deuda externa y sectores dominantes desde mediados del siglo XX a la actualidad*(Buenos Aires: FLACSO-Siglo XXI, 2nd ed., 2006), pp. 53–63; and F. Amico, "Notas sobre la industrialización por sustitución de importaciones en la Argentina: buscando adentro la fuente de competitividad externa," H-Industri@ n° 9, Buenos Aires, 2011.

series" of production, a high level of diversification, and scarce development in process and product technology.[7] This second stage comprised the decade with the greatest uninterrupted growth that the country had seen thus far in industrial production and in the economy in general, with a significant growth in productivity, employment, and the average size of factories.

This change in the short cycle is crucial because it indicates an increasing macroeconomic sustainability and not a progressive weakness or exhaustion of the import substitution stage. These transformations did not alter the nature of the accumulation pattern, but necessarily entailed changes in economic variables and, particularly, in those that until that moment had caused the GDP to drop in absolute terms during the contraction phase of the cycle.

Those changes were associated with the growth pace of exports, which grew at a rate above the GDP.[8] Manufacturing industries saw the most dramatic growth (with an annual cumulative rate of 20 percent from 1962 to 1975), but even agricultural products were above the average economic growth (at an annual cumulative rate of 7.1 percent for the same period).

The sharp growth in exports, both agricultural and industrial, was linked to the nature of this industrialization. In manufacture it was undeniably tied to a tight control by foreign capital and the collapse of national companies. The severe retraction of textile exports (which dropped to an annual cumulative rate of 18.1 percent between 1962 and 1975) was a sign of the declining national bourgeoisie of the Peronist era, while the increase in foreign sales of machinery, materials and electrical equipment (which grew at an annual 37.5 percent during that same period), and especially of transport equipment (which reached a cumulative annual rate of 64.7 percent), expressed the foreign capital boom. There were, of course, other productions that also significantly expanded their export activities (including the chemical, petrochemical, and metallurgy industries), but they were all characterized by the predominance of foreign oligopolistic companies.[9]

The role played by foreign sales was a key factor in the alteration of the short cycle of the import substitution period, but it was not the only factor, as the external debt also contributed in this sense. As the second import substitution period advanced, the country's external debt grew, especially in the public sector, which continued

7 On the shortcomings of the import substitution industries of that period, see J. Katz, "Estrategia industrial y ventajas comparativas dinámicas," *Cuaderno n° 1*, Fundación Eugenio Blanco, Buenos Aires, 1983.

8 See the studies by ECLAC: "Estadísticas de corto plazo de la Argentina. Sector externo y condiciones económicas internacionales," *Documento de Trabajo* n° 20, Buenos Aires, CEPAL, 1986; and "Exportación de manufacturas y desarrollo industrial. Dos estudios sobre el caso argentino (1973–1984)," *Documento de Trabajo* n° 22, Buenos Aires, 1986.

9 Empirical evidence for this is provided in ECLAC (CEPAL), "Exportación de manufacturas."

to have the largest debt, together with a growing private external debt. It should be emphasized that, because of the process that began with the military dictatorship, the evolution of both public and private indebtedness was tied to industrial growth.[10]

The combination of these phenomena – export growth and foreign indebtedness – caused an upward trend in the reserves available in Argentina's Central Bank (Banco Central de la República Argentina, BCRA) that indicates a significant advance in the sustainability of the process of industrialization. This fact undoubtedly contradicts the established commonsense conviction that assesses, as noted previously, this process of import substitution as definitely exhausted by the mid-1970s.

The differences between the two stages of the second import substitution period were not only economic but also political and social. This is so because throughout this period substantial changes occurred in the prevailing relation of forces between popular sectors and the dominant power bloc.

There is a general belief that International Monetary Fund (IMF) adjustment policies were applied for the first time after the coup that deposed the Peronist government[11] and that this fact was the beginning of the harshest stage of Peronist resistance owing to the dictatorship's repression of popular sectors. This situation continued throughout the developmental government as, after winning the elections because of Peronist support, it implemented the State Internal Unrest Plan (Conmoción Interna del Estado, CONINTES) with the aim of repressing the numerous strikes and labor actions that were being staged, especially in the metallurgy and textile industries. In 1961, during the government of Arturo Frondizi, there was also an attempt to implement a railroad restructure plan that triggered bitter labor conflicts, as it involved the elimination of 50 percent of the railway system, selling lands, dismissing 75,000 workers, privatizing equipment maintenance and manufacture, and modifying employment conditions. Among the leading beneficiaries of the privatization proposed were the companies from the automotive sector – Fiat, General Motors, and General Electric – and the economic group Acindar, whose majority shareholder, Arturo Acevedo, was the Labor Minister.

10 There are several quantitative estimates from international agencies and academic and political authors, including: World Bank, *World Debt Table*, 1976–1977; ECLAC, "Estadísticas de corto plazo de la Argentina"; G. O'Donnell, *El estado burocrático autoritario: 1966–1973* (Buenos Aires: Editorial de Belgrano, 1982); and A. Cafiero, *De la economía social-justicialista al régimen liberal-capitalista* (Buenos Aires: Eudeba, 1974).

11 One of the first measures of the dictatorship that toppled Perón was Argentina's incorporation into the IMF and the World Bank. In that respect, the BCRA's 1956 Annual Report (*Memoria*) notes: "Ending the country's isolation in the field of international financial cooperation, it was decided by Decree 710, of April 19, 1956, that . . . the necessary steps would be taken for the Republic of Argentina to join the International Monetary Fund and the International Bank for Reconstruction and Development" (*Memoria*, p. 40). Membership was formalized on August 31, with the adoption of the Articles of Agreement of the IMF And the IBRD by Decree-Law 15,970.

As popular sectors and the dominant power bloc faced each other in a heightened and uneven conflict, their respective representations changed, in a reconfiguration that is key for understanding the accumulation pattern and the nature of the March 1976 military coup.

In 1957 and 1962, as part of popular resistance, the La Falda and Huerta Grande programs were launched. Both were critical milestones in the process of differentiation between combative unionism and labor bureaucracy led by Augusto T. Vandor. This rift deepened in 1968 with the founding of an offshoot of the General Confederation of Labor (Confederación General del Trabajo, CGT), the CGTA (CGT de los Argentinos), when the popular offensive began. It was consolidated in 1969 during the *Cordobazo* uprising and, once the cycle of military dictatorships was defeated, it was furthered during the third Peronist government, which began in 1973, with the irruption of the Peronist Working Youth (Juventud Trabajadora Peronista, JTP).

Following the defeat of Peronism, the armed forces became the party that expressed the interests of the ruling classes. In the late 1950s and early 1960s, in the context of the cold war and the Alliance for Progress launched by John F. Kennedy, the National Security Doctrine prevailed, based on the argument of the "war on communism," the equivalent to the fight against "internal subversion." This came to replace the conception of the "nation in arms" that had been predominant in the 1940s and 1950s, which understood that the duty of the armed forces was to defend national borders from foreign enemies, and that this required an economic self-sufficiency based on national control over a domestic economy built on the country's own industrial development.

One of the main lines of this new doctrine was to ensure economic growth to address social contradictions and defeat the internal enemy. Foreign capital was essential for achieving economic growth.[12] The other line was the repression of that subversive enemy, although – as often happens with the application of transnational doctrines – counterrevolutionary war was understood *all'uso nostro*, as for the Argentine ruling classes and, consequently, for the military party Peronism was a real or potential variant of communism.

While the military party agreed on the content of this doctrine, in its political practice it split into two opposing factions: *Azules* and *Colorados*. The core of the

[12] In this respect, the words spoken by Division General J. Iavícoli at the Seventh Conference of American Armies, held in Buenos Aires in October 1966, are eloquent: "Development can be defined as the expression of a number of changes in structures and in the social behavior of a people that puts that people in a state of permanently increasing its general real product. Development is to security what cause is to effect, origin to consequence, principal to secondary. Without development, security is utopian, [both] at the individual or national level and at the general or international level" (*Clarín*, November 3, 1966; quoted in Portantiero, "Clases dominantes").

Azules was in a way concentrated in the cavalry division, constituted to a great extent by descendants of the provincial and Pampas-based oligarchy that had opposed Juan Domingo Perón in his first governments. Militarily, it had close ties with the high commands of the air force and, politically, with the Intransigent Radical Civic Union (Unión Cívica Radical Intransigente, UCRI). The Colorados instead were mostly formed by mid-ranking officers of the infantry and artillery divisions, and had provided the military support for the first Peronist administrations. This faction's allies included most notably the navy and, among political parties, the Radical Civic Union (Unión Cívica Radical, UCR) and conservative sectors.[13]

The most significant difference between the two factions was in their approach how to deal with the popular movement and particularly with Peronism. The Colorados believed it was necessary to wipe out Peronism, as it meant the penetration of communism in the country; the Azules, instead, understood that it had to be politically neutralized, a goal that could be achieved by breaking it. Except for brief intervals, the military party was controlled by the Azules, who acted organically, both in consolidating their project – during the government of General Juan Carlos Onganía and its alliance with labor bureaucracy – and in retreating, once that attempt failed – under the leadership of General Alejandro Lanusse, who had to hand the government over to the Peronists in the midst of widespread popular unrest.

The Colorados, who during that time lacked a project comparable to that of the cavalry division, had their historical opportunity – in terms of doctrine but also of personal chances in many cases – when the armed forces were defeated by popular action and by the return of Perón to Argentina. As of that moment, the National Security Doctrine was subjected to a thorough review within the armed forces, which would lead to the war hypotheses that would be applied during the dictatorship that began on March 24, 1976. This new doctrine, inspired by the ideas of the Colorado faction and the French experience in the Algerian War (1954–1962),[14] would rest on an unprecedented repression to achieve the annihilation of the popular movement through what came to be known as the "dirty war" (the disappearance, torture, and murder of popular activists). In this way, the previous goal of economic growth was replaced by an economic restructure that would interrupt industrialization as a way

13 For a detailed analysis of the factions of the military party, see the classic studies on the subject: A. Rouquié, *Poder militar y sociedad política en la Argentina*, vol. 2: 1943–1973 (Buenos Aires: Emecé, 1982); and R. Potash, *El ejército y la política en la Argentina, 1962–1973. De la caída de Frondizi a la restauración peronista. Primera parte, 1962–1966* (Buenos Aires, Sudamericana, 1994).

14 In respect of the French influence in repression, it is interesting to recall the words of the then army commander, General Carlos Severo Toranzo Montero: "Closer ties between the armies of Argentina and France would be beneficial. If the French doctrines cannot be adopted purely and simply, they at least demand a more in-depth study to … adapt them to our particular case, considering our possibilities and needs" (*La Nación*, June 29, 1960; quoted in Rouquié, *Poder militar*).

of eliminating the structural conditions that gave way to social alliances and enabled the emergence of national and popular governments.[15]

THE INCOME REDISTRIBUTION AND ECONOMIC POLICIES OF THE MILITARY DICTATORSHIP

In the framework of the application of the new repressive doctrine, the dictatorship installed an unprecedentedly harsh redistribution of income to the detriment of workers, with a monetarist economic policy that cut short the process of industrialization and put financial valorization at the center of the country's restructure and macro- and microeconomic behavior. The combination of these processes defined a new pattern of accumulation that can be viewed as a homegrown variant of the neoliberal position that prevailed in the global economy as of the late 1970s, when class-based revenge reached its cruelest point.

As was to be expected, with the emergence of this model a new power bloc was formed, and the one corresponding to the second import substitution stage, formed by productive transnational capital and fractions of the Pampas-based oligarchy, was dissolved. The foreign industrial capital that had prevailed during the period of industrialization was fractured, and some transnational companies aligned themselves with the new power bloc while others repatriated their capitals. This new alliance was composed of local economic groups (the diversified fraction of the Pampas-based oligarchy) and international financial capital, which included private banks and international bodies (the political representatives of financial capital).[16]

The diversified fraction of the Pampas-based oligarchy took the helm of the state and, so as to ensure its hegemony, appointed its own organic intellectuals to key positions in the government. It was a capital fraction formed by, among others, economic groups such as Pérez Companc, Bridas, Acindar, Techint, Arcor, Loma Negra, Clarín, Macri, Bemberg, Bunge & Born, which had control of the state throughout the application of this accumulation model and succeeded in prevailing economically during its development (1976–2001).[17]

[15] For a rigorous analysis of this doctrine, see H. Verbitsky, *Malvinas, la última batalla de la tercera guerra mundial* (Buenos Aires: Sudamericana, 2002).

[16] About the dominant power bloc during the dictatorship and in particular on the diversified oligarchy, see D. Azpiazu, E. M. Basualdo, and M. Khavisse, *El nuevo poder económico en la Argentina de los años ochenta* (Buenos Aires, Siglo XXI, 2004).

[17] The following quote by Nicos Poulantzas on ruling alliances, hegemony, and their relationship with economic control is of interest here: "In talking of the bourgeoisie as the dominant class, it must not be forgotten that we are really dealing with an alliance between several dominant fractions of the bourgeoisie sharing in political domination. … This alliance between several classes and fractions which are all dominant can only function regularly under the leadership of one of those classes or fractions. This is the hegemonic fraction which unifies the power alliance under its leadership. The hegemonic fraction is the one that guarantees the general interest of the alliance and whose specific

The necessary condition for the development of the new accumulation pattern was income redistribution, which took on an unprecedented magnitude. Between 1976 and 1977, real wages fell by more than 40 percent, causing a sharp reduction in the participation of wage earners in the national income, which went from 45 to 25 percent, remaining throughout the dictatorship far below the level of 1969, the worst year in the second stage of import substitution.

With the coup d'état, workers lost the most basic and fundamental labor rights that they had gained through hard struggles over the previous decades.[18] During the military dictatorship, the government took control of the CGT; wage bargaining, the right to strike, and all other labor actions were suspended indefinitely; trade union privileges were eliminated; dismissal without cause was authorized for state employees; military supervisors were appointed to control the leading trade union organizations; the Ministry of Education was authorized to totally or partially suspend the application of the Teachers' Statute; and the Residence Act was reintroduced, enabling the expulsion from the country of anyone suspected of antinational security activities.

Particularly brutal were the disciplining actions against industrial workers, which formed the dynamic core of the working class. Not only were they repressed and denied their most basic social rights, like all other workers, but they also suffered under a systematic downsizing of employment in manufacture. Industrial employment dropped steadily over twenty-seven consecutive quarters (from the second quarter of 1976 to the fourth quarter of 1982) generating an increase of almost 70 percent in the rate of exploitation (productivity/labor cost).[19]

This downsizing of the working class occurred in the framework of the process of deindustrialization and the ensuing displacement of industry as the driving force of the economy and of the expansion of oligopolistic capital. From then on, wages ceased to be a determining factor in ensuring the level of aggregate demand and the

interests are particularly guaranteed by the state. While the dominant fractions' internal contradictions and their internal struggle to occupy the hegemonic place have a secondary role vis-à-vis the principal contradiction (bourgeois/proletariat) their role is still important . . . the various forms of state and forms of regime are marked by the changes in hegemony between the various bourgeois fractions. Still less can economic domination and political hegemony be identified in a necessary and mechanical fashion." (N. Poulantzas, "Las clases sociales," in *Las clases sociales en América Latina. Problemas de conceptualización*, Mérida Seminar, Yucatán (Mexico: Siglo XXI, 1975); quoted in E. Gálvez, *Crisis, economía y hegemonía en Argentina*, 1999–2003, PhD diss., Buenos Aires: FLACSO, and Paris: EHESS (2008).

18 See, Comisión Provincial por la Memoria, "La clase trabajadora durante la última dictadura militar argentina," *Dossier* n° 13, La Plata, (2011).

19 On employment adjustments carried out primarily by large corporations, see Azpiazu, Basualdo, and Khavisse, *El nuevo poder económico*, and L. Beccaria, "Distribución del ingreso en la Argentina: Explorando lo sucedido desde mediados de los setenta," (1991) *Desarrollo Económico*, n° 123, Buenos Aires, IDES.

realization of surplus value, and increasingly became a production cost that had to be reduced to a minimum to guarantee a greater profit for business.

In the context of this unprecedented income redistribution, the dictatorship implemented a financial reform through the decentralization of deposits and through regulations governing financial institutions (Law 21,526). This was another decisive step toward introducing a qualitative change in the economic and social structure, as through this reform the state yielded control over the intersectoral transfer of resources to the dominant power bloc.

This reform was followed by a succession of three monetarist policies that were intended to control inflation: an orthodox monetary policy (from June 1977 to April 1978), based on a contraction of the monetary base; a policy aimed at dampening inflationary expectations (from May to December 1978); and the monetary approach to the balance of payments (from January 1979 to February 1981), in which the financial reform converged with external openness in the product and capital markets.[20]

The first two policies were failed attempts. The monetary approach to the balance of payments, however, was decisive and brought about lasting structural changes. It was an organic policy because it contained the necessary instruments to benefit some capital fractions and to markedly damage others, by combining an exchange rate set on the basis of a devaluation that decreases over time with import liberalization – by lowering tariff and para-tariff barriers – and free capital outflows.

The free movement of capital was a key aspect for defining the nature of the economic and social restructure that the new economic policy entailed. The persistence of a domestic interest rate that systematically exceeded the cost of external debt – owing to, among other reasons, the revaluation of the peso introduced by José Martínez de Hoz's *tablita* – accelerated the foreign indebtedness of the dominant fractions, with the aim of valorizing that mass of resources in the domestic financial market to then take them out of the country.

As of 1979, the policy of the dictatorship found the key for achieving the restructure it sought, by driving out significant sectors of the national bourgeoisie – and even numerous foreign industrial companies that did not conform to the new guidelines – while simultaneously expanding the dominant capital fractions that formed its economic and social base. Just as industrial downsizing was implemented through a combination of tariff reform and the revaluation of the peso, the expansion of the dominant fractions was installed through fixed capital transfers and the dying off of companies in the real economy, and particularly through the appropriation of financial returns derived from the difference between domestic and international

[20] For an analysis of these policies, see R. Frenkel, "El desarrollo reciente del mercado de capitales en la Argentina," (1980) *Desarrollo Económico*, nº 78, Buenos Aires, IDES.

interest rates, which enabled these fractions to be the main recipients of the income derived from the reduced participation of wage earners and of the weaker business sectors.

FINANCIAL VALORIZATION: THE NEW CAPITAL ACCUMULATION PATTERN IMPOSED BY THE MILITARY DICTATORSHIP

In the new functioning of the Argentine economy, both foreign and public debt played an instrumental role. The local oligopolistic capital (mainly the large economic groups, but also foreign capital) contracted external debt, used those funds to purchase financial assets in the domestic market (securities, bonds, deposits, etc.) valorizing them through the positive differential of the domestic interest rate over the foreign interest rate, and finally send them out of the country. External debt ceased to be an instrument for financing productive investments or working capital to become a means for obtaining financial returns. The flip side to this indebtedness was capital flight and, consequently, there was a high correlation between the two.

The importance of the state in this stage, in which the economy was controlled by a diversified oligarchy, was decisive and it was expressed in at least three critical aspects. One aspect was public indebtedness in the domestic financial market – where the state was the national economy's largest borrower – which put the interest rate in that market systematically above the cost of indebtedness in the international market. Another aspect was the external debt contracted by the state, which supplied oligopolistic capital with the foreign currency it needed to take local capital outside the country. The last aspect consisted in the nationalization (absorption by the state) of the private external debt through the various exchange rate insurance regimes that were implemented as of 1981.

A factor that cannot be ignored is that the strategic leadership of the dictatorship – the economy cabinet – imposed a restructure of state-owned companies that served the interests of local economic groups. The so-called peripheral privatization allowed this capital fraction to seize a significant portion of the income of state-owned companies. It was a specific form of privatization that is not an antecedent to the privatization imposed by foreign creditors in the 1990s, but a different form, because it did not involve transferring the ownership of state companies but only their profitable operations through contracts. It was inspired in the modus operandi introduced by Krieger Vasena for public works during the Onganía dictatorship, which was the origin of the "contractor nation."

The oil and gas company Yacimientos Petrolíferos Fiscales (YPF), which during those years was the country's highest grossing company, constitutes an emblematic case, as between 1977 and 1980 the state awarded private contracts for twenty-one areas of oil extraction, paying contractors an oil price that greatly exceeded the original costs of the state-owned company.[21] Under these contracts, various local economic groups took over production in those areas, while the participation of foreign companies made that strategy viable within the dominant sectors. Among the economic groups that most benefited were Pérez Companc,[22] Bridas, Astra, Soldati, and Macri (SOCMA).[23]

Another line of action imposed on state companies was the obligation of contracting debt abroad to supply the foreign currency that would enable capital flight. This entailed a heavy load for state companies and for the post-dictatorship constitutional government. YPF is once again an emblematic case[24] in that process. According to available data, the US$375 million debt it had at the end of 1975 ballooned into a US$6 billion debt toward the end of the dictatorship, thus showing that the company's external debt was equal to the sum of all of its assets.[25]

An analysis of the evolution of key variables of the new accumulation pattern reveals a significant expansion in all of them, most intensively as of 1979, following

[21] On the specific characteristics of this process, see M. Barrera, *La entrega de YPF. El proceso de fragmentación y privatización* (Buenos Aires: Cara o Ceca, in press, 2014).

[22] The Pérez Companc group, a senior member, along with the Techint group, of the contractor nation (*la patria contratista*), was one of the leading YPF contractors. Oscar Vicente, an executive of the group, said in an interview: "The year 1958 is when the company decides to go into oil. Pérez Companc, at that time, had a turnover of less than US$10 million. 1967: sales increased threefold when the company began operating in oil drilling and production; that's when the Entre Lomas contract was secured. 1976, 1977, 1978: these are the years of the great privatization of oil contracts, when we bought Sade-General Electric. By then we were grossing well above US$100 million. 1981, '82, and '83: Sade was in full operation. And we were grossing US$300 million to US$400 million." L. Majul, *Los dueños de la Argentina. Vol II: Los secretos del verdadero poder* (Buenos Aires: Sudamericana, 1994).

[23] In 1982, with Reynaldo Bignone as dictatorial president and Alieto Guadagni as energy secretary, the original contracts were renegotiated. The journalist Marcelo Bonelli analyzed this renegotiation and among other issues noted: "The power group of the three Argentine sisters, formed by the influential economic conglomerates that make up the Bridas group, the Pérez Companc consortium, and Astra corporation, had no qualms about placing its men in government positions, using the media, and even buying opinions to overcome the legal, technical, and economic resistances that prevented the amendment of the agreements signed by YPF. ... These three sisters also operated with a few cousins, the SOCMA group and Soldati holding. ... From 1977 to 1981, period in which all the areas renegotiated by the military dictatorship were awarded, twelve of the twenty-one contracts in question were awarded to the three sisters, three went to cousin SOCMA and one to the Soldati group. In sum, the family obtained 76 percent of the areas awarded, including seven of the most important contracts, such as the 25 de Mayo-Medanitos contract, which is jointly operated by the two eldest sisters: Bridas and Pérez Companc." M. Bonelli, *Un volcán en llamas. Los contratos petroleros* (Buenos Aires: Corregidor, 1984).

[24] It should be noted that José A. Cosentino, former president of YPF, declared in court that the company "was forced to contract, or it was determined that it would contract new loans in foreign currency ... but YPF received pesos instead of dollars. The order to increase its debt was given over the telephone by finance ministry officials, usually Juan Alemann." J. Ballesteros. Legal decision by Judge Ballesteros on court case n° 14467: 'Olmos, Alejandro s. denuncia,' Buenos Aires, 2000, quoted in Barrera, *La entrega de YPF*.

[25] See Barrera, *La entrega de YPF*.

the adoption of the monetary approach to the balance of payments. In 1983, the external debt was 6.6 times greater than in 1975 (going from US$7.7 billion to US$45.9 billion in that time). Local capital flight in 1983 was almost seven times that of 1975 (increasing from US$5.4 billion to US$37.1 billion) and the interests paid to foreign creditors were 5.4 times the interests paid in 1975 (from US$2.5 billion to US$13.5 billion).[26]

In addition to the notable growth of these variables in an economy that was stagnant or in crisis, there were other relevant phenomena. Not only did capital flight increase vertiginously but its importance with respect to external debt also rose. From this empirical evidence it can be inferred that at the start of the period analyzed, when capital flight amounted up to US$5.4 billion, for every US$100 of debt there were US$70.1 that were taken out of the country. In 1983, with an external debt of US$37.1 billion, for every US$100 of debt the country lost US$81.7 owing to capital flight. This confirms how financial valorization was consolidated during the dictatorship, and particularly as of the application of the monetary approach to the balance of payments.

More significant still is the relation between the interests paid and capital flight. In 1975, for every US$100 that left the country in the form of capital flight, US$46.3 were paid to foreign creditors; in 1983, for that same amount of capital flight, the country paid US$36 to foreign creditors. As capital flight is directly associated with local capital and the interests paid to creditor banks, this obviously contradicts the commonly held assumption that the country's depletion was only attributed to the extraction of surplus by transnational banks for payment of interests and repayment on the principal of the external debt. It is clear that while that was one of the factors behind it, it was not the most important; instead, the key driving force in that depletion was the capital flight in which the hegemonic fraction engaged, draining the country of capital.

These processes also reveal a phenomenon that points to the nature of the power bloc that introduced financial valorization. While the hegemonic capital fraction formed the central core of private foreign debtors, transnational banks and international credit institutions were the creditors of both private and public external debt. Hence the instability of the new accumulation pattern, as the disputes within the dominant power bloc were at the heart of the great crises of the dictatorship, which will be replicated during the constitutional governments that followed, and

[26] On the evolution of these variables over the period considered, see E. Basualdo, "El nuevo funcionamiento de la economía a partir de la dictadura militar (1976–1982)," in *La construcción de la Nación Argentina. El rol de las Fuerzas Armadas. Debates históricos en el marco del Bicentenario 1810–2010* (Buenos Aires: Ministerio de Defensa de la Nación, 2010).

which will all find transitory reconciliation with the repeated adjustments that were implemented against workers and the transferring of state assets to the private sectors.

The final major step taken by the dictatorship to further the economic dominance of the hegemonic fraction was the nationalization of the private external debt. With the exhaustion of the monetary approach to the balance of payments, the resignation of Martínez de Hoz as economy minister, and the change of dictators (with Roberto Viola replacing Jorge Rafael Videla) in early 1981, a cycle of devaluations was triggered by the shortage of foreign currency.

It was under these circumstances that the absorption of the private external debt by the state began. It was not that the economic groups, as the leading private external debtors, were facing a critical economic or financial situation and tried to solve it through an economic policy. On the contrary, their debt was clearly less than the resources that had been drained from the country, so that their intention was to further increase their assets by transferring their debt to the state, while the resources transferred abroad were left untouched.

The transfer of private external debt to the state was done through a system of exchange rate insurances: these were contracts between private debtors and the BCRA that guaranteed the debtor a fixed exchange rate and repayment of the debt in pesos at the end of the contract, provided they extended the maturity with the creditor bank. The modification of relative prices produced the transfer over time, while the exchange rate would be the most dynamic price in Argentine economy because of the exchange rate lag.[27] According to World Bank estimates,[28] the subsidy that the indebted companies received until 1983 amounted to US$8.243 billion, equivalent to 58 percent of the total private external debt and 67 percent of the private external debt with exchange rate insurance. Its effect was even greater given that the exchange insurances were valid until 1985 and 1986, with the implementation of the first external debt capitalization regime with that insurance.

FINAL CONSIDERATIONS

The imposition of financial valorization entailed deep long-term transformations both in the country's economic structure and in social and political relations. The first such transformation was the great deindustrialization that began during the dictatorship and continued into the constitutional governments up until 2001. It was not only driven by capital flight, as such transfers are fed primarily with resources

[27] For a detailed analysis on how the exchange rate insurance operated, see Basualdo, "El nuevo funcionamiento."

[28] World Bank, "Economic Memorandum on Argentina," *Report* n° 4979-AR, Washington, DC, June 22, 1984.

intended for investments in production, but also by the acute liberalization that was implemented as part of the monetarist policies. That was how the radical downsizing of the national bourgeoisie occurred, and even of the foreign capital invested in manufacture, which in the 1980s saw the largest repatriation of capital in history.

It should be noted, however, that this process was not the result of a contradiction between the financial and industrial sectors. On the contrary, the hegemonic fraction that led and was benefited by this new accumulation pattern was a major actor in industrial production, which significantly increased its influence in production by displacing other business fractions and boosted its fixed assets by centralizing capital.

Financial valorization not only redefined capital relations favoring large economic groups to the detriment of the national bourgeoisie and broad sectors of industrial foreign capital. It also affected the relationship between capital and labor, in favor of the former naturally, like never before in the history of Argentina, through the redistribution of income away from workers, the reduction of employment, the deterioration of working conditions, and, in general, the loss of basic rights, which gave way to a vast unprecedented class-based revenge.

6

Public Finances

Alfredo Fernando Calcagno

INTRODUCTION

Public finances constitute a determining factor in the country's economic performance during the 1976–1983 dictatorship. The policies applied in this sphere not only had a decisive impact on the economic results of that period, they also shaped the following decades. Among the most significant consequences of these policies are the rapid increase of public debt and the deterioration of the financial situation of state-owned companies, which would later facilitate their privatization. Other results that stretched beyond the dictatorship were an increasingly regressive system of taxation, the deterioration and decentralization of public services, and the transferring of assets to certain business groups.

However, to understand how public finances evolved during the last dictatorship, they must be considered in the framework of the economic policies of that period, as public finances were one aspect – albeit a central one – of a larger political and economic project that sought to refound the Argentine economy on new bases. The aim was to do away with an economic structure on which rested a convergence of interests of workers and national businesses, and an economic functioning whereby the demands of organized and politicized social forces were channeled toward the state, which sought to respond to those demands through the application of controls and incentives. What was seen as a "statizing interventionism" had to end, the state had to withdraw from economic decision making and leave that role to open and deregulated markets, and to the network of decentralized private dealings and market relations.[1]

This paper expresses the opinions of the author and does not in any way reflect the opinions of the institution he works for.

[1] See the speech delivered on April 12, 1976 by José A. Martínez de Hoz to representatives of leading companies, in Ministerio de Economía, *Memoria 29/3/1976 a 29/3/1981*, vol. 3, first part, Buenos Aires,

This project, in turn, had different stages. In the first stage, an orthodox stabilizing adjustment was attempted, in addition to the implementation of some structural reforms, most notably the financial reform of 1977. In the second stage, which began in 1978, economic policy focused on combating inflation by setting certain prices in advance – in particular those of public utilities and the exchange rate (with the *tablita*, as the regime of the predetermined exchange rates was known) – and stepping up trade liberalization and capital movements. The third stage corresponds to the management of the crisis. Although the challenges faced at each stage were different, the direction of the economic policy did not change in essence – that is, in the determination of which sectors were to be benefited and which were to be negatively affected. This chapter shows how the handling of public finances furthered those goals.

PUBLIC FINANCES IN THE ORTHODOX ADJUSTMENT STAGE

When the coup d'état was staged in March 1976 the economy was suffering an acute crisis with high inflation and strong imbalances in external and fiscal accounts. The crisis had erupted in June 1975, as a consequence of the adjustment attempt known as the *Rodrigazo*, which included a mega devaluation and steep rises in public utility rates and gasoline.

Argentina had already undergone several recurring crises since the 1950s. Economic growth followed a "typical cycle" that began with a comfortable external situation and idle capacity, which made it possible to increase public spending, raise wages, and boost domestic demand. This led to the expansion of industrial production, credit, and employment, with a moderate inflation that benefited industrial prices. In the following stage, the balance of trade began to show signs of tightening as a result of the increase in imports of industrial inputs and the reduction in exportable agricultural product surpluses owing to greater domestic consumption. With the real appreciation of the peso and the outflow of capital, a crisis in the balance of payments ensued, followed by a devaluation, the acceleration of inflation (in particular in agricultural prices), a regressive redistribution of income, and falling domestic demand. This, in turn, contracted industrial production and employment, which led to an improvement in the balance of trade as imports of industrial inputs dropped. The conditions were thus met for inflation to be moderated and for the start of a new cycle.[2]

1981, p. 16. Also, A. F. Calcagno, *Politiques monétaristes et dynamiques financières, les expériences de l'Argentine et du Chili*, PhD diss., Université Paris 1 (June 1984), pp. 104–105, 174–179; and M. Rapoport, *Las políticas económicas de la Argentina. Una breve historia* (Buenos Aires: Booket, 2010), pp. 288–289.

2 This "typical cycle" is partially inspired by R. F. Bajraj, "La inflación argentina en los años setenta" October-December 1977, 44, 176 (4), *El Trimestre Económico*, 947–996.

The usual adjustment was based, then, on altering income distribution through changes in relative prices and a reduction in real wages. The anomaly of 1975 and early 1976 resided in the political inability to apply that reduction in real wages, a failure that gave way to a distributive struggle that caused inflation to surge. At the same time, high inflation eroded tax revenues, increased the financing of the government by the Central Bank, and led to new devaluations, which in turn encouraged the purchase of foreign currency by the private sector, further complicated the fiscal and balance of payment imbalances, and pushed inflation up.

Some of the first measures of the government of the dictatorship included breaking up trade unions, repressing social demands, and freezing wages for three months. It also liberated prices and unified the exchange rate at a level that entailed an increase of 354 percent from December 1975 to December 1976, compared to 348 percent for the consumer price index (CPI) and 153 percent for basic wages covered by agreements. With a "realistic" exchange rate and the inflow of foreign credits (including a stand-by loan from the International Monetary Fund [IMF]), the government succeeded in turning the expectations of speculators around and stopping the run to the dollar. It thus implemented a new scheme of relative prices (from April to December 1976, agricultural prices increased 25 percent with respect to nonagricultural prices) and income distribution, which brought about an unprecedented drop in the share of wage earners in the GDP.

Reducing the fiscal imbalance was another key measure of the orthodox adjustment. In 1975, tax revenue had fallen by more than 6 percentage points of the GDP, bringing public sector financing needs to 15 percent of the GDP, two thirds of which were covered by financing from the Central Bank of the Republic of Argentina (BCRA). The government adopted a number of measures to recover both tax and nontax revenue. For the former, it indexed tax credits and expanded the scope of indirect taxes. For the latter, it increased public utility rates and brought the revenue of state companies up from 8.4 to 11.1 percent of the GDP. The result was a recovery of public sector resources of more than 12 points of the GDP in only three years, going from 24.4 percent of the GDP in 1975 to 36.9 percent in 1978 (see Table 6.1). At the same time, these measures intensified the regressive nature of the public revenue system.

On the expenditure side, the steep drop in real wages resulted in a notable compression of spending on employee compensation; in particular, in 1976 and 1977: real wages in the public sector fell by 34 percent from 1975 to 1977. The reduction of public sector employment also contributed, although to a lesser extent: –4.1 percent in that same period. The lower salaries were reflected in a drop in spending in transfers for social security benefits in 1976–1977, although recovering in 1978 because of the increase in the number of benefits and a partial improvement in real

TABLE 6.1. *Savings-investment-financing scheme in the public sector, 1974–1983 (in % of GDP)*

	1974	1975	1976	1977	1978	1979	1980	1981	1982	1983
Current revenue	30.7	24.3	27.9	32.8	36.5	33.2	35.5	34.7	32.3	34.1
Tax	19.7	13.5	15.8	19.2	20.9	20.6	23.3	20.4	18.7	18.4
Nontax	11.0	10.8	12.0	13.6	15.6	12.6	12.3	14.3	13.5	15.7
Current expenditure	30.4	30.6	26.7	24.6	30.8	29.9	34.4	39.4	39.6	40.1
Compensation of employees	15.4	15.9	10.4	9.4	11.6	11.5	13.4	12.5	9.9	12.8
Use of goods and services	5.4	6.2	8.3	7.0	8.0	7.2	7.1	7.5	9.6	10.9
Domestic debt interests	0.8	0.7	1.6	1.4	2.5	2.6	2.6	5.2	5.7	0.9
External debt interests	0.4	0.5	0.5	0.6	0.6	0.5	0.8	2.2	4.7	5.0
Other current expenditures	0.8	0.3	0.3	0.2	0.7	0.3	1.2	1.2	1.2	1.1
Transfers	7.6	7.0	5.6	6.0	7.5	7.7	9.4	10.8	8.6	9.4
Capital revenue	0.5	0.2	0.2	0.4	0.4	0.3	0.3	0.3	0.5	0.2
Capital expenditure	8.8	8.9	13.1	13.3	12.5	10.5	9.5	9.7	8.6	9.7
Surplus from previous periods						0.4	0.6	0.9	0.3	0.3
Total revenue	31.2	24.4	28.0	33.2	36.9	33.9	36.4	35.8	33.1	34.6
Total expenses	39.2	39.5	39.7	37.9	43.4	40.4	43.9	49.0	48.2	49.7
Financing needs	8.1	15.1	11.7	4.7	6.5	6.5	7.5	13.2	15.1	15.2
Net use of domestic credit	1.0	1.8	3.0	1.5	3.5	3.8	1.5	4.0	5.1	−1.9
Net use of foreign credit	0.9	0.1	1.1	1.3	1.9	1.8	1.9	4.3	1.3	0.6
Net use of advances							−0.4	−0.2	−0.1	−0.3
BCRA	5.6	9.7	3.4	2.4	0.9	−0.3	3.6	5.3	7.3	16.6
Variations of net short-term financial debt	0.6	3.5	4.1	−0.6	0.2	1.3	0.9	−0.1	1.5	0.2

Source: Ministry of the Economy (Ministerio de Economía, Secretaría de Hacienda, *Sector público, esquema ahorro-inversión-financiamiento 1961–1986*, Buenos Aires, May 1988).

wages of the public sector.[3] The abrupt reduction in current spending was partially offset by an increase in investment, in particular by state companies, but also with significant contributions by the national and provincial governments.

[3] R. Carciofi, *La desarticulación del pacto fiscal. Una interpretación sobre la evolución del sector público argentino en las dos últimas décadas*, Documento de trabajo no. 36, (Buenos Aires: CEPAL, March 1990), pp. 22–24.

In this way, the fiscal deficit was significantly reduced during the first two years of this stage: the primary deficit decreased to 2.7 percent of the GDP in 1977, and the financial deficit to 4.7 percent, representing more than 10 percentage points below 1975 levels, and financing of the public sector by the Central Bank also fell. This evolution saw a reversal as of 1978, attributed to a gradual recovery in wages of the public sector – although public employment continued to drop – and a still limited but growing incidence of the interest burden on public debt.

THE "EXCHANGE ANCHOR" STAGE

The government had succeeded in deactivating the hyperinflationary process of early 1976, bringing the inflation rate down from 38 percent in March and 34 percent in April to a monthly average of a little more than 8 percent over the rest of the year. However, it was still well above what was considered acceptable.

It then went on to apply a recessive adjustment with a restrictive monetary policy that, with the coming into force of the new Financial Institutions Act in July 1977, was translated into a rise in real interest rates to previously unseen levels: in late 1977, a thirty-day deposit paid an annual equivalent interest of 247 percent, while consumer prices grew at an annual rate close to 150 percent. This monetary shock, however, had a greater effect on economic activity than on prices: the GDP contracted by 3.4 percent in 1978, while inflation remained at 170 percent, slightly above 1977 levels. This failure prompted a new revision of the anti-inflationary policy.

For the government, the inflation inertia was evidence that business operators still had the same mentality of "the last thirty years":

> While the typical and normal effect of a recession anywhere in the world is to push down prices, which is why inflation is combated with recession ... we, in the middle of a quite important recession, have found that the less companies sold, the more they raised their prices to recover the same income with less units, instead of trying to sell more at lower prices. Companies have, once again, displayed a completely atypical behavior.[4]

With the implementation of the Economic Readjustment and Intensification Plan of December 20, 1978, the government sought to limit the price-setting power of business operators, forcing them to focus on their costs, in particular salaries. This once again reaffirmed the project that sought to break the prior functioning mechanism of the economy – which had enabled a more or less

[4] Speech delivered on December, 27, 1978 by José A. Martínez de Hoz to the Association of Business and Commerce Leaders (Asociación de Jefes de Empresa y de Comercio), quoted in Ministerio de Economía, *Memoria 29/3/1976 a 29/3/1981*, vol. 3, second part, Buenos Aires: 1981, pp. 455–456.

tacit alliance between industrial entrepreneurs and workers – and to replace the state's role as arbitrator in the distributive struggle with the market's impersonal disciplining force.

The plan's leading measures consisted of a significant reduction in customs tariffs, which would gradually bring nominal protection to 15 percent in average by 1984; the liberalization of capital movements; and the adoption of a calendar of mini exchange rate devaluations at decreasing rates: the price of the dollar would fall from a 5.2 percent monthly increase in January 1979 (considerably below inflation, which stood at 9.1 percent in December 1978) to a 3.4 percent in August. This calendar would extend to March 1981, when the nominal exchange rate was expected to be definitely fixed. These measures were accompanied by others aimed at discouraging inflationary expectations and easing costs: a monthly minimum wage progression of at least 4 percent was set; the Central Bank would announce its monetary expansion program every six months, starting with a monthly 4 percent expansion; and the readjustments of public utility rates would accompany the pace of devaluations.

These measures generated a sharp distortion in relative prices, as prices increased more rapidly than the exchange rate – and public utility rates – throughout 1979 and 1980 (see Table 6.2). The fact that wholesale prices rose faster than the exchange rate evidenced an inflationary inertia that the exchange "anchor" could not eliminate instantaneously, not even in the "tradable" sectors exposed to international commerce. But prices rose even more rapidly in the protected sector (basically services, with a large weight in the CPI), which explained why the CPI grew more rapidly than the wholesale price index.

The difference in the pace of inflation and that of devaluation was also reflected in the interest rate structure, as interest rates were much greater for domestic transactions, which basically followed inflation, than for foreign transactions, the cost of which was determined largely by devaluation. The incentive to contract debt abroad was not an option available to everyone, as only the state, the largest companies, and banks with international connections – and their leading clients – could access foreign credit.

The immediate impact of the new economic package was not negative for economic activities, as they were stimulated by a great inflow of foreign credit, the growth of domestic credit, and an improvement in real wages associated with the increasing exchange-rate lag. However, within a few months, that same lag affected the profitability of tradable sectors and produced an explosion of imports, which led in 1980 to the first trade deficit since 1975. The loss of profitability, combined with the high financial costs of companies that did not have access to cheap foreign financing, pushed certain business groups to insolvency, dragging with them the

TABLE 6.2. *Selected economic indicators, 1975–1983*

	1975	1976	1977	1978	1979	1980	1981	1982	1983
Gross domestic product[a]	–1.7	–1.7	4.9	–3.4	6.7	0.7	–6.2	–5.3	2.8
Consumer prices[b]	335	348	160	170	140	88	131	210	434
Wholesale prices[b]	348	386	147	143	129	58	180	311	411
US dollar[b]	542	344	114	70	63	24	284	503	365
Industrial real wage[a]	–3.9	–32.7	–1.5	–1.7	14.7	11.8	–10.7	–10.3	25.4
Current account position[c]	–1286	657	1127	1836	–536	–4768	–4714	–2358	–2438
External debt[d]	7.9	8.3	9.7	10.8	19.0	27.2	35.7	38.9	45.5

[a] Annual rates of change.
[b] December-to-December rates of change.
[c] Millions of dollars.
[d] Billions of dollars.
Sources: BCRA, *Memoria anual*, several years, and Calcagno, *Politiques monétaristes*.

banks they controlled and used to finance themselves through "self-loans."[5] In March and April 1980, the economy was further deteriorated when the government took control of four major private banks, which subsequently declared bankruptcy. As it became clear that a devaluation in the near future was inevitable, the domestic interest rate was raised in an effort to stop capital outflows.

These measures and their macroeconomic consequences had a strong impact on public finances. On the revenue side, the insufficient readjustment of public utility rates brought nontax revenue down by 3 GDP points. Moreover, in an effort to compensate the loss of profitability suffered by companies, in late 1980 the government decided to eliminate company contributions to the social security system and the National Housing Fund (Fondo Nacional de la Vivienda, FONAVI), thus shrinking public revenues by 2.5 points of the GDP. This reduction was partially compensated by an increase in indirect taxes, which included the extension of the value added tax (VAT) to a broad base of products and services. Goods and services taxes doubled their incidence as a percentage of the GDP (from 4.7 percent in 1976

[5] See Calcagno, *Politiques monétaristes*, pp. 334–348.

to 9.7 percent in 1981), and they became, by far, the main source of tax revenue, collecting 3.5 times the sum of income and wealth taxes. Export taxes, which in the first half of the 1970s accounted for almost 2 points of the GDP, were eliminated. To prevent the social security system from being depleted after the elimination of employer contributions, it received a portion of the taxes, which was taken from the co-participable mass (i.e., the funds to be shared by central and provincial governments). In this way, current revenue of the provinces and the Municipality of the City of Buenos Aires dropped from 9.5 percent of the GDP in 1980 to 8 percent in 1981 and 6.5 percent in 1983.[6]

With respect to spending, current expenditures increased from 30 percent of the GDP in 1978–1979 to 34.4 percent in 1980 and 39.3 percent in 1981. The greatest factor behind this increase was the interests paid by the central government and state companies. By contrast, public investment fell from an average of almost 13 percent of the GDP in 1976–1978 to a little under 10 percent in 1979–1981. It should be highlighted that these were historically high levels, which nonetheless did not lay the groundwork for sustained growth.

Several factors can explain the poor contribution of that investment to the country's production capacity: the existence of surcharges may have resulted in an overestimation of the actual investment; some works of scarce productive impact were very costly, such as the 1978 World Soccer Cup and the urban highways; other large infrastructure works – especially in the field of energy, such as the Atucha II and Yaciretá works – took much longer to complete, and cost much more, than was initially planned; and the area with the greatest growth in public investment was military and security spending, which represented a fifth of all public investment in 1979.[7]

Another important aspect was the decentralization of a portion of social spending: the provinces now covered the costs of public preschools and primary schools, hospitals, and potable water services, but without receiving either the corresponding resources nor the decision making power to manage them. Combined with a reduction of co-participable resources, this measure contributed to the deterioration of provincial accounts, whose need for financing increased from 1.3 percentage points of the GDP in 1977 to 3.9 points in 1981.

A number of decisions must also be mentioned, which, although not clearly reflected in fiscal accounts, generated heavy loads on the public treasury, both during that period and in the following decades. One of these decisions had to do with the industrial promotion regimes implemented between 1979 and 1983, which favored the provinces of La Rioja, San Luis, Catamarca, and San Juan. Through these

[6] Ministerio de Economía, Secretaría de Hacienda, *Sector público, esquema ahorro-inversión-financiamiento* 1961–1986, Buenos Aires, May 1988.

[7] See Carciofi, *La desarticulación*, pp. 30–31, and Rapoport, *Las políticas económicas*, p. 312.

regimes, industrial projects benefited from national tax exemptions, in particular the VAT, not only for the project investment itself but also for the purchases that were later made by beneficiary companies, so that the subsidy could amount to more than the value of the project itself. Another subsidy program consisted in the substantial guarantees granted to a small number of large private companies to enable them to access foreign credits for a total of almost US$3 billion between 1976 and 1983.[8] Many of these credits were channeled through the National Development Bank (Banco Nacional de Desarrollo, BANADE) and, as a general rule, were difficult to recover, despite the numerous facilities and restructures granted (in addition to the foreign exchange insurances), or were directly uncollectible.[9]

Lastly, the subsidies, bailouts, and costs assumed by the Central Bank generated an important quasi-fiscal deficit. A component of the quasi-fiscal spending were the payments that the Central Bank made to commercial banks under the Monetary Regulation Account (Cuenta de Regulación Monetaria, CRM), established in 1977. This account compensated commercial banks for compulsory reserves in respect of interest-bearing fixed-term deposits and charged a fee on the lending capacity generated by demand deposits, with the aim of providing equal profitability conditions for banks with different funding structure.[10] The CRM had a large negative balance in 1978 and 1979, equivalent to 2.8 percent and 0.9 percent of the GDP, respectively; and in those same years, the CRM accounted for 37 percent and 19 percent of the issue of base money.

As of the 1980 banking crisis, the Central Bank began massively funding the financial sector, with credits equal to 3.8 points of the GDP in 1980 and 5.5 points in 1981. Part of that monetary emission had to cover the withdrawal of deposits

[8] Carciofi, *La desarticulación*, p. 38 and Table II.14.

[9] In late 1983, of the fifty leading clients of BANADE (which concentrated half of its portfolio), thirty-eight were large private companies, and only six of them were not in arrears with their bank payments. Among the largest private debtors were companies in the fields of cellulose and paper (Alto Paraná, Celulosa Argentina, Papel del Tucumán, Papel Prensa, Massuh), oil, petrochemical, and chemical (Astra, Polisur, Petroquímica Bahía Blanca, Inanclor, Pluspetrol, Induclor, Monómeros Vinílicos, Indupa, Bridas, Petropol, Copetro, Electroclor, Petrolífera del Carmen, Alcalis de la Patagonia), steel and metallurgy (Aluar, Acindar, Dalmine-Siderca, Pescarmona, Aceros Bragado, Astilleros Alianza), textile (Fabril Financiera, Uzal, Alpargatas), and agro-industrial (Cía. Azucarera Concepción, Cía. Azucarera del Norte, Ventura), and companies connected with public works and construction (Corcemar, SOCMA).

[10] The greater costs faced by the banks that received relatively small demand deposits would have been compensated in a simpler and less costly way by establishing different reserve requirements for demand deposits and fixed-term deposits. This alternative was rejected because movements from one type of account to another would have modified the "monetary base multiplier" and that would have affected monetary supply management (BCRA, *Memoria anual* 1977, Buenos Aires, 1978, p. 27). It was, thus, a refinement of the monetarist policy that failed to take into account that the CRM could have deficits and consequently generate costs for the Central Bank and an unwanted expansion of the monetary base.

from the institutions that came under government control in March and April 1980 (Banco de Los Andes, Banco de Intercambio Regional, Banco Internacional, and Banco Oddone, which ranked first, second, seventh, and ninth among private banks in terms of deposits). In February 1980, these banks combined held 19.5 percent of all private bank deposits, which was equivalent to US$3.4 billion and 3 percent of the GDP. A significant part of these advances was never recovered by the Central Bank.

MANAGING THE CRISIS AND PUBLIC FINANCES

The banking crash of 1980 was not an isolated event resulting from poor management by a handful of businessmen. It was the most visible consequence of the failure of the economic policy. Domestic and external financial deregulation had failed to efficiently assign credit to the most profitable productive activities. The result was quite the opposite, in fact, as credit was used for speculative operations, consumption of imported goods and services, self-loans, and capital flight. This, combined with the exchange policy and regressive income redistribution, led to the dismantling of the postwar industrialization model supported by the internal market, without replacing it with another model. The GDP began to drop in the last quarter of 1980, ushering in a lasting economic depression (it would not be until 1992 that the GDP would climb back up above 1980 levels).

In 1980, the economic situation reached a breaking point: currency appreciation produced a strong deficit in the balance of trade despite the economic recession, and this was compounded by the increasing burden of interests paid on the external debt. The private sector, for its part, anticipated devaluation and engaged in capital flight. In an attempt to stop the hemorrhaging, banks increased their interest rates, thus dealing a new blow to production without succeeding in stemming capital outflows.

However, two sources of foreign currency remained open. On the one hand, the public sector continued to contract long-term loans to stem the loss of international reserves, even if it was not financially rational. Thus, the government acquired a US$3.4 billion debt in 1980 and 1981, and state companies had to take out more than US$4 billion in debt over that two-year period, of which 77 percent was acquired prior to the April 1981 devaluation. On the other hand, private banks and companies, both national and foreign, set up a back-to-back loan system, whereby a foreign bank granted a loan in dollars to an agent with residence in Argentina, secured with the deposit that that same client had outside the country. The agent could then make a short-term investment to take advantage of the interest rate differential – as interest rates were still much higher in the country than abroad – and later withdraw the money, buy dollars and deposit them in the bank outside the country, and, with the guarantee provided by that deposit start the process all over again.[11] The agent could even pay off the debt with the foreign bank without having to report that payment to Argentine authorities, who were well aware of what was going on: "These unreported transactions, performed by companies or individuals, involve the accumulation of assets – including hoarding – and possibly the reduction of the foreign liabilities of residents."[12]

In this game of registered inflows and non-registered outflows, the net balance was negative. In 1980, the net inflow of loans to private companies amounted to US$3.9 billion and the outflow of "short-term capital" amounted to US$4.6 billion. In the first quarter of 1981 another US$2.9 billion left the country as short-term capital; in addition, the negative balance was worsened as a result of US$2 billion in import financing (advance payments), and US$1.6 billion in export-related loans.[13]

Thus, while the private sector was protecting itself in preparation for the imminent devaluation, the public sector's debt in dollars was growing quickly. With the successive devaluations beginning in 1981, this indebtedness would result in significant fiscal costs. Interest payments on external debt increased from 0.5 percent of the GDP in 1979 to around 5 percent in 1982 and 1983. The external debt service was thus added to the already considerable service of the domestic debt. In 1982, the total burden of interest payments was more than 10 points of the GDP and absorbed 32 percent of the current revenue of the nonfinancial public sector (compared to only 1.2 percent and 5 percent in 1975, respectively).

While the increasing interest burden was the leading factor in the deterioration of the public accounts of this last period of military dictatorship, it was not the only factor. There was also a reduction of tax revenues in real terms, partly as a result of the economic recession and partly because of the elimination of employer social contributions, as mentioned earlier. As for spending, in addition to the service of the debt itself, the national treasury and the provincial governments had to cover the collaterals of secured private debts.[14] In this way, despite a reduction in social spending of about 25 percent in constant values between 1980 and 1983,[15] public sector spending increased with the crisis from 43.9 percent of the GDP in 1980 to 49.7 percent in 1983.

11 For example, Eduardo Halliburton, José Mauro Bianco, and Carlos Villalba show how Citibank actively promoted this business among its clients. See their article "Deuda externa privada. El destino de una investigación," (1989) 87 *Realidad Económica*, 72–113.

12 BCRA, *Memoria anual* 1980 (Buenos Aires, 1981), p. 13.

13 Ibid., pp. 91–92.

14 See ECLAC, "Nota sobre la evolución de la economía argentina en 1983," *Documento de trabajo* no. 12, Buenos Aires, July 1984.

15 Secretaría de Política Económica, Ministerio de Economía de la Nación, "Gasto público consolidado," available at www.mecon.gov.ar/peconomica/basehome/serie_gasto.html (accessed March 16, 2014).

The fiscal balance was disastrous: the financial deficit amounted to 13 points of the GDP in 1981 and slightly more than 15 points in 1982 and 1983, and was covered increasingly by monetary financing from the Central Bank. The deficit affected both the central government (4.1 percentage points of the GDP in 1983) and the provinces (4.9 points that same year) and state companies (6.3 points).

That imbalance was aggravated by the enormous transfer of wealth from the public sector to the private sector through the external debt. This was done through various mechanisms. The first mechanism was explained earlier: the contracting of ruinous external debt by the public sector, shortly before devaluation, so that private agents with international connections could obtain financial profits, buy cheap dollars, and export capital. The second was the granting of foreign exchange insurances to individuals and companies, many of which, as it turned out, did not need them, as they were already self-insured with assets abroad. In February 1981, the dollar increased 10 percent more than what was preannounced by the *tablita*, which was finally abandoned in April. Another devaluation ensued, pushing the dollar up 29 percent, followed by another one that same month (3.6 percent), one in May (3.6 percent), and one in June (30 percent). The government granted a peculiar ex post foreign exchange insurance for the last devaluation, benefiting loans entered or renewed between January and May, provided they were renewed for terms of no less than a year, and it established a foreign exchange insurance regime for new loans entered or renewed for terms exceeding 540 days. The premium to be paid for these insurances was a monthly 2 percent during the first six months, very inferior to the devaluations they were meant to cover. In addition, the government agreed to grant a compensation over the devaluations prior to June 1981 (not covered by foreign exchange insurance), equivalent to 23 cents per dollar of debt.[16]

In November of that same year, the foreign exchange insurance regime was replaced by a system of swap operations, whereby private agents could contract external debt for 180 days with foreign exchange guarantee, at a monthly cost of 5 percent. At maturity, as of May 1982 (in the midst of the Malvinas/Falklands war), these swap operations were accepted for renewal along with new demands, with a premium that went down to a monthly 3 percent. These monthly premiums of 2 to 5 percent for the foreign exchange insurance must be compared to the price of the dollar, which from January 1981 to June 1982 increased at an average monthly rate of 12 percent (jumping to 20 percent in the second half of 1982 and almost 14 percent during 1983).

In July 1982, when debts covered by exchange insurance began to mature, the government, presided by General Reynaldo Bignone, and with Domingo Cavallo heading the Central Bank, encouraged their renewal with a new foreign exchange

[16] Rapoport, *Las políticas económicas*, p. 322.

insurance for debts renewed for terms of one to five years. This time, the premium was higher, as it depended on the difference between the evolution of domestic and external prices, but because it was lower than the devaluation during those months, the system still amounted to a considerable subsidy.

The subsidy involved in those exchange insurance mechanisms has been calculated to have been equivalent to a reduction of about 65 percent of the principal of the ensured debt.[17] As of October 1982, the government assumed a large part of the burden of the private debt when it was nationalized: the credits with exchange insurance not renewed by that date were assumed by the national government against a payment in pesos at the ensured exchange rate, but well under the market price. In the following years, the nationalization of the private debt continued with subsidies to the debtors that had contracted it.

It should be highlighted that state companies were excluded from all exchange insurances and other compensations.

THE LEGACY OF THE DICTATORSHIP

Managing public finances is much more than just the more or less orderly administration of fiscal revenue and spending, and its consequences greatly exceed the macroeconomic results of deficit or surplus.

It is a central mechanism for reallocation of resources among social agents, activity sectors, and economic aims (consumption, investment, and transfers), that evidences the economic role assigned to the state and contributes decisively to form a certain mode of development.

Any evaluation of public finances during the last dictatorship must take into account two aspects: its macroeconomic sustainability, and its function in the structural changes imposed by that government.

With respect to the former, the failure could not have been more complete. In 1982 and 1983, the deficit in the nonfinancial public sector was slightly more than 15 percentage points of the GDP, its 1975 level. This imbalance was compounded by a quasi-fiscal deficit of the Central Bank, which, while difficult to estimate accurately, was of a similar magnitude. Indeed, the subsidies channeled to private debtors between January 1981 and December 1983, through the exchange insurances, were estimated at US$8.24 billion, or 10 to 11 points of the GDP of any of those years.[18] The quasi-fiscal deficit also includes the deficit of the monetary regulation account, the subsidized and/or not recovered BANADE credits, and

[17] See E. Basualdo, *Deuda externa y poder económico en la Argentina* (Buenos Aires: Nueva América, 1987).

[18] See World Bank, "Economic Memorandum on Argentina," *Report* no. 4979-AR, Washington, DC, June 22, 1984.

the costs of the banking crisis noted previously, whose effects continued well into democracy.

This deterioration of public accounts, in contrast with the deterioration of 1975, was attributed to lasting factors that were difficult to reverse. In particular, the service of the public debt would represent a heavy burden on fiscal accounts for decades to come. The public debt had also been, to a large extent, unnecessary, as it had not been used to finance a great expansion of the country's physical infrastructure or production capacity. Argentina, in fact, brought its external debt up from US$9.149 billion at the end of 1975 (23.4 percent of the GDP of that year) to US$45.1 billion (70.5 percent of the GDP) in late 1983, despite having accumulated a US$6.8 billion surplus in foreign trade of real goods and services during that period. Normally, this should have reduced Argentina's external debt. The bulk of this growth in the debt was the result of US$24.7 billion in capital outflow – in particular private capital flight – and, as of 1980, of the need to contract debt to pay interests: the financial services accumulated between 1976 and 1983 amounted to US$18 billion, of which US$15.4 billion corresponded to the years 1980–1983

However, the public finance policy was notably efficient in dismantling the previous mode of development and implanting neoliberalism. By assuming most of the burden of the external debt (and eventually practically nationalizing it),[19] the state radically reduced its capacity to implement active policies. The burden of the public external debt was a key factor in the quasi-hyperinflationary episodes that took place over the coming years and that served to legitimize the reforms of the 1990s. Moreover, the need to renegotiate maturities and resort to the IMF would condition the economic policy of the post-dictatorship governments.

In this way, in addition to its severe macroeconomic consequences, these public-finance-related decisions deeply restructured Argentine economy and society.

On the revenue side, they gave way to a more regressive tax system, with a greater prevalence of indirect taxes over direct taxes and the elimination of employer contributions to the social security system. This, in turn, forced a reallocation, with that aim, of part of the co-participated taxes and affected the revenue of the rest of the public sector, in particular of the provinces.

On the expenditure side, interest payments increased their participation to the detriment of the compensation of employees and investment spending. Budgetary cuts and low wages affected the quality and coverage of public services, both those performed by the general government and those provided by state companies. This deterioration was later used as proof of their intrinsic inefficiency and as an argument for their privatization. More generally, the shrinking of the state's social role gave way to the expansion of the private sector in the fields of health, education,

[19] In 1989, of the US$63.3 billion in external debt, 58.4 was public and only 4.9 billion was private.

and security, weakening the integrating function of public policies in these areas. The lesser incidence of social and personnel spending by the state and the increase of interest payments to bondholders contributed to the deterioration of income distribution in Argentina, which between 1974 and 1981 saw its Gini coefficient increase from 0.35 to 0.41.[20]

No less important was the incidence of these policies in the economic power structure. We have reviewed some of the decisions that transferred significant public resources to certain groups and sectors of the economy. Those benefits tended to concentrate on a relative small core formed by companies and individuals connected with international banks and by those companies that were awarded public works contracts, received industrial subsidies, or were granted loans by BANADE under highly advantageous conditions. Based on this and with the financial resources accumulated abroad, these favored groups were able to take advantage of the policies implemented over the following years, including access to new forms of subsidized credit, lending transactions, debt capitalization, and low price privatizations.

In sum, public finance management during the last dictatorship was intimately connected with the national project that the dictatorship tried to impose. On the one hand, it gave a regressive tone to the structure of both spending and revenue; and, on the other, it sought to redefine Argentine economy and society by eliminating the integrating role of the state and consolidating the national and foreign financial sector and large economic groups.

[20] Standardized World Income Inequality Database (SWIID). The Gini coefficient is a synthetic measure of income inequality: perfect equality (for example, if every inhabitant in a country receives the same income) would yield a Gini value of 0, whereas absolute inequality (if one individual concentrates all income) would yield a Gini coefficient of 1. A country is considered equal if its income distribution presents a Gini of 0.30 or less (for example, Japan at 0.30, or Denmark at 0.27) and very unequal if the coefficient is 0.50 (as in Chile) or more (South Africa, higher than 0.60).

7

Complicity of the Lenders

Juan Pablo Bohoslavsky

FINANCIAL COMPLICITY: A RATIONAL AND HOLISTIC ANALYSIS

In the context of the more general debate on whether or not the economic factors that caused or facilitated human rights violations committed by authoritarian governments must be incorporated into the universe of transitional justice, there is a particularly underdeveloped area, connected with the role and responsibility of the lenders who contribute to the financial side of this type of regimes. The reasons for the scarce theoretical and judicial development on this subject have to do with the controversy over the possibility of considering non-state actors as subjects of international law, the complexities presented by financial activities and the fungibility of money, and the political power that financial institutions have accumulated in the past decades.

Analyzing the financial dimension of authoritarian regimes is, in any case, useful as it contributes to attain justice, reparation, historical memory, and deterrence objectives. What are, specifically, the implications of such an investigative exercise? First, it enables a better understanding of the causal link between the financing of a criminal state, its consolidation, and human rights abuses. Second, it makes that link visible, transparent. And, lastly, it allows for the development of appropriate legal answers in a transitional context.

This chapter explores the case of Argentina. Did the financial aid received by the dictatorial government affect the country's economy and its political life, and if so,

This chapter expands on and updates the research published in the *Harvard Human Rights Journal*, vol. 23, 2009, and in the *International Human Rights Law Review*, vol. 1, 2012. The theoretical aspects of the financial complicity have been further elaborated by the author in his "Report on Financial Complicity: Lending to States Engaged in Gross Human Rights Violations," UN Doc. A/HRC/28/59, submitted to the Human Rights Council (HRC) on December 22, 2014, available online at the HRC web site. The author would like to thank Martín Schorr for his comments on the draft of this text. The opinions and conclusions in this chapter are solely those of the author and do not reflect in any way those of the institutions with which he is affiliated.

to what extent? What specific forms did that influence take? In what concrete ways was financial aid linked to human rights violations?

A theoretical framework of rational choice and analytical narrative is used to explore possible answers to these questions, in an approach that focuses not only on a presumed search for maximization of profit but also on a casuistic analysis that can prove that theoretical-rational explanation and, in turn, feed back into it to further develop it.

To stay in power and carry out a massive campaign of human rights abuses, the regime in question must have the financial means to apply policies that will ensure it a certain measure of political support (the purchasing of loyalties) and/or have an efficiently functioning bureaucratic apparatus to be able to control and repress. A steady and reliable source of financing is, therefore, necessary to support this policy over a long period.

Determining whether the financial support a criminal regime receives can be causally linked to the crimes that regime perpetrates requires a holistic, interdisciplinary, and casuistic study. It requires delving into the functioning of the state apparatus itself and into its context to fragment and defragment, through a dynamic approach, any causal link that may exist between the sovereign financing received by the Argentine dictatorship and the gross human rights violations it committed. This approach thus considers not only the micro-relations (between death squads, their financiers, and the victims) but also the more general dimension connected with the structures, processes, and dynamics of a concrete authoritarian regime.

THE ARGENTINE CASE: EXTERNAL FINANCIAL AID

Purchasing Loyalties

Since their abrupt entry into the international financial market in the 1970s, developing countries have all been, to a greater or lesser degree, constantly dependent on foreign capital. The massive sovereign moratoriums of the early 1980s and the financial crises demonstrate that economic vulnerability, from which the external financial dependency of these countries stems. This, among other reasons, results in capital markets having a significant influence in the decision making processes and even in the fate of their governments.

Although this trend was already a concern at the time of the Bretton Woods conferences, in the 1970s the deterioration of the terms of trade affected raw material exporting countries, aggravating their financial imbalance. In Argentina, this general trade phenomenon, which predated the military coup, was compounded by a growing external debt during the period of study, which in turn prompted a greater external financial dependency.

Between 1976 and 1982, Argentina received an increasing volume of credits from states and multilateral bodies, during a brief initial period,[1] and later, mostly from major commercial banks based in a range of industrialized countries. There is no consolidated data available on loan volume and lender identity, but some of the banks that granted credits include Lloyd's Bank International Ltd., Citibank N.A., Morgan Guaranty Trust Co., Manufacturers Hanover Trust Co., Chase Manhattan Bank N.A., European Banking Co. Ltd., Bank of Tokyo, Libra Bank Ltd., and Bank of Montreal, among others.[2]

The channeling of such a huge mass of money has been attributed to the expansion of the European market and the massive recycling of "petrodollars." In that context, lending banks implemented a pressure policy to further the indebtedness of states that lacked adequate repayment capacity for the debts they were contracting, and which, in addition, used public resources, in part, to repress their own populations.

It should be highlighted that, without prejudice to the effects these loans had in terms of consolidating the regime, the fact that these creditors ignored the most basic rules of credit risk assessment laid the groundwork for the debt crisis that would erupt in 1982.

Creditor banks, which from 1982 to 1989 were reluctant to acknowledge losses from debtor insolvency, also benefited by later participating in the Brady Plan,[3] that led to a highly advantageous use of the new bonds during the process of dismantling of the state through the deluge of privatizations of public companies and other state assets in the 1990s, in line with the reshaping of Argentine society and its economy and state launched and furthered by the dictatorship.

In the Argentina of the 1970s these credits were inserted in a typically monetarist policy, which involved a broad economic and financial liberalization, the elimination of tariff protections, high domestic interest rates, and an exchange rate lag, and later the overvaluation of the national currency through targeted official policies. External debt played a key role in this scheme.

This financial dependency was even more acute if we consider that, in its application of an economic policy that involved allocating domestic resources by following the signals of international market prices, the military government

1 "Estados Unidos reconoció a la junta. Crédito del FMI," *Clarín*, March 27, 1976; D. Albín, "España financió a la dictadura de Videla," October 20, 2014, *Público*, available at www.publico.es/politica/espana-financio-dictadura-videla.html (accessed December 10, 2014).

2 See E. Calcagno, "Los bancos transnacionales y el endeudamiento externo en la Argentina," *Cuadernos de la CEPAL*, LC/G.1483 (Santiago, Chile: November 1987), pp. 25 and 108; and Juzgado Nacional en lo Criminal y Correccional Federal no. 2 de la Capital Federal, "Olmos, Alejandro s. denuncia," June 13, 2000, *Jurisprudencia Argentina*, January 31, 2001.

3 M. Monteagudo, "The Debt Problem: The Baker Plan (1985) and the Brady Initiative (1989). History, Experience, Practice and Prospects," in D. Carreau and M. Shaw (eds.), *La dette extérieure. The External Debt* (Leiden: Martinus Nijhoff Publishers, 1995), p. 157.

adjusted domestic relative prices based on international prices, and promoted the de facto dollarization of the economy. With a domestic market demanding dollars and an insufficient foreign trade balance, the state increased its debt with foreign banks to supply dollars. Once those dollars were poured into the domestic market, at a value below their real cost through the application of an exchange rate methodology known as the *tablita* (a system that established a calendar of preannounced exchange rates below real values), they initially (1976–1979) swelled the country's international reserves to later feed the capital flight circuit, and ultimately they often ended up being deposited in the very same banks that granted the credits, thus benefiting the country's major economic groups.

Table 7.1 shows how the external debt increased during the military dictatorship.

The country's external debt with non-banking creditors grew by 161 percent between 1975 and 1981, whereas the debt with international private banks increased by 615 percent during that same period. In 1983, bank loans represented more than two-thirds of the external debt, not counting the US$5 billion in bonds that are believed to have been held by banks.

The drop in domestic demand and industrial activity during the 1976–1983 period brought the country's GDP down, and therefore, it is not surprising that the average fiscal deficit from 1976 to 1980 was 7.4 percent of the gross domestic product (GDP), whereas in the 1981–1983 period (Malvinas/Falklands war) that ratio reached 14.6 percent. With such deteriorated macroeconomic variables, the external financial support received by the regimes appears to have been critical for its survival.

A high public deficit and the deceleration of real economic activity, as occurred in Argentina, can lead a country to bankruptcy, usually leaving the government in a

TABLE 7.1. *Evolution of the external debt (in billions of dollars)*

	State	Private	Total
1975	4.021	3.854	7.875
1976	5.189	3.090	8.279
1977	6.044	3.635	9.679
1978	8.357	4.139	12.496
1979	9.960	9.074	19.034
1980	14.459	12.703	27.162
1981	20.024	15.647	35.671
1982	26.341	14.362	40.703

Source: Calculated by the author based on data from BAI and the IMF.

no-way-out situation, as it must implement budget adjustments or debt moratoriums, with all the internal political and social costs such measures entail. Thus, external financing appears to have been instrumental in temporarily sustaining this monetarist system, which, at an extremely high economic cost for the country, maintained financial stability, provided the government with liquidity, and enabled it to stave off various domestic economic and social actors, whose demands would grow both in number and in intensity over time, while at the same time buying loyalties from key economic actors (see in particular Chapters 3, 5, 6, 16, 17, and 21 in this book). It should be noted, moreover, that the bulk of external debt not only maintained the *tablita* regime and facilitated and funded capital flight, it also furthered the process of deindustrialization and the regressive restructuring of the industrial sector, which benefited certain powerful groups.[4]

The importance of the private financial support received by Argentina was explicitly mentioned in a document approved by high-ranking officers of the U.S. Department of State:

> The Argentine strategy for relations with the U.S. has been based on the following assumptions.... Argentina can survive U.S. hostility because of access to alternate suppliers of military aid and economic and financial opportunities. ... Negative IFI votes are a political embarrassment to Argentina, but such votes do not block access to critical financing. The Videla government's economic success in the external sector has ensured the availability of financial opportunities from a variety of foreign sources.[5]

Adopting a pro-cyclic behavior, the banks' decision to cease granting credits to Argentina as of 1982, the eruption of the debt crisis, and the collapse of the local economy as a result of the country's recession (which eroded the little social support base that the dictatorship had managed to retain, as more and more local businesses went bankrupt and workers faced massive layoffs) coincided in time with the beginning of the transition to democracy. This shows that, even with other factors that influence the possibilities of such a transition, large-scale financial aid can play a major role by making it easier for the state to carry out its criminal plan. Recent quantitative studies indicate that the greater the financial aid an authoritarian regime receives, the less likelihood there is of a democratic opening.[6]

4 In this regard, see Chapter 5 in this book.

5 Department of State Report, Bureau of Intelligence and Research, September 11, 1978, Subject: "Evolution of U.S. Human Rights Policy in Argentina," State Argentina Declassification Project (1975–1984), available at foia.state.gov/documents/Argentina/0000AA65.pdf.

6 J. P. Bohoslavsky and A. Escriba-Folch, "Rational Choice and Financial Complicity with Human Rights Abuses: Policy and Legal Implications," in J. P. Bohoslavsky and J. Černič (eds.), *Making Sovereign Financing and Human Rights Work* (Oxford: Hart Publishing, 2014), pp. 17–32.

As discussed in other chapters, there were sectors that profited from the monetarist policy applied by the dictatorship, which was based on external financial aid and which distributed funds selectively. The political support pledged explicitly to the dictatorship by certain corporate groups and business associations must be read as an acknowledgment and commitment to the regime motivated by the economic benefits obtained during that period thanks to the country's external indebtedness.

The impact of external financial aid in Argentina can thus be visualized from two perspectives. The first is a more general, macroeconomic and political perspective, whereby the leading actors in the country's economy and political life benefited from a host of economic instruments deployed by the government, the feasibility of which rested, to a large extent, on the huge amounts of foreign currency made available by the state. These same actors, in turn, compensated those benefits by giving their support to the regime, thus furthering its political consolidation, with the ensuing costs in terms of human rights. (This mechanism of selective purchasing of support is described in detail in other chapters.) The other perspective of analysis of the impact of financial aid has to do with military spending associated with repression.

MORE RESOURCES FOR REPRESSION

A massive supply of foreign currency can enable and/or enhance the regular operations of the bureaucratic apparatus of the state (including military and repressive logistics). In the case of Argentina, the loans appear to have financed a policy of greater military spending that in the initial years of the dictatorship – which were also the most brutal in terms of human rights abuses – was not associated with any real hypothesis of war with other countries, but instead with internal security issues that in practice entailed the repression of the population.

Table 7.2 shows how military spending evolved over these years, representing a growing participation in the country's GDP.[7]

Despite the economic recession that characterized the *años de plomo* (or "lead years," as the period of greatest repression is known), military spending increased steadily year after year during the dictatorship, both in absolute terms and as a percentage of the GDP.

The thesis that posits that the greater military spending registered in 1976 and 1977 was motivated by internal security concerns is to a large extent substantiated

7 See T. Scheetz, "Gastos militares en América del Sur," in *Proliferación de armamentos y medidas de fomento de la confianza y la seguridad en América Latina* (Lima: Centro Regional de las Naciones Unidas para la Paz, el Desarme y el Desarrollo en América Latina y el Caribe, 1994).

TABLE 7.2. *Evolution of military spending (in billions of dollars and as a percentage of the GDP)*

	Military spending	% of the GDP
1975	1.2780	2.04
1976	2.2933	3.79
1977	2.4833	4.01
1978	2.6991	4.73
1979	2.8137	4.67
1980	2.5611	4.20
1981	2.7003	4.72
1982	2.2005	4.00
1983	2.4994	4.39

by the specific evolution of defense imports spending. Conservative estimates put spending on arms imports at US$1.5696 billion in 1975, US$1.1924 billion in 1976, and US$626.1 million in 1977. After that, these imports pick up again as a response to the potential conflicts with Chile and the United Kingdom.[8]

In sum, during the initial years of the dictatorship, while overall military spending grew, arms imports (to prepare for external military attacks) actually went down, from which it can be inferred that the increase in military spending was applied, in part, to financing the role assigned to the armed forces in the *war against subversion*, under which the human rights abuses were committed.

These numbers contradict the idea that the loans were contracted by the Argentine state with the sole purpose of buying weapons to defend the country in the event of a military conflict with Chile or with the United Kingdom. The loans and the increase in military spending began before the possibility of these conflicts appeared, and until 1978 the military junta prioritized areas unrelated with external attacks.

THE ACTIONS OF THE UNITED STATES GOVERNMENT AND (THE WITHHOLDING OF) FINANCIAL AID

In what was a major departure from the Gerald Ford administration, which had supported dictatorships that could serve as allies against communism, with Jimmy Carter's victory in the 1976 elections, the United States entered a new stage in terms of human rights, in particular with respect to its Latin American policies. Carter's

8 Ibid.

four years in office coincided with the most vicious phase of human rights violations in Argentina.

In that context, the public and open work undertaken by various human rights groups in the United States, together with the international efforts to raise awareness among both the general public and politicians regarding the human rights abuses that were being perpetrated in Latin America in general, and in Argentina in particular, did not fall on deaf ears. The U.S. Congress and the Carter administration adopted several financial measures seeking to prevent these abuses, which entailed a recognition of the gravity of the situation and of how vital granting monetary aid – or denying it – could be for a military government and its criminal activities.[9]

Following the official acknowledgment by the Department of State regarding the situation of extreme human rights abuses that prevailed in several ally countries, and especially in Argentina, the United States distanced itself from the initial support that the Ford administration had given the just-established military government. Carter furthered an aggressive human rights foreign policy with the aim of preventing those crimes through diplomatic pressure and conditional assistance. This involved reducing financial and military aid to the Argentine dictatorship, with the tacit expectation that those cuts would generate certain economic and military difficulties that would force the junta to improve its human rights record.

The 1974 Foreign Assistance Act already required that, "except under extraordinary circumstances," military aid to governments engaged in "consistent patterns of gross violations of internationally recognized human rights" be reduced or suspended (Section 502B). On February 24, 1977, Secretary of State Cyrus Vance announced to the Senate that the government would be reducing its aid to Argentina, Ethiopia, and Uruguay because of the repeated human rights violations in those three countries.

That year the U.S. Congress banned military aid to Argentina in the form of donations, credits, guaranteed loans, sales, and export licenses, effective as of September 30, 1978. As of August 1978, the Department of State had rejected requests for military exports to Argentina for a sum estimated at US$1.25 billion (including eleven Export-Import Bank transactions valued at US$600 million), based on the country's human rights situation.

The Overseas Private Investment Corporation (OPIC) also had to consider the human rights record of the country where a U.S. company applying for OPIC

9 See in more detail R. Bejesky and J. P. Bohoslavsky, "Contemporary Lessons from Carter's Incorporation of Human Rights into the Financing of Southern Cone Dictatorships," in J. P. Bohoslavsky and J. Černič (eds.), *Making Sovereign Financing and Human Rights Work* (Oxford: Hart Publishing, 2014), pp. 303–322

financing planned to invest. By the end of 1978, it had already made the decision not to grant insurance coverage to companies seeking to invest in Argentina, because of the serious violations committed there.

Moreover, when it expanded its original Harkin initiative (PL94-161, 1975),[10] Congress ordered U.S. representatives in multilateral development banks to oppose the granting of loans to countries whose governments were violating the fundamental human rights of their citizens (PL94-302, 1976, and later PL95-118, 1977). Thus, the U.S. government exposed the severity of the situation in Argentina, abstaining or voting against numerous multilateral loans requested by the military junta.[11] In fact, between 1976 and 1980, Argentina was the country that the United States most voted against in development banks, representing a fourth of its rejections and abstentions in credit applications.

This policy was explained in the following terms: the United States felt it had to use its voice and voting power in the six multilateral development banks it was a member of to further the cause of human rights in countries whose governments were implicated in consistent human rights violations, including torture and cruel, inhuman, or degrading treatment.[12]

In the case of the Chilean dictatorship, the U.S. government went as far as warning private banks that their policy of credit support to the Pinochet regime was inconsistent with the foreign policy of the Carter administration, which viewed human rights as a variable that had to be taken seriously.[13]

While the human rights policy of the Carter administration was not sufficiently strong and consistent and had a limited impact on the situation in Argentina, it is also true that even before Ronald Reagan won the elections, U.S. foreign policy had already taken a conservative turn and was giving more importance to commercial and geopolitical interests. These facts, however, do not obliterate the political and legal significance of the legislative and administrative decisions adopted by the United States during the bloodiest years of the Argentine dictatorship, which corroborate that there was a clear awareness of the link that existed between financial aid and human rights violations.

[10] This norm prohibited economic aid to any country that committed gross human rights violations, unless it could prove that such aid would benefit poor people in need.

[11] A. Avenburg, "Entre la presión y el apoyo a los 'moderados.' La política de derechos humanos de Carter y el régimen militar argentino (1976–1978)," Master's thesis in International Relations and Negotiations (Buenos Aires: FLACSO, 2009), pp. 77–83 and 124–129.

[12] U.S. Congress House, Committee on Banking, Finance, and Urban Affairs, Subcommittee on International Development Institutions and Finance, International Development Institutions-1977, 95th Cong. 1st sess., March 1977, p. 9.

[13] "Reuss: Rights Policy not Helped by Loans to Chile from Banks" *The Washington Post*, April 13, 1978, p. a19.

CONCLUSIONS AND PROSPECTS OF ACCOUNTABILITY FOR FINANCIAL COMPLICITY

In a context of fiscal deficit and poor performance of the national economy, the options available for financing are limited, and thus any potential source of financing that the state may access becomes even more critical. Ultimately, the regime must be capable of implementing efficient economic instruments to secure the support of key sectors of the country's economic and political life, and/or of executing a budget that will enable an effective repressive apparatus, which translates into greater spending in the military and police sectors charged with this task. From a general perspective, while political institutions determine the level of state indebtedness (in absence of citizen control, an authoritarian government will tend to contract unlimited loans), the loans that a state receives also shape its political institutions, including those that carry out criminal activities (in terms of consolidating the regime).[14]

In the Argentine case, under a situation of economic stagnation, the government implemented a monetary and financial policy dependent on foreign assistance. It was able to face the serious economic and financial challenges that compromised its political existence, and purchase decisive loyalties and political supports, because it had a source of solid financing. This also enabled it to apply a budgetary policy that strengthened the military apparatus.

All of this was achieved during a time in which not only were the reports of human rights violations widely known in various national, regional, and international forums, there was also awareness of the causal link that existed between human rights violations and the financial aid to the regime. According to public reports from the United States and from human rights NGOs and to news articles featured in international media, the seriousness of the human rights situation was not something of which banks – vectors of information in international markets – could have been unaware. Moreover, considering that the United States in numerous opportunities blocked financial (both bilateral and multilateral) and military aid to the Argentine dictatorship, based expressly on its human rights violations, the factual connection between financial aid and the regime's consolidation was already evident at that time.

The approach proposed in this chapter is not new. In 1977, Professor Antonio Cassese was appointed by the United Nations Commission on Human Rights as special rapporteur mandated with assessing the relationship between the financial aid received by the Pinochet regime at that time and the human rights violations suffered by the Chilean people. In his more than 260-page report, Cassese set out

[14] T. Oatley, "Political Institutions and Foreign Debt in the Developing World" (2010) 54 *International Studies Quarterly* 1, 175.

a sophisticated methodology for integrally measuring the impact of that aid on the country's human rights situation:

> Foreign economic assistance largely serves to strengthen and underpin the economic system adopted by the Chilean authorities, which in turn needs to rely on the suppression of civil and political rights. The findings confirm that the mass of the current economic assistance is instrumental in the consolidation and perpetuation of the ongoing crackdown on those rights.[15]

Far from being a theoretical question, the issue of accountability for financial complicity has prompted legal actions in international and domestic courts.[16] Although the legal aspects of accountability for complicity are addressed more thoroughly in three other chapters in this book (8, 9, and 10), it still merits mentioning here that in 2009 and 2010 relatives of victims of the dictatorship brought legal actions in Buenos Aires against several foreign banks, accusing them of complicity in the crimes committed by the junta against their parents, who are still disappeared.

These actions invoked international, U.S., and Argentine laws and jurisprudence, and argued that banks must be made accountable in civil courts for lending huge sums of money to the military regime and thus enabling it to function economically and supporting its systematic and mass repression.[17] In one of these civil actions, further and more in-depth information on the impact that the loans had on the human rights situation during the dictatorship was requested, proposing a broad and thorough analysis that includes not only the economic, financial, and budgetary aspects of the military regime, but also its political and institutional dimensions, which enabled it to implement the process in which serious crimes were perpetrated on a massive scale. In March 2010, the University of Essex in England, together with the Center for Legal and Social Studies (Centro de Estudios Legales y Sociales, CELS) presented an amicus curiae explaining why both international law and Argentine law suggest that the banks must be made accountable for complicity.[18]

As for the judicial chances that this claim has, given that the criminal trials against repressive agents are still underway and the Argentine state has implemented a

[15] A. Cassese, "Study of the Impact of Foreign Economic Aid and Assistance on Respect for Human Rights in Chile," E/CN.4/Sub.2/412, vol. 4, 1978, p. 24, available at http://business-humanrights.org/en/corporate-complicity-and-finance-as-a-killing-agent-the-relevance-of-the-chilean-case-full-text-requires-subscription-0#c56126 (accessed December 10, 2014) and recently republished in a summarized format by the Texas International Law Journal, Vol. 50, Issue 4, 2015 (forthcoming).

[16] See the cases explained in the articles cited in note 2 in this chapter.

[17] Juzgado Nacional de Primera Instancia en lo Civil no. 34, "Ibáñez, Manuel Leandro y otros casos s. diligencia preliminar," Buenos Aires, proceeding no. 95,019/2010; Juzgado Nacional en lo Contencioso Administrativo Federal no. 8, "Garramone, Andrés c. Citibank N. A. y otros" (2010), Buenos Aires, proceeding no. 47,736/2010.

[18] The amicus curiae can be consulted at www.business-humanrights.org/Links/Repository/1000191/link_page_view (accessed December 10, 2014).

standardized and limited system of compensation to benefit victims (which, as it is paid with bonds, was eroded first by the effects of the default and then by the debt restructure), the legal and economic responsibility of the accomplices that facilitated the commission of crimes is an open issue in Argentina's judicial system.

The question of accountability of the banks is raised at a time in which both Argentine society and the field of human rights could benefit from such an investigation, not only because Argentina's transitional justice experience is still ongoing, but also because international law has evolved and reached a point in which it can effectively address and resolve complex questions connected with corporate complicity. These two factors make analyzing bank responsibility timely and relevant at several levels. First, recognizing the material links between corporate behavior and human rights violations could encourage mechanisms of transitional justice that would attribute responsibility to economic factors and in that way have a dissuasive effect on future illegal conduct by corporations. Second, it would allow for the construction of a more complete narrative of the crimes, with new evidence in both historical and judicial terms,[19] and would provide additional funds to compensate the victims and their families, if it were determined that banks should be held accountable.

The victims of state terrorism who are asking Argentine courts if the dictatorship's lenders are responsible for having supported it financially, at the same time they demand to know the truth about the workings of that dimension of complicities, summarize the argument that was set forth in this chapter: "I want to know who gave money to the military junta that governed a country that was bankrupt but could pay a salary to my parents' killers and buy the instruments with which to torture them."[20]

[19] It should be noted that in June 2013 the São Paulo Municipal Truth Commission summoned Brazil's former finance minister (1967–1974), Antônio Delfim Netto, to give testimony on a scheme set up by São Paulo business operators to finance repression during the Brazilian dictatorship. See "Ex-ministro Delfim Netto vai depor na Comissão da Verdade," *Estadão*, June 5, 2013, available at http://politica.estadao.com.br/blogs/roldao-arruda/ex-ministro-delfim-netto-vai-depor-na-comissao-da-verdade/ (accessed December 10, 2014).

[20] "Los prestamistas de la muerte," *Página/12* (Buenos Aires), June 21, 2011, available at www.pagina12.com.ar/diario/elpais/1-121607-2009-03-16.html (accessed December 10, 2014).

PART IV

Complicity and the Law

8

Corporate Complicity and Legal Accountability: Report of the International Commission of Jurists

International Commission of Jurists Expert Legal Panel

In March 2006, the International Commission of Jurists (ICJ) convened an Expert Legal Panel on Corporate Complicity in International Crimes commissioned with studying when companies and their officials could be held legally responsible under criminal or civil law in cases in which they are involved with other actors that perpetrate gross human rights violations, and with providing criteria to identify the kind of situations that should be avoided by companies to ensure they are not complicit in human rights abuses.

The final report was issued in 2009 in three volumes. In the first volume, the Panel synthesizes its understanding of civil and criminal law based on the studies contained in volumes 2 and 3. Using public policy language, it describes the kind of behavior companies should avoid if they do not wish to be complicit with gross human rights violations and put themselves in an area of legal risk as a result of such complicity.

The Panel was formed by eight prominent jurists from all regions of the world, renowned in their different fields of expertise, and representing both the common law and civil law legal traditions. The panel members are Andrew Clapham, Claes Cronstedt, Louise Doswald-Beck, John Dugard, Alberto León Gómez-Zuluaga, Howard Mann, Usha Ramanathan, and Ralph G. Steinhardt.

The ICJ is a nongovernmental organization that promotes understanding and respect for the rule of law and the protection of human rights worldwide. It was established in 1952 and is headquartered in Geneva. It is formed by fifty-five eminent

ICJ, *Corporate Complicity and Legal Accountability. Report of the International Commission of Jurists Expert Legal Panel on Corporate Complicity in International Crimes*, vols. 1, 2, and 3 (Geneva: ICJ, 2008), available at www.icj.org/report-of-the-icj-expert-legal-panel-on-corporate-complicity-in-international-crimes/. The editors would like to thank the ICJ for granting authorization to include selected extracts of the report in this book, and, in particular, Carlos López, ICJ Senior Legal Advisor, for his collaboration and for revising this chapter. For the purposes of this book, the text is reproduced with a format different from the original publication.

jurists, representing all the legal systems in the world, and has ninety national chapters and affiliated legal organizations. Its prestige has earned it consultative status in numerous international bodies.

This chapter reproduces extracts from the report issued by the Panel, focusing on the first volume, which presents the "general theory of accountability for complicity," and to a lesser extent on the second volume, on "criminal law and international crimes." In choosing the fragments reproduced here, we considered how representative they were of the contents of the report and at the same time their relevance with respect to the context of Argentina.[1] The aim is to contribute to the legal debate in Argentina on the subject of economic complicity by drawing on the ideas discussed by the ICJ, one of the most prestigious institutions in the field of international law.

The Report: Corporate Complicity and Legal Accountability

> Six decades ago senior company officials were convicted for actively helping the Nazi regime to commit some of the worst war crimes imaginable. These business leaders, often working through their companies, supplied poisonous gas to concentration camps knowing it would be used to exterminate human beings; actively sought slave labor to work in their factories; acquiesced or helped in the deportation, murder, and ill-treatment of slave workers; donated money to support the criminal *Schutzstaffel* (SS); and enriched their companies by plundering property in German-occupied Europe.
>
> Reports of business participation in gross human rights abuses did not stop with the end of the Second World War. The recognition that thriving trade and business investment can help to raise people's standards of living has not allayed concerns that businesses can also do considerable harm. …
>
> Oil and mining companies that seek concessions and security have been accused of giving money, weapons, vehicles, and air support that government military forces or rebel groups use to attack, kill and "disappear" civilians. Private air service operators have reportedly been an essential part of government programs of extraordinary and illegal renditions of terrorist suspects across frontiers. Private security companies have been accused of colluding with government security agencies to inflict torture in detention centers they jointly operate. Companies have reportedly given information that has enabled a government to detain and torture trade unionists or other perceived political opponents. Companies have allegedly sold both tailor-made computer equipment that enables a government to track and discriminate against minorities, and earth-moving equipment used to demolish houses in violation of international law. Others are accused of propping up rebel groups that commit gross human rights abuses by buying conflict diamonds,

[1] The full report is available on the ICJ web site at www.icj.org.

while some have allegedly encouraged child labor and sweatshop conditions by demanding that suppliers deliver goods at ever cheaper prices.

Although these abuses are, unfortunately, not new, what has changed is the renewed insistence by victims and their representatives on accountability when companies are involved in gross human rights abuses. This is driven by several related developments.

...

In its discussion in Volume 2 of international and domestic criminal law the Panel refers not to complicity, but to "involvement" in crimes. This is intended to take account of two things. First, that in criminal law complicity has a particular and limited legal meaning. Second, that because this criminal law concept does not necessarily correspond to the full remit of the policy concept of "business complicity in human rights abuses" described above, the Panel chose to focus on other headings of criminal responsibility in addition to "aiding and abetting," in order to properly reflect the zone of potential legal risk which it believes may exist for companies who are involved with other actors in gross human rights abuses.

Although the title of the Panel's report uses the phrase "corporate complicity," throughout its inquiry the Panel has considered all business entities irrespective of structure or composition, of whether they are large or small, multinational, transnational or national, state or privately owned. The Panel's analysis and findings are intended to apply across the board to all business entities and throughout its report the Panel uses the terms *company* and *business* interchangeably in order to capture the extent of its inquiry.

Furthermore, throughout the report, when the Panel refers to the legal accountability of companies or businesses, it should be understood as referring to the legal liability of a company entity and/or company official, bearing in mind that whether one or both may be held liable will depend on the jurisdiction and body of law at question. Criminal law will often (though not always) only apply to individuals (natural persons), and therefore in many jurisdictions, including at present the International Criminal Court, only company officials (and not company entities) can be prosecuted. On the other hand, across all types of jurisdictions, civil liability can arise for both company entities (legal persons) and for company officials (natural persons).

...

Conduct that gives rise to gross human rights abuses will also often involve breaches of international criminal law, and therefore will often constitute a crime under international law. International criminal law creates criminal offences in respect of an ever broadening range of acts, known as crimes under international law. It also imposes obligations on governments to prosecute and punish these crimes. In Volume 2 of its report, the Panel looks in detail at the ways in which criminal responsibility may arise for companies when they are implicated with another actor in the commission of gross human rights abuses amounting to crimes under international law. It also looks briefly at national criminal accountability in relation to such crimes.

...

In terms of the bases on which criminal responsibility may be imposed, the report has focused on aiding and abetting, common purpose and superior responsibility. These bases of criminal liability are explored in detail in Volume 2.

While no international forum yet has jurisdiction to prosecute a company as a legal entity, it is widely accepted that corporate officials could face trial for crimes under international law at the international level. Indeed, even at its conception after the Second World War, international criminal law was applied to the sphere of company activity, and business officials who had become involved in crimes under international law, perpetrated by the Nazis in the course of their business transactions, were held criminally accountable. Furthermore, as national legal systems incorporate international criminal law into their domestic legislation, they often include legal entities, including companies, in the list of potential perpetrators.

Conduct at the heart of gross human rights abuses will often also contravene the domestic law of tort in common law jurisdictions and the law of non-contractual obligations in civil law jurisdictions. In Volume 3, the Panel explores the comparative law of domestic civil liability and the ways in which, across jurisdictions, civil liability could arise for companies and/or their officials when they are complicit in gross human rights abuses.

The laws of tort and non-contractual obligations are hundreds of years old, in both common law and civil law traditions. The interactions of different actors in society, including businesses, have been regulated in all jurisdictions long before international human rights standards were developed. They are intended to protect personal interests, such as bodily and mental integrity, personal liberty, dignity and property and provide for liability in situations where harm is caused to someone's interests as a result of another actor's behavior and where that actor and the victim are not in a contractual relationship. These bodies of law have always applied to the conduct of businesses, and it is clear that business conduct can cause harm to the interests the law of civil remedies protects, and that both business entities and individual business officials can be held legally liable.

...

The Principles: Causation, Knowledge, and Proximity

The panel considers that a prudent company should avoid the following conduct, because it crosses a threshold beyond which the company and/or its individual representatives could be held responsible under criminal law and/or the law of civil remedies, for complicity in gross human rights abuses committed by a government, armed group, or other actor.

A company should avoid a conduct if:

First, by such conduct, the company or its employees contribute to specific gross human rights abuses, whether through an act or failure to act, and whatever form of participation, assistance or encouragement the conduct takes, it:

1. Enables the specific abuses to occur, meaning that the abuses would not occur without the contribution of the company, or
2. Exacerbates the specific abuses, meaning that the company makes the situation worse, including where without the contribution of the company, some of the abuses would have occurred on a smaller scale, or with less frequency, or
3. Facilitates the specific abuses, meaning that the company's conduct makes it easier to carry out the abuses or changes the way the abuses are carried out, including the methods used, the timing or their efficiency.

Second, the company or its employees actively wish to enable, exacerbate or facilitate the gross human rights abuses or, even without desiring such an outcome, they know or should know from all the circumstances, of the risk that their conduct will contribute to the human rights abuses, or are willfully blind to that risk.

Third, the company or its employees are proximate to the principal perpetrator of the gross human rights abuses or the victim of the abuses either because of geographic closeness, or because of the duration, frequency, intensity and/or nature of the connection, interactions or business transactions concerned. The closer in these respects that the company or its employees are to the situation or the actors involved the more likely it is that the company's conduct will be found in law to have enabled, exacerbated or facilitated the abuses and the more likely it is that the law will hold that the company knew or should have known of the risk.

. . .

As described above, the Panel considers that there will usually be a sufficiently close link in law between a company's conduct and gross human rights abuses if the company's conduct has "enabled," "exacerbated," or "facilitated" the abuses. If a company helps to cause gross human rights abuses in these ways, the company or its officials enter a zone in which they could be held legally liable, under criminal law as an aider or abettor of a crime or as a participant in a common criminal plan, or under the law of civil remedies for intentionally or negligently causing harm to a victim.

As long as the company's conduct provides a sufficient level of assistance or encouragement to the gross human rights abuses (by enabling, exacerbating, or facilitating), it does not matter what the nature of the conduct is. The company could give advice or support that encourages the principal perpetrator to commit the act; purchase, hire, or provide goods or services such as weapons, tools, financing, fuel, computer systems, vehicles or transportation, security or infrastructure. The contribution of a company to human rights abuses could be in the form of a business agreement, through which the company makes a deal in which it is foreseen that in fulfilling its side of the agreement, the business partner will commit acts that amount to gross human rights abuses. The company's conduct could be a positive act, or it could be an omission – failure to act – such as deciding not to refuse government imposed forced labor and therefore contributing to gross human rights abuses. In today's global marketplace, therefore, every company, no matter what its core business, needs to consider whether there are situations in which its conduct could contribute to the perpetration of gross human rights abuses.

...

"Enables": Without the Company's Conduct the Abuses Would Not Have Occurred

This is the clearest scenario. A company could be responsible under both criminal law and the law of civil remedies if the specific abuses carried out by the principal actor would not have happened without the company's contribution. There are always many causes that contribute to a particular outcome, but in this situation, the company's conduct must be at least one such crucial ingredient – a necessary, though usually not the only, factor in the perpetration of the abuses.

"Exacerbates": The Company's Conduct Makes the Abuses and the Harm Worse

A company could also be responsible under both criminal law and the law of civil remedies where the principal perpetrator would still have carried out the human rights abuses, but the company's conduct either increased the range of human rights abuses committed by the principal actor, the number of victims, or the severity of the harm suffered by the victims (i.e. exacerbated or aggravated the harm). Such scenarios fulfill the test under the law of civil remedies in that at least some of the harm would not have occurred without the involvement of the company. They would also satisfy the aiding and abetting test under criminal law if the company's conduct had a substantial negative effect by increasing the number or scale of the crimes committed or the number of victims or the severity with which they are harmed.

...

"Facilitates": The Company's Conduct Changes the Way the Abuses Are Carried Out

A company could also be responsible under criminal law and the law of civil remedies where the human rights abuses would still have occurred without the assistance or encouragement of the company, but where the company's contribution made it easier to carry out the abuses or changed the way in which the abuses were carried out, even if it did not aggravate or exacerbate the harm.

Under the law of aiding and abetting in international criminal law, it is not necessary to show that the crime would not have occurred without the assistance or encouragement of the accomplice, only that the crime would not have happened in the same way. The assistance or encouragement would still be said to have had a "substantial effect" if it changed, for example, the methods used to carry out the crime, or the timing or location, or if it resulted in it affecting more or different people, or increased its efficiency.

...

The Causation "Continuum"

Although in different types of situations the process of assessing whether a company's conduct was linked sufficiently to the perpetration of gross human rights abuses may be difficult, the Panel believes it to be possible if the three-fold analysis above is applied, to assess whether the conduct of the company is sufficiently implicated in the human rights abuses.

Some of the clearest situations may arise when a company's conduct is used directly by the principal perpetrator to commit the abuses. For example, this could include situations in which police arrest an agitating unionist worker because of a tip-off by a company, or an armed group uses vehicles or aircraft provided by a company to attack civilians, or a company hires and pays a government or private security force, renowned for human rights abuses, to suppress local protests. In such situations, the involvement of the company is often very tangible and the link between its conduct and the ability of the principal perpetrator to carry out the gross human rights abuses is relatively clear.

More complex are situations where the contribution made by the company is not necessarily used directly by the perpetrator, but nevertheless it builds up the general capacity of the perpetrator – in the form of much-needed revenue, products, infrastructure such as roads, railways, communication systems, or power stations. Sales of conflict diamonds by the rebel group *União Nacional para a Independência Total de Angola* (UNITA) were said to be essential to its survival, including providing it with the finances necessary to continue the war, in which its forces systematically committed war crimes. Direct links have been made between the oil revenue the Sudanese Government receives and its ability to purchase military hardware used to forcibly displace civilians.

The different degrees to which businesses contributed to the perpetuation of apartheid in South Africa and the associated gross human rights abuses illustrate the complexities of analyzing whether company conduct is sufficiently close to the human rights abuses to be said to have enabled, exacerbated or facilitated the abuses. The South African Truth and Reconciliation Commission (TRC) concluded that business was central to the economy that sustained the apartheid state. It distinguished three levels of moral responsibility. Companies that actively helped to design and implement apartheid policies were found to have had "first-order involvement." This included, for example, the mining industry which worked with the government to shape discriminatory policies such as the migrant labor system for their own advantage. Companies which knew the state would use their products or services for repression were considered as having "second-order involvement," that is, more indirect assistance. An example would be the provision by banks of covert credit cards for repressive security operations or the armaments industry's provision of equipment used to abuse human rights. This contrasted with more indirect transactions that could not have been reasonably expected to contribute directly or subsequently to repression, such as building houses for state employees. Finally, the Commission identified "third-order involvement," ordinary business activities that benefited indirectly by virtue of operating within the racially structured context of an apartheid society.

...

Silent Presence

...

Under existing criminal or civil legal principles, the fact that a company is present in the country or area of the country where gross human rights abuses are being committed, without more, would not usually make the company responsible for involvement in the human rights abuses committed in the country or region. However, in some situations, presence and silence are not neutral in law. Although as yet untested in court, the Panel considers there might be special situations in which a company or its individual officials exercise such influence, weight, and authority over the principal perpetrators that their silent presence would be taken by the principal to communicate approval and moral encouragement to commit the gross human rights abuses. In such a situation, depending on the circumstances, the company could be responsible for aiding and abetting any crime that occurs. The greater the political and economic influence wielded by the company, the more likely that company executives could find themselves in such situations. Furthermore, under the law of civil remedies, there will be situations in which the law considers that a company has an obligation to take proactive steps to protect an individual, or a class of actors, from harm, and that a failure to do so would be a cause of the harm suffered. This is more likely to be the case where there is a close relationship between the company and the other actor, for example, in the context of a business partnership or parent-subsidiary relationship. Also, in cases where a company has a particularly close relationship with the victims of gross human rights abuses, a company's failure to intervene, speak up or take proactive protective steps could possibly place the company in a zone of legal risk.

...

Receiving an Economic Benefit

Closely related to the question of silent presence is the accusation that a company should be considered complicit because it benefits commercially from a business relationship with those who commit gross human rights abuses (usually also being silent about the abuses). There are at least two situations in which this might arise. First, a company might earn a profit from buying or selling goods or services to or from an actor that is committing gross human rights abuses. Second, a company might benefit commercially from a favorable business environment created in a country by another actor, enabling it to establish lucrative operations in the country. For example, a government might commit gross human rights abuses that provide the company with an infrastructure or access to resources.

...

Although companies may not in general incur legal responsibility solely for making a profit in a business environment built on human rights abuses, in reality "mere passive economic benefit" can quickly slide into a more active contribution that enables, exacerbates, or facilitates gross human rights abuses. For example, a company that indicates to a government, in a country where it plans to set up operations, that trade union activity or continuing anti-development protests by local communities would be a major obstacle to it investing in the country may have more of an impact on the abuses that may be committed to remove such obstacles. In other situations, companies may have actively assisted a government to create the commercial environment from which they benefit, such as companies in South Africa that helped the government create the apartheid system, which thereafter produced large quantities of cheap labor.

...

In addition to having helped to cause the gross human rights abuses, to be legally responsible in relation to such abuses, a company must also have the necessary state of mind. This raises questions of intention, knowledge, or foreseeability of risk, which, as discussed more fully in Volumes 2 and 3, are dealt with differently by the criminal law and the law of civil remedies.

...

Therefore the Panel considers that in today's world, where communication processes, information sources, and expertise are continuously developing, expanding, and multiplying, it is unwise for a company that is seeking to avoid legal liability to fail to take steps to regularly and carefully assess the potential human rights impacts of its conduct and inform itself about the risks – thereby providing itself with the opportunity to change its conduct.

Where a company shares with the principal actor the wish or desire to commit at least some of the gross human rights abuses perpetrated, both the principal actor and the company could always (as long as the requirements of causation are fulfilled) be responsible in both criminal law and the law of civil remedies.

If the company's contribution to the gross human rights abuses is sufficient, criminal law could treat the company officials as principal perpetrators, responsible for crimes of violence such as murder. Where a company participates with others in the commission of a crime, criminal law places more emphasis on the shared criminal intent of the company and less on the size of its contribution to executing the plan. Under international criminal law and most national criminal systems, each member of a group that comes together intentionally to perform a criminal plan could be held responsible for the foreseeable crimes committed by the others as part of that common plan, even if any particular individual only in practice assisted in a minor way and did not realize that the others in the group would commit the other offences.

...

Even where a company does not actively wish to contribute to gross human rights abuses, it may still be legally responsible if it knew or should have known that its conduct was likely to help cause such abuses.

...

For a company to be liable, it is not necessary that it knows or should have known the full extent of the gross human rights abuses to which it contributes, provided that some of the abuses are known. Under international criminal law, it is not necessary for the company to know the precise crime the principal offender is committing, as long as the company knows that it is contributing to one of a group of crimes being committed. Under the law of civil remedies, the company will be liable for harm that is a reasonably foreseeable consequence of its conduct. For example, if a company provides security forces with information that enables them to torture and forcibly disappear trade unionists working in the company, in law it would be sufficient if violence and resulting personal injury was reasonably foreseeable, even if it was not clear at the time that the security forces would specifically inflict torture or forcibly disappear the trade unionists.

...

As long as a careful actor in the company's shoes would have appreciated the risks, then what the company itself did or did not know about the risk (purposefully or otherwise) will be irrelevant. In defining what a company should have known, the law of civil remedies will often hold that a reasonable company's level of knowledge would have been based on due diligence, including risk assessment, and will include the information such steps would have brought to light in its assessment of what a company should have known.

Although in many instances a criminal court would need to go further and examine whether the company had in fact sufficient awareness that its conduct could contribute to one or more particular gross human rights abuses, nevertheless, the Panel considers that a criminal court will often be able to infer from the surrounding circumstances that a company did in fact know that its conduct was enabling, exacerbating or facilitating gross human rights abuses. With fewer places to hide and claim "we did not know," a prudent company would avoid trying to construct false walls of willful blindness between itself and the impact of its actions.

...

Companies are often exhorted to support and respect human rights within their "sphere of influence." This concept of "sphere of influence" is still rather vague. It shares with proximity the notion of closeness, and can be useful in encouraging companies not only to "do no harm" (including avoiding complicity) to those to whom they are closest, but also to proactively promote human rights in relation to those within the concentric circles of its influence. However, for the purposes of analyzing when legal responsibility for complicity might arise, the Panel has used the separate, more expansive, and more descriptive concept of "proximity," the content of which mirrors more closely existing legal reasoning.

It makes sense that the closeness of a company to the principal perpetrator, to the victims, or to the harm inflicted on the victims, is highly relevant in determining legal responsibility. First, the closer the company is, the more likely it is that it will have the power, influence, authority or opportunity necessary for its conduct to have a sufficient impact on the conduct of the principal perpetrator to establish legal responsibility. Secondly, it is more likely that the company will know or could have foreseen what is really going on.

Corporate Complicity and Legal Accountability: Criminal Law and International Crimes

Labeling a perpetrator as an accomplice and not a principal in the commission of a crime under international law does not necessarily diminish their legal liability. The concept of accomplice liability is especially important in international criminal law because of the often large-scale and complex nature of the crimes and, consequently, the number of people who participate in them. Indeed, the main focus of the international criminal courts and tribunals since Nuremberg has not been the perpetrators on the ground, such as executioners, torturers, and rapists, but those who conceived, led, controlled or facilitated their acts, whose responsibility may be even greater than that of a principal perpetrator who directly or physically committed the crime.

9

Corporate Responsibility for Complicity: International and Local Perspectives

Juan Pablo Bohoslavsky

TWO KEY QUESTIONS

In recent decades, companies have wielded increasing power over economic, social, and political events within national territories and globally. Corporate responsibility, including responsibility for complicity, has evolved significantly in the past ten years, in an effort to adapt to this growing influence.[1] This evolution has taken various forms, including the adoption of codes of business conduct (some of which were already in place before the Argentine dictatorship), numerous business and human rights guidelines issued by the United Nations (UN),[2] reports by nongovernmental organizations, a growing body of academic research, and a series of court actions at the national level.[3]

This trend has been synthesized, explained, and documented in the report on corporate complicity and legal accountability prepared by the International Commission of Jurists (ICJ) in 2008,[4] as shown in Chapter 8. This report highlights

This chapter expands and updates previous research by the author conducted in conjunction with Mariana Rulli, published in *Anuario de Derecho Público*, Universidad Diego Portales, Santiago de Chile, 2011. The author would like to thank Agustín Cavana, Juan Justo, and Sabine Michalowski for their comments to earlier versions of this chapter. The views and conclusions presented in this chapter are solely those of the author and are in no way intended to reflect those of the institutions with which he is affiliated.

1 D. Weissbrodt and M. Kruger, "Norms on the Responsibilities of Transnational Corporations and Other Business Enterprises with Regard to Human Rights," (2003) 97 *American Journal of International Law*, 901–923.

2 United Nations, *Declaration on the Establishment of a New International Economic Order*, G.A. Res. 3201, UN GAOR, sixth special session, Supp. (No. 1), at 527/8, UN Doc. A/9559 (1974); E.S.C. Res. 1913, UN ESCOR, 57th session, Supp. (No. 1), UN Doc. 5570/Add 1 (1975).

3 For an extensive list of cases in Latin America, Canada, and the United States, see C. Hutto and A. Jenkins, "Report on Corporate Complicity Litigation in the Americas: Leading Doctrines, Relevant Cases, and Analysis of Trends," in *Human Rights Clinic* (Austin: University of Texas, 2010).

4 ICJ, *Corporate Complicity and Legal Accountability Report of the International Commission of Jurists Expert Legal Panel on Corporate Complicity in International Crimes*, vols. 1, 2, and 3 (Geneva: ICJ, 2008).

the responsibility of companies that provide support in gross human rights violations by enabling, facilitating, or exacerbating the commission of such crimes.

In that context, and to begin discussing the legal essence of the subject matter of this book, this chapter attempts to answer two key questions:

1. From the perspective of international law and Argentine law, does contributing economically to the perpetration of human rights abuses involve illegal conduct?
2. What circumstances are required for there to be a case of civil responsibility for corporate complicity?

IS IT UNLAWFUL TO CONTRIBUTE ECONOMICALLY TO A CRIMINAL REGIME?

International Law

Several international human-rights-related conventions and instruments expressly penalize complicity in general terms[5] – that is, in the sense of facilitating or contributing to the commission of crimes against human rights. These multilateral conventions and instruments have been accompanied for the most part by an expanding regulatory and administrative development in the field of human rights, both at the international and national levels, crystallizing customary international law on the subject, which has not been limited by the persistent objections from national governments, in terms of opposing the idea that it is illegal to contribute to the violation of fundamental rights.

When that contribution takes the form of corporate inputs (goods or services), is it still unlawful? And if so, are only states responsible for complicity in human rights abuses or can non-state subjects be responsible too?

Even though it has been argued that there is no norm that specifically prohibits the complicity of corporations, the above conventions and instruments make no distinctions between natural and legal persons when prohibiting complicity in

5 Convention against Torture and Other Cruel, Inhuman or Degrading Treatment or Punishment (Art. 4); International Convention on the Suppression and Punishment of the Crime of Apartheid (Art. 3(b)); Supplementary Convention on the Abolition of Slavery, the Slave Trade, and Institutions and Practices Similar to Slavery (Art. 6); Convention on the Prevention and Punishment of the Crime of Genocide (Art. 3(e)); Convention on Combating Bribery of Foreign Public Officials in International Business Transactions (Art. 1(2)); United Nations Convention against Transnational Organized Crime (Art. 5(1)(b)); International Convention for the Suppression of the Financing of Terrorism (Art. 2(5)(a)); International Convention for the Suppression of Terrorist Bombings (Art. 2(3)(a)); Protocol against the Smuggling of Migrants (Art. 6(1)(b)); Statute of the International Criminal Court (Art. 25(3)); and the Statutes of the International Tribunals for Rwanda (Art. 6) and for the Former Yugoslavia (Art. 7).

human rights abuses, whether the principal crime is committed by the state or by non-state subjects. Neither are contributions in the form of certain goods or services excluded. Excluding the provision of commodities from the general prohibition established is not an option that emerges either explicitly or implicitly from these conventions and instruments.

The Charter of the Nuremberg International Military Tribunal already penalized cooperation or contribution in the commission of major crimes and provided for the possibility of declaring that when individual members of a group were found to have perpetrated such crimes, the group such individuals belonged to would be considered a *criminal organization*.[6] The *industrial cases* heard by this military tribunal, in which several businessmen were convicted on charges of contributing to the Nazi extermination campaign, confirmed the principle that companies themselves can be found to have breached international law even when their officials were criminally convicted, although only in one exceptional case was the death penalty applied to a company.[7] Among other business operators, these proceedings – which were founded on customary international law – convicted individuals who had contributed commercially (Bruno Tesch, for supplying gas to the Auschwitz concentration camp) and financially (Friedrich Flick, the German industrialist who used slave work and donated money to the *Schutzstaffel* [SS]) to the acts of genocide perpetrated by the Nazi regime.[8]

Non-state subjects can, technically, breach international human rights law, with which the different consideration of states and non-states is, in practice, a chapter of legal theory (in crisis) and an issue that requires a casuistic analysis more than a mandatory or innate definition of international law. Corporations are, in fact, increasingly regulated by international law (consider, for example, bilateral investment treaties), so that the scope of their rights and obligations is more the result of political decisions than of deductions derived from their subjectivity in international law, as occurs in the domestic sphere.

In that way, corporations, like natural persons and states, are not exempted from the duty of respecting the fundamental human rights that, depending on the case, concern them. This is the general spirit behind the Guiding Principles on Business and Human Rights adopted by the United Nations Human Rights Council in 2011.[9]

6 *Charter of the Nuremberg International Military Tribunal*, Art. 9, August 8, 1945, 59 Stat. 1544, 82 UNTS, 279.

7 On the dissolution of IG Farben ordered precisely because of its implication in serious violations of international law during World War II, see *Control Council Law* no. 10, *Punishment of Persons Guilty of War Crimes*, December 20, 1945, in *I Enactments and Approved Papers of the Control Council and Coordinating Committee*, p. 306.

8 "*In re* Tesch (The Zyklon B case)," 13 Ann. Dig 250 (Brit. Mil. Ct. 1946), reprinted in 1 United Nations War Crimes Comm'n, *Law Reports of Trials of War Criminals*, 93, 1947; *United States v. Flick* (The Flick case), December 22, 1947, in *Trials of War Criminals Before the Nuremberg Military Tribunals Under Control Council Law* no. 10, 1, 1952.

9 UN Human Rights Council, Resolution No. 17/4, UN Doc. A/HRC/17/L.17/Rev.1, 2011.

This new way of conceiving the link between human rights and companies responds to two concurring phenomena. The first is a humanist view of international law, which has been explicitly adopted by the International Criminal Tribunal for the Former Yugoslavia:

> A state-sovereign-oriented approach has been gradually supplanted by a human-being-oriented approach. Gradually, the maxim of Roman law *hominum causa omne jus constitutum est* (all law is created for the benefit of human beings) has gained a firm foothold in the international community as well.

The second is an integral and horizontal notion of human rights, which – with very few exceptions in which the presence of the state is essential – govern not only the relations between states and individuals but also the relations between individuals. This responds to the definition that the Universal Declaration of Human Rights itself establishes in its preamble, which applies to every individual and every organ of society, including corporations. If an international tribunal or a domestic court specifically demands that that duty be met, then it is a jurisdictional matter.

Although in the current state of international law legal persons do not specifically fall under the jurisdiction (*ratione personae*) of international criminal tribunals, that does not mean they are exempted from the principle that prohibits contributing to acts of serious human rights abuses, in particular when *jus cogens* norms are involved. Admitting that option would entail accepting that corporations can be employed as useful vehicles for breaking the law and for profiting by facilitating serious crimes, an assumption that is unacceptable for international systems for the protection of human rights. It would also put corporations in a position of absolute immunity vis-à-vis peremptory norms, a position to which states, as legal persons, could not aspire.

DOMESTIC LAW

Given that international responsibility is not synonymous with jurisdiction or with a mechanism in place for its enforcement, it is ultimately up to domestic legal systems[10] to incorporate, recognize, translate, and define the specific implications arising from certain general principles derived from international public law. Of interest here is the principle that recognizes the responsibility of non-state accomplices that contribute to the commission of serious human rights violations. Consequently, a comparative analysis on this subject gains particular relevance.

[10] UN Human Rights Council, "Business and Human Rights: Further Steps Toward the Operationalization of the 'Protect, Respect and Remedy' Framework," *Report of the Special Representative of the Secretary General on the issue of human rights and transnational corporations and other business enterprises, John Ruggie*, UN Doc. A/HRC/14/27, April 9, 2010.

The basic international postulates concerning responsibility for complicity are primarily reflected in the domestic systems of law of each country, which specifically regulate and give a concrete response when corporate responsibility for damages caused within the territory of a given state (*lex loci delicti*) is discussed, thus significantly reducing the field of application of the *forum non conveniens* doctrine.

Even though criminal responsibility in the case of legal persons has been recognized by only a few legal systems, the vast majority – both in the common law and civil law traditions – admits civil responsibility in the case of damages arising from the complicity of legal persons, in particular in respect to human rights abuses.[11] Numerous constitutions have incorporated integral human rights protection systems, including against harmful actions by states, individuals, and legal persons. This same reasoning is applied in several branches of the law, including labor law, environmental law, child protection law, and native peoples law: all of these materialize in some way the protection and remedies required under certain international principles. Argentina, Australia, Canada, France, India, Japan, the United Kingdom, and the United States have applied both international and domestic law in civil actions for complicity in human rights violations. These solutions are consistent with the international principle that penalizes the contribution to acts that violate *jus cogens* norms.

Given that in the past fifteen years the courts of the United States have been the most active courts in terms of corporate complicity lawsuits and have had a great influence in the development of global standards in this area, it is useful to look closely at this country's legal system and jurisprudence.[12] The U.S. Restatement (Second) of Torts § 876 (1979) establishes civil responsibility for complicity. Recovered in modern times in 1980, the Alien Tort Claims Act (ATCA) has been used frequently in U.S. courts to bring civil actions against individuals and corporations for facilitating and contributing to serious human rights abuses outside the country.[13] These civil responsibility actions were possible because it is recognized that *jus cogens* norms must be respected by both state and non-state actors, even in civil cases for damages.

[11] A. Ramasastry and R. Thompson, *Commerce, Crime and Conflict: Legal Remedies for Private Sector Liability for Grave Breaches of International Law. A Survey of 16 Countries* (Oslo: FAFO, Institute of Applied International Studies, 2006).

[12] For a list of these lawsuits, see UN Human Rights Council, "Promotion and Protection of All Human Rights, Civil, Political, Economic and Cultural Rights, Including the Right to Development. Clarifying the Concepts of 'Sphere of Influence' and 'Complicity,'" *Report of the Special Representative of the Secretary General on the issue of human rights and transnational corporations and other business enterprises, John Ruggie*, UN Doc. A/HRC/8/16, May 15, 2008.

[13] R. Faulk, "The Expanding Role of the Alien Tort Claims Act in International Human Rights Enforcement," *Class Action Litigation Report* 10 (2009): 304, available at works.bepress.com/richard_faulk/24 (accessed February 8, 2010).

The confusion regarding which law is applicable – international, domestic, or both – emerged basically by influence of the ATCA debate. First, because of its reference to the *law of nations*, which is connected with the unique criterion adopted under U.S. jurisprudence when it must decide how international law relates to its own domestic law. And, second, because of the jurisdictional (extraterritorial) implications generated by the application of the ATCA. In any case, the actions brought in the United States under the ATCA pursue, to a certain extent, the same aims as civil actions available under various domestic law systems that can be brought in cases of human rights violations, even if they are identified under diverse labels. These aims are, namely, to effectively punish the abuses perpetrated, to dissuade similar conducts in the future, and to grant reparation to the victims.

Although there are significant regressions in U.S. jurisprudence in the resolution of cases of corporate responsibility for complicity (for example, when the extraterritorial application of the ATCA is limited, as in the 2013 Supreme Court decision),[14] there is currently a growing judicial consensus that companies must follow certain minimum standards of conduct when doing business with governments that are publicly known for perpetrating human rights violations.[15] Unfortunately, this has not translated into a *justice cascade* – to use the term coined by Kathryn Sikkink – to protect victims of human rights abuses from companies.

When focusing on Argentina's legal system, as the crimes committed during the last dictatorship compromised *jus cogens* norms, it is necessary to compare this system to determine if it is consistent with the customary international law that prohibits contributing to the commission of serious human rights violations. In general terms, the Argentine legal system admits this type of responsibility.

Sections 45 to 49, 210, 277 and ff. of the Argentine Criminal Code stipulate penalties for anyone who helps or cooperates with the perpetrators of a crime, whether or not that collaboration was essential to the perpetration. They also punish anyone who motivates others to commit those crimes (instigators), anyone who benefits from the consequences of a crime, anyone who takes part in an association formed to commit crimes, and anyone who can be directly considered the intellectual or material perpetrator of crimes.[16] However, these criminal categories are only applicable to individuals, not legal persons.

Moreover, the interaction of Sections 1067, 1081, and 1109 of the Argentine Civil Code reveals that actions for damages can be brought against the principal perpetrator

14 *Kiobel v. Royal Dutch Petroleum Co.*, No. 10–1491, April 17, 2013.

15 See Chapter 8 in this book.

16 On the charges against former Ford executives for their role as primary participants in the commission of serious crimes against plant workers, see Juzgado Federal en lo Criminal y Correccional de San Martín no. 2, "Riveros, Santiago Omar y otros s/privación ilegal de la libertad, tormentos, homicidios, etc.," May 20, 2013.

of a crime and against accessories after the fact and accomplices, be they individuals or legal persons. This is based on an assumption of civil responsibility attributed to intention (*dolus*) or negligence in which the classic requirements of civil liability apply: an act or omission; accountability; contrariness to the law; a harm; and a causal link between the behavior and the harm sustained. The diligence that is expected of any individual – a standard of conduct determined by the nature of their profession – influences the duties of precaution that each person must meet (Sect. 902, Civil Code). Professional activities naturally require greater due diligence in the exercise of one's duties.

CIVIL RESPONSIBILITY REQUIREMENTS

For reasons of space, it is not possible to go into detail here regarding the requirements of criminal and civil responsibility for complicity. Therefore, we focus on civil responsibility, because it is the least developed in Argentine legal theory and jurisprudence, and because, in contrast to criminal responsibility, it applies both to individuals (acting in a personal capacity or as company managers or representatives) and to legal persons (Sect. 43, Civil Code). Moreover, other chapters in this book examine the criminal criteria applied in trials that investigate the conduct of numerous business operators and military officers who agreed to perpetrate – technically – premeditated crimes against workers or against other business operators. As explained earlier, given that international law establishes minimum standards in this subject, we examine the requirements of responsibility from an Argentine legal perspective in light of applicable international law.

CORPORATE CONTRIBUTION AND THE CAUSAL LINK

The Relevance of Context

Corporate assistance to a criminal regime can consist in the provision of various kinds of goods and/or services (transportation, logistic support, input supply, computer services, money, personnel, etc.). The company must have been in a situation of *proximity* with the principal perpetrator of the crime, in terms of nature of the connection, business transactions, and duration and frequency of the relationship. The closer the company and its contribution are to the commission of the crimes, the more likely it is that it will have had the "power, influence, or opportunity necessary for its conduct to have a sufficient impact on the conduct of the principal perpetrator."[17] The key is in determining if without that ingredient the causation continuum would have been

[17] ICJ, *Corporate Complicity and Legal Accountability*, vol. 1, p. 24.

interrupted, or if, alternatively, it had a substantial effect on the development of the criminal activity in question.

The following factors, among others, must be taken into account when defining whether there was a substantial contribution from the collaborator: the nature of the activities promoted or supported; the extent of the collaboration provided; the presence of the collaborator at the time the harm was done; the collaborator's relationship with the principal perpetrator of the harm; knowledge of the facts by the collaborator; and the duration of the assistance provided.

The aim, when analyzing the causal link, is to encapsulate a contribution that, far from benefiting the population in terms of human rights, harmed it, a harm that could have been foreseen by the company if it had conducted a conscientious assessment of the probable use to which the goods and services in question would be put. The *dolus* (intention), therefore, lies in having foreseen the effects of the collaboration that would contribute substantially to cause the harm and in having prioritized the profit that would be gained from that business activity, accepting in that way the high likelihood that such harmful consequences would occur.

What the vast majority of legal systems – including Argentina's – require to recognize the legal potentiality of the causal link in civil responsibility is for the action attributed to have been efficient with respect to the harm caused (Sects. 512, 901–905, 1109, and 1072, Civil Code). This means that the reproached result would normally occur as a foreseeable consequence of that action. The question, then, is to determine, in each case, if it is feasible to expect that the commodity supplied to the criminal state will substantially influence, facilitate, or give continuity to the criminal practices.

The courts of the United States have been very active in discussing this specific issue. The final ruling issued in "*Re* South African Apartheid Litigation" – a trial in which thousands of apartheid victims brought claims against companies that helped maintain South Africa's segregationist regime[18] – does not appear to share the criterion of foreseeable use of the commodity. To determine if there was a substantial effect, the court considers the *inherent quality* of the good or service provided to the perpetrator of the crime. Without even a basic empirical analysis of the concrete effects of the loans in question (the defendants in this trial were the banks that financed apartheid), the judgment establishes that money can never be sufficiently linked to crimes because it is not a *lethal commodity*.

This distinguishing criterion, which rests on the intrinsic qualities of the good or service provided (instead of considering its actual use and impact), not only ignores developments in international law in the field of corporate responsibility for complicity, it is also put into question by the judgment itself, as it accepted that

[18] "South African Apartheid Litigation," SDNY, April 8, 2009.

the computers provided by IBM to the apartheid regime for implementation of the denationalization policy against black South Africans represented an inherent risk and were a sufficient link to the crimes, while at the same time recognizing that lethal gas could be used with legitimate purposes.[19]

Denying a priori and categorically that a commodity that is not *intrinsically lethal* can, in fact, contribute, facilitate, or enhance the effectiveness of a campaign of human rights abuses entails ignoring the way in which authoritarian governments make rational decisions based on the resources available to them, as well as the importance of those resources in terms of the consolidation, operation, and legitimation of such governments, as explained in the introduction to this book.

Analyzing the complicit role – and in particular the causal link between corporate contributions and human rights abuses – played by companies in Argentina requires looking at the political, social, and economic factors that enabled the military junta to stage the coup, move forward, consolidate itself, and survive while it carried out its plan. A strictly legal analysis must be complemented by an interpretation of the structures, processes, and dynamics of the authoritarian regime, in order to understand the context of the causal mechanism of the complicity. The theory of rational choice can help identify the structural reasons for which the regime and its economic accomplices behaved as they did, and the way in which those behaviors affected the operation of the regime and its repressive apparatus.

Thus, if we look at how the national product was distributed during the dictatorship and how military spending evolved, we can see, on the one hand, why numerous businesspersons and the trade associations that represented them publicly declared their support to the regime; and, on the other, how the economic assistance provided to the government facilitated an effective repressive budgetary policy. This information regarding the context is useful for complementing the assessment of the micro-relations of that complicity, which may include anything from express requests to kidnap workers or participating in company theft operations and other forms of economic crimes, to condescending media policies, financing the regime, intellectual contributions,[20] etc.

[19] S. Michalowski and J. P. Bohoslavsky, "*Jus Cogens*, Transitional Justice and other Trends of the Debate on Odious Debts. A Response to the World Bank Discussion Paper on Odious Debts," (2010) 48 *Columbia Journal of Transnational Law*, 95.

[20] On the legal responsibility of intellectuals in the commission of criminal acts, see Nuremberg International Military Tribunal, *United States of America v. Josef Altstoetter et al.* (Justice Case), 1947, 3 T.W.C. 1 (1948), 6 L.R.T.W.C. 1 (1948), 14 Ann. Dig. 278 (1948); and the amicus brief submitted by the European Center for Constitutional and Human Rights in the criminal trial against U.S. officials who authorized the use of torture in interrogations, Audiencia Nacional de Madrid, Case 134/2009, September 2012.

THE SUBJECTIVE ELEMENT

Internationally, a controversial question is whether it is reasonable to require the accomplices' knowledge that with their actions they would be facilitating the commission of the crime, or if, instead, the accomplices must also have willingly sought to facilitate the crimes. Most international statutes and jurisprudence have required knowledge of the crime, even if the main goal pursued is not the commission of the principal criminal act. This was the conclusion arrived at by various rulings of the British Military Tribunal and the Military Tribunal at Nuremberg, the Draft Code of Crimes against the Peace and Security of Mankind prepared by the International Law Commission in 1996, and the interpretations of the International Criminal Tribunal for the Former Yugoslavia and the International Criminal Tribunal for Rwanda.

The Rome Statute of the International Criminal Court, instead, requires that an intent to facilitate the crimes must exist for there to be responsibility (Art. 25(3)), but that such an intent may be secondary or nonexclusive, in the sense that a different prior aim (such as profiting) could have been sought. This thesis appears to be supported by the fact that Article 25(3)(d) of the Rome Statute establishes that the criminal responsibility of a member of a group involved in criminal activities is determined merely by that member's knowledge of the group's intention to commit the crimes, and not necessarily by the aim of contributing to the perpetration of the crime.

Alternatively, the report of the ICJ mentioned earlier demands knowledge – and acceptance – of the consequences of the corporate contribution or concurrence with the criminal intention of the principal perpetrator. Although the company and the perpetrator of the crime may not share the same criminal intent, knowledge by the company of the critical nature of its contribution in terms of enabling the commission of the abuses, and, thus, the likelihood that they will be occur as a result of such contribution, entails accepting that course of action:

> Even where a company does not actively wish to participate in gross human rights abuses, it may still be legally responsible if it knew or should have known that its conduct was likely to help cause such abuses.[21]

Gross negligence can serve as an indication to prove the collaborator had knowledge of the consequences of its contribution.

In the sphere of civil responsibility, and considering that domestic legal systems must incorporate, at the very least, the fundamental standards of international

[21] ICJ, *Corporate Complicity and Legal Accountability*, vol. 1, p. 20.

human rights law, if those same domestic systems are even more protective of victims of human rights abuses than international law, these are valid, and in fact advisable, legislative options. This means that, specifically in the sphere of Argentine law (Sects. 1072, 1077, and 1109, of the Civil Code), the subjective element in civil responsibility may consist of the intention or negligence of the accomplice, who knew or should have known the foreseeable consequences that collaborating with the regime would have.

To establish whether a company knew or should have known the consequences of its contribution, it is necessary to analyze the information that was reasonably available at the time. Large corporations are characterized by their high degree of sophistication and generation of numerous externalities, which require them to meet rigorous obligations regarding their means (that is, their duty is to act with prudence at all times but without guaranteeing any given result) toward determining the implicit risk involved in their operations. In this way, if a company is aware that a harm may occur as a result of its conduct and, even acting in the hope that such harm will not materialize, it prioritizes the profit it may derive from the transaction, then it consents to the harm by moving forward with its actions: it acts with oblique intent. Knowledge can be attributed either directly or indirectly, inferring it from objective facts, as has been established by specialized jurisprudence. Similarly, the facilitator can be judged based on what is presumed that such facilitator knew or should have known. Responsibility can also be established if the facilitator was negligent – by not complying with the obligations of means in terms of due diligence – when assessing the consequences of its actions.

COMPENSABLE DAMAGES

Pursuant to international law, civil responsibility is activated when there is a contribution to the violation of fundamental human rights. In that case, any recoverable personal damages must be connected with the crimes that violated human rights. This repertoire of crimes includes, among others, genocide, slavery, torture, and other crimes against humanity, all of which were present in Argentina during the years 1976–1983. Additionally, Argentine law grants the right to bring claims for any unfair damage.

As specified under UN General Assembly Resolution 60/147 adopted in 2006,[22] compensation for victims of gross human rights violations should be provided for any economically assessable damage, and such compensation must be proportional

[22] United Nations, "Basic Principles and Guidelines on the Right to a Remedy and Reparation for Victims of Gross Violations of International Human Rights Law and Serious Violations of International Humanitarian Law," UN General Assembly, UN Doc. A/RES/60/147, March 21, 2006, par. 20.

to the gravity of the violation and the circumstances of each case. The "individual circumstances" of each victim must be taken into account (par. 18). At the same time, this resolution calls for reparation in the form of "satisfaction," in the sense of finding out and disclosing the facts connected with the human rights abuses perpetrated, which entails uncovering complicities (paragraphs 22 and 24). The Rome Statute stipulates that reparation shall not "be interpreted as prejudicing the rights of victims under national or international law" (Art. 75(6)).

Under the law of damages in Argentina, the damage must be certain, lasting, concrete, and ascertainable. When the reparation granted by the very state that perpetrated the crimes is limited and standardized, owing to the need to adjust reparations to budgetary constraints (as was the case in Argentina), the responsibility of the accomplices may remain a pending issue.

Even though court actions aimed at making corporations accountable in this way require a casuistic analysis of the damages, the experience of U.S. courts has shown that such actions can be harmonized with the practicality of the administrative approach of compensation programs that follow authoritarian periods: the reparation funds for Holocaust victims were managed outside the tribunals, although they operated under their supervision.

The case of business operators who were divested of their properties is unique in that they have not received any compensation, either from the state or from accomplices or those who benefited economically. Recognizing the responsibility of the accomplices necessarily entails recognizing the responsibility of the principal perpetrator of the crime (the state agent). The criteria for calculating compensable damages will probably depend, to some extent, on whether the compensation should be paid by the state or by the companies or business operators involved. As with state reparations granted to victims of the most serious human rights abuses, compensations for companies divested of their property must take into account the actual budgetary capacity of the state, the determination of which may include political and social justice considerations. In contrast, companies involved as accomplices must provide compensation in the same measure as the damage caused.

CONCLUSIONS

As the crimes committed under state terrorism in Argentina have been placed in the legal category of maximum severity (violation of *jus cogens*), the attempt to analyze the conduct of business operators who collaborated with the dictatorship using the same prism of the standards of corporate responsibility for complicity is not merely an exercise of historical narrative, it is also a technical and legal evaluation aimed at providing an adequate legal answer to the victims. The implications of this are further heightened in light of the conclusions drawn in the next chapter, which discusses the statute of limitations for this kind of actions.

Both international and domestic law clearly prohibit contributing to the violation of human rights. Argentine law is particularly nuanced in terms of capturing a wide variety of economic conducts that can be considered complicit and thus either criminally punishable or compensable through civil remedies. The challenge is clearly judicial, and consists in defining how rules are to be applied and determining the requirements of responsibility in concrete cases.

An appropriate criterion for assessing such complex scenarios as are those presented by economic complicity is to observe the use given to and the foreseeable consequences of the commodities, instead of their intrinsic nature. This is the criterion primarily applied in U.S. jurisprudence to determine if someone who has provided assistance to terrorist groups in the form of money can be considered an accomplice of those groups' actions.[23] Information on the context is necessary to render the specific conducts to be judged economically and politically meaningful, and to understand the complexity of the causal mechanism linking corporate contributions, the regime's operation, and the perpetration of the crimes.

A relevant and intricate question that has not yet been incorporated into the discussion proposed in this book is whether accomplices can bring an action for recovery against the principal perpetrator of the damage (the state). The answer to that question must be given on a case-by-case basis, as it will depend on the nature of the participation of the accomplice in causing the damage (it could be a co-perpetrator, a negligent collaborator, an instigator, a beneficiary, etc.).

Another issue that must be addressed is to what extent parent companies can be held accountable for the complicit acts of their subsidiaries. In principle, if the company involved as an accomplice was merely a means to break the law, disrupt the public order, or act in bad faith, or if it was a means to damage the rights of others, the partners or controlling companies that made it possible will be held directly accountable, and will have to respond jointly and unlimitedly for the damages caused (Sect. 54 of the Commercial Companies Act).

[23] S. Michalowski, "No Complicity Liability for Funding Gross Human Rights Violations?" (2012) 30(2) *Berkeley Journal of International Law*, 451–524.

10

Statute of Limitations in Actions for Complicity

Juan Pablo Bohoslavsky, Agustín Cavana, and Leonardo Filippini

SPHERES OF RESPONSIBILITY AND THE CHALLENGE OF THE PASSAGE OF TIME

The process of memory, truth, and justice continues to move forward in Argentina. This is accompanied by a growing interest, at the institutional and legal levels, in properly addressing the complicity of individuals and companies in state terrorism. During the first years of democracy, the expression "military dictatorship" could have perhaps reflected the prevailing understanding of the recent past. The political, economic, institutional, and legal changes that have taken place since then – and the greater information available – appear to contribute now to favor, instead, the use of expressions such as "civilian-military dictatorship" to reflect in a more precise way a process that involved both the repressive action of security forces and the participation of numerous civilians, often in their capacity as judges, government officials, religious authorities, lawyers, doctors, journalists, intellectuals, trade unionists, bankers, and business operators.

However, this civilian component of the dictatorship has not been analyzed as thoroughly as the role played by members of the security forces. The magnitude and cruelty of the repression may perhaps condition our interest and lead us to focus on behaviors that affected in a very direct way the life and dignity of individuals. And perhaps the debates over the validity of the amnesty granted for these crimes went on for too long and postponed other discussions. Neither has there been an integral institutional effort to detect, record, analyze, and systematize the relevant conducts deployed by individuals and legal persons in this sense.

In any case, the progress achieved in learning the truth enables and demands new questions and a reexamination of certain decisions, as has been done with other

The views and conclusions presented in this chapter are solely those of the authors and are in no way intended to reflect those of the institutions with which they are affiliated.

aspects of state terrorism that were also initially avoided. What is under discussion today is not the actual existence of civilian involvement in state terrorism, but how to properly articulate a collective response to the injustices perpetrated with that complicity or for the benefit of individuals or legal persons.

This chapter aims to highlight the importance of reflecting on this and at the same time to contribute to the debate around the question of the statute of limitations of civil actions significantly associated with state terrorism. In other words, the aim is to discuss how long we can go on debating in court about responsibility for civil complicity. Although this is just one aspect to consider when reflecting on civil complicity, it is a critical aspect, because it entails defining a time limit for demanding judicial decisions regarding events dating back decades. It is also key for examining whether Argentina's legal system is permeable to the expansion of international law in the field of corporate responsibility for complicity.[1]

The main aspects of this discussion have been resolved in the criminal sphere, both by international law and Argentine law, as established by the National Supreme Court (Corte Suprema de Justicia de la Nación, CSJN) in the 2005 Simón case. Criminal actions against individuals charged with crimes against humanity are not subject to statutes of limitations and can always be brought no matter how much time has passed since the commission of the crime.[2] In other areas, however, there is still controversy. For example, this issue is not so clear when it comes to dealing with cases of claims for compensation brought against companies that used their connections with the dictatorship for their own economic advantage. The answer that would normally be given according to the law suggests that after a certain time has elapsed the possibility of bringing a claim in court is exhausted. But, is that the right solution for cases of civil complicity? Or should we conceive a broader system, or even the non-applicability of statutory limitations for this kind of cases?

STATUTORY LIMITATIONS TODAY

As noted earlier, the non-applicability of statutory limitations for crimes against humanity is recognized in criminal justice, but it is an issue that has not been

[1] ICJ, *Corporate Complicity and Legal Accountability*, vols. 1–3 (ICJ: Geneva, 2008); and UN Human Rights Council, "Business and Human Rights: Further Steps Toward the Operationalization of the 'Protect, Respect and Remedy' Framework," *Report of the Special Representative of the Secretary General on the issue of human rights and transnational corporations and other business enterprises, John Ruggie*, UN Doc. A/HRC/14/27, April 9, 2010. See, also, Chapters 8 and 9 in this book.

[2] Juzgado Federal en lo Criminal y Correccional de San Martín no. 2, "Riveros, Santiago Omar y otros s/privación ilegal de la libertad, tormentos, homicidios, etc." (action against former Ford executives), May 20, 2013.

definitively resolved in other areas. In civil law, for example, there is a time limit of two years for bringing claims (Sections 1067, 1109, 1081 and ff., Civil Code). After that term, the right to demand compensation in court is exhausted, with the sole exception of cases stipulated under Section 3980 of the Civil Code, which gives judges discretion to compute a different time limit in consideration of the claimant's difficulties or actual impossibility.

In practice, the system poses a barrier to anyone who wishes to bring a noncriminal action after the established two-year term. This is particularly so if the claim is brought against a legal person, whose criminal responsibility is highly limited. Indeed, and despite a certain trend that seeks to expand the scope of corporate criminal responsibility, no current theories expressly incorporate criminal responsibility of legal persons for serious human rights violations, nor do we know of any judicial application of it.

Very broadly speaking, then, civil claims brought against natural or legal persons for their complicity with state terrorism lapse after the two-year term normally established. As legal persons are not even criminally accountable, this greatly limits the scenario of civil and corporate responsibility, which is very small in comparison to the almost 1,000 criminal convictions obtained since 1983.

Even so, as will be shown in this chapter, Argentina's Supreme Court has to a certain extent escaped this general rule by providing, in different cases, more flexible solutions, in particular with respect to the starting point from which to start computing the term. Moreover, recent rulings by lower courts have proposed an alternative reading of the law that is more sensitive to the situation and the rights of the victims, and which we understand is what international human rights law currently demands.

THE DISCUSSIONS IN ARGENTINE JURISPRUDENCE

The Supreme Court defined its position basically in three cases: Olivares (1988), Tarnopolsky (1999), and Larrabeiti Yáñez (2007). The first case dealt with the situation of a former detainee (Olivares) who had been held in custody under the authority of the Executive Branch, without being legally charged, and who sought compensation. A federal court in Río Cuarto had ruled in favor of Olivares, despite the fact that the term established under statutory limitations had lapsed. The court found that the term had to be calculated as of the start of the constitutional government in 1983, basing its decision on Section 3980 of the Civil Code. Thus, it rejected the statutory limitation defense presented by the state.

This decision, however, was reversed on appeal by the Federal Court of Appeals (Cámara Federal de Apelaciones) of Córdoba. That reversal was confirmed by the majority of the court, under the argument that the circumstances required for the application of Civil Code Section 3980

> must be assessed ... in relation to the defendant and not merely based on general considerations concerning the situation of the country, the existence of a de facto government, or the application of a state terrorism regime by that government.
>
> Adding:
>
> The argument that a system of government constitutes *in genere* an intimidating apparatus ... [such] that the course of statutory limitation can only begin after the elimination of that system, would entail establishing a parenthesis in Argentine life in which the passage of time would be suspended in terms of the protection afforded by legal certainty, a conclusion that is not possible without a specific law that establishes it.

Justices Enrique Petracchi and Jorge Bacqué, instead, highlighted that the counsel for the defense (representing the state) had himself admitted the existence of state terrorism from 1976 to 1983, and that that element had been omitted from the appealed ruling. They also criticized the Federal Court's assertion that as of August 30, 1982, with the adoption of Laws 22,627 (the Political Parties Organization Act) and 22,847 (convening general elections for October 30, 1983), citizens were already "in a position to act and express themselves freely and ... exercise all their rights without any impediments." In these judges' opinion, the Federal Court failed to explain how these laws by themselves could have enabled victims of human rights abuses to fully enjoy their rights.

Over the years, more and more claims emerged and were reported to the Inter-American Commission on Human Rights (IACHR). Based on Articles 8 and 25 of the American Convention on Human Rights (ACHR), it was held that the Supreme Court's decision violated the right to access justice and the argument of the Inter-American Court of Human Rights in the Velásquez Rodríguez case, where it ruled that states had an obligation to provide "effective judicial remedies to victims of human rights violations, ... remedies that must be substantiated in accordance with the rule of due process of law."[3] This led to an offer by the Argentine state and the matter was resolved through a friendly settlement.[4]

Other cases, however, did not have the same outcome. A year before the Olivares case, Daniel Tarnopolsky had brought a suit against Armando Lambruschini, Emilio Massera, and the Argentine state for damages suffered as a result of the kidnapping and disappearance of his family in July 1976. Both the first and second instance courts ruled in his favor. The federal court, while exonerating Lambruschini of all

3 Inter-American Court of Human Rights, judgment on the preliminary objections, June 26, 1987, par. 92.

4 IACHR, Report No. 1/93.

responsibility, rejected the state's defense with respect to the statutory limitation, arguing that it was not until the ruling handed down in "Causa 13" (the 1984 military junta trial) that Daniel Tarnopolsky was able to identify the individuals against whom he could bring his action, and thus the federal court found the national state and Massera guilty.

All the parties brought the case to the Supreme Court, where the state insisted with its argument that the term for statutory limitation had to be computed as of the date of the crime. This time, the minority opinion in Olivares prevailed and the Supreme Court ruled unanimously that as the plaintiff did not know what had happened to his family he could not know the magnitude of the damage. The Supreme Court underlined that as the state had not provided information on the fate of the plaintiff's relatives, nor had they been found alive, the starting point of the term for statutory limitation had to be established on the date on which, based on a fiction, the state of uncertainty legally ended. Moreover, for the Supreme Court, the term should not be computed as of the judicial declaration of the presumed death of the victims, but instead as of the ruling that effectively defined the situation and put an end to an ongoing illicit act.

The same discussion was repeated again in 2007. The siblings Victoria and Anatole Larrabeiti Yáñez filed a civil action demanding compensation from the state for the forced disappearance of their parents. The action filed by Victoria was admitted by the majority of the Third Chamber of the Federal Court of Appeals for Administrative Matters (Sala III, Cámara Nacional de Apelaciones en lo Contencioso Administrativo Federal), but her brother Anatole's claim was rejected because it was filed more than two years after he reached the legal age and after the term established under Section 3980 of the Civil Code. Both parties appealed the decision, expressly requesting the application of the jurisprudence established in the Tarnopolsky case.

This time, the Supreme Court explained that, if the damage was determined late or the illicit conduct was ongoing and it was not possible to assess it until it ended, the term for statutory limitation, which normally begins with the damaging event, could have a different starting point. Nonetheless, it held that the non-applicability of statutory limitation in crimes against humanity could not be assimilated to that of a compensation action as monetary claims are "renounceable and waivable matter," while the prosecution of crimes is founded on "the need to prevent crimes of such nature from going unpunished, that is, on reasons that go beyond the property interest of affected individuals."

According to the Supreme Court, the criterion on which the Tarnopolsky ruling was based was not applicable because the forced disappearance of the parents of the plaintiffs was recorded in the final report of the National Commission on the Disappearance of Persons (Comisión Nacional sobre la Deparación de Personas, CONADEP) and there had been no evidence that the adoptive parents had been prevented in any way from bringing a claim until then. Moreover, it added that, even if there had been any obstacle in that sense, Section 3980 of the Civil Code established a three-month grace period to be computed as of the moment the obstacle was removed, which, under the most favorable hypothesis, had begun on May 29, 1995 when the plaintiff granted a general power of attorney to her legal representatives. For this reason, it ruled that the statute of limitations of the claim brought by Victoria Larrabeiti Yáñez had also expired.

With a similar approach, the Supreme Court of Justice of the Province of Buenos Aires (Suprema Corte de Justicia de la Provincia de Buenos Aires, SCBA) analyzed the issue in the Cebrymsky case (2007). In this case, the widow of a disappeared factory worker, who had been kidnapped on his way to work, filed a civil action for compensation for her husband's death, basing her claim on sections 1 and 8(a) of Law 9,688 and section 248 of the Employment Contract Act. Expressly citing the Tarnopolsky case, the SCBA admitted the claim, although it ruled that the term had to be computed as of the moment in which the victim was declared "absent and presumed dead."

More recently, the prevailing approach to this issue was questioned by the Fifth Chamber of the National Court of Appeals for Labor Matters (Sala V de la Cámara Nacional de Apelaciones del Trabajo), in the Ingegnieros case (2012), in which, distancing itself from the criteria discussed earlier, it declared the non-applicability of statutory limitations for compensation actions. Judges Oscar Zas and Enrique Arias Gibert clearly held that if a crime against humanity is not subject to statutory limitation it follows that the same applies to its effects, as there is no reason to distinguish between punitive and compensable consequences of a crime of this kind.

THE DEBATE IN COMPARATIVE JURISPRUDENCE

The complexities of this kind of actions are not exclusive to Argentine courts. Instead, it has been a complicated issue in all the jurisdictions where they have been brought. The United States, in particular, has been the forum chosen by numerous groups of victims to bring their claims, by virtue of a number of circumstances, including the U.S. legal tradition and the options offered by its legislation (for example, the Alien Tort Claims Act). What follows is a brief overview of the discussions that have arisen around the issue of statutory limitations in some of the more prominent cases.

The experience of the Holocaust victims who brought civil actions against financial agents of the Nazi regime and the companies that took advantage of prisoner labor is considered one of the most salient cases because of its results and influence. Starting in 1996, a number of class actions were brought against Swiss banks that had collaborated with the Nazi regime by receiving unlawfully obtained property and concealing its origin, or that once the war was over failed to return deposits made by victims. In general, they overcame the statutory limitation defenses by arguing that, as it was an ongoing illicit act, the term had to be computed as of the moment in which the act ended (that is, with the recognition of the act and the delivery of the funds) and that the banks had acted in bad faith by concealing their right to bring suit and refusing to release their files or provide information on their accounts, and thus the actions ended in multi-million-dollar settlements.[5]

Most of the claims against Austrian, German, and French banks and the companies that used prisoner labor had the same outcome, although some of the latter faced difficulties when five actions against German and U.S. companies failed because of procedural obstacles. In one of these actions, Judge Joseph Greenaway dismissed the case against Ford Motor Company on the grounds that the statute of limitation had expired. He found that the postwar treaties that suspended the term to sue German companies did not apply in this case as it was a U.S. company with a German subsidiary, and he denied that the statements issued by the company in 1974 and 1988 were sufficient to support an allegation that the company had maliciously concealed its responsibility.[6] Ultimately, however, as a result of public pressure, before the appeal was decided, the German government and the companies involved established a foundation to pay compensation to the victims (2000).[7]

The cases against insurance companies that defrauded Holocaust-era policyholders by associating with the Nazi regime and paying them only a fraction of the compensations they were due concluded with the establishment of an international commission mandated with identifying and compensating the victims. By June 2007, this commission had received 91,558 claims, resulting in 48,000 offers from insurance companies. Sometime later, the claims brought by relatives of Armenian genocide victims against U.S. and European insurance companies were similarly settled through a law that benefited claimants by extending the term to bring actions and helped them overcome statutory limitation defenses.[8]

Independently of the feasibility of these claims, their success is attributed to the pressure exerted by part of the political community, including the federal government, on the defendant companies.[9] The importance of these factors is evidenced by the failure of the actions that were not backed by the U.S. government. Thus, for example, the actions attempted by World War II forced labor victims

5 M. Ratner, "Factors Impacting the Selection and Positioning of Human Rights Class Actions in United States Courts: A Practical Overview," (2001–2003) 58 *New York University Annual Survey of American Law*, 628.

6 *Iwanowa v. Ford*, 67 F. Supp. 2d 424, 1999.

7 J. Authers, "Making Good Again: German Compensation for Forced and Slave Laborers," in P. de Greiff (ed.), *The Handbook of Reparations* (Oxford: Oxford University Press, 2006), pp. 420–448.

8 Ratner, "Factors Impacting the Selection," 628.

9 M. J. Bazyler, "The Holocaust Restitution Movement in Comparative Perspective," (2002) 20 *Berkeley Journal of International Law*, 17–28.

against Japanese companies were dismissed on the grounds that the statute of limitations had expired despite the fact that – as with the Armenian experience – the term to claim compensation was extended by a state law, which would later be declared unconstitutional.[10]

These experiences, in turn, prompted new litigations, such as the actions brought by descendants of African-Americans who were enslaved during the Civil War, which after a first wave of suits against the federal government were brought as class actions against private defendants. To avoid being dismissed on statutory limitation grounds, these descendants argued, among other things, that the harm caused to their rights became evident a long time after it happened, and, in those cases in which it was known, they lacked essential information necessary to bring their claims, through no fault on their part, as it was an ongoing illicit act and the defendants had maliciously concealed information.[11] As of 2011, however, none of these lawsuits for slavery reparation had found any success.[12]

SOME PROBLEMS OF ARGENTINE JURISPRUDENCE IN LIGHT OF INTERNATIONAL STANDARDS

As shown previously, the issue of statutory limitations has been a frequent, although not insurmountable, obstacle encountered by this kind of action, and often the outcome has been determined by extrajudicial factors, such as the capacity of the victims to act as a pressure group or the historical situation or the interests involved. Moreover, jurisprudence reveals that in such cases general statute of limitations rules are applied and that the discussion focuses on establishing the starting point for calculating the term, in an attempt to contemplate, through positive laws that do not refer to the specific case of state terrorism, the unique situation of those who were victims of human rights violations. Lastly, the responses given by the courts in this issue are also often not conclusive.

One possible reason for this is the acritical application of principles and notions associated with civil actions, which is characterized as an area of disputes between individuals who are considered to have the responsibility of furthering this kind of claims. This is evident, for example, in the CSJN ruling in the Larrabeiti Yáñez case, which categorically states that an exclusively individual monetary interest is involved and draws a sharp dividing line between the consideration of the statute of limitations of a civil action and that of a criminal action, when it is, at the very least,

[10] R. Brooks, "The Slave Redress Cases," (2004–2005) 27 *North Carolina Central Law Journal*, 136.

[11] A. Sebok, "Two Concepts of Injustice in Restitution for Slavery," (2004) 84 *Boston University Law Review*, 1421.

[12] K. Wenger, "Too Big to Remedy? Rethinking Mass Restitution for Slavery and Jim Crow," (2010–2011) 44 *Loyola of Los Angeles Law Review*, 191.

doubtful that a civil action for damages inflicted as a result of a serious human rights violation can be comparable – in terms of absolute loss – to an ordinary action for damages.

The Statute of the International Criminal Court stipulates that crimes within its jurisdiction are not subject to any statute of limitations and establishes that reparations for the victims falls under its jurisdiction (Articles 29 and 75). This formula is in line with the Basic Principles and Guidelines on the Right to a Remedy and Reparation for Victims of Gross Violations of International Human Rights Law and Serious Violations to International Humanitarian Law, adopted in 2005 by resolution of the United Nations General Assembly.[13] Under Section IV, paragraph 7, this instrument establishes:

> Domestic statutes of limitations for other types of violations that do not constitute crimes under international law, including those time limitations applicable to civil claims and other procedures, should not be unduly restrictive.

The Inter-American Court of Human Rights suggests that there is a very close connection between the obligation to investigate and the obligation to repair the damage caused, which does not appear to have been fully reflected in the distinction proposed by the CSJN. In its jurisprudence, none of these obligations can be ignored by invoking domestic regulations (see, for example, the *Barrios Altos v. Peru* and *Bulacio v. Argentina* cases). In this way, it puts into question the conclusions of the CSJN and the possibility that the authorities or other individuals may have of presenting a defense based on ordinary statutory limitation regulations.

There is also a social and collective interest in providing reparation for the pain and harm suffered by the victims of these crimes and enabling them to access the truth, as well as in avoiding a hasty resolution for unfair situations in those cases that merit special consideration and time. Victims have an inalienable, autonomous, and imprescriptible right to learn the facts, which could be realized through civil actions with the specific objective of knowing the truth. For example, an investigation concerning economic accomplices can be – under a transitional justice approach – a tool for completing a historical narrative and providing an integral and coherent reparation.[14]

The analyses of the CSJN, however, are limited to a dogmatic consideration of the issue based on domestic laws conceived for matters unrelated to systematic violations of fundamental human rights. They also fail to address this dimension, as they sidestep the fact that these are cases obviously affected by the passage of

[13] UN General Assembly Resolution 60/147, December 16, 2005, UN doc. A/RES/60/147, Annex, par. 7.

[14] P. de Grieff, "Los esfuerzos de reparación en una perspectiva internacional: El aporte de la compensación al logro de la justicia imperfecta," (2005) 7 *Estudios Socio-Jurídicos*, Universidad de Rosario, 2005, 187; C. Nash Rojas, "Las reparaciones ante la Corte Interamericana de Derechos Humanos (1988–2007)," *Centro de Derechos Humanos*, Universidad de Chile, 2009, p. 86.

time, but which also involve exceptional and very serious circumstances that call for a fair solution, as suggested by the American Convention on Human Rights by recognizing the right of the victims to "fair compensation" (Article 63(1)). As we know, ordinary provisions regarding statutory limitations in civil cases are aimed at guaranteeing legal certainty and predictability in legal relations and reducing risks in private contracts; they seek to protect debtors who, as a result of the passage of time, may have lost the means that could exonerate them from an obligation, or else sanction those who failed to diligently exercise their rights or who may have tacitly waived them.

These objectives, however, do not appear to be realized here, so that the unqualified application of such provisions can lead to unfair solutions. In this sense, it has been noted that:

> In such scenarios, we cannot, without a certain degree of cynicism, preach the need to preserve the certainty of legal situations created by those abhorrent acts, or to preserve social peace; or maintain that the victims have tacitly waived compensation for damages that are in most cases irreversible. Much less can we admit that victims deserve to be penalized or punished for not moving quickly to activate their claims, nor can we invoke, in cases involving crimes against humanity, a social requirement that rests on the public order or on economic efficiency. The public order consists, precisely, in the unrestricted observance of human rights (*jus cogens*).[15]

These arguments must be treated with caution, and their importance wanes if we consider the context in which many claimants would have been forced to litigate, pursuant to such provisions. The victims saw the possibility of bringing those responsible for illegal repression to justice precluded, and many of the institutions involved have been unwilling to collaborate or have even pressured to have such proceedings halted. Moreover, the task of gathering evidence has been a difficult one, even for government agencies, and has led to instances of investigation and coordination with the judicial system. Evidence of civil complicity, in particular, emerged much later, after the initial obstacles were removed. To speak of negligence or maintain that the burden of proof should have been on the victims or their relatives seems excessive.

FINAL REFLECTIONS

At this point in Argentina's transition, no one doubts that there was an active involvement of the private sector in state terrorism. Nonetheless, the bulk of the

[15] J. B. Justo, *Dos desafíos para los derechos humanos del siglo XXI: restitución a las víctimas y responsabilidad de las corporaciones* (Río Negro, 2013, unpublished).

state's interventions is highly associated with a criminal justice approach to the issue that pushes the focus of attention away from reprehensible corporate practices or actions, while privileging the analysis of individual criminal responsibility over an assessment of other possible effects and consequences. The path thus taken poses insurmountable obstacles, as the judicial sphere is greatly constrained by statutory limitations in all noncriminal areas and by a system of criminal responsibility that only exceptionally holds legal persons accountable.

The judicialization of the examination of the role of the private sector during the dictatorship is, moreover, unfolding outside the framework of a more or less shared documented narrative, in contrast to what happened with the crimes documented by CONADEP, which were executed under a criminal plan that was proven in court as early as 1985 in the military junta trial. With the phenomenon of private and corporate complicity we may still not have a documented description comparable to that of the Never Again report. In principle, it may be debatable to assert that there are institutions capable of generating similar results in this field. With the exception of cases such as that of Papel Prensa,[16] or the recent report by the National Securities Commission,[17] investigations in most cases have been furthered only by spontaneous efforts from relatives of victims and survivors.

The growing variety of claims, both labor and civil, national and transnational, then, may give an idea of the ongoing discussion around how to address this issue. It may require a process of trial and error, similar to what the criminal prosecution of human rights abuses went through a decade ago, as well as the emergence of social consensuses and more solid government actions. The fairness itself of setting any kind of time limit on the possibility of claiming damages has, in fact, been put into question again with the ruling on the Ingegnieros case, which reopened an unavoidable discussion.

Reducing the obstacles for accessing justice, or examining them more carefully on a case-by-case basis, taking into account not only the difficulties and fears experienced by the victims, but also the historical dynamics involved in considering the two decades it took for criminal proceedings to move firmly forward against those responsible for human rights abuses, or the fact that the details of the economic accomplices of the dictatorship are only now being made public, are necessary steps toward allowing these claims to be judged on their merits, instead of consolidating situations that were determined by undue pressures, delays, and silences.

Under this perspective, equating the renounceable nature of a compensatory action derived from a serious human rights violation to a tacit waiver resulting from the mere passage of time entails adopting a criterion that seems to ignore

[16] See Chapter 20 in this book.
[17] See Chapter 19 in this book.

that truth, justice, and reparations are complementary aspirations rather than alternative responses to serious human rights abuses.[18] The pressing morality of the claims involved forces us to provide the possibility of obtaining a reparation, instead of ensuring a legal coverage for the atrocities of our history,[19] and demands, for example, that we harmonize the statutory limitation regimes of criminal and civil actions.

Not providing a fair criterion that facilitates compensatory actions brought against the economic accomplices of gross and systematic human rights violations generates incentives that are doubly damaging for the aims of transitional justice. On the one hand, the economic accomplices will seek to delay as much as possible any measures aimed at furthering truth, memory, and justice, so as to benefit from the passage of time and the ensuing expiration of the statute of limitations of civil actions for complicity. On the other hand, the aim of guaranteeing the non-repetition of these abuses is hurt by this course of action, as being an accomplice is rendered both profitable and highly unlikely to result in legal and monetary consequences for those involved. The monetary immunity of those who profit greatly from criminal contexts is thus ensured.

POSTSCRIPT

In October 2014, the Argentine National Congress passed Law 26,994, which completely reformed the Civil and Commercial Code and, among other important amendments, established the non-applicability of statutory limitations to civil claims derived for crimes against humanity (Section 2561, Civil Code). This new legal framework will come into effect in August 2015 (Section 7, Civil Code). Even when it establishes that its provisions do not apply to the liability of the state itself, which is regulated separately by Law 26,994, it shows a great deal of potential in terms of truth, memory, justice, and compensation from the perspective of the responsibility of civil accomplices.

Its consequences are yet to be seen, but considering that the National Securities Commission report disclosed hundreds of cases of businesspersons who were illegally dispossessed of assets and properties to favor economic accomplices of the military government, a new wave of lawsuits against private defendants is to be expected. Other victims of gross human rights violations including, for example, workers and/ or their relatives kidnapped, tortured, and killed by military personnel who were

18 UN, Office of the High Commissioner for Human Rights, "Rule of Law Tools for Post Conflict States: Amnesties," HR/PUB/09/1, Geneva, 2009.

19 Brooks, "The Slave Redress Cases," 133.

asked by corporate employers to carry out these crimes to repress labor claims are also expected to bring more and broader actions.

As there is no limitation in terms of time, indigenous people may pursue this path as well; and the fact that Argentine courts have accepted the principle of universal jurisdiction could also encourage victims from other countries to file suits under Argentine jurisdiction.

PART V

Company-Ordered Disappearances

11

The Cases of Ford and Mercedes Benz

Victoria Basualdo, Tomás Ojea Quintana, and Carolina Varsky

For decades, and especially in the past few years, trade unions and social and human rights organizations have been denouncing the role played by business groups in the repression. This chapter discusses two emblematic cases that evidence the complicity between a number of large companies and the armed forces during Argentina's last military dictatorship, which have given rise to legal proceedings in the country and abroad: the cases of the car manufacturers Ford Motor SA and Mercedes Benz. After taking a brief look at the particularities of each case, we point out aspects shared by both so we can identify the characteristics of the relationship between the companies and the armed forces in the last dictatorship, and how legal action was taken. Lastly, some of the impacts of these cases on the judicial, historical, and political fronts are briefly analyzed.

THE CASE OF FORD MOTOR ARGENTINA

Ford Motor Company opened its first branches in Argentina in the early twentieth century, initially in Barracas and later in La Boca; the current plant in General Pacheco, in the province of Buenos Aires, was inaugurated in 1961. Toward the mid-1970s, following a period of growth in the country's automotive industry, workers at the Pacheco plant began mobilizing and organizing at the rank-and-file level, represented by some 200 factory delegates who not only stepped up their demands to management but also increasingly confronted their own national leadership at the Union of Automotive Transport Mechanics and Related Workers (Sindicato de Mecánicos y Afines del Transporte Automotor, SMATA). Pedro Troiani, a factory worker and delegate, and a member of the internal commission, was kidnapped and tortured inside the General Pacheco plant in April 1976. Later, when he testified in court, he talked about the implications and the impact of trade union activism on the way the company operated. In his testimony, he clearly explained that the internal commission received worker complaints that were not only about wages but also had to do with the working conditions and the pace at which they were forced to work, and that in 1975 the commission succeeded in signing an agreement that was highly beneficial to the workers. All of this, he said, had consolidated the commission's position and the workers' bargaining power in the company.[1]

It was in that context that repressive policies were implemented, with increasing force after the March 24, 1976 military coup. Between March and May of that year, twenty-five workers in the plant were kidnapped, most of them members of the internal commission and the rest active unionists, who remained "disappeared" for thirty to sixty days. Some of them were kidnapped from their homes and taken to the Tigre police station, which operated as a clandestine detention center, while the rest were seized directly at the factory, where they were held for hours and then taken to the Tigre police station.

The relationship between company and armed forces in this process of repression of workers became apparent in different ways in the Ford case. First, the kidnapping victims have testified that they were picked up in F100 pickup trucks supplied by the company to the military. Second, there are numerous testimonies indicating that, as well as supporting the armed forces, the company asked the military to kidnap workers and trade union delegates. Arcelia Luján de Portillo, the wife of one of the victims, stated in her testimony that during a meeting she had with a military officer responsible for the kidnappings, whose last name was Molinari, the officer "opened a drawer and pulled out a list typed on a sheet of paper with the Ford logo, which he told me had 'all the names that the company gave us of workers it wanted us to *chupar*,'" using the repression slang term for kidnapping and disappearing (literally, "suck up").[2]

In their statements, several people have testified that the company had "marked" the workers who were to be kidnapped, and that this was done not only by means of the list, but also by providing the workers' IDs bearing their photos, so the military could identify them.

Additional testimony, such as that by Jorge Ernesto Berguier, a conscript who was doing his military service during the years of the dictatorship, have provided a

[1] Written statement by Troiani, dated October 14, 2004, given in the case "Rivero, Santiago Omar y otros s. privación ilegal de libertad, tormentos, etc.," on folios 449/450, case file 142, Juzgado Federal en lo Criminal y Correccional no. 2, San Martín.

[2] Request for preliminary statements in the case "Molinari, Antonio, personal Ford s. privación ilegal de la libertad," brought by Troiani with the legal counsel of Tomás Ojea Quintana. The statement by Arcelia Luján Portillo appears on folio 44 of the case file. Numerous additional testimonies are included, such as that of Elisa Josefa Charlin, the wife of another kidnapping victim who met with Molinari, "who had a list with approximately twenty or thirty typewritten names. I remember the paper had the Ford logo on it." Molinari made it clear then that "'this is the list they gave me,' putting his hand on the list mentioned above" (folios 465/466).

picture of the exchange of favors between the company and the armed forces.[3] The constant presence of military personnel on factory premises was confirmed in very similar terms by other workers, such as Daniel Hagelin, who worked at the factory during the dictatorship:

> There was a strong military presence on the premises, in fact, the sports area, which included the football ground, tennis courts, barbecue area, and workers' changing rooms, was turned into a military barracks; this section was off-limits to workers. But, in addition to that, the plant cafeteria had a specific time in which it only opened for the members of the military posted there; there were even kids doing military service in the factory, as if it were just another unit. I can't say there was a regiment, but there were more than 100 people posted there, there was at least a military company in the factory, and they weren't exactly manufacturing cars. … They weren't providing security in the installations, the company itself took care of that; their task was specifically repression. The military acted at the request of management, and the one calling the shots there was Galarraga, the institutional relations manager. We can't say that the military gave orders to the workers, but they were there in case any wage demands or other forms of trade union complaints came up. The company's management was pro-military. The situation in the internal commission hit by the coup was notorious: months before the government of Isabel [Martínez de Perón] collapsed, they had an argument with Galarraga, who told them verbatim: "I'm not arguing with you people anymore; from now on take it up with Camps." No one knew who this Camps guy was; after the coup he became chief of police of the province of Buenos Aires, and was responsible for the disappearance of two members of the internal commission.[4]

The company's participation in the repression was not limited to providing logistical support or requesting the detention of some of its own workers. As in other extreme cases, such as the Acindar steel plant (analyzed in Chapter 12), it was a highly organized support. It has been proven that a military barracks operated on factory premises, set up in the sports grounds (in the *quincho* or enclosed barbecue area), with the alleged purpose of combating subversion as part of the criminal plan whose existence was judicially proven in "Causa 13/84" (the 1984 military junta trial) in the Federal Court of the city of Buenos Aires. Some of the workers were illegally detained in that quincho, while others were held in the Tigre First Police Station, and in the Ingeniero Maschwitz police station in the province of Buenos Aires, where they were tortured.

3 Testimony by Berguier, given on August 25, 2005, on folio 712 of the case "Molinari, Antonio, personal Ford s. privación ilegal de la libertad."

4 Quoted in F. Domínguez and A. Sayus, *La sombra de Campo de Mayo*, available at www.desaparecidos.org/nuncamas/web/investig/saydom/lasombra/lasombra.htm (accessed March 31, 2013).

Among those detained on factory premises was Juan Carlos Conti, a SMATA delegate who had worked for Ford since 1965 and was kidnapped on April 14, 1976. He was taken in one of the company's pickup trucks to the plant's quincho, with his hands bound together with wire. After his kidnapping, the company accused him of "walking out on the job," and when his wife responded by saying what happened (of which the company of course was aware), he was fired.[5]

Also, Ford personnel members participated in the interrogations of the kidnapped delegates, to extract information regarding trade union activities in the factory. One such interrogation was that of detainee Francisco Guillermo Perrotta, who was not a factory worker but one of the administrative employees, a category that until the mid-1970s had not been represented by a union. As an employee in the cost, material, and inventory analysis division, Perrotta had access to key information about the factory's internal matters. He and another delegate from the financial area were tortured with an electric prod. During the torture session, in which his interrogators mentioned details and names that only very well-informed employees of the firm could know, Perrotta, who was wearing a hood, was able to identify the voice of the factory's security chief, Héctor Francisco Sibilla, among the people present. Sibilla was a member of the armed forces and on July 26, 1978, after the kidnapping of workers, he was promoted to the rank of lieutenant colonel. After his time in the company, he was hired to work in security at the U.S. Embassy, a position he held until 2004.[6]

All of these elements show a clear pattern of a relationship between the company and the repressive forces. In fact, this evidence is added to previous reports indicating that in the past Ford was an accomplice of other authoritarian regimes. In this sense, it has also been reported that during World War II it used prisoners as slave labor. Although the legal action brought in that case was not successful, the company acknowledged the facts and helped compensate the victims. In the case of Argentina, the history of the legal actions brought by workers is a lengthy one, and began as soon as the dictatorship came to an end.

After the return to democracy, Pedro Troiani decided to sue the carmaker for wrongful dismissal, as a few days after his kidnapping his family received a telegram notifying them that he had been fired for walking off the job, like other people

5 See the report filed in 1998 by the Federation of Workers of Argentina (Central de Trabajadores Argentinos, CTA) in the trial conducted in a Spanish court by Judge Baltasar Garzón for the forced disappearance of persons during Argentina's last dictatorship (p. 14).

6 A. Dandan, "Ford Falcon modelo 76," *Página/12* (Buenos Aires), February 26, 2006. One of the lines of investigation followed by the workers and their legal representatives is the relationship between the Argentine branch and the parent company, with the aim of determining the latter's degree of knowledge and participation in the repression.

abducted by the company. The lawsuit was rejected by the Supreme Court of Justice in the 1980s, on the argument that the statute of limitations had expired. In other words, Troiani, according to the Court, should have sued Ford during the military dictatorship.

Despite the fact that legal action appeared to be impossible because of the Full Stop and Due Obedience acts, other trade union delegates also sued Ford for wrongful dismissal. These cases, however, were successful, as the Supreme Court modified its jurisprudence by applying interruptions to the statute of limitations.

Although the lawsuits involved labor claims, they were underpinned by the conviction that Ford was responsible for abductions and torture. This was made clear in Conti's labor trial, when Judge Juan Carlos Morando concluded:

> Dr. Capón Filas, with his vote, has shown that the defendant corporation acted, in the emergency, with exemplary bad faith. What is more, in the course of the proceedings, it attempted to assume the inadmissible position of a disinterested third party with regard to the circumstances in which the claimant and the other delegates were detained, an episode in which, as these proceedings have established to a moral certainty, its officials acted as instigators.[7]

After the impunity laws were declared unconstitutional in 2001, the possibility of bringing criminal action against the perpetrators of the crimes was opened, and Pedro Troiani appeared as private prosecutor (*querellante*) in a criminal case brought in November 2002.[8] From the start the objective of the private prosecution (*querella*) brought by Troiani, accompanied by the rest of the trade union delegates, was to accuse and penalize the Ford managers, who according to the evidence were civilian accomplices of the crimes committed.

Establishing the company's responsibility with concrete proof was a gargantuan effort from the start. The case was prosecuted in the Federal Court presided by Judge Daniel Eduardo Rafecas, but the investigation had been delegated to the prosecutor's office headed by Federico Delgado. However, it was the private prosecution and the Ford workers that furthered and deepened the investigation: they gave testimony along with their family members, called on experts to add elements to analyze the company's track record, requested a search and an on-site inspection of the plant (a measure that was not accepted by the judge or the state prosecutor), and offered documents that were in their possession. One of these documents, containing a

7 See the court ruling in "Conti, Juan Carlos c. Ford Motor Argentina SA s. cobro de pesos," court file 26,091.

8 With regard to the unconstitutionality, see Juzgado Federal en lo Criminal y Correccional no. 4, "Simón, J. H. y otros," resolution of March 6, 2001.

speech given by the president of Ford on May 13, 1980, during the inauguration of a truck factory, can serve as an example of the kind of evidence provided:

> As of March 1976 we were facing a challenge. In Argentina a process had begun, a change of system, a complete change in philosophy, which covered individual behaviors and the collective behavior of society as a whole. A change in mentality was necessary. In our case, we had to make a business decision and, with our actions and procedures, we showed what that decision was. Those representatives of destruction with no love of country and no God – whose eradication has cost the nation so much, and who still persist in small numbers – deserve only scorn from the decent men who work and study, day in and day out, to build this nation.

It took several years to gather solid legal proof, and in 2006 the private prosecutors felt that they were ready to call four Ford managers, who had been clearly identified as participants in the crimes, to give their statements in the preliminary investigation. The four officers were: the president of Ford Argentina, Nicolás Enrique Courard; the general manager of the plant, Pedro Müller; the manager of labor relations, Guillermo Galarraga; and the plant's security chief, Héctor Francisco Sibilla. The private prosecutors filed a specific petition to gather their preliminary statements, but the process was delayed by jurisdictional disputes, and the case was finally assigned to a federal court in the district of San Martín under acting judge Juan Manuel Yajl and federal state prosecutor Jorge Sica, where it was stalled, despite repeated petitions and complaints that went unheeded.

In that context, and despite the difficulties and failed attempts, this group of Ford workers was strengthened and took part in other coordinated actions. For example, in one of the traditional March 24 demonstrations, in 2006, the group decided to march carrying a flag where they presented themselves to society as "the Ford disappeared," thus vindicating their history.

In 2012, Alicia Vence was appointed to the bench in the Federal Court of San Martin (Juzgado Federal de San Martín). A few months later she admitted the private prosecution's longstanding request and ordered an on-site inspection of the Ford plant in General Pacheco. This measure was very important from both a procedural and humane point of view. After decades, the workers were able to return to the place from which many of them had been removed at gunpoint by military personnel and to the spot where they had been held after the abduction – the quincho area that had been modified to serve as a detention center. Furthermore, this measure was a clear signal that the Ford case would finally start to move forward.

In late 2012, Judge Vence ordered the four Ford managers identified by the private prosecution as participants in the crimes to appear in the preliminary investigation. The support of the National Secretariat of Human Rights, which also appeared as a private prosecutor and had backed the request for preliminary statements, played an important role. In March 2013, after two cancellations, they were finally summoned. Nicolás Courard, as noted in the case file, had died by then. Guillermo Galarraga refused to give a statement, as did Pedro Müller. Héctor Sibilla, instead, gave a statement and denied the accusations.

After these preliminary statements, a decisive breakthrough was made in the case. On May 20, 2013, Judge Vence initiated criminal proceedings against the three former Ford executives for their criminal involvement in the illegal deprivation of liberty of the factory delegates and workers and the torture inflicted on them. This was a significant step forward in the case, even though the pretrial detention of the defendants was not ordered and they remain free. The next objective is to hold a public, oral trial, where the human rights violations that were committed will be exposed to society.

Meanwhile, in 2004, a U.S. law firm represented by Paul Hoffman agreed to sue Ford Motor Company under the Alien Tort Claims Act (ATCA), which enables foreigners to seek remedies in U.S. courts for violations to the law of nations committed by individuals and companies abroad.[9] This firm worked with the lawyers who had brought the private prosecution, and together they prepared a lawsuit on behalf of the trade union delegates, which was filed in a California court of first instance. The expectations raised by the filing of this case were shot down when the U.S. lawyers decided to withdraw, shortly before the company was notified of the lawsuit. Their decision had been prompted by a recent U.S. Supreme Court ruling that seriously limited future ATCA cases.[10] From Buenos Aires, the workers insisted on moving forward with the lawsuit, but the lawyers' decision was final. The trade union delegates have since been seeking a U.S. law firm interested in filing a lawsuit under the ATCA.

Despite the U.S. Supreme Court's decision in the Kiobel case, which set serious limitations on this kind of lawsuit, the Ford case has an important element in its favor, given that the defendant firm is a U.S. company, a fact that strengthens the question of territorial jurisdiction. In this sense, it is clear that Ford Argentina was a subsidiary of Ford Motor Company and, consequently, the latter is responsible, at least objectively, for the illegal actions of its subsidiary. Two examples that are incorporated in the criminal proceeding serve to illustrate this corporate relationship. First, a few years before the 1976 coup d'état, the president of the U.S. company, Henry Ford III, visited Ford Argentina and toured the General Pacheco plant, taking part in a general inspection. In addition, declassified U.S. State Department documents reveal that the president of Ford Argentina had to make trips to Washington, DC to try to arrange exports of Ford Falcon cars to Cuba, a trade operation that is still banned today under the U.S. embargo.

9 See Chapter 9 in this book.

10 See Kiobel v. Royal Dutch Petroleum Co., 133 S.Ct. 1659 (2013).

The Ford trade union delegates also feel certain that the parent company based in the United States was ultimately responsible for the illegal actions of which they were victims.[11] However, the enormous challenge faced now is to unravel and promote the necessary mechanisms that will allow justice to be done.

THE CASE OF MERCEDES BENZ

The Mercedes Benz car manufacturer, founded in Germany in 1890, is one of the biggest industrial companies in Europe. Its close ties with the Nazi regime played a major role in its growth and expansion; it not only obtained extraordinary profits by supplying war vehicles and materials, it also benefited from slave labor. The plant in Argentina, the company's first branch overseas, was built in González Catán, in the province of Buenos Aires, in 1951.

The repression in the factory in the mid-1970s was a reaction to the harsh disputes between the company's workers and management. Like workers in other plants, the Mercedes Benz workers mobilized in October 1975 in rejection of the representatives appointed by SMATA, which they considered did not defend their interests. The plant's 4,000 workers held an assembly and elected a new internal commission, made up of nine representatives, who were known as the "group of nine."

SMATA disputed the validity of the election and of the internal commission, and the company dismissed more than 100 workers, including those who would later be kidnapped and disappeared during the dictatorship, with the support of the national automobile union and its secretary general, José Rodríguez.[12]

During the union actions staged to demand the reinstatement of the dismissed workers, on October 24, 1975 the Montoneros guerrilla organization kidnapped the plant's production manager, Heinrich Metz.

The company finally gave in and announced that the workers would be rehired, after which the Montoneros demanded payment of a ransom, which according to the parent company was a sum of US$7 million, while local management said it was US$4 million and the Montoneros's heads of finance claimed was US$2 million. The investigation into the amount that was paid in ransom exposed the fraudulent practices of the company, which took advantage of the kidnapping to claim a much higher amount in its tax declaration in Germany, enabling it to increase its profit margin.

Of the sixteen Mercedes Benz Argentina workers who were kidnapped during the dictatorship, only two reappeared, and their testimony was key in reconstructing

[11] With respect to a parent company's civil responsibility regarding the activities of its subsidiaries in the context of complicity under Argentine law, see Chapter 9 of this book.

[12] See Chapter 14 in this book.

what happened. The two survivors are Juan Martín (detained in April 1976 at the factory, imprisoned and tortured in the San Justo police station, and released nineteen days later) and Héctor Aníbal Ratto (detained in August 1977, also at the factory, by an armed group belonging to the Argentine army, held in clandestine captivity and tortured in the Ramos Mejía police station and later in Campo de Mayo, and released in March 1979). Although they both consider themselves lucky to have survived, they still suffer physical and psychological effects from their time in captivity. There was also a third survivor: Alfredo Martín, who was not a worker but a foreman, and who was detained in December 1976, tortured by Rubén Lavallén in the San Justo police station, and freed a few hours later.

The company's involvement in the repression has been documented in the testimony of several individuals. On August 12, 1977, Héctor Ratto was called to the office of the production manager, Juan Tasselkraut, and that same afternoon he was kidnapped. While in his office, Ratto heard Tasselkraut reveal the address of trade union delegate Diego Núñez to the police. The next day, Núñez was abducted by the security forces. Ratto was tortured with electric shocks, which caused permanent damage. He and Núñez were transferred to the Campo de Mayo detention center, along with other fellow factory workers, where they were all tortured. Ratto was freed, but Núñez and the other delegates are still disappeared today.

Several of these workers were arrested in their workplace without any kind of protest from the factory's managers, who instead cooperated with the repressive groups. Tasselkraut himself revealed the effects that the repression had on the company's internal operations, when in the context of the Truth Trials in the La Plata courts he was asked if he believed there was a link between the reduction in conflicts in the factory, the rise in productivity, and the disappearance of workers and trade unionists. The answer he gave was: "Well … there's no such thing as miracles."[13]

The case of Rubén Luís Lavallén illustrates the depth of the ties between the company and the repressive forces. In the first few years of the dictatorship, Lavallén was in charge of the commando of the San Justo Investigations Brigade, where a clandestine detention center operated. He was identified by the wife of Alberto Gigena, a Mercedes Benz worker, as one of the men who kidnapped her husband, who remains disappeared. With that service record, Lavallén was hired by Mercedes Benz in 1978 as security chief in the González Catán plant.

After the return to democracy, he was sentenced in 1998 to four years in prison for forging the birth certificate of Paula Logares, the daughter of a Uruguayan couple abducted in Montevideo and held in the San Justo Investigations Brigade, under

[13] Statement by Juan Tasselkraut in the Truth Trials (Juicios por la Verdad) held in La Plata, November 21, 2001.

Operation Condor. The couple was never seen alive again, and the girl was taken by Lavallén and registered as his daughter.[14]

The close relationship between the company's management and the military leadership is best illustrated by the fact that the Argentine army was Mercedes Benz's top client, from which it purchased Unimog trucks, and that Mercedes Benz was in turn one of the twenty highest grossing companies in Argentina and had one of the largest industrial complexes in the country.

According to the information provided by management personnel, as part of its gestures toward the army, the company donated obstetric equipment to be used in Campo de Mayo. The only obstetric installations present in that military center were illegal and were set up for the pregnant disappeared women who gave birth in clandestine captivity.

Mercedes Benz's involvement in the repression of its workers during the last military dictatorship has been investigated by the German journalist Gabriela Weber, and her findings were laid out in two books and a documentary film.[15] Legal action seemed impossible after the Full Stop and Due Obedience Acts were passed. However, since these crimes could not be tried in Argentina, human rights movements sought to launch investigations and legal proceedings in Europe, not only with the aim of bringing those directly responsible to justice, even if it were outside the country, but also to pressure the Argentine justice system to reconsider the reopening of trials in the country. It should be underlined, however, that while these cases involved direct perpetrators of torture and murder, the broader structure, which had held up the dictatorship, did not figure in the investigations.[16]

In this sense, based on these investigations, in 1999 an action was brought in Germany on behalf of Héctor Ratto, against Juan Tasselkraut, on charges of collaborating and allowing the murder of other kidnapping victims.

Due to the characteristics of the German legal system, it was only possible to file charges against that Ford manager.[17] The Nuremberg-Fuerth public prosecutor began the investigation of the case, which included interviews with several witnesses in the German embassy in Buenos Aires. But on November 27, 2003, the public prosecutor's office suspended the proceedings on grounds of insufficient evidence. It was held that Ratto's testimony had been contradictory, while Tasselkraut

[14] G. Weber, *La conexión alemana. El lavado del dinero nazi en la Argentina* (Buenos Aires: Edhasa, 2005).

[15] Ibid.; G. Weber, *Die Verschwundenen von Mercedes-Benz* (Hamburg: Assoziation A, 2001); and the documentary *Milagros no hay. Los desaparecidos de Mercedes Benz* (color, 113 min., 2003; there is an updated version: 85 min., 2005).

[16] W. Kaleck, "International Criminal Law and Transnational Businesses: Cases from Argentina and Colombia," in S. Michalowski (ed.), *Corporate Accountability in the Context of Transitional Justice* (London: Routledge, 2014).

[17] On the impossibility of holding legal persons criminally responsible, see Chapter 9 in this book.

emphatically denied the allegations. In addition, the public prosecutor's office maintained that the murder of Diego Núñez could not be proven because it was not possible to verify his fate (given that the law in Germany distinguishes between murder and disappearance).[18]

As noted earlier, there is evidence indicating that Mercedes Benz – the Argentine branch – collaborated with illegal repression by identifying the workers who were to be kidnapped. That was revealed by the testimony of different people that implicated Tasselkraut in the events and pointed to his shared responsibility. Giving the police Núñez's address would be, at the very least, an act of collaboration. Given the dates on which the company's workers were disappeared, Tasselkraut could not have been unaware of what the security forces were doing. In statements to Gabriela Weber, Tasselkraut said, referring to that period of time: "Anyone who knew anything about Argentina knew that against all human sense, against human rights, people were being eliminated in Argentina." Nevertheless, the prosecutor's office in Nuremberg concluded that there was not enough evidence of his participation to bring charges.

The prosecutor's office has not considered the need to continue investigating, even though the fate of Diego Núñez and the rest of the disappeared Mercedes Benz workers has not been determined. The office's resolution indicated a reluctance to delve deeper into the reported events. International doctrine and jurisprudence universally holds that the only possible response to systematic human rights violations is to exhaust all possibilities of investigation to uncover the truth about what happened and determine criminal liability.

In this sense, the Nuremberg prosecutor's office has not explored all of the possible leads for investigating what happened and holding those responsible for the disappearance of the workers accountable.

Despite these limitations and difficulties, the legal proceedings had the positive effect of bringing together a group of Mercedes Benz workers and trade unionists who launched numerous activities to bring attention to the case, with initiatives such as placing commemorative plaques at the spots where the kidnappings took place and the holding of public events. At the same time, in 2002 this group initiated legal proceedings in Buenos Aires. On the basis of evidence collected after the Truth Trials held in La Plata, Mercedes Benz was accused of establishing a criminal alliance with then Labor Minister Carlos Ruckauf, and with the SMATA national leadership to kidnap and murder "undesirable" trade union representatives. The Centre for Legal and Social Studies (Centro de Estudios Legales y Sociales, CELS) also joined the action as a private prosecutor in representation of the company's

18 See Kaleck, "International Criminal Law," and G. Weber, "Mercedes Benz Argentina," available at www.gabyweber.com/prozesse_mba.php (accessed February 21, 2013).

group of victims (case no. 17735/02, "NN s. Asociación ilícita con peligro vigencia Constitución nacional. Homicidio simple, homicidio agravado").

After five years of investigations, the Federal Criminal and Correctional Prosecutor's Office of the city of Buenos Aires (Fiscalía Federal Criminal y Correccional de la ciudad de Buenos Aires) concluded that certain key representatives of Mercedes Benz and SMATA had been aware of the crimes, but considered the evidence to be insufficient to demonstrate their role in them. At this point the case was referred to the Federal Court in San Martín, in the province of Buenos Aires (as the crimes had been committed in that jurisdiction), the same court hearing the action of the delegates of the Ford Pacheco plant, which is currently halted.

Owing to these difficulties, in 2004 a group of workers and delegates decided to file a civil lawsuit in the United States against DaimlerChrysler AG, the name of the Mercedes Benz parent company at the time, to demand reparations for the serious human rights violations committed by the firm during the military dictatorship. Although the court of first instance in the district of San Francisco dismissed the case, the court of appeals reversed the decision, and finally, on April 22, 2013 the U.S. Supreme Court agreed to hear the appeal, to decide whether DaimlerChrysler AG had to respond in a U.S. court for the lawsuit against its branch in Argentina. This represented a major step forward for the case.

CONCLUSIONS

The cases of Ford Motor Company and Mercedes Benz are high-profile examples of the close collaboration that existed between a number of large companies and the armed forces in the repression of workers during the last dictatorship. Both clearly show the direct involvement of top executives in the kidnapping and disappearance of representatives of rank-and-file workers who had fostered new lines of organization and activism. These workers not only questioned the orthodox union leadership of SMATA, they also introduced major changes in the internal functioning of the factories, altering the previous balance of labor relations, a change that had important repercussions beyond their specific workplaces. These developments make it possible to conclude, furthermore, that an essential motivation underlying corporate complicity with crimes against humanity was the aim of strengthening the position of corporate management, with the objective of exercising a tight control over workers and their trade union representatives, increasing work paces, and boosting the profit margin in the industrial activity that the two carmakers carried out in Argentina during that time period.

The two cases also show the enormous difficulties that workers had to overcome when it came to bringing legal action against their employers for their involvement in the events of that time. In a context that was especially adverse for trials regarding crimes against humanity in Argentina, they turned to courts in other countries with the aim of obtaining justice and reparations for the serious human rights abuses that were committed. Although to date no sentence has been handed down in any of these cases, there have been advances in the framework of the criminal justice system. For instance, the possibility of holding legal persons, including companies, responsible for these crimes is an issue that is now being debated. Under Argentine criminal law, these collective actors cannot be charged. But progress has been made toward making managers or owners accountable in the case of companies involved in crimes against humanity perpetrated against their workers.

From our perspective, any civil action seeking reparations for crimes against humanity must also follow the principle of non-applicability of statutory limitation that governs criminal actions. This is particularly necessary in the case of legal persons, which, as such, were involved in some way in this kind of crimes, beyond the responsibility of individuals who held executive positions. Otherwise there would be scant possibilities of effectively bringing legal persons to justice and, consequently, of generating mechanisms to prevent further abuses.

Both cases have made it possible to identify collusion with the repression on the part of civilian actors belonging to economic groups, which not only benefited from the dictatorship's economic and labor policies, but were also accomplices in the kidnapping and torturing of workers and trade union delegates and leaders. The crimes committed during the dictatorship must be thoroughly investigated, and that entails investigating what happened, who was directly responsible, and also what the collaboration from other sectors of society was.

Because they are crimes against humanity, forced disappearances entail an obligation to investigate them, prosecute the perpetrators and bring them to justice, and reveal to the families of disappeared individuals and to society everything that can be established about the fate and whereabouts of the victims – an obligation that continues to exist as long as there is uncertainty about what happened to them.

To these are added other cases, including, most notably, the November 15, 2012 prosecution of the president of the Ingenio Ledesma sugar mill, Carlos Blaquier, and the company's manager, Alberto Lemos, for home invasion, unlawful deprivation of liberty, torture, and homicide in a case involving thirty-two victims; a sentence handed down in March 2012 ordering an investigation into the responsibility of the board of directors of the Loma Negra cement plant and its complicity with the military dictatorship; and the prosecution, confirmed by the Salta Federal Court (Cámara Federal de Salta) on April 8, 2013, of businessman Marcos Levin, owner of La Veloz del Norte, accused of instigating the kidnapping of trade union delegate Víctor Manuel Cobos, who was tortured. Lastly, the ruling handed down in the V. Cuerpo case by the Bahia Blanca Federal Oral Tribunal (Tribunal Oral Federal de Bahía Blanca), ordering the extraction of testimony about publications by the newspaper *La Nueva Provincia* with the aim of investigating the commission of crimes against humanity by its directors.[19]

The cases involving the responsibility of companies in the commission of crimes against humanity not only open a new dimension in the trials for human rights abuses perpetrated under state terrorism, they also underscore the importance of incorporating economic and social dimensions into the analysis of the impacts of the last military dictatorship in Argentina.

LATEST JUDICIAL DEVELOPMENTS

With respect to the Mercedes Benz case, after five years of investigations, the Sixth Federal Criminal and Correctional Prosecutor's Office of the city of Buenos Aires (Fiscalía Federal Criminal y Correccional de la ciudad de Buenos Aires) concluded that certain key representatives of Mercedes Benz and SMATA had been aware of the crimes that were being committed, but considered that the evidence furnished was insufficient to demonstrate their role in the crimes, and therefore the victims and their families are currently trying to obtain additional evidence. It also considered that the justice system of the Federal Capital did not have jurisdiction to investigate the crimes. As a result, by court order, the case was referred to the Federal Court of San Martín, Buenos Aires province, which was the jurisdiction in which the crimes had been committed. As noted earlier, this is the same court prosecuting the Ford Pacheco plant case. The defendants in the Mercedes Benz case – members of the armed forces – are Santiago Omar Riveros, Reynaldo Benito Antonio Bignone, Ángel Rubén Omaechevarría, José María González, Carlos Eduardo José Somoza, Julio San Román, and Hugo Miguel Castagno Monge. However, on July 21, 2014, the Federal Court of San Martín declared the partial lack of jurisdiction with respect to certain victims in the case and its referral to La Plata, thus confirming the lack of jurisdiction declared by Judge Vence, in line with the decision adopted by the La Plata Federal Court. Meanwhile, in August 2014, the private prosecutors were summoned under Section 346 of the National Code of Criminal Procedure and requested to state whether they agreed to bring the case to trial.

At the same time, the U.S. Supreme Court, which had accepted the case to consider whether DaimlerChrysler AG could be sued in that country based on charges against its branch in Argentina, finally decided in January 2014 that the company could not be sued in California for crimes in which Mercedes Benz Argentina was implicated, because the alleged offenses had occurred outside U.S. soil.

[19] See Chapter 21 in this book.

With respect to the Ford case, as of September 2014, the criminal case against three managers of the Argentine branch for complicity in crimes against humanity committed during Argentina's last dictatorship is in the preparation stage for the public oral trial. All of the parties have presented to the court the list of evidence that they hope will be produced. The court must now decide which evidence it will admit and which it will reject. Subsequently, the court will have to set a time and date for the start of the trial.

Originally, the parties involved in the investigation were the state prosecutor's office and the Ford workers as private prosecutors – that is, as a sort of accusing parties. Later, the National Secretariat of Human Rights and the Secretariat of Human Rights of the Province of Buenos Aires joined as private prosecutors, or accusing parties. The three prosecuted managers, along with their private defense lawyers, are the three defendants. Thus, in total, there are seven parties in the Ford trial.

The number of parties and, consequently, the volume of evidence that has been furnished will undoubtedly require that the court take more time in deciding on the admissibility of the evidence. Taking this into account, and the court's involvement in other trials currently underway, the prospects are that the Ford trial could start in February 2015; that is, if the defendants refrain from using any more dilatory tactics, as they have already attempted by asking for the annulment of the investigation, which was duly rejected.

In December 2014, the trial court took the testimony of two unionists who are in delicate health and who might not be in a condition to participate in the coming trial. In their testimonies, they highlighted how they were kidnapped and tortured inside the Ford factory in the locality of Pacheco. These early testimonies have had the effect of generating the necessary climate to begin the trial.

The holding of the Ford trial and the progress in the Mercedes Benz case are essential for completing the process of memory, truth, and justice in Argentina, given that nearly forty years after the events in question, and with abundant evidence of the involvement of business sectors in the repression against workers, no sentences have yet been handed down for the responsibility of corporate executives in crimes against humanity. The efforts to move the Mercedes Benz case forward and to reach the stage of a public oral trial in the Ford case have been enormous; but an even greater effort will be needed to achieve a conviction. If that is accomplished, the legal channels to hold the Argentine subsidiaries, and possibly the parent companies, accountable will be more accessible. Ultimately, it is the companies themselves that will have to be held accountable for what happened, above all, so that these companies will never again, here in Argentina or anywhere in the world, seek profits at any cost.

12

Acindar and Techint: Extreme Militarization of Labor Relations

Victorio Paulón

Another clichéd expression, hanging like a sword of Damocles over our legitimate right to defend ourselves from the cunning attacks of international subversion, is this trite business of human rights. Its loudest champions demand that they be respected in noncommunist countries, but remain silent when communism savagely crushes even the tiniest attempt of the population to shake off the totalitarian pressure that stifles it and deprives it of any of kind of freedom.[1]

THE COMPANIES AND THEIR PLAYERS IN HISTORICAL PERSPECTIVE

This chapter explains the importance of the companies Acindar and Techint in the economic life of the country, as well as their evolution before, during, and after the dictatorship, with the aim of providing additional background elements to help understand the rationale and scope of the complicity of these two companies in the repression of workers. The coincidences in terms of field of industry, location of factories, corporate histories, trade union movement, and collaboration with military and police forces to repress their own workers merit a joint examination of both companies.

As in other chapters in this book that describe the close collaboration that existed between companies that sought to discipline their workers and the military and police forces that repressed the population, the cases of Acindar and Techint clearly show the economic rationale behind repression and the extreme involvement of business in the commission of the crimes. So evident is this involvement that a recent court ruling declared the non-applicability of statutory limitations in a

The author would like to thank Victoria Basualdo for her comments on earlier versions of this chapter, as well as for the research material provided.

1 *De las frases hechas y la impaciencia. Carta política, agosto de 1976. Acindar. Su pensamiento empresario 1976–1992*, Buenos Aires, 1992, p. 23.

labor action brought against Techint for its collaboration in the kidnapping and disappearance of one of its own plant workers.[2]

It seems inadequate to speak of "corporate complicity" in the gross and systematic human rights abuses committed during the last civilian-military dictatorship. The progress achieved in state terrorism trials and the evidence provided in the court proceedings currently underway have clearly established that there was a truly integral strategic plan devised by the most powerful economic interests to do away with what was known as "the second import substitution industrialization plan."[3] Rather than complicity, then, it would be more accurate to talk of corporate planning and direct involvement in state terrorism, as the cases of Acindar and Techint blatantly show.[4]

Abandoning this characterization would entail reducing what happened – as was intended in the 1980s and 1990s – to alleged excesses in repression, instances of abuse of authority, or police and military brutality, ignoring the class nature of such actions. Only from that assumption can corporate complicity be analyzed. These were not merely minor partners who took advantage of the dictatorship to impose increasingly lower wages, arbitrary dismissals, unlimited work hours. These corporate actors also *competed* against other business sectors, which they succeeded in *eliminating* from the market, forcing them to sell their factories and sign over their export contracts, often under torture in concentration camps. Papel Prensa is an emblematic example of these practices, but it is only the most notorious of the more than 100 cases reported to the National Secretariat of Human Rights.

As of the late nineteenth and throughout the twentieth century, Argentina's iron and steel industry saw major developments, such as the first installation of a Siemens-Martin furnace. With World War II, as developed countries were unable to meet their greater supply needs, Argentina's local industry received a major boost,

[2] Enrique Roberto Ingegnieros started working at Techint on May 17, 1976 and almost a year later, on May 5, 1977, he was kidnapped at his workplace by a task group on the payroll of the national government, during an operation known as "Ampliación Dalmine." According to testimony given in the proceedings in the labor appeals court, on the day he was kidnapped he was called into the factory's administration office where he was told a relative was waiting for him, and once there he was kidnapped. See Cámara Nacional de Apelaciones del Trabajo, Sala V, "Ingegnieros, María Gimena c. Techint SA Compañía Técnica Internacional s. accidente. Ley Especial," February 2, 2012, available at http://diariojudicial.com.ar/fuerolaboral/Se-le-vino-la-noche-a-empresas-donde-hubo-desaparecidos-20120215-0002.html (accessed November 9, 2014).

[3] E. Basualdo, *Estudios de historia económica argentina. Desde mediados del siglo XX hasta la actualidad* (Buenos Aires: Siglo XXI, 2006). All references to socioeconomic transformations during the period analyzed are drawn from this book.

[4] The factual information concerning the repression of Acindar and Techint workers provided in this chapter is drawn primarily from the research published in V. Paulón, *Una larga huelga. Historias de metalúrgicos* (Buenos Aires: Desde el Subte, 2012). The author of this chapter was a trade union delegate during the strike studied and spent five years in jail as a result. All the accounts of that episode and subsequent developments are based on the author's firsthand knowledge of the events.

furthering the import substitution model and marking another major milestone for steel production.

State initiatives such as Fábrica Militar de Aceros (1935) and Altos Hornos Zapla (1943) joined the private companies Tamet, Acindar, and Santa Rosa in this field of industry. However, this period of development would no doubt reach its height with the passing of Law 12,987 and the adoption of the National Steel Industry Plan, which included the establishment of Sociedad Mixta Siderúrgica Argentina (SOMISA), the great national iron and steel company, for the production of pig iron, steel, semi-finished steel products, and hot rolled steel sheets. There were some 150 businesses devoted to the production of pig iron, steel, cast iron, and finished pieces, but this only covered 10 percent of domestic demand.

In the 1950s, 1960s, and 1970s this industry experienced a period of significant growth in production, driven by the state's investment in SOMISA (developed in the belief that the ironworks industry was key, a "mother of industries"), which supplied semi-finished billets and slabs for steel production in the various private companies. The combination of short supply and increasing concentration contributed to shape a conglomerate in which the duopoly Techint-Acindar went from being dependent on state production to competing with it.

Acindar, whose board was headed in the 1970s by José Alfredo Martínez de Hoz, who would later be one of the leading political officials supporting the military dictatorship, had carried out one of the period's most direct crackdowns on trade unionism in 1975. It seized the opportunity afforded by a labor power dispute – which pitted the factory's internal commission (left-leaning) against the leadership of the national union (headed by Lorenzo Miguel, a major representative of orthodox Peronism) – to spearhead a new trend in business. In March 1974 it set up a federal police unit within the premises of the Villa Constitución plant, and, by the middle of that year, it had practically militarized the company, to such an extent that it has since been proven that after the March 24, 1976 coup a clandestine detention center operated in the nearby "bachelor's residence." In March 1975, a strike, which would continue for two months, broke out after the national government took control of the local union and the members of the union steering committee and internal commissions of the Acindar, Metcon, and Marathon plants were arrested. On March 20, 1975, a caravan of more than 150 military vehicles arrived from the national capital to occupy the city and arrested 100 unionists, including leaders of the internal commissions and delegates. The assemblies of the various factories responded by electing a struggle committee and calling an indefinite strike, demanding the release of the arrested leaders and the reestablishment of the union.

Parapolice command units were a permanent presence throughout the city of Villa Constitución, in addition to the rural police of Santa Fe (known as the Pumas), which stood guard around the company. More than 150 workers were arrested.

Acindar maintained this situation for the entire duration of the strike, and it fired 1,000 workers once the strike was lifted.[5]

The scope of this repressive plan, of which Acindar was the leading actor and beneficiary, can be gauged by the fact that 300 metallurgy workers in that city, which at the time had a population of less than 30,000, were arrested between March 20, 1975 and March 24, 1976. As a result of the company's offensives against its workers, more than thirty people died, several of whom are still disappeared. There were also armed attacks against the sites where the struggle committee operated and several simultaneous kidnappings of workers, whose bodies were later found mutilated and with signs of torture. This was the case of Carlos Ruescas, Julio Palacios, and the lawyers María Concepción de Grandis, found in November 1975, and Carlos Tonso, Pedro Reche, and Jorge Andino, found in early January 1976.

The criminal involvement of corporations in state terrorism is without a doubt most clearly exemplified by José Alfredo Martínez de Hoz. The grandson of one of the founders and the first president of the Argentine Rural Society, at the time of the military coup, when he was appointed economy minister, Martínez de Hoz was serving as acting chairman of the board at Acindar, whose majority shareholder was Arturo Acevedo, a representative of the "diversified oligarchy" that had branched out into industry during the import substitution process of World War II. The position left by Martínez de Hoz at Acindar when he took the helm of the economy ministry at the beginning of the dictatorship was filled by the retired general Alcides López Aufranc, one of the first Argentine military officers trained in the French "school of counterinsurgency."[6]

The fact that José Alfredo Martínez de Hoz left the board to head the economy ministry of the civilian-military dictatorship is not a minor detail. The existence of some thirty companies connected with the sector at the time of the coup reveals a process in which competition had already eliminated the state and private companies that had not kept up with technological development.

In Acindar's case, the loan that had been requested during the last Peronist government to install the new electric steel mill and the direct reduction plant was granted under Martínez de Hoz's term as economy minister, and it would later be absorbed by the state in the last stage of the dictatorship, when Domingo Felipe Cavallo headed the Central Bank.

The subsidies, which were reflected strongly in the prices paid for SOMISA products, gave way to significant state credits, which enabled both Acindar and Siderca to install their own electric steel mills, with a direct reduction system,

5 Paulón, *Una larga huelga.*

6 M. M. Robin, *Escuadrones de la muerte. La escuela francesa* (Buenos Aires: Sudamericana, 2005), p. 225.

based primarily on gas consumption. The two companies opened new plants in the early years of the dictatorship: first Techint in 1976, in Campana, followed in 1978 by Acindar, in Villa Constitución. At the same time, after the 1976 coup, Acindar took over the leading companies of the competition (Santa Rosa, Genaro Grasso, Gurmendi, Tamet, Navarro Heredia, Lamimfer, Bonelli Hnos.), and gained control of the smaller companies, which it supplied with semi-finished products.

The regressive transformation involved in that economic plan sought, and partly achieved, an economic concentration based on the elimination of the vast network of small and medium-sized companies that existed at the time of the coup and which represented more than 60 percent of the country's private sector employment. The indiscriminate liberalization of the economy prevented Argentina's industry from competing with the products that entered the country subsidized by a favorable exchange rate, and the lack of credits weakened the national business community. The process of financial valorization absorbed savings through term deposits, and the debt inherited at the time of the coup increased sevenfold as external indebtedness grew.

In line with this economic and financial policy, both steel production and consumption plummeted during the years of the dictatorship (1976–1983). Direct jobs in the industry dropped from 45,000 to 17,000, and currently stand at 10,000, following the reconversion of Acindar and Techint in the early 1990s and the privatization of SOMISA, which reduced jobs from 14,000 to approximately 3,500.[7]

Throughout the military dictatorship, the company was notoriously controlled by civilian personnel of the armed forces who "worked" the different shifts at the plant spying on company employees. As a result of the information obtained through this intelligence work, several workers were fired without legal cause. The climate that was set on that day in March 1975 would continue unchanged until December 10, 1982, when workers left their stations to join the general strike called by the General Confederation of Workers (Confederación General del Trabajo, CGT).

The steel industry is the area that most clearly shows the consequences of Martínez de Hoz's plan, the role played by the state in its first stage of development, and its dismantling in the second stage, known as the "market policy" stage. Without the military dictatorship, which maintained the course of that economic program, it would have been impossible in the 1990s to further the policies of the Menem government, which brought that plan to fruition under the leadership of Domingo Cavallo, now in the role of economy minister.

In the 1990s, the steel market fell under the control of Acindar and Techint, two economic groups that had built their power during the military dictatorship and

7 The reconversion in 1990–1991 entailed a reduction of approximately 30 percent of the permanent workforce and the application of new forms of organization of labor while maintaining the same levels of production.

consolidated it under Menem, in an industrial activity of great strategic importance and with a major impact in terms of energy, as the technological changes introduced entailed a high level of consumption of gas and electricity. In 1991, at a time of great labor unrest, it was estimated that Acindar alone consumed the same amount of gas as the entire province of Entre Ríos and as much electricity as all of the city of Rosario. Siderca's situation was very similar. That decade saw the consolidation of the Techint-Acindar duopoly, following Techint's acquisition of SOMISA, which was privatized in 1992.

Techint became the other leading player in the steel industry, under the direction of Agostino Rocca, until his death in 1978 when he was succeeded by his son Roberto. This Italian engineer, who was very active in the development of Italy's steel industry, played a key role in the Mussolini years, specializing on the link between the state and private business. A major weapon manufacturer during World War II and exonerated in the postwar trials, he came to Argentina with Torcuato Di Tella, with the aim of developing seamless pipe production.

Through Siderca first and Propulsora Siderúrgica later, Rocca's position in industry grew, making him one of the country's leading businessmen by the time of the coup. Used to dealing with totalitarian governments, don Agostino expertly combined industrial know-how with worker control. As in Acindar, in Rocca's companies there was an anti-bureaucratic and combative labor faction among the union's rank-and-file delegates. When the possibility of eliminating this faction presented itself, he did not let the opportunity pass.

Several dozen workers and some foremen, including delegates and members of internal commissions, suffered the effects of state terrorism directly, often targeted as they left the factory and even in their own homes. Among the most notorious cases were the abduction of Enrique Roberto Ingegnieros,[8] previously mentioned, and the repressive action known as "Noche de los tubos" (Night of the Pipes), in which four of the company's factory workers were kidnapped on September 22, 1976.

Another well-known fact is that, immediately after the March 24 coup, the company provided lodgings in its hotel (currently the city hotel) for several high-ranking army officers responsible for Security Area 400, which covered Zárate and Campana.

In both cases, an important rank-and-file labor organization emerged in the early 1970s. The rank-and-file delegates and internal commissions of these companies belonged to the hegemonic Metal Workers' Union (Unión Obrera Metalúrgica, UOM), headed by Lorenzo Miguel, and were part of the generation that opposed

[8] "Una indemnización que no prescribe," *Página/12* (Buenos Aires), February 4, 2012. On the Ingegnieros case and the non-applicability of statutory limitations in labor claims concerning workers who were disappeared as a result of actions carried out with the complicity of their employers, see Chapter 10 in this book.

the prevailing labor bureaucracy line. In Acindar, this contradiction was resolved through the intervention of the government of Isabel Martínez de Perón, who sent the federal police to occupy the city, supported by far right-wing groups. After a long sixty-day conflict, that labor experience was effectively crushed through "fire and sword" by the company, which then positioned its representative, Martínez de Hoz, in the front lines to enable the application of state terrorism as of March 24, 1976.

The process opened by the military dictatorship clearly forged a relationship between Arturo Acevedo and Agostino Rocca, and later his son Roberto, which would afford them many advantages and favors. Only a few of those connected with the military government survived the four years of Martínez de Hoz's term as economy minister and were the beneficiaries of the enormous economic concentration that occurred during that time.

A generation later, Arturo Acevedo's and Roberto Rocca's sons, "Arturito" Acevedo and Paolo Rocca, inheritor of the Rocca empire after the death of his brother Agostino, would take different paths. The former played a minor role in the privatization policies of the 1990s; his attempt to expand beyond borders (in Chile, Brazil, and Uruguay) ended in a resounding failure and he finally succumbed during the 2001 crisis. In less than a decade, Acindar was acquired by Belgo Mineira, a Brazilian steel company belonging to the Arlet group. Originally Belgian and based in Luxembourg, Arlet had merged with Usinor – a privatized French steel company – and with Aceralia – a Spanish company, also privatized – to form the second largest steel producer in the world, called Arcelor. Shortly after this merger, the Indian company Lakshmi Mittal – the world's leading steel producer – absorbed Arcelor, and today Acindar's annual production represents barely 1 percent of the 150 million tons of steel that Lakshmi Mittal produces worldwide.

The Rocca family, founder of Siderca in Campana and Propulsora Siderúrgica in La Plata, acquired the SIAM pipe plant in 1977 (called Siat) and, at the time of Acindar's purchase by Belgo Mineira (in 2000), it bought up that company's pipe plants: the former Marathon in Villa Constitución, Lamimfer in Rosario, and Ipeco in San Luis. Its expansion as a global company enabled it to purchase Usiminas in Brazil, Sidor in Venezuela (later renationalized by Hugo Chávez), Tansa in Mexico, Algoma in Canada, La Dalmine in Italy, and NKK in Japan. It now controls 35 percent of all seamless pipe manufacture in the world.

In this way, Techint became a major multinational corporation in the steel market and Acindar disappeared in the mergers and acquisitions of the globalized world.[9]

[9] On the evolution of the steel industry in Argentina, in Latin America, and in the world, see D. Azpiazu, E. Basualdo, and M. Kulfas, *La industria siderúrgica en Argentina y Brasil durante las últimas décadas* (FETIA, 2005), available at www.funcex.org.br/material/REDEMERCOSUL_BIBLIOGRAFIA/biblioteca/ESTUDOS_ARGENTINA/ARG_176.pdf (accessed November 9, 2014).

The evolution of the steel industry in Argentina also explains the country's political history. Judging corporate complicity in terms of practices such as the reporting of union activists to the police, layoffs, wage cuts, or the persecution of workers only covers part of the picture, as the analysis must also include the planning and implementation of the economic program that defined the country's social, economic, and political profile for decades to come.

Moreover, civilian complicity is not circumscribed to what happened between March 24, 1976 and December 10, 1983. In the months leading up to the coup, the Argentine Business Council (Consejo Empresario Argentino, CEA), of which both companies were members, saw the Peronist government as erratic, maintaining that it had lost its course with the death of Perón, when his widow Isabel Martínez took the reins of the country. As the country fell deeper and deeper into an acute governability crisis and repression escalated, the coup became inevitable, spurred by, among other factors, these business sectors through a succession of boycotts and increasingly explicit calls for military intervention, echoed in the media, as a clear witness of this policy deployed by business. On February 16, 1976, the Permanent Assembly of Business Associations (Asamblea Permanente de Entidades Gremiales Empresarias, APEGE), led by the CEA, declared an industry-wide lockout.

Later, after the return to democracy, both Siderca and Acindar acted as powerful pressure factors, exercising increasing control over the domestic market, setting prices, and generating conditions to bring back neoliberal recipes after the failure of Raúl Alfonsín. The auctioning off of state assets to a handful of economic groups cannot be understood without taking into account the power that was concentrated – and wielded – by these groups during the military dictatorship.

REPRESSION OF WORKERS IN AND FOR THE BENEFIT OF COMPANIES

In the case of Acindar, once the 1974 conflict was over, having ended with general elections in the Villa Constitución division of the UOM, the company adopted a practice that was intensified over the following months and culminated, after the coup, in the installation of a clandestine detention center in the "bachelor's residence," within factory grounds.

This residence was initially used to provide lodgings for federal police troops, paid for by the company itself. A year later – on March 20, 1975 – following the city's occupation by the police, these troops were joined by the Pumas, the special provincial police formed to combat cattle rustling in northern Santa Fe.

Throughout the 1975 strike, Acindar maintained a rigid stance, refusing any agreement with the strikers and holding out firmly for the unionists' defeat while preparing to retaliate. The hundreds of workers fired as soon as the strike ended and the kidnapping and murdering of workers associated with the jailed union leaders clearly show the active complicity of the company. The threats received by the victims, who were told they would be killed if they did not leave the city within hours, were in many cases made in the plant through notes left with the workers' time cards so that they would find them when they punched in or out of work. In addition, as mentioned earlier, the growing number of undercover agents posing as workers in the different shifts, who were planted to spy on real workers, reveals more than the simple consenting of repression.

In the months spanning from the end of the strike on May 20, 1975 and the March 24, 1976 coup, several metal industry workers were kidnapped and murdered. Thus, the coup did not mark the beginning, but the consolidation of Acindar's role in state terrorism. It was not the opposition in parliament that capitalized on the deterioration of the Peronist government of Isabel Martínez de Perón but the country's most concentrated and powerful economic forces, among which Acindar occupied a central position.

It should be noted that, in contrast to similar contemporary experiences, the Acindar phenomenon was met with significant action from workers and the local labor movement. It was practically the only case in which, despite the brutal repression that began in March 1975 and continued until the end of the dictatorship on December 6, 1982, the workers gathered in an assembly to join a strike called by the CGT and began a process of union reconstruction that would culminate in January 1984.

Throughout the years that followed, and to this day, there was a strong presence of the union and the factory's internal commission, and this meant that management had to negotiate each of the changes it introduced. The UOM-Villa Constitución experience is, even today, an example of democratic and participatory rank-and-file labor activism.

As of the occupation of the plant after an assembly that called for elections of union representatives on March 16, 1974 and until the resumption of union activities following the end of the military dictatorship, in January 1984, Acindar deployed a range of repressive tactics against its workers.

The complicity of the national UOM leadership, headed by Lorenzo Miguel, is undeniable. The role that the government of Isabel Martínez de Perón played against this rank-and-file experience of the workers is evidenced in the decision to occupy the city on March 20, 1975, by decree of Ministry of the Interior Alberto Rocamora, Minister of Labor Ricardo Otero, and the President herself.

In pursuing that goal, the government faced strong resistance from workers. The strike that was called on that same day, and which lasted sixty-one days, brought steel production in that city to a halt, and the workers were able to continue the strike thanks to the solidarity and support of the local population and anti-bureaucratic labor organizations from across the country, despite the escalating repression.

Seconded by Ford, which owned the Metcon plant – adjacent to Acindar – and is also responsible for the disappearance of the members of the internal commission of its leading plant in Pacheco,[10] repression spread to all the factories in the area. Proportionally, the number of Metcon workers arrested or fired was the same as in Acindar. This repressive strategy was imposed to such an extent that even the company Villber, a manufacturer of cold storage equipment for supermarkets, owned by a businessman linked to the Communist Party, contributed to the jailing of workers. The more than twenty workers arrested from 1975 to 1976 and another thirty or so who were forced to flee in a workforce of two hundred evidences the extent and intensity of the repression. Villa Constitución was, without a doubt, the testing ground for the repressive operations that would be implemented throughout the country's leading private companies after the coup.[11]

It is important to observe this corporate behavior during the year prior to the 1976 coup. The growing role of the business associations in the boycotting measures against the declining Peronist government and the ongoing demands to restore order and impose the state's authority were a constant reality, repeated like a daily litany, calling for the suspension of democratic institutions. These business operators were not convened the day after the coup to collaborate, as they were involved beforehand in the preparation, execution, and implementation of an economic program that would deal a death blow to the import substitution industrialization process. These were not isolated actions but a systematic plan to seize power by force and impose a social, economic, and political reengineering program.

The year after the coup, Chief Inspector Carlos Rampoldi was assigned to Villa Constitución to head the local police's intelligence office. In the significant testimony he gave Comisión Nacional sobre la Desaparición de Personas (CONADEP), describing the repressive plan carried out against the workers of these two companies, he recounted how he joined the Villa Constitución police in 1977 as superintendent in charge of the Information Division. When he arrived, the Pumas were already stationed at the Acindar factory and were carrying out their tasks. This group, which was based in Santa Felicia, near Vera, was joined by another force formed by some forty men from various coastal region brigades, which remained there for a month until they were

[10] See Chapter 11 in this book.

[11] For additional references, see E. Basualdo, M. Á. Fuks, and C. Lozano, *El conflicto de Villa Constitución. Ajuste y flexibilidad sobre los trabajadores. El caso Acindar* (Buenos Aires: IDEP-CTA, 1991); V. Basualdo, "Complicidad patronal militar en la última dictadura," FETIA. *Revista Engranajes de la Federación de Trabajadores de la Industria y Afines* no. 5, special edition, March 2006, available at comisionporlamemoria.net/bibliografia2012/dictadura/Basualdo.pdf; C. del Frade, "Matar para robar, luchar para vivir. Historia política de la impunidad. Santa Fe, 1976–2004," Rosario, 2004, available at desaparecidos.org/nuncamas/web/investig/frade04/frade04_00.htm (accessed November 9, 2014); and V. Paulón and others (comps.), *El Villazo. La experiencia de una ciudad y su movimiento obrero* (Villa Constitución: Revista Historia Regional Libros, 1999).

replaced by another unit. They were commanded by low-ranking officers. A section of that group was assigned to watch over Rosario. In practice, they directed procedures, such as arrests or guarding a place, and requested collaboration from the Information Division of the Villa Constitución police of which they were in charge.

Rodolfo Peregrino Fernández, for his part, a former federal police chief, told the Argentine Human Rights Commission (Comisión Argentina de Derechos Humanos, CADHU) that "management of the metalwork industries established there, most prominently the chairman of the board of Acindar, engineer Arturo Acevedo, forged close ties with the police forces through bonus payments in cash," and he clarified, "he paid an extra bonus in cash to the entire police staff, chiefs, mid-ranking officers, and troops, supplementing the bonus that the state already paid them." In another statement he added, "Acindar turned into a sort of military fort surrounded by barbed wire. The police officers that stood guard at the factory stayed in houses reserved for company executives."[12]

The Siderca case presents similar characteristics.[13] One out of three of the more than 150 individuals who were disappeared from the Zárate-Campana area were metal industry workers, most of them employed by the company Dalmine-Siderca, by companies with corporate ties to it, or by contractors who provided it with various services.

As pointed out, the company hotel, located very close to the industrial plant to provide accommodations for guests of the company, housed the high-ranking officers of Security Area 400 in the early days. This was no simple "company courtesy" paid to the military authorities but a deliberate collaboration with them.

The company's collaboration with military intelligence and the bodies that carried out the illegal repression emerges very clearly. In their testimonies, survivors vividly describe the brutal repression unleashed on the very night of March 24, 1976: the free access given to the military by the company, the kidnapping of workers on their way to and from work, and management's lack of concern for the fate of the victims. Accounts by plant workers reveal a permanent presence of plainclothes officers infiltrated among workers in every shift. It mirrored the situation at Acindar. These reports have not been denied by either company.[14]

Acindar and Siderca were deeply involved with the regime that took power on March 24, 1976. However, they were certainly not the exception, but part of a group

[12] Testimony given to CADHU, Madrid, March 8, 1983, and statement to the Working Group on Enforced or Involuntary Disappearances, United Nations Commission on Human Rights, Geneva.

[13] See Basualdo, "Complicidad patronal militar."

[14] On the case of Propulsora Siderúrgica, see M. A. Esponda, "De la dictadura a los '90, y de los '90 a la dictadura. Legados e impactos sobre la clase trabajadora y sus posibilidades de organización en el lugar de trabajo," Buenos Aires, 2011, available at conti.derhuman.jus.gov.ar/2011/10/mesa_1/esponda_mesa_1.pdf (accessed November 9, 2014).

of large companies, both national and international, that includes Ford, Mercedes Benz, and Ledesma. In all these cases, workers were continuously repressed, with the support of the companies themselves.

More than thirty-five years after those crimes, numerous common features can be identified in the cases of Acindar and Techint: a repressive strategy facilitated and executed by management together with military and police forces, aimed at disciplining workers, who resisted through representative and democratic organizing. As a result of their collaboration, these companies obtained a direct economic benefit that was translated into enormous growth during and after the dictatorship and which afforded them impunity for their complicity.

13

Between Historical Analysis and Legal Responsibility: The Ledesma Case

Alejandra Dandan and Hannah Franzki

The responsibility of the Ledesma sugar mill for crimes committed during Argentina's last dictatorship erupted as a major issue in the national media's agenda in 2012 after two members of its board of directors were summoned for questioning in a preliminary judicial investigation: Carlos Pedro Blaquier, the chairman of the board and majority shareholder, and Alberto Lemos, the manager. In this way, Ledesma's role in the repression of the labor movement of Jujuy, which had been part of local memory since the first kidnappings, now emerged as part of a new juncture that seeks to investigate corporate responsibility[1] in the crimes committed in the 1976–1983 period.

In this chapter we propose an analysis of the Ledesma case that will identify the place that the trial against the sugar mill's executives occupies in the representation of the economic dimension of state terrorism. We look at how the court action has progressed and then focus on the files produced by the legal proceedings to explore how corporate responsibility is addressed in this particular case. Two core themes emerge from the documents: (1) the relationship between Ledesma and the terrorist state; and (2) the repression of the labor movement and the economic project of the last dictatorship. We examine how this historical dimension is "translated" by legal language in the establishment of responsibilities during the 1976–1983 period.

THE LONG PROCESS OF JUDICIAL PROCEEDINGS

In November 2011, a public prosecutor in Jujuy called for a judicial investigation of two executives of Ingenio Ledesma, an agro-industrial consortium and the country's

The authors would like to thank Juan Manuel Sivila, Pablo Pelazzo, and the editors for their comments.

1 We use the term "corporate responsibility" in its general sense, as responsibility "pertaining or related to companies or business operators," and not in the legal sense that limits it to the "responsibility of the company."

leading sugar producer, in connection with two cases: the kidnapping of four labor leaders from the Union of Sugar Workers and Employees of Ingenio Ledesma (Sindicato de Obreros y Empleados del Azúcar del Ingenio Ledesma, SOEAIL) on March 24, 1976; and the detention and disappearance of approximately twenty-six people – the number is still uncertain – who were kidnapped between July 20 and 27, 1976, in three towns near the sugar mill, on power-cut nights that are remembered as the "Blackout Nights." In both cases company vehicles were used for the abductions.

Although these court cases had been reopened in 2003, for years the local courts both failed to examine the responsibility of the company and to assess the responsibility of the armed forces in these or any other cases. In 2011, the National Public Prosecutor's Office defined the situation of the court actions in Jujuy as "outrageous": the court presided by Judge Carlos Olivera Pastor refused to move the proceedings forward and join the dockets, which in 2008 had reached a total of 115 cases and 158 victims.[2] Thus, in 2012, while oral trials were being held across the country, Jujuy had yet to hold its first trial and had halted the most important investigations.

In March of that year, the news of the request for a judicial investigation of Blaquier and Lemos and the judge's delay in responding prompted grassroots groups and human rights organizations to mobilize in protest. On March 24, the anniversary of the coup, 70,000 people marched to demand a decision from the court. Four days later the judge stepped down from the bench. To replace him, the court appointed a judge from Tucumán, Fernando Poviña, who began serving on April 16 and within twelve days had issued a warrant for the first search of company premises. The search uncovered files that revealed the company had spied on Jorge Osvaldo Weisz, a worker and class-based unionist who had headed the Ledesma union healthcare program and who was arrested in 1975 and disappeared in 1976. On May 10, Judge Poviña ordered the preliminary investigation and in November he charged Blaquier and Lemos.

The defense lawyers representing the Ledesma executives appeared for the first time in the proceedings after Poviña took the bench. One of them had been the first federal judge in the case, his co-counsel had been clerk of the court, and the lawyer who was called in as assistant counsel in Buenos Aires had sat on the federal court that heard the military junta trial in 1985. Thus, the Ledesma case could also serve as an example to illustrate the complicity of the judicial system in the stalling of

[2] See *Informe sobre las causas por violación a los derechos humanos durante el terrorismo de Estado en Jujuy*, Buenos Aires, Unidad Fiscal de Coordinación y Seguimiento de las Causas por Violaciones a los Derechos Humanos cometidas durante el Terrorismo de Estado, Procuración General de la Nación, 2011, p. 3.

trials and to show the link between these two influential groups. Or to point out the characteristics of a process that moved forward thanks to the coordination of different social forces. In any case, this text seeks to reflect on how the legal system builds meanings regarding the business community's involvement in the dictatorship.

Blaquier and Lemos are currently on trial, facing charges of first-order and second-order complicity, respectively, in the illegal deprivation of freedom of twenty-nine people. The case has some similarities with another operation carried out in Jujuy, which involved the abduction of twenty-seven workers of the Mina El Aguilar mining company between March 24 and 26, 1976. The workers were taken from their homes or from company premises on company vehicles, in raids under the command of officers of the Gendarmerie Subdivision "El Aguilar."[3]

CONSIDERING CORPORATE RESPONSIBILITY FROM THE PERSPECTIVE OF THE LEDESMA CASE

In our opinion, the importance of the Ledesma case in part lies in the way in which it incorporates the context of the events that are investigated. The order to initiate criminal proceedings issued by the court in November 2012 devotes significant space to the historical framework, as, according to the judge, such background "would enable an understanding of the true dimension of the events."[4] It thus introduces a procedural objective that goes beyond establishing whether the defendant is guilty or not. It seeks to offer an explanation that would help us "understand." Hence, it provides a historical interpretation that contributes to the country's social struggles aimed at constructing meaning about the recent past. And it does so from the privileged space of legal authority. Thus, in contrast to what some criminal law experts may think, the historical context included in a case file is not merely a misplaced historiographic study, but gains legal relevance. "An obligation presupposes a relationship," Joseph Jenkins reminds us when he says that the decision regarding what constitutes the historical context is the first moment in the judgment of obligations.[5]

Against this backdrop, we analyze the way in which context operates in the Ledesma case, based on two aspects: on the one hand, the historical account of the economic dimension of state terrorism as it is constructed in the case; and, on the other, the "translation" of this historical analysis into a (possible) responsibility

3 For an analysis of the common logic behind these two operations, see "Un patrón común de la complicidad civil," *Página/12* (Buenos Aires), March 11, 2011.

4 See resolution in the case "Burgos, Luis y otros s. procesamiento a Blaquier y Lemos" (hereinafter, "Burgos case"), Juzgado Federal no. 1, San Salvador de Jujuy, Auto de procesamiento, November 15, 2012, p. 72.

5 See J. Jenkins, "Inheritance Law as Constellation in Lieu of Redress: A Detour through Exceptional Terrain," (2003) 3 *Cardozo Law Review*, 1043–1065, 1046.

of the economic actors. Two main issues that cut across the case are considered: the place occupied by the company with respect to the state; and the repression of the labor movement as one of the leading goals of the dictatorship.

Whereas our analysis is based on elements of the judicial proceedings, the impact of the trial on the public sphere exceeds what happens "inside" the case: the demonstrations that accompany the hearings, the press reports issued by the parties, the interviews. As at the time of writing, the trial was at the pretrial investigation stage, the material assessed is still not final. Therefore, what follows is not meant to be a conclusion but a contribution to the discussion on the possible role of trials in the construction of the representations of the socioeconomic dimensions of the last dictatorship.[6]

THE STATE AND LEDESMA

In December 2012, in what was the first conviction of a civilian government official of the dictatorship, a court of the city of La Plata convicted Jaime Smart, interior minister of the province of Buenos Aires, who was in charge of the police structure under the command of the army. Smart was sentenced to life in prison in an unprecedented legal perspective that considered his role as "civil servant" to situate him as "perpetrator" rather than "accomplice" of the repressive apparatus. One of the judges described the ruling as a "change of paradigm": the figure of "perpetrator" – he said – makes it possible to think of a "macro-criminal" state formed by civilian authorities, civil servants, and military officers with the same degree of perpetration.[7]

The question regarding how the "macro-criminal state" should be understood opens new perspectives for thinking about the Ledesma case. It sheds light on how to position the role of companies with respect to the state. Throughout these proceedings there have been various narratives that question the liberal separation of state and company – that is, the separation of the political and economic spheres.

6 For the Argentine case, see M. Osiel, *Mass Atrocity. Collective Memory, and the Law* (New Brunswick-New Jersey: Transaction Publishers, 1997). The author stresses the pedagogical purpose that trials serve in that they affirm the fundamental values of a liberal society (pp. 2, 23, 28). For an evaluation of the limits of legal narrative to give an account of the recent past, see E. Kaufman, "El ritual jurídico en el juicio a los ex comandantes. La desnaturalización de lo cotidiano," available at www.esterkaufman.com.ar/wp-content/uploads/2010/02/desnaturalizacion-de-lo-cotidiano.pdf (accessed May 7, 2013). For a general discussion, see L. Douglas, *The Memory of Judgment. Making Law and History in the Trials of the Holocaust* (Yale: Yale University Press, 2005); D. Bloxham, *Genocide on Trial. The War Crimes Trials and the Formation of Holocaust History and Memory* (Oxford: Oxford University Press, 2001); and R. A. Wilson, "Judging History: The Historical Record of the International Criminal Tribunal for the former Yugoslavia" (2005) 3 *Human Rights Quarterly*, 908–942.

7 See interview with Roberto Falcone, "Tener un uniforme o tener un traje es lo mismo," *Página/12* (Buenos Aires), December 23, 2012.

As shown in this chapter, when seen in its historical context, the Ledesma sugar mill emerges as part of the macro-criminal apparatus.

THE SUGAR MILL/STATE

The Ledesma sugar mill is located in the province of Jujuy, in a town called Libertador General San Martín, in the department of Ledesma. Two other settlements grew around the sugar mill (Ledesma and Calilegua), in the way of company towns, built on lands granted by or expropriated from the company.[8] Blaquier built a neighborhood just feet from the plant, and in the middle of the neighborhood he erected a huge mansion, which the locals call *La Rosadita* (the little pink house): "Their administration is at the Rosadita, by assimilation to the *Casa Rosada* [the seat of the national government]. It all has to do with power, with showing people what it is."[9] The court file incorporates this social space of the mill, among other aspects, when it includes as one of its main points the 1973 and 1974 struggles waged by workers demanding the construction of housing.

The SOEAIL called for the implementation of Law 1,814, of 1947, which required companies with more than 200 employees to build housing, schools, and hospitals for their workforce and which had never been enforced. As a result of these demands, the provincial government signed a resolution in 1974 ordering the mill to build some 5,000 houses with funds from Banco Hipotecario (the mortgage bank) and the National Housing Fund (Fondo Nacional de Vivienda, FONAVI). The court file draws a connection between this conflict and the disappearances in 1976. It describes one of the two important conflicts that occurred before the coup, and among its participants it identifies the names of several leaders who were jailed as of 1975 and who were disappeared a year later.

The discussion that arises in this sense in the proceedings is interesting because it offers a unique reading of the relationship between state and company. Once again, there is a portrayal of Ledesma as the state, this time by the company itself. In a statement given during the investigation, Blaquier noted:

> Ledesma SAII went beyond its role as company and performed duties that were more typically performed by the state in its role of social assistance and development, such as housing construction and urbanization, and contributing financially to health and education institutions.[10]

[8] F. Neiburg, *Fábrica y villa obrera: historia social y antropología de los obreros del cemento*, 2 vols. (Buenos Aires: CEAL, 1988), p. 84.

[9] "Testimonio de Olga Márquez de Aredez," in F. Krichmar, *Diablo, familia y propiedad, documental histórico* (color video, 90 min., Argentina, 1999).

[10] Preliminary statement given by Blaquier in the Burgos case, pp. 19–21. See also the preliminary statement by Alberto Lemos in the same case, p. 107.

In an interview, one of Blaquier's lawyer, Jorge Valerga Aráoz, stated, "Blaquier has held that Ledesma operated always as a true socialist government."[11]

In response to this self-representation of the company as "sugar mill/state," in the order initiating criminal proceedings Judge Fernando Poviña countered with a different reading:

> The provision of housing and health services for Ledesma workers and employees cannot be attributed to the gracious predisposition and disinterested good will of its [the company's] executives and owners and their desire to improve the housing conditions of its workers and employees as was claimed by the defendants, but, essentially, to an obligation arising from a law.[12]

By framing the discussion in terms of compliance with a law (and evaluating whether or not the company complies), Poviña establishes Ledesma as an actor, like the rest, with the obligation of obeying the law. In that way, he also attributes to the state the power and will to effectively enforce the law. However, this distinction between state and private actor appears to fade shortly after:

> The Company, then, exercised a dominant control over the majority of the population of these towns, through the employer-employee relationship, which, without a doubt, must have made it very difficult [for workers] to oppose any resistance or make any complaints against management that could jeopardize their economic interests.[13]

Thus, in the order initiating criminal proceedings Ledesma appears as a device for controlling a population over which it wields "dominant" power. Both the statements by the Ledesma executives and this last analysis by the judge thus put into question the idea of the modern state with a strict division between state and private institutions. In the two narratives, the company, Ledesma, is the place where economic and political power converge. In this sense, the traditional ways of thinking about corporate responsibility are challenged by the judicial analysis, which: (1) reveals "power" mechanisms that go beyond the bureaucratic structures of the administrative and military apparatus; and (2) poses the question of who has control over the local armed forces, as is discussed later in this chapter in reference to the Gendarmerie.

THE GENDARMERIE

Another core issue in the court file is the kidnappings of March 24 and of July 1976. The two operations involved "joint forces" that, according to testimonies,

[11] See interview with Jorge Valerga Aráoz, *Perfil*, August 12, 2012.

[12] Preliminary statement given by Lemos in the Burgos case, pp. 107.

[13] Burgos case, p. 88.

used Ledesma vehicles and drivers to transport the victims. The men kidnapped on March 24 were known leaders of the union or the union-run healthcare program, who had been blacklisted, and they were snatched from their homes and taken to the Villa Gorriti prison. The July operations were conducted during power cuts in the three towns located around the mill; in this case, there were no union leaders, only rank-and-file unionists, relatives, and individuals who had participated in the mobilizations and protests.

Under this point, the court file discusses the role of the Ledesma vehicle fleet and the relationship between the company and the security forces. What is of interest here is how the focus on the vehicles shows how the link between Ledesma and the security forces is visualized and prioritized in the proceedings.

In the workers' account, Ledesma is placed at the scene of the kidnappings through the vehicles used and the way the company refers to the security forces. For example, in the testimony given by Carlos Héctor Brandan, as told by the judge:

> Brandan recounts how he was held against his will during the night of July 20, 1976 in Calilegua, how he was bound and blindfolded and taken to the Calilegua police station, where he was labeled with the number 19, and from there he was transported to the *Gendarmería del Ingenio Ledesma*, and then to Guerrero, to the penitentiary, and to La Plata.[14]

This idea of the "Gendarmería del Ingenio Ledesma" (the Ledesma Mill Gendarmerie) is taken up again by Blaquier and Lemos's defense counsels, who argued that there was a "confusion" there, produced by the way the town was organized, whereby everything is associated with Ledesma.

> That the *confusion* caused by the use of the terms "Ledesma" and "Ingenio" to denote both the Company, the town, the police station, and the neighborhood that bears its name, does not mean that there are security forces stationed within the premises owned by the Firm.[15]

The court examines this idea of "confusion." After comparing documents and testimonies, it cites Decree 2,379 of 1966, whereby the national government established the Ledesma Division of the National Gendarmerie on company property. According to the judge:

> Based on the documentary and testimonial evidence gathered in the proceedings, the Ledesma Division of the Gendarmerie was created to control the border security zone, using the building infrastructure facilitated by the Mill, even though, at 160 km from the Republic of Bolivia, it was beyond the limits of what was considered

[14] Resolution in the Burgos case, p. 79 (emphasis added).

[15] Burgos case, p. 22 (emphasis added).

> border area for that situation.... Thus, since its inception the new division did not have much of an infrastructure and much less its own vehicles, so that they were provided by the Company as compensation in exchange for security services... including, among other things, control and repression of trade union activities.[16]

Under this interpretation, "confusion" becomes "relationship." The decree gave way to a series of exchanges between the company and the gendarmes in a territory that was at the same time classified as a "border zone." In another part of the file, the judge explains what he understands is meant by "border zone" in Ledesma:

> According to the military, the boost to the development of the Ledesma mill in Jujuy would enable the strengthening of a border zone, which was key in the struggle against communism.[17]

Here the separation between state and company is again blurred. Through the decree, the company was, at the same time, provided with a repressive force typical of the state, which it would use to "control and repress trade union activities." In a similar way, the testimonies of the victims that refer to the "Mill Gendarmerie" ("Gendarmería del Ingenio") also describe something that is confused, turning everything into one and the same thing: they testify to the fact that what is actually confused is, above all, the limits between the company and state forces.

As seen earlier, the historical context provided in the order initiating criminal proceedings places Ledesma in a position that seems to go beyond the figure of "accomplice." Not only does the presumed dividing line between repressive state and company fade, but economic interests are also presented as the reason for repression.

However, when the historical reading of the process is incorporated into the legal framework of the accusation, several ruptures can be observed in the way Ledesma's responsibility is conceived. First, the judge turns to the context again to refer to the economic reasons for the repression. In this sense, he repeats that the "the compensation in the form of security provided by the Gendarmerie to the company was in fact provided to contain growing and organized union demands in the region," and then concludes that "in that way, in practice, the symbiotic relationship forged between the company and the security forces that participated in state repression was able to keep in check anyone who was considered as being against their plan for economic expansion."[18]

Then, in the legal classification of the facts of the case, the judge provides a different solution for the "symbiotic relationship" between company and state

[16] Burgos case, p. 182.
[17] Burgos case, p. 95.
[18] Burgos case, p. 133.

which he examined throughout the case: he decides to consider the facts as subsumed under paragraph 1, Section 144 bis of the Criminal Code, which defines the penalties for the crime of deprivation of liberty perpetrated by civil servants.[19] The perpetrator of the crime is thus considered to be part of the state apparatus. The judge sees General Luciano Benjamin Menéndez, head of the Third Army Corps, as having the "highest responsibility in the chain of command of all the security forces in this jurisdiction"[20] and as being the indirect perpetrator, and places Blaquier and Lemos in the position of "accomplices." In legal language, context is reduced to "participation" in a crime committed by another person through the provision of vehicles:

> Therefore, with the contribution of company vehicles, there is a "co-causality" between the actions carried out by the accused Blaquier and Lemos and the result of the act by the perpetrator (unlawful deprivation of liberty of the victims), according to the application of the theory of objective accusation.[21]

Thus, when defining the legal responsibility of Blaquier and Lemos, the separation between state and company reappears, a separation that does not match the perception of the local people and even most of the construction of the arguments in the case.

The theory of indirect perpetration (*autoría mediata*) offers the possibility of constructing the idea of the control over the act through organized power structures. Emphasizing hierarchical structures, however, reduces the state to its institutions and separates it from economic and social forces. This concept of state is, in any case, more a statement of how the modern state is supposed to operate in society than a description of how it actually operated.[22] Under this perspective, economic power appears as "accomplice" of the state, but it does not explain the rationale of its actions. Thus, the initial narrative that interprets the use of physical violence as a tool to protect economic interests is transformed into a narrative that describes the responsibility of Blaquier and Lemos in terms of a "conduct of cooperation in an act perpetrated by another through the facilitation of means of transportation."[23]

The Ledesma case, therefore, shows the difficulties faced by criminal law in including the complex interactions between armed forces and economic actors under its forms of commission, perpetration, and participation. This raises the

19 Burgos case, p. 114.
20 Burgos case, p. 2.
21 Burgos case, p. 135.
22 R. J. Michalowski, "In Search of 'State and Crime' in State Crime Studies," in W. J. Chambliss, R. J. Michalowski, and R. C. Kramer, *State Crime in the Global Age* (Cullompton: Willan Publishing, 2010), pp. 13–30, 14.
23 Resolution in the Burgos case, p. 132.

question of the extent to which the legal norms applied can influence the meaning attributed to economic power in state terrorism.

LABOR MOVEMENT, REPRESSION, AND ECONOMIC PROJECT OF THE LAST DICTATORSHIP

It is hardly surprising that the labor movement and its repression in the 1970s is starting to be thematized as a major issue of the trials for the crimes committed against Ledesma workers. Already in the oral trial conducted at the province level against three military perpetrators, the testimonies from Ledesma workers (and also from workers of Mina El Aguilar) refer to conflicts between the company and its workers and the difficult conditions under which they had to exercise their right to unionize. In the pretrial investigation stage of the Blaquier and Lemos case, the private prosecutors, the public prosecutor's office, and the judge place the physical violence committed against workers during the dictatorship in the framework of the permanent opposition between capital and labor. The repression of the labor movement is thus no longer merely *a dimension of* state violence and gains *explanatory force*: the participation of workers in the labor struggle not only explains the violations of their individual rights (kidnapping, torture, deprivation of liberty), but also the establishment of the dictatorship as a collective, political, and economic project.

The first aspect, labor activism as an explanation for the violence suffered, is evidenced above all in the testimonies. The "Aredez, Luis and others" case, which includes former Ledesma workers, is heard under the oral trial against the three military officers. In their testimonies, several of the workers clearly state that their trade union involvement was the reason they were victims of repression. This was also declared by relatives of Luis Aredez, who in 1973 was advisor to the SOEAIL healthcare program and town mayor, elected with the support of the union. In their accounts, they explain that they see the struggle for their labor rights as the reason for their disappearance.[24]

Similarly, in the pretrial investigation stage of the Blaquier and Lemos proceedings, when asked why he thought he had been arrested, Luis Alfaro Vasco replies:

> When I was studying at the university in Tucumán, I participated in the "LIA" [Liga Independiente Antiimperialista (Anti-Imperialist Independent League)] and my activism there led me to the city of Ledesma to work at the union level, and I think the reason I was arrested was that that work entailed a shift in the union's leadership, which went from a management-centered leadership to one

[24] See, in particular, the statements by Ramón Luis Buen, Carlos Alberto Melián (12th day, August 17, 2012), and the Aredez family (13th day, August 24, 2012).

> that defended the workers.... We confronted Ledesma management and that's the reason why all the union leaders were thrown in jail.[25]

However, it is in particular in the section devoted to the historical context that these personal accounts are incorporated into a "structural" explanation of the dictatorship. The judge contextualizes the conflict between the trade union and the company by recounting different moments in the labor struggle in the sugar mills of Argentina's Great North and the repression by the de facto governments and under the Isabel Martínez de Perón administration. He highlights the use of the National Security Act (Law 20,840) as a means for repressing the labor movement as of September 1974, which in Ledesma made it possible to take control of the union in March 1975 and make the first arrests of union leaders who were members of the Communist Vanguard Party (Vanguardia Comunista).[26] At different points, the judge highlights the intellectual and material support provided by the company to the military and the economic gain it obtained as a result of the weakening of the labor movement. The section on the historical context concludes in this sense that

> the jailing, torturing, murdering, and disappearing of individuals by the security forces during the last civilian-military dictatorship were, thus, not only motivated by the desire to preserve a given ideology, but rather the purpose of the illegal repression was to establish and defend an economic model with neoliberal overtones that would be free of threats from labor demands and claims.[27]

In this way, the judicial account participates in a discursive field in which various historical narratives regarding the *why* of the dictatorship compete. It places the violence practiced during those years within the framework of the violent relationship between capital and labor and it stresses the consequences that the repression and the labor policy measures implemented by the military regime have had for the organization of workers today.[28] In this sense, it challenges readings that until recently had depoliticized repression victims. But, also, the dictatorship and the human rights violations committed do not appear as ends in themselves, but as means. By interpreting the abuses as an extreme expression of the physical violence required at a time in which economic power was threatened by demands of the working class, the account based on the Ledesma case questions those who posit political violence under the dictatorship as a state of exception between two periods of "democracy."

[25] See "Trabajadores y empresarios," *Página/12* (Buenos Aires), September 23, 2012.
[26] Resolution in the Burgos case, p. 78.
[27] Burgos case, p. 92.
[28] On the consequences that the labor policies adopted by the military regime have had on the labor organization of workers, see D. Azpiazu, V. Basualdo, and M. Schorr, *La industria y el sindicalismo de base* (Buenos Aires: Cara o Ceca, 2010).

By presenting the coup as just another point in a process of repression of workers who defended their rights, the historical context re-signifies labor struggles in a positive light. Besides providing former workers and their relatives with a space in which they can tell their stories, and forcing the accused to listen to them, the trials now allow them to reaffirm their activism as a legitimate struggle, instead of omitting it. The argument presented by the National Secretariat of Human Rights as private prosecutor in the oral trial of the military perpetrators serves a "social function," which, among other things, "enables these small great *tributes* that many of the witnesses come here to pay to their absent fellow activists."[29] Considering that in many towns in the province of Jujuy the workers who were involved in social activism and the relatives of the disappeared are still stigmatized today, that statement is not a minor one.[30]

By claiming the legitimacy of the labor struggles of the 1970s, these trials also enable – by contrast – another observation: the fact that many of their demands are still ignored. The day of the last march on the anniversary of the *Noche del Apagón*, most of the people of the Ledesma neighborhood hid inside their houses; they felt that hundreds of demonstrators were "invading" their town. They perceive the trial against Blaquier and Lemos as a threat to the company that provides them with jobs, housing, and school supplies. In the symbolic "hugging" of the mill, a demonstration organized by people of the town in defense of the company, the workers who participated carried signs that read "Right to Work" and "Ingenio Ledesma, We're with You."[31] The high unemployment rate in the region has made those who are still employed by the company fearful that they will be replaced if they join the union, whose leaders still feel persecuted by management.[32]

In this sense, the political potential of the memories of the labor struggles in the framework of the trials in Jujuy consists precisely in making visible the distance between the social struggle of the 1970s – committed to the cause of social equality – and the persistent influence of economic power in local politics. In this framework, Walter Benjamin's concept of history takes on meaning. Benjamin criticizes historicism for choosing certain events in history and organizing them according to a logic of cause and effect, so that they suggest a certain inevitability of the status quo. He confronts the traditional historiography of the victors with a concept of history

[29] This is voiced by the lawyer representing the National Secretariat of Human Rights as private prosecutor, Juan Manuel Sivila, Querella Secretaría de Derechos Humanos de la Nación, Ministerio de Justicia y Derechos Humanos de la Nación, pleading in case 93/11, entitled: "Fiscal Federal n° 1 – Solicita acumulación [Aredez, Luis Ramón y otros]," San Salvador de Jujuy, p. 8.

[30] E. López, "Las cabezas revueltas" (2012) 2 *Otros Territorios*.

[31] Burgos case, p. 22.

[32] See "SOEAIL acusa a Ledesma de usar métodos de la dictadura para interrogar a los trabajadores," *El Libertario de Jujuy*, February 27, 2013.

that breaks with homogeneous time and puts the stress on discontinuity.[33] According to him, a fact acquires historical relevance only when it enters into a constellation with the present that allows us to recognize moments of the past that had until then been "forgotten," not included in official historiography. The possibility of perceiving those images of the struggles of the past, according to Benjamin, endows the present generations with a "weak Messianic power": while they cannot change the past, they can change history, provided they assume and take up again the unfinished struggles of the defeated.[34]

The accounts by Ledesma workers and their relatives of the strength of the labor movement in the 1970s and of the reasons for their struggles and the disappearances enable an understanding of the contingency of the relations of power that structure the field of labor in the present. They offer a historical explanation of the current capital-labor relationship (the repression of the labor movement in the last dictatorship that enabled the privatizations, among other economic measures, and the changes in labor legislation), but also evidence that that relationship is not at all "natural," but contingent, and that there is still an unfinished struggle.

THE MEANING OF JUSTICE IN THE ECONOMIC RESPONSIBILITY TRIALS

Seen from this last perspective, the meaning of justice in the trials on economic responsibility acquires another dimension. If companies participated in and benefited from the repression of the labor struggle and from the economic policies implemented by the dictatorship, is it enough to prosecute members of its executive bodies in the sphere of criminal law? Or should ways also be found to redistribute the benefits obtained? Is it enough to recognize that the struggle of the former workers of Ledesma was legitimate or should their various political demands be taken up again and updated? What role could criminal law play in this search for justice? We would like to posit briefly two possible scenarios.

From a more skeptical approach, the criminal trials against business operators could ultimately result in the legitimization of the current power relations. If Blaquier and Lemos are sentenced, that fact would give the workers a moral victory, but the material effects of the repression would not necessarily be affected. A criminal ruling in itself does not exclude the company from its position in the market, nor does it take any of its economic power away from it, or force it to change its labor policy. By prosecuting the crimes committed against organized workers, those same "crimes"

33 W. Benjamin, *Tesis de filosofía de la historia* (Madrid: Taurus, 1973), Thesis XVII.

34 M. de Wilde, "Benjamin's Politics of Remembrance: A Reading of 'Über den Begriff der Geschichte,'" in R. J. Goebel (dir.), *A Companion to the Works of Walter Benjamin* (Rochester, New York: Camden House, 2009), pp. 177–194.

are placed in the past, they are expelled from the present. Judging that the past was bad implies agreeing that the "bad" is now past. In summary, thematizing economic responsibility via criminal law can, thus, entail reducing human rights abuses to individual behaviors that are prohibited or not allowed by law while at the same time leaving the structural and material causes and consequences of repression aside.[35]

But there are also signs that allow us to trace a different scenario. Even though the ruling itself cannot independently fulfill the demand for justice in the broad sense noted earlier, the trials have triggered actions that can be interpreted as an expression of the "Messianic force" of the present generations. On March 24, 2013, the commemoration of Memory Day in Jujuy gathered local human rights organizations, social organizations, and – for the first time – a SOEAIL delegate. It was the trial against Ledesma, accompanied by the strong social mobilization, that opened the debate on the possible transformation of the mechanisms for appointing magistrates and employees in the local judicial branch, positions that were traditionally reserved for members of groups connected with the local oligarchies. As the proceedings moved forward, the workers who are currently members of the union sought spaces in the national media to voice their demands.[36]

There are also symbolic effects. On July 13, 2012, the Town Council of the Ituzaingó district, in the province of Buenos Aires, declared the city "free of purchases of Ledesma products." In March 2013, the Space for Memory, which operates under the former clandestine detention center Escuela de Mecánica de la Armada (ESMA), followed suit.

By way of conclusion, we would like to highlight some observations that can be gathered from our analysis of the Ledesma case. First, the collaboration between economic and military actors in the crimes perpetrated in Jujuy is used by the court to reflect extensively on the role of economic power, and of Ledesma in particular, in the last dictatorship. In that framework, the testimonies on the labor struggle of the 1970s gain greater importance. The historical context presented in the order initiating criminal proceedings supports, then, the historical narratives that explain in economic terms the state violence practiced during that dictatorship. Second, the case also shows the difficulties that arise when it comes to translating the structural analysis of the link between company and state into the legal logic of individual responsibility. The filter effects, which in the case analyzed here are expressed in the separation between the structure of the state and the economic actors,

35 On the tension between mass crimes and individual responsibility in international criminal law, see also M. Koskenniemi, "Between Impunity and Show Trials," (2002) 6 *Max Planck Yearbook of United Nations Law*, 1–35, 16; and G. J. Simpson, *Law, War and Crime: War Crimes Trials and the Reinvention of International Law* (Cambridge: Polity Press, 2007), pp. 67–70.

36 See "Las irregularidades del Ingenio Ledesma," *Pagina/12* (Buenos Aires), February 4, 2013.

establish which causes and dynamics of state terrorism can be captured through the legal prism.

Third, the Ledesma case (and this could be applied to other cases of corporate responsibility) allows us to see the continuities that exist in the labor and economic spheres between the dictatorial past and the democratic present. This connection raises a doubt regarding the meaning of "justice" when it comes to corporate responsibility and regarding the capacity of criminal proceedings to have an effect in the consequences of repression. Thus, it appears that the transformative power generated by the trials will depend to a great extent on how much the demand for *recognition* of the rights of workers, their suffering, and the legitimacy of their struggle in the past will be connected with demands for social justice and *redistribution* in the present.

14

Contributions to the Analysis of the Role of Labor Leadership in Worker Repression in the 1970s

Victoria Basualdo

INTRODUCTION

Studies on Argentina's last military dictatorship have evolved over the past decades, accompanying structural, political, intellectual, and disciplinary changes. The analyses of the brutal human rights abuses that dominated interpretations during and immediately following the dictatorship gave way, gradually and from different perspectives, to approaches that addressed a number of changes and economic, political, and social impacts that had taken place in that stage of local history. In particular, in the past decade, various lines of research have highlighted the need to study that period taking into account the role and responsibilities not only of the armed forces, but also of the other actors and sectors that participated in an intricate web that sustained the dictatorship, which would, therefore, not be merely a military dictatorship, but a civilian-military dictatorship.

In this framework, the aim of this chapter is to contribute to the analysis of the relationship between trade unionism and dictatorship, with a special focus on the role played by some sectors of top union leadership in the repression of the combative sectors during the 1970s.

This study is part of a long-term line of research that deals with the history of labor organization in Argentina, which draws on a range of primary and secondary sources, and suggests that the dictatorship constituted an attempt to refound economic and social relations in a context of strong economic, political, and social confrontations that were aggravated in the first half of the 1970s. This approach requires that we look further back, to the previous period, to explore these confrontations, in which there was a major involvement of the labor movement.

Although there is a vast and rich literature on workers and unionism from 1973 through 1976, these works have been dominated by analyses of the Peronist government, its leader, and the movement as a whole, and this has often tended to shift the focus of study and blur the specific issues of the working class and the labor movement. Another issue to be considered is that the history of the labor movement in the periods before and after the coup d'état has been explored by different currents of thought and authors, and in most cases in isolation from each other, which makes it difficult to visualize the continuities and ruptures between the pre- and post-1976 periods.

Lastly, even the most recent bibliography has generally ignored the revisionist views of the dictatorship and the role of the labor movement in that process, so that these studies do not provide direct information on this aspect. For all these reasons, this chapter proposes a few possible lines of approach to address the subject more thoroughly.

There is general agreement that Argentina's labor movement was nowhere close to achieving unity in the period prior to the dictatorship – that is, from the late 1960s to the early 1970s – and that the confrontation of "orthodox" and "combative" sectors became more acute and vicious as of 1973.[1] A clear example of the level of confrontation and the link between the labor and political struggles is the incident that took place on June 20, 1973, a major episode during those years that is known as the Ezeiza Massacre and which crystallized a violent confrontation at the heart of the Peronist movement. The various labor factions played a central role, as José Ignacio Rucci, general secretary of the General Confederation of Labor (Confederación General del Trabajo, CGT) and head of orthodox unionism, was one of the leading instigators of the repression of the radicalized sectors, and given that the "assault forces" drew their members from the right-wing factions of several unions. The confrontation between the various factions of the labor movement from 1973 to 1976 was closely linked to the repressive processes that disarticulated the various attempts at organization and mobilization by the combative sectors, a factor that played a relevant role in the historical process that culminated in the military dictatorship. As it would be impossible to review that history in its entirety here, I focus on the evidence available in one case in particular, that of the Union of Automotive Transport Mechanics and Related Workers (Sindicato de Mecánicos y Afines del Transporte Automotor, SMATA).

[1] "Orthodox" and "combative" sectors opposed each other in two leading fronts. With respect to the internal dynamics of labor organization, the former supported vertical and hierarchical structures (a preference that earned the members of this sector the label of "bureaucratic"), whereas the latter favored democratic union practices and ongoing contact with and engagement of the rank-and-file. In terms of the objectives pursued by union activity and the definitions adopted, the orthodox line privileged negotiation over conflict and believed that the ultimate goal of labor organizations was to achieve improved conditions for workers without questioning the basis of the system or the authority of management; combative groups, instead, adhered to a range of radical political ideologies and, without abandoning demands for partial economic improvements, they also sought, in the vast majority of cases, to promote radical social and economic changes.

This example is relevant and interesting for several reasons. First, because the automobile industry was strategically important for the second stage of import substitution industrialization, a factor that is without a doubt crucial for explaining the power, presence, and influence of a union that in the mid-1960s had some 120,000 members and aspired to successfully challenge the position of the Metal Workers' Union (Unión Obrera Metalúrgica, UOM) as leader of the industrial labor movement. Second, in the first half of the 1970s, there were interesting processes of combative unionism and activism in factories, which were opposed by the national steering committee of SMATA and its top leader, José Rodríguez. This was the case, for example, of two large corporations, Ford and Mercedes Benz,[2] whose workers denounced the union's involvement in the persecution of workers and combative delegates. Moreover, SMATA participated in the repressive crackdown on the Córdoba division, which began in 1974 and culminated in the dismantling of a combatant group that was key at the national level. Even though a brief analysis of these processes is not enough to draw general conclusions on labor leadership and unionism during this period, it can at least help us visualize a pattern of operation.

THE SMATA CÓRDOBA DIVISION

René Salamanca, a worker at IKA-Renault and an activist of the Revolutionary Communist Party (Partido Comunista Revolucionario, PCR), became the face of a major victory in April 1972, when in an election of authorities in the Córdoba division of SMATA the Brown Ballot defeated the traditional leadership represented by the Green and Blue Ballot, headed by Elpidio Torres. With Roque Romero, who defined himself as *clasista* (or class-based, in reference to a focus on the defense of class interests), as candidate for assistant secretary, the Brown Ballot obtained 3,089 votes, against 2,804 votes of the Green and Blue Ballot. This victory had a huge impact, both locally and nationally, in terms of strengthening the combative union line, which had had a major milestone in 1968 with the forming of the CGT offshoot, the Argentine CGT (CGT de los Argentinos, CGTA). During that period, SMATA-Córdoba secured local alliances with other combative leaders, such as Agustín Tosco, of the union of electricity workers (Luz y Fuerza), and Atilio López, of the Automotive Tramway Workers' Union (Unión Tranviarios Automotor, UTA), with whom it formed the Combative Labor Movement (Movimiento Sindical Combativo), which had a profound influence on combative union sectors across the country. Under the direction of Salamanca, the Córdoba division also introduced big changes in the union's organization and internal dynamics: it turned for support to the delegates and internal commissions of the leading plants, viewed rank-and-file

[2] See Chapter 11 in this book.

assemblies as key discussion and decision making instances, and established a system of rotation for the members of the steering committee.

Because of all of these factors, the *clasista* victory met with growing opposition from the two major figures in the union at the national level, the general secretary, Dirk Kloosterman, and José Rodríguez, who headed the Buenos Aires division. On May 22, 1973, Kloosterman was murdered, joining a number of orthodox union leaders who had been "executed," starting with Augusto Timoteo Vandor, on June 30, 1969. José Rodríguez took his place at the head of the national steering committee of SMATA, and from his position there he maintained a firm confrontation with the Córdoba division, in the framework of the increasing growth of right-wing groups in the province, which culminated in February 1974 with a coup staged by the former chief of the provincial police, Antonio Navarro, who ousted the constitutionally elected governor, Ricardo Obregón Cano, and his assistant governor, Atilio López.

The conflict between the Córdoba division and the national steering committee of SMATA was aggravated when Salamanca was reelected that same year. This time, the Brown Ballot obtained a resounding victory, with 4,027 votes against the 2,770 obtained by the ballot formed by Rodríguez supporters.

Finally, a union action questioned by the Ministry of Labor, and to which Renault responded by suspending more than 3,000 workers, gave Rodríguez and the national division of SMATA the opportunity to neutralize the Córdoba union. On August 6, 1974, Salamanca spoke to an open assembly of 6,000 workers from the sector, rejecting the mandatory conciliation, and was supported by the vast majority of the workers, who voted to continue with the strike. Two days later, SMATA expelled him, along with twenty-two other members of the Córdoba steering committee, and decreed the suspension of the division, appointing a monitoring committee from Buenos Aires to take control of the division.

Following government orders, the Central Bank froze all union funds deposited in national accounts. At the same time, the Labor Ministry of Córdoba ignored the petitions to have the measures adopted by the central division of SMATA revoked. Rodríguez moved swiftly to legitimize the central union's control over the Córdoba division. That same day, the central division of SMATA took out full-page ads in Córdoba and Buenos Aires newspapers denouncing the *clasistas*, characterizing the strike as proof of their "defense of foreign ideologies," and accusing them of involving the entire labor movement of Córdoba in a "conspiracy of the mercenary Left" at the service of the great corporations.[3] This offensive escalated further after the murder of Atilio López at the hands of the Triple A (the Argentine Anticommunist Alliance), on September 16, 1974, which was followed by a wave of murders in the province.

3 *La Voz del Interior*, August 8, 1974, quoted in J. Brennan, *El Cordobazo* (Buenos Aires: Sudamericana, 1996), p. 364.

When, on October 10, the recently appointed Federal Interventor of Córdoba, Raúl Oscar Lacabanne, visited the central headquarters of SMATA, he was applauded by José Rodríguez for "getting rid of the image of a Marxist Córdoba, which is actually a Peronist province through and through." Lacabanne, in turn, expressed his thanks and admitted that they "could not have achieved anything were it not for the support of the sixty-two organizations and the local CGT," and he assured them that they were "cleaning up the city, removing what little is left."[4]

These events marked the end of the class-based union experience in SMATA-Córdoba, as Lacabanne banned union assemblies, allowed the raiding of the union's files and library, and supervised the suspension of all union activities, including social-welfare-related activities. After being expelled from the union and forced to go underground, from 1974 to 1976 Salamanca denounced the coup preparations underway and called to defend the government of Isabel Martínez de Perón, while maintaining contact with workers through any means available to him. In the early hours of March 24, 1976, right before the coup, Salamanca was kidnapped by the armed forces and disappeared.

The SMATA-Córdoba case is one of the leading events that underscore the fact that the repression of workers, and particularly of its combative groups, did not begin with the military coup, but instead existed and had been growing in intensity since 1974. After the division came under the control of SMATA-Buenos Aires, and as Agustín Tosco was trying to regroup his supporters and join forces with other unions across the country, the Tucumán Sugar Industry Workers' Federation (Federación Obrera Tucumana de la Industria del Azúcar, FOTIA) was banned by the government, its top leaders were arrested, and Tosco himself was persecuted. These developments were accompanied by a crackdown on several focal points of labor mobilization and radicalization, which were quashed by police and military forces, while some of their organizations were taken over by the government and their leaders persecuted and jailed.[5] This offensive of the security forces reached its height with the "occupation" of the city of Villa Constitución on March 20, 1975 and the detention of almost all the union leaders of the area. This was followed by murders and disappearances after the military coup.[6]

4 "SMATA recibió la visita del gobernador interventor de Córdoba, compañero brigadier mayor Raúl Oscar Lacabanne," *Avance* no. 30, October 1974, pp. 40–41, quoted in Brennan, *El Cordobazo*, p. 370.

5 For a list of the leading union organizations that came under government control before the coup, see A. Fernández, *Las prácticas sociales del sindicalismo (1976–1982)* (Buenos Aires: CEAL, 1985), p. 135.

6 That day the city was "invaded" by what eyewitnesses described as an endless convoy of vehicles of the security forces, whose aim was to stop an alleged conspiracy of "industrial guerrilla groups" that supposedly sought to overthrow Isabel Martínez de Perón. The accusations were completely unfounded, but the repression claimed dozens of arrests and various acts of violence against workers and their families. See, for example, V. Paulón and others (comp.), *El villazo. La experiencia de una ciudad y su movimiento obrero* (Villa Constitución: Revista Historia Regional Libros, 1999).

THE CASES OF FORD AND MERCEDES BENZ

In this context, the experiences of Ford Motor Company and Mercedes Benz serve to illustrate how, immediately after these events, Rodríguez dealt with other worker attempts to organize at the rank-and-file level. At these factories, the more significant processes took place in 1975, with the consolidation of dissident groups that began to forge ties with other combative sectors and make demands on the national leadership of SMATA. This process took a major turn on October 6, 1975 when then Labor Minister Carlos Ruckauf promoted and signed a decree to "wipe out subversion in industrial centers," whereby all worker struggles were equated with industrial guerrilla activity.[7]

SMATA's support to the policy imposed by the government was evidenced in the signing of an agreement with the automotive companies, under which one percent of the price of every vehicle sold would go to a special fund for the "eradication of negative elements" from the plants. This fund was to be managed by the union steering committee, and would not be subject to audits, and in exchange the union, which supposedly represented the interests of workers, would guarantee that they were effectively repressed.

The period between late 1975 and early 1976 saw a deterioration in the situation of workers and activists who had succeeded in consolidating their presence in the plants, promoting democratic union practices, forging ties with radicalized sectors, and participating in mobilizations and significant processes, such as the meetings held in June and July 1975 to protest the adjustment plan furthered by Economy Minister Celestino Rodrigo. At Ford, where nearly 5,000 workers were represented by some 200 delegates, repression was particularly harsh. Ford employees have given valuable testimony on how José Rodríguez and the national leadership of SMATA kept up their part of the bargain with the government and zealously combated the so-called industrial or factory guerrillas. The union's steering committee even appealed to the Green Ballot delegates to do away with the new opposing rank-and-file leaders. Pedro Troiani, one of the delegates who survived, explained this as follows:

> One time, they called all the members of the internal commission and the better-known delegates … they called us all in to the union, and José Rodríguez

[7] The decree was signed by Ítalo Argentino Luder (provisional president of the National Senate, acting as head of the Executive Branch), seconded by Ministers Manuel Arauz Castex (Foreign Affairs and Worship), Tomás Vottero (Defense), Carlos Ruckauf (Labor), Carlos A. Emery (Social Welfare), Antonio Cafiero (Economy), and Ángel Federico Robledo (Interior). It read: "In view of the need to address the activity of subversive elements that have been disturbing the country's peace and stability with their actions.… The Interior Security Council is hereby mandated with: a) Conducting national efforts to combat subversion."

> started talking to us about the leftist groups; he wanted us to mark them. He said: "The leftist groups are gaining ground here and they want to take over the union; what we need to do here is defend the union, and we're not going to let them have it."... And at one point, still talking about this, he says: "Alright, let's see who has the guts to defend the union." And they took us down to the basement, where they showed us a pile of weapons they had.... I believe the union collaborated with the Triple A.[8]

Other testimonies, such as that given by former plant delegate Luis Degiusti, describe the impact that the union's campaign had on combative activists, as it limited enormously their capacity for action and organization in the plant and even outside it. Referring to how they were seen by their superiors, Degiusti said: "There, at Ford, we were [seen] as rapists are now, we were the bomb-throwing terrorists, we were against work, against everything."[9] The testimonies refer to the weight of that discourse, which twisted any labor demands that could interfere with company production, turning them into subversive actions. Guerrillas and organized workers, armed groups and rank-and-file delegates were thus confused and presented as one and the same and accused of undermining the foundations of the social structure, hence legitimizing the repression carried out by the state in conjunction with business.

This concern over "industrial guerrillas" was so widespread that the issue was studied and monitored by the U.S. Embassy, at the request of the Defense Department. In this respect, a December 2, 1975 document notes:

> Terrorism is a fact and a way of life in Argentina. The guerrilla activities in the rural areas of Tucumán and the urban areas of Córdoba and Buenos Aires have been the subject of world-wide comment and endless analysis. However, another and possibly even more insidious form of guerrilla warfare, to which little attention has heretofore been paid, is in full operation in Argentina. It is the war being carried out by the industrial guerrilla, who operates on the factory floor, in the union hall.... He aims to radicalize the workers, alienate them from their legitimate leaders and their government, and win their sympathy so that they become his willing accomplices or docile followers.[10]

8 Interview with Pedro Troiani, conducted by Marina Lascano, quoted in M. Lascano, *Cambios y continuidades en la clase obrera argentina (1973–1983). El caso Ford*, Master's thesis, Universidad Nacional de Sarmiento, Buenos Aires (2013).

9 Interview with Luis Degiusti, conducted by Marina Lascano, February 2012, in Lascano, *Cambios y continuidades*.

10 "Industrial Terrorism: Guerrilla Warfare on the Factory Floor," extracts from a document issued by the U.S. Embassy in Buenos Aires, on December 2, 1975, for the Defense Department and diplomatic posts in Latin American countries. Available at www.nosdigital.com.ar/2011/11/docqhicieronhistoriaii (accessed February 3, 2013), quoted in Lascano, *Cambios y continuidades*.

The document also stressed the radicalization of broad sectors of the rank-and-file and the difficulties encountered by several orthodox leaders to contain their actions and conflicts:

> Embassy reporting has consistently pointed out the increasing alienation of the Argentine organized labor leadership from its rank-and-file. With the exception of only a handful of unions, the current national union leaders are now virtually divorced from the workers they represent. Their authority has eroded to the point that rank-and-file parallel unions, usually called plant "Struggle Committees" or "Coordinating Committees," have virtually replaced elected union delegates in negotiations at the plant level. Invariably, these grass-roots committees are far more militant than their legitimate leaders.... Their only suggested "solution" is for the police and military forces to suppress any "unauthorized" act of the workers. While the Military is not yet prepared to enforce trade union discipline, it is becoming increasingly concerned with the subversive aspects of the problem. But, as with all the other sectors, the Military also has difficulties distinguishing between real subversion and more legitimate workers militancy.[11]

The offensive against "industrial guerrillas" was, in fact, greatly intensified after the 1976 military coup, with the wave of kidnappings of workers and activists that followed in Ford and Mercedes Benz, which were, nonetheless, only a portion of such crimes in the country. In Ford's case, between March and May 1976, twenty-five workers were kidnapped and "disappeared" for thirty to sixty days. Half of them were picked up in their homes and taken to the Tigre police station, which operated as a clandestine detention center, while the other half was detained directly at the General Pacheco plant, which for a long time housed a First Army Corps garrison.[12]

Some testimonies highlight how repression was stepped up at the plant after the coup: "The Ford plant was surrounded by trucks and jeeps, [with men] armed to the teeth; they frisked us one by one, and they arrested a lot of our fellow workers. They would go through our lockers, the changing rooms, they were constantly conducting searches." Others recount how "they took the delegates, sub-delegates, and activists away. They decimated the body of delegates, and, shortly before the coup, or during the coup itself, many were pressured by the company into resigning"; "we'd be working and there'd be a soldier next to us with a rifle."[13]

The investigation of the company's actions during the last dictatorship gave way to a criminal proceeding and to a civil lawsuit against its executives, furthered by some surviving workers, in particular by Pedro Norberto Troiani, as is analyzed in Chapter 11 in this book.

11 Lascano, *Cambios y continuidades*.
12 Á. Abós, *Las organizaciones sindicales y el poder militar (1976–1983)* (Buenos Aires: CEAL, 1984), p. 12.
13 Ibid., p. 43.

The role played by SMATA was also denounced by Mercedes Benz workers.[14] Similar to what was happening in other plants, in October 1975 4,000 workers mobilized and, gathered in an assembly, they questioned the union leadership and elected a new internal commission, formed by nine representatives, which became known as the "group of nine." SMATA denied the validity of the election and the internal commission, and the company fired more than 100 workers (including the workers who would later be kidnapped under the dictatorship) with the support of the union and its secretary general, José Rodríguez.

In contrast to statements by Rodríguez, who in the framework of the Truth Trials claimed that that strike had been "a conflict in one of the many factories represented by SMATA" and that "the union had nothing to do with the dismissals," the group of surviving workers declared instead that it was "a conflict with the union over the discussion in the joint assembly and over internal elections, as SMATA had taken control of the internal commission more than a year earlier, and had filled the plant with thugs." They maintain that what Rodríguez described as "a conflict artificially promoted by agents of chaos and subversion" was actually "such a unique experience in union democracy that just remembering any aspect of it, any gesture, stirs the heart":

> Like what happened on October 8, 1975, when news of the dismissals spread and 4,000 workers marched out of the plant shouting "All 4,000 in or all 4,000 out"; or the workers at the thermal power plant, whose collective bargaining agreement prevented them from striking, but who donated their entire salary to the strike fund; or the solidarity shown [to the workers] when the union reacted by leaving all Mercedes Benz workers without healthcare program; or the thousands of signatures that accompanied every effort to find our disappeared fellow workers throughout the dictatorship.[15]

These workers and survivors also pointed out that José Rodríguez used the involvement of the Montoneros in the conflict to report workers, accusing them of being guerrillas. On October 24, 1975, the Montoneros kidnapped the plant's head of production, Heinrich Metz, demanding the reinstatement of the dismissed workers and payment of a ransom, to which the company ultimately agreed. In this context, on November 5, 1975, Rodríguez sent a letter to Minister of Justice

[14] This case was researched extensively by Gabriela Weber, who wrote two books with her findings: *Die Verschwundenen von Mercedez-Benz* (Hamburg: Assoziation A, 2001) and *El lavado del dinero nazi en la Argentina* (Buenos Aires: Edhasa, 2005), and produced the documentary *Milagros no hay. Los desaparecidos de Mercedes Benz* (color, 113 min., 2003; there is an updated version: 85 min., 2005).

[15] Ex Trabajadores de Mercedes Benz por la Memoria y la Justicia (Former Mercedes Benz Workers for Memory and Justice), "José Rodríguez y los desaparecidos de Mercedes Benz," document signed by Ricardo Hoffmann, Eduardo Olasiregui, Héctor A. Ratto, Ramón Segovia, and Daniel Suárez. Available at labournet.de/branchen/auto/dc/ar/ehemal-s.html (accessed February 3, 2013).

Corvalán Nanclares requesting that the government take control of Mercedes Benz on account of the company's payment of the ransom to the Montoneros, and describing the workers as a "group of agitators allied with subversion," the internal commission as a "commission alien to the union and fostered by subversion," the actions conducted by the workers as a "strike without cause; a provocation whose sole aim was to use workers as guinea pigs in a seditious experience," or a "strike with subversive motivations," "a typical act of the industrial guerrillas," furthered by "mercenaries of enslaving Marxism."[16] Very similar expressions were used in the two ads taken out in the newspaper *Clarín* on October 22, 1975, signed by the steering committee of SMATA and the Green Ballot, associated with José Rodríguez.

The March 24, 1976 coup triggered successive waves of repression at the plant. In April, Juan José Martín was kidnapped from his place of work and was only released after some 1,000 workers mobilized and protested at La Tablada barracks. A second repressive stage began in December 1976, when Miguel Griecco, José Vizzini, and Alfredo Martín were kidnapped. In January 1977, after a bargaining process with management, Esteban Reimer and Hugo Ventura were kidnapped; and in August 1977 the abductions of Héctor Ratto and Diego Núñez were perpetrated, along with other workers (including Gigena, Mosquera, Arenas, Leichner, and Delcontte, in addition to Juan José Ratto, who was taken by mistake). Most of them had been on the lists of "radical elements" and had been fired by the company in 1975.

During these years, when increasing numbers of workers from major factories were being disappeared, and despite the fact that SMATA was under military control, José Rodríguez continued living in Argentina and even sat on the Executive Committee of the International Metalworkers' Federation. In his statement to the Federal Court, Rodríguez claimed he "honestly, only found out about what happened in Mercedes Benz with CONADEP" in 1984. Moreover, he said that after the coup d'état the military controllers "decided everything" in the unions and "there was nothing [he] could do," a claim that stands in stark contradiction to the importance of the position he occupied, which went beyond national borders.

Recent research into organization and resistance attempts in Mercedes Benz during the military dictatorship, based on documents of the Intelligence Division of the Buenos Aires Province Police (Dirección de Inteligencia de la Policía de la Provincia de Buenos Aires, DIPBA), sheds light on the role played by SMATA:

> The files not only reveal the collusion of union bureaucracy with management, in this case Mercedes Benz' executives – a phenomenon that was also established in the cases of Volkswagen and Ford – they also evidence their favorable position toward military authorities with the aim of preventing the growth of opposition groups within the labor movement.... Considered from this perspective, it is not

[16] Ex Trabajadores de Mercedes Benz por la Memoria y la Justicia, "José Rodríguez y los desaparecidos."

> surprising to find the regional direction of SMATA repeatedly mentioned in police records as confronting the Internal Demands Commission and workers in general in assemblies held at the factory after the former's intention to suspend union actions or temper the methods used to protest.[17]

The evidence available suggests, then, that the collusion with management and the confrontation of part of the leadership of SMATA with rank-and-file delegates was not limited to the early days of the dictatorship, but instead continued throughout it.

TOP UNION LEADERSHIP AND DICTATORSHIP: ELEMENTS FOR A DISCUSSION OF THE "SOCIAL CONSENSUS" VIEW

This brief review of some of the cases connected with SMATA suggests that the repressive process of the mid-1970s was not carried out against a unified labor movement, which jointly resisted the onslaught from government, corporate management, and repressive forces, but instead, on the contrary, both before and after the March 24, 1976 coup d'état, sectors of the "orthodox" union leadership supported, legitimized, and actively collaborated with the repression of combative groups. Although there are no systematic and comprehensive studies yet to enable an analysis of this phenomenon in all its complexity and across the entire period, the evidence gathered with respect to the national leadership of SMATA and, in particular, to the actions of José Rodríguez as general secretary exposes the existence, at least among some sectors of top union leadership, of a policy of collaboration with management and the repressive forces in their efforts to discipline and control workers and rank-and-file union delegates.

Still pending, however, is a discussion of what this line of analysis can contribute in terms of the interpretation of the dictatorship and the intricate web of social, political, and economic relations that supported it. In this sense, I want to focus here, in particular, on the corollaries and implications of Hugo Vezzetti's book *Pasado y presente. Guerra, dictadura y sociedad en la Argentina*, published in 2002, which has become a reference work for the movement that over the past decade has undertaken the revision of the history of the dictatorship. The central hypothesis of this work is that Argentina's last military dictatorship "put leaderships, the state, and the country's institutions to the test, and, in general, brought to light the very worst of society." From this perspective, that "acute episode of political barbarization and state degradation would not have been possible without the commitment, the support, the agreement of many," so that Vezzetti proposes analyzing "the responsibilities of society."[18] He posits that "the image of a society predominantly and permanently

[17] H. Barbero, "La resistencia obrera en los anales de la Policía Bonaerense. El caso Mercedes Benz Argentina," Buenos Aires, Centro Cultural de la Cooperación, 2006, pp. 37–38.

[18] H. Vezzetti, *Pasado y presente. Guerra, dictadura y sociedad en la Argentina* (Buenos Aires: Siglo XXI, 2002), pp. 12–13.

terrorized by widespread violence present in everyday life" is erroneous, and puts forward instead the idea that "a majority accompanied or contributed through passive conformity to the actions of the dictatorship."[19] In this respect, he says:

> A society must take responsibility not only for what it actively promoted and supported but also for what it failed to prevent.... Moreover, if we look at the conditions under which the dictatorship was established, we cannot but recognize that it was furthered by an escalation of illegal violence, factionalism, and anti-institutional exaltation that involved a broad spectrum of civil and political society, both to the right and left.

This book, which in the words of its author "is not a work of historical research, in the sense of a systematic investigation of political, economic, and military events of that period," but "a study of social memory"[20] (and in fact draws little explicit support from primary or secondary sources), operated as a call to steer history and memory studies on the dictatorship in that direction, and was echoed enthusiastically by a wide scope of productions on the subject in the field of history and the social sciences.

This line, which holds all of society accountable for what happened during that period, analyzes its behavior, makeup, and history with a strong tendency toward generalization and a notable disregard for basic structural dimensions. In particular, the resistance to incorporate the links between political history and the transformations in the economic and social structure are especially negative. Vezzetti argues, for example, that "when it is said and repeated that the massacre in Argentina was necessary to implement an economic model that required wiping out, exactly in that manner, any opposition, no real evidence is given for that assertion."[21]

As the facts and events analyzed here could be interpreted along such lines, I propose a different reading, highlighting two main issues. First, with respect to disregarding the importance of structural factors, it is important to analyze the complicity of a sector of union leadership with the repression within the context of the central division of this period, which is essential to understand the causes of the dictatorship and its main policy lines – that is, the high level of confrontation between capital and labor, which peaked at historical levels in the mid-1970s. Second, with respect to holding all of society responsible for the origin and development of the Process of National Reorganization, as the dictatorship called itself, it is essential to underline that, in addition to expressions of complicity, there were also strong movements that opposed, questioned, and resisted the dictatorship.

19 Ibid., p. 43.
20 Ibid., p. 12.
21 Ibid., pp. 161–162.

The SMATA case revealed the existence of divisions and clashes between different factions within trade unions, which not only had different approaches to union activity, they had different political goals. However, it should be recalled that the working class as a whole – which during the Peronist decade had succeeded in consolidated a far-reaching union structure and a prominent position in the economy and in society – far from being marginal during this period, as the excessive emphasis placed on political conflict and armed struggle could sometimes suggest, played a key role as labor unrest increased in line with political conflict.

The strength of the working class – even with its acute internal divisions and confrontations – is evidenced, for example, by the fact that in 1974 wages represented about 47 percent of the total national income. This strength was rooted not only in the characteristics of the industrialization model and in the role played by workers in the production and consumption of goods, but also in the mechanisms of representation and organizations available to it. As of its – partial, contradictory, conflictive, but critical – association with a range of political organizations closely connected with the process of radicalization in Latin America and the Third World, and with significant developments in the central countries, the labor movement set out to fight to improve the conditions of the working class, and, in many cases, supported projects that called for radical transformation. This was influenced by the vitality of union delegates and internal commissions during the second stage of import substitution. The high degree of organization at the rank-and-file level is a decisive factor that explains the roots of that strength of labor vis-à-vis capital, which was translated both in economic terms in the struggles in the sphere of production, and in the great confrontations at the political and social levels.

The measures introduced as of the mid-1970s, although marked by multiple contradictions and tensions among the various actors and social forces that were directly or indirectly involved in the dictatorial government, were clearly aimed at overcoming the challenge posed by the convergence of the process of political and social radicalization and the strength of the working class. In contrast to the types of solutions attempted during the second import substitution stage, which had been implemented against a backdrop of the persisting model of industrialization and its structural relations, the various policies deployed as of March 1976 not only made it possible to attack the forms of organization of the working class and its political ties, they also simultaneously promoted economic transformations that deeply altered the structural foundations of labor strength.

In this sense, it is essential to bear in mind that, in the context of a profound restructuring of global capitalism and the crisis of the Fordist paradigm, the dictatorship introduced major changes in the country's economy and altered the foundations of the strategic power that the industrial working class had had in previous decades. The process of industrial restructuring and deindustrialization was accompanied by an exponential growth of the external debt, which, in contrast to what had happened in previous stages, did not finance productive activities but was used increasingly for financial valorization.[22] At the same time that the wage and employment policy of Economy Minister José Alfredo Martínez de Hoz entailed in just a few months a 40 percent drop in wages as compared to 1974 levels, basic labor rights were severely curtailed, including the right to collective agreements, the right to bargaining, and the right to protest.

With respect to labor policies, the military dictatorship promoted a series of laws aimed at legalizing repressive actions and government control in the sphere of union organization, which constituted a major turning point in the history of labor.[23] These laws were accompanied by the government's control over most of the large trade unions and federations, starting with the CGT and followed by the leading second-tier union organizations, which represented 50 percent of the working class, thus fracturing the centralized national structure of the labor movement.[24]

Lastly, in terms of repression, the military coup imposed a new scheme, which was characterized by the existence of detention camps and the disappearance of persons, combined with the murdering and jailing of political opponents, and which penetrated deep into the workplace, through the presence of police officers, the control of all political and union activities, different forms of repression and disciplining, the control of the recruitment process, and political and ideological surveillance.[25] A favorite target of this repression were union delegates and members of the internal commissions – that is, the rank-and-file representatives of workers, who for decades had played a very important role in the defense of labor rights and in organizing and furthering actions to achieve gains and negotiate with management.[26]

At the same time, while repression was led and carried out primarily by the armed forces, it enjoyed not only the connivance but also the active support of large corporations, which reported their workers to the police, supplied funds to the repressive forces, and, in the cases of Ford and the steel company Acindar,

22 For a thorough analysis of the economic context, see E. Basualdo, *Estudios de historia económica argentina. Desde mediados del siglo XX hasta la actualidad* (Buenos Aires: Siglo XXI, 2006).

23 B. Gallitelli and A. Thompson, "La política laboral en la Argentina del Proceso," in M. Barrera and G. Fallabella (comps.), *Sindicatos bajo regímenes militares. Argentina, Brasil, Chile* (Santiago, Chile: CES-Naciones Unidas), 1990, pp. 28–30. See also Chapter 15 in this book.

24 For a list of the leading trade union organizations that came under government control after March 24, 1976, see Fernández, *Las prácticas sociales*, pp. 135–137.

25 F. Delich, "Después del diluvio, la clase obrera," in A. Rouquié (comp.), *Argentina, hoy* (Mexico: Siglo XXI, 1982), p. 140.

26 For a synthesis of the history of delegates and internal commissions, see D. Azpiazu, V. Basualdo, and M. Schorr, *La industria y el sindicalismo de base en la Argentina* (Buenos Aires: Cara o Ceca, 2010).

for example, authorized the establishment of clandestine detention centers in the premises of their factories.[27] This repressive policy spread across all economic activities, but it focused particularly on industrial activities (and within industry, the metal and mechanical workers' unions were especially persecuted) and essential public services (transportation, railroads, energy) – that is, on strategic sectors that had, in addition, been pillars of labor organization.

It was in the framework of enormous transformations and confrontations that the repressive processes, the murders, and disappearances in SMATA-Córdoba, Ford, and Mercedes Benz occurred. The labor movement was, thus, critically remapped. Leaders and workers of the combative factions were among the main targets of dictatorial repression and most of them were jailed, disappeared, or forced into internal or external exile. However, even in this context of brutal repression and changes in working and organizational conditions, there were strong movements that resisted, opposed, and questioned the dictatorship, with different approaches and perspectives within the working class, strongly impacting this historical period and the definition of the transition to democracy. Therefore, during the dictatorship the tendency toward "participation," dialogue, or agreement with the regime on the part of one sector of the union spectrum coexisted with another, "confrontational" tendency in the heart of the labor movement, although, owing to the impact of repression, it was furthered by union lines different from those that had been predominant before 1976.[28] From this perspective, the support and involvement of unionists in the repressive process should not be seen as additional proof of a supposedly widespread social support to the policies of the dictatorship, but instead as examples of complicity of sectors of the leadership with a regressive model of social, political, and economic transformation that ultimately, in many cases, also affected their own position. The analysis of the role of the labor leaders who collaborated in the repression of workers must be conducted, then, through interdisciplinary research and a careful historical contextualization that will make it possible to show the different dimensions and conflicts, and the forms they took on before and after the military coup. This is important so that the focus on certain union leaders and structures that betrayed their mandate and position and repressed those they were

[27] V. Basualdo, "Complicidad patronal-militar en la última dictadura argentina. Los casos de Acindar, Astarsa, Dalmine-Siderca, Ford, Ledesma y Mercedes Benz," *Engranajes*, special supplement on the thirtieth anniversary of the coup, FETIA-CTA, March 2006, available at comisionporlamemoria.net/bibliografia2012/dictadura/Basualdo.pdf (accessed February 3, 2013).

[28] For an analysis of the various union sectors and the different lines of action during the dictatorship, see V. Basualdo (with the collaboration of I. Barragán and F. Rodríguez), "La clase trabajadora durante la última dictadura militar argentina (1976–1983): apuntes para una discusión sobre la resistencia obrera," Dossier no. 13, Comisión Provincial por la Memoria, 2011, available at www.comisionporlamemoria.org/investigacionyensenanza/dossiers/con%20issn/dossier14versionfinal.pdf (accessed February 3, 2013).

supposed to represent will not obscure, confuse, or blur the major role played in this history by the dispute between capital and labor, or that of the repressive forces and of important fractions of economic power, or the role of significant sectors of the working class and the labor movement that defied the alliance woven around state terrorism and its attempt to refound the country's economic and social structure.

15

Suppression of Workers Rights

Héctor Recalde

In this chapter, I attempt a historical review of the role played by the civilian-military dictatorship that held de facto power in Argentina between 1976 and 1983, with special emphasis on the measures introduced in the field of labor law to regulate both individual worker-management relations and collective affairs – that is, the links among unions, between unions and business chambers, and between labor organizations and the state. I undertake this analysis in the understanding that this regulatory evolution perfectly illustrates the *iter criminis* taken by the brutal dictatorship and exposes the ultimate aim of these essentially instrumental measures – that is, the suppression of rights and the disciplining of organized workers were conceived as necessary means for imposing a distinctly neoliberal economic plan.[1] This chapter thus seeks to identify the objectives pursued by the civilian-military dictatorship, which presented itself as the Process of National Reorganization, with the aim of fostering memory and honoring truth, toward establishing justice as a good in itself and as a means to guarantee that these events will not be repeated.

According to this reading, the designs for the 1976 coup d'état started to develop on July 1, 1974, with the death of General Juan Domingo Perón. In historical hindsight, the warning signs are evident. Two such signs were the ad taken out in the press by the Permanent Assembly of Business Associations (Asamblea Permanente de Entidades Gremiales Empresarias, APEGE)[2] in December 1975 and the lockout that followed on February 16, 1976, called by this business organization with the aim

[1] On this aspect in particular, see Chapters 5 and 16 in this book.

[2] The executive secretariat of this business association was formed by representatives of the Argentine Rural Society (Sociedad Rural Argentina, SRA), the Argentine Rural Confederations (Confederaciones Rurales Argentinas), the Argentine Chamber of Commerce (Cámara Argentina de Comercio), the Industrial Federation of the Province of Córdoba (Federación Industrial de la Provincia de Córdoba), the Economic Federation of the Province of Buenos Aires (Federación Económica de la Provincia de Buenos Aires), the Argentine Construction Chamber (Cámara Argentina de la Construcción), the Chamber of Corporations (Cámara de Sociedades Anónimas), and the Argentine Commerce Association (Unión Comercial Argentina).

of paving the way for the military.[3] It is no coincidence that the sectors represented in the board of APEGE would later be the leading beneficiaries of the measures implemented by the de facto government.

In a press release issued before the lockout – the first action of its kind in the history of the country – APEGE declared:

> The Permanent Assembly of Business Associations, which has put the business community on a state of alert, warns Public Authorities that the adoption of these measures, along with the excessive tax increases in provinces and municipalities, will trigger reactions and actions from business that are not what the business community wants but that it will be forced to resort to in order to ensure its survival.

In other words, as Claudius would say of Hamlet, diseases desperate grown by desperate appliance are relieved. Moved by that logic, the sectors represented in APEGE sought to generate an atmosphere of great imminent danger by playing the survival card to justify extreme measures such as the lockout and later the coup d'état. The speech delivered by Jorge Rafael Videla on December 24, 1975 is another such sign.

This shows that civilian-military complicity, as noted earlier, was present at the very conception of the coup and in its planning and subsequent execution; which is why the dictatorship cannot be considered as merely military as it was a civilian-military enterprise. Thus, the dark process launched on March 24, 1976 did not emerge from a simple decision by the military commands, and instead involved representatives from different sectors of society, in particular, concentrated economic groups, even before the coup.

The infamous day chosen to stage the coup was March 24, 1976 and the de facto "Program" was the speech by the later convicted and now deceased former economy minister, José Alfredo Martínez de Hoz, where he called for the shrinking of the state and economic liberalization. In this sense, some significant passages of that speech serve to illustrate the argument put forward in this chapter:

> Argentina has been mired in a sterile ideological debate of "isms" with stereotyped labels with which some sectors have tried to discredit others. It is absolutely crucial that we overcome this situation, adopting an attitude of great pragmatism, and considering and taking without delay all the practical measures necessary,

[3] See H. Recalde, *Una historia laboral jamás contada* (Buenos Aires: Corregidor, 2012), in particular, chapter 3: "La última dictadura cívico-militar y su alianza con los grandes grupos empresarios," which reproduces portions of the speeches delivered by APEGE, the SRA and some of its members, the Association of Argentine Banks (Asociación de Bancos Argentinos, ADEBA), and Jorge Rafael Videla. It also contains brief accounts of complicity between management and the armed forces in the companies Astarsa, Acindar, Siderca, Ford, Ledesma, Mercedes Benz, Loma Negra.

> without wasting time or efforts in having to justify ideological and doctrinaire categorizations.[4]

There is nothing fortuitous in this choice of words, calling to ignore an ideological debate that was, in fact, and still is, necessary to enable the political participation of the population and to raise worker awareness concerning the defense of their rights. This passage reflects the military dictatorship's intention of prohibiting any space for social organization and reflection, with the aim of plunging people into a state of passivity, of pure authoritarian pragmatism, and thus precluding any questioning of the prevailing state terrorism.

A clear sample of the shrinking of the state announced by Martínez de Hoz are the massive layoffs in the public sector, including the personnel cuts in the National Administration of Roads and Highways, which from 1975 to 1981 reduced its workforce by 44 percent. The "disciplining" effect of the dismissals is evident.[5] This economic model also brought with it an acute drop in the participation of state-owned companies in the overall sales of large companies, as they went from representing 34.3 percent in 1976 to 24.3 percent in 1983,[6] and a notable growth in external indebtedness, which in the same period increased by 363 percent, from US$8.085 billion to US$45.087 billion.[7]

Moreover, between 1976 and 1982, industrial production dropped by 11.3 percent, and the number of workers employed fell by 36.7 percent. This also entailed an increase in "workforce productivity," which in this case is a euphemism for worker exploitation, as the reduction of employment was far greater than the reduction of production – that is, a smaller number of workers had to produce the same volumes.[8]

In sum, this period was marked by a falling gross domestic product (GDP), the destruction of national industry, the selling off of state property, and a growing external debt, among other ailments.

In the specific case of labor legislation, the aim of the reform was to spread fear so as to paralyze union activism: it simultaneously produced a regressive shift in income distribution while boosting the power of management in the workplace, bringing workers to the point of subjugation, and attacking the dignity of wage

[4] Speech delivered by Martínez de Hoz on April 2, 1976, in the presentation of the economic plan. Instituto Argentino para el Desarrollo Económico – IADE, "A 30 años del golpe militar," July 12, 2006.

[5] L. D. Iramain, "Intervención estatal, desempeño empresario y ámbitos privilegiados de acumulación. El caso del sector vial durante la última dictadura militar. Argentina (1976–1981)" (2006) 6 *Revista H-industria*.

[6] M. Schorr, "La industria argentina entre 1976 y 1989. Cambios estructurales regresivos en una etapa de profundo replanteo del modelo de acumulación local," *Perspectivas cruzadas sobre los estudios sociales de la economía*, Dossier no. 1 (Buenos Aires: IDAES-UNSAM, 2007).

[7] M. Rapoport, "Mitos, etapas y crisis en la economía argentina," *El pensamiento político, económico y social en la construcción nacional, regional y provincial*, Seminar held in Catamarca, August 2007.

[8] Schorr, "La industria argentina."

earners. The means employed included dismissing workers, cracking down on labor activism, and repealing or amending existing legislation to enable certain business sectors to maximize their profit.

While advocating noninterventionism, the state nonetheless intervened in capital-labor relations, but paradoxically it did so to enhance the lack of assets of labor with respect to capital, thus tending to what has been called "savage capitalism," which privileges the market over human life and dignity. The omnipresent device was terror. The images reproduced on television showing soldiers pulling workers from buses by force were tools used for social subjugation and control and they illustrate eloquently the prevailing atmosphere of an era marked by fear.

This process began, no less, with the government taking control of the Confederación General del Trabajo (CGT), the country's most representative labor confederation, and of the leading trade unions and union-run healthcare programs. The dictatorship spared no expense when it came to kidnapping, torturing, disappearing, and jailing combative labor activists, in many cases with the direct involvement of business directors and executives.[9] It continued with the criminalization of the constitutional right to strike through the adoption of explicit state rules, such as Law 21,400,[10] or simply by acting without the backing of any law, unconstitutional or otherwise.

The government's involvement in work relations was so important for the ends sought by the civilian-military dictatorship that, on the very day of the coup, the military junta passed and enacted Decree-Law 21,261, suspending, effective nationwide, the right to strike and any other labor action, stoppage, interruption, or reduction of work or the performance of work in any way that could affect production.

Simultaneously, it eliminated trade union privileges enjoyed by union representatives and, in addition to seizing control of the CGT, it ordered the freezing of its funds, bank accounts, and assets (Law 21,270).

Five days later, on March 29, 1976, the government implemented a regime that established the dispensability of civil servants (Law 21,274), which went manifestly against the constitutional guarantee of stability in public employment and which would serve to further this goal of shrinking the state. Under paragraph 6, section 6, this law stipulated that anyone who "may represent a real or potential factor of disturbance of the normal operation of the body they belong to shall not be entitled to compensation" if fired.

[9] See Chapters 11, 12, 13, and 14 in this book.

[10] Although, as noted by professor Rodolfo Capón Filas, these should be referred to as "state rules" or "de facto state rules," in this chapter I use the terms "laws" or "decree-laws" to refer to these rules, but such use does entail giving them a legal status that they do not, by law, have.

Less than a month after the coup, the dictatorship adopted its Law 21,297, which repealed – "disappeared" – twenty-seven sections and amended – "tortured" – another ninety-nine sections of the Employment Contract Act (Ley de Contrato de Trabajo, LCT). The LCT had been passed under the toppled democratic government through the law-making procedure established in the national constitution and with broad popular participation. The main author of this law, the lawyer Norberto Centeno, was kidnapped on July 7, 1977, along with other labor lawyers, and murdered after two torture sessions.

Before detailing the amendments made to the LCT, a general, and obvious, observation is in order: all the eliminations and changes to this law damaged worker rights that had been secured by the law passed under the democratic government, and most of them unquestionably violated guarantees and rights established by the national Constitution, primarily under section 14 bis.

By Law 21,307 of July 7, 1976, collective wage bargaining was banned, and only the national Executive Branch was authorized to grant general raises. Under Law 21,371, of July 30 of that same year, the government ordered the suspension of all assemblies, congresses, and election processes in trade unions, and the Ministry of Labor was given the power both to revoke the mandates of employee delegates and internal commissions and to take control of unions or employer associations, where it was authorized to appoint representatives through resolutions that were not subject to appeal.

Under Law 21,400, of September 3, 1976, workers were prohibited from making use of their constitutional right to strike and take any other direct action. In this way, such actions were turned into crimes punishable by prison. The same law stipulated that when union representatives were taken into custody under authority of the National Executive, their work contracts were suspended for three months and their employers were authorized to fire them without severance pay once that term was over.

It should be stressed that this series of measures was imposed within the first six months of the dictatorship, so that the government wasted no time in stripping away gains that had been achieved through centuries of social awareness-raising and activism. The dictatorship's brutal targeting of trade unions is evident, as it recognized that the labor movement had the capacity for organized struggle necessary to protect workers' rights and sustain democracy in general, and therefore it sought to wipe it out. This focused attack on trade unions and the individual rights of workers had the evident purpose of benefiting business – the other side of the dispute between antagonistic interests.

On September 17, 1976, Law 21,418 voided all collective work agreements applicable to the public sector (yet another measure tending toward the shrinking of the state) and, by Law 21,476 of December 16 of that year, the most beneficial rights protected under collective work agreements were eliminated for activities in both the public and private sectors.

Decree 385 of February 11, 1977 canceled all memberships to unions and established that workers would have to reapply for membership if they wanted to join. Curiously enough, this measure resulted in labor unions increasing their number of members when workers flocked to apply for membership, as – despite being afraid – they refused to passively accept the trampling of their rights and found (sometimes silent) ways to protest and stand up against the dictatorship. This phenomenon of massive reapplication for membership led the labor movement to dub this norm the "referendum decree."

On November 15, 1979, Law 22,105, the Workers' Union Associations Act (Ley de Asociaciones Gremiales de Trabajadores), was enacted, banning joint unionization of upper-level employees with lower-level personnel, imposing the fractioning of unions, which prevented unions from operating together beyond the scope of a province (or of a region, if they had prior authorization to operate at the provincial level), setting geographic limits for federations, and dissolving confederations (the CGT). If in union there is strength, atomization was the death blow the dictatorship was seeking to deal.

This law also banned unions from participating in political activities and providing direct or indirect support to parties or to anyone who conducted such activities, and limited their purpose solely to the defense of the union and labor interests of workers. It also prohibited them from engaging in the operation and administration of healthcare programs or granting welfare benefits. The law stipulated that union officers and delegates could only stand for immediate reelection once and established that 50 percent of workers had to participate in an election of delegates for it to be considered valid. It enabled arbitrary dismissals – without cause – of union delegates and leaders and stipulated only a compensation surcharge. In what was a clearly interventionist measure, which also violated the principle of union autonomy, it authorized the Labor Ministry to suspend the rights of trade union associations, cancel their registration or union standing, disqualify union representatives so that they could not perform their union duties, take control of unions by removing their authorities and appointing replacements, and oversee the handling and managing of union funds.

On July 10, 1980, the National Rural Work Regime Act (Law 22,248), which until recently was still in force, was enacted, excluding rural workers from the scope of application of the LCT and curtailing their rights.

Law 22,310 eliminated the service charge provision applicable to the restaurant and hotel industry. Most significant were the consequences this law had in wealth distribution in the sector, as it produced a steep drop in wages while at the same time boosting business profitability. A modest and restrictive estimate puts this transference of wealth from hotel and restaurant workers to their employers at approximately 26 billion pesos, some US$5 billion, between 1980 and late 2012. These amounts explain the strong suspicion that the adoption of this law generated, favoring as it did one side while damaging the other.

Then, by Law 22,425 the Private Bank Employee Statute and the Insurance Company Employee Statute were annulled. This clearly evidences that another of the business sectors that benefited from the dissolution of the rule of law was the financial and banking sector, as these annulled regulations contained gains for workers of the sector.

AMENDMENTS TO THE EMPLOYMENT CONTRACT ACT

The mutilation of the Employment Contract Regime contained in the 1974 LCT merits a separate consideration. Under the pretext of eliminating "excesses with respect to the balance of behaviors that must be observed" in "the harmonic relations between workers and employers,"[11] the dictatorial government sought to do away even with the spirit behind the LCT by repealing its section 19, which established: "The inequalities that this law will create in favor of one of the parties can only be understood as forms of compensating other inequalities that occur naturally in the [labor] relationship." This provision was recovered in 2010 by Law 26,592, along with many more that contained similar provisions, in a process of reinstatement of labor laws that began around 2006.

That was the teleological framework that led the dictatorship to suppress and curtail worker rights. For reasons of space, all twenty-seven eliminations and ninety-nine amendments to the LCT, which, as noted earlier, targeted rights gained by the working class, are not detailed here, and only the more relevant ones are reviewed. In addition to the provision mentioned previously, the most significant provisions eliminated include:

- the prevalence of uses and practices more favorable to workers or of company practices based on legislation, collective agreements, and employment contracts (sec. 17);
- the presumption of dismissal when there is proof that a work relationship existed and ceased (sec. 63);
- the obligation of informing workers of all personnel controls adopted by management (sec. 77);

[11] See the grounds for State Rule 21,297, drafted through intense discussions between an admiral, a general, and a brigadier who were members of the substitute national parliament – that is, the Legislative Affairs Commission – with technical support from lawyers representing the business sector, whose names even today are kept under a disgraceful confidentiality.

- the obligation of prioritizing, under equal conditions, workers already employed by the company when filling higher positions, and workers hired under temporary or seasonal contracts when filling permanent positions (sec. 90);
- the requirement of regularly updating the adjustable minimum living wage based on the variations in the cost of living without admitting reductions by zones (sec. 120);
- the minimum wage for professionals (secs. 131 and 132);
- the right of workers to consider themselves fired – and entitled to severance pay – in cases in which they have been suspended for less than thirty days, if such suspensions have been damaging or harmful (sec. 242);
- the requirement of submitting any decision concerning dismissals, suspensions, or contract modifications affecting several workers to a prior procedure and request for authorization, with participation of the union (sec. 276);
- the possibility of receiving, in the case of male workers, a compensation bonus – equivalent to one year in wages – in the case of dismissals within the marriage protection period (sec. 299).

Also particularly significant was the elimination of sections 243, 244, and 245, on the right to strike. Section 243 stipulated that strikes and other direct union actions only suspended the effects of the labor relation (as opposed to extinguishing it), that a worker's participation in such actions was in no way cause for dismissal, and that not reinstating any portion of the workforce involved in a strike once it was lifted constituted unequal and discriminatory treatment. Section 244 prohibited employers from hiring workers to substitute or replace striking workers (strikebreakers, popularly known as *esquiroles*, *crumiros*, or *carneros*), and from adopting disciplinary measures against them, or altering their situation or position in the company. Section 245 established the right of workers to receive compensation for days on strike when the strike was caused by a fault of the employer. These three sections were eliminated.

Among the ninety-nine changes made to the LCT, the most significant included suspending the application of the LCT to activities governed by special statutes (for example, journalists, traveling salespersons, managers of rental houses, etc.) if the law's provisions were more favorable than the provisions of the statutes (sec. 2). This suspension was extended to contracts executed in Argentina to be implemented abroad, as it was established that LCT provisions that were more favorable than the corresponding foreign provisions would not be applied (sec. 3).

Another aspect eliminated was the application of the rule of *in dubio pro operario* (when in doubt, the decision is to be made in favor of the worker): when evidence furnished in court is inconclusive, in which case – according to this principle – the judge has to decide in the most beneficial way for the worker (sec. 9, recovered in

2008 by Law 26,428). Also taken out of the law was the requirement that in cases for which prior notice is not duly given, compensation must be paid for the term that would have corresponded to the prior notice (sec. 21).

In the case of outsourcing, the joint responsibility of the main companies was limited, with the modification of the scheme established under the LCT (sec. 32). Two situations were contemplated for outsourcing: (1) when the services outsourced were essential to the main or accessory activity of the main company, the law established the joint solidarity of both companies vis-à-vis the worker hired by the contractor; and (2) when what was outsourced were works, tasks, or services corresponding to the regular and specific activity of the main company, and within its field, it was stipulated that the main company was to be considered the employer, especially for the purposes of implementing collective work agreements and of union representation. Law 21,297 replaced both provisions, eliminating the main company as employer when the subcontracting corresponded to a specific activity of the company, establishing for such cases only the joint solidarity of the main company and eliminating that joint responsibility when the subcontracting corresponded to the main or accessory activity.

In the case of economic groups, the LCT established that all the companies that were part of the group were jointly responsible for the obligations contracted by each of them with their workers and the social security agencies (sec. 33). Law 21,297 limited that joint responsibility to cases that involved fraudulent operations or negligent management. It goes without saying that the beneficiaries of the scope of this provision were large corporations gathered in economic groups. This provision affected the rights of workers, as the solvency of the economic group was segmented and the insolvency of one company in the group – whichever had the worker registered as its dependent – enabled the rest to avoid responsibility. In this way, corporations maximized their profit at the expense of the rights of their workforce and also of the state, which they sought to shrink.

With respect to books, records, payrolls, and other auditing elements that by law or under collective work agreements employers were required to keep, observing certain formalities, the LCT provided that when kept without due care and without meeting the established formalities, such documents would have no value in court as evidence in favor of the employer and could not be used to prove that their obligations had been met (secs. 57 and 58). The same consequences were established if the formalities required for paychecks were not observed or if they failed to match the corresponding documentation (sec. 158). Law 21,297 modified the consequences in all these cases, giving the court discretion to determine the validity of any documentation that failed to meet the required formalities.

Whereas the LCT established that when there was a claim over wages (in terms of either the amount to be paid or the payment itself), the burden of proof was on the employer (sec. 60), Law 21,297 stipulated that in such situations the judge was to set the amount to be paid.

Law 21,297 also eliminated worker participation and union representation in the organization of the company (sec. 69), denied the free access they previously had to company books and documentation to control sales and income in cases in which there was a system of commissions and percentages over sales (sec. 120), and took away the right of unions to be consulted regarding personnel monitoring systems (sec. 78).

With respect to personnel monitoring systems, the law eliminated the need for them to be approved by the Labor Administrative Authority (sec. 78), and that body's power to issue rules, either general, by area, by activity, or by field of activity, and to resolve specific cases prior to consultation with union organizations (sec. 79). This measure, among others, lends support to the assertion that these amendments were not purely economic in nature, but also targeted the dignity of the worker as an individual.

The law also eliminated the right of workers to bring legal action for the reestablishment of any working conditions modified unilaterally by employers, exceeding the limits that the law imposes on that power, called *ius variandi* (i.e., that the modification not alter essential conditions under the contract, that it not cause material or moral damage to the worker, and that it not be implemented unreasonably – that is, that it be grounded on functional needs of the company's organization), and leaving workers the only alternative of considering themselves as indirectly dismissed (sec. 71, provision recovered in 2006 by Law 26,088).

As for the disciplinary powers of employers, the law eliminated the right of workers to be heard before the application of penalties, it set a term of thirty days for the worker to challenge the penalty ([sec. 72] no such time limit existed under the LCT), and removed the clause that established that suspensions were to be expunged from a worker's records twelve months after their application (sec. 75).

The law also eliminated the prohibition imposed on employers of conducting surveys or inquiring about the political, religious, or labor views of workers when hiring them, as well as the right of workers to freely express such opinions in the workplace, provided such expression did not involve misconduct or interfere in the normal performance of their tasks (sec. 81).

By modifying section 85, the law suppressed the right of workers to say no to certain tasks (to refuse to work), without loss of pay, when such tasks posed an imminent risk of harm or when the employer failed to adopt the necessary measures to protect the psychological and physical safety (prior notice of noncompliance), or when the employer failed to carry out repairs or provide elements required by the administrative authority after declaring a workplace unfit for health reasons.

With respect to the obligation of equal treatment, the LCT stipulated (sec. 89) that unequal treatment was to be considered arbitrary when the employer discriminated based on any nonobjective reason. Law 21,297 replaced that text, limiting the consideration of unequal treatment to arbitrary discriminations based on gender, religion, or race.

As regards seasonal employment contracts (contracts for cyclic activities), it exempted employers from notifying the start of a new season (sec. 107). It also extended to ninety days the term of expiration – which the LCT set at thirty – for employers to bring liability action against workers for serious and intentional damages caused by them to shops, instruments, or work materials (sec. 149).

As for vacation time, it eliminated the right of workers to receive compensation if the company closed for vacation for a period of time longer than the worker's annual leave (sec. 167); it reduced to forty-five days the sixty-day period set under the LCT for employers to give notice of the start date of vacations; it gave the administrative authority the power to authorize the granting of vacation time in periods other than those stipulated by law (from October 1 to April 30 [sec. 168]), and repealed the provision that established that, if the worker had pending vacation time at the termination of a contract, the employer was to pay the worker a compensation equivalent to two and a half times the value corresponding to the periods owed (sec. 170).

It also eliminated the consideration of the days established under collective work agreements as national and nonworking holidays (sec. 180).

Concerning maternity protection, the LCT established the right of pregnant workers to stability in the workplace as of the moment of conception, while Law 21,297 established it as of the moment management is notified of the pregnancy. It also repealed the *iuris et de iure* presumption (whereby no proof to the contrary is admitted) for dismissals during the ninety days of maternity leave, which meant that it was not possible to claim that such dismissals were motivated by anything other than the maternity itself; it cut in half (from two years to one) the extent of compensation for aggravating circumstances in cases of dismissals within the seven months prior to or following the birth (secs. 193 and 194); and it limited to a term no longer than a year the daily breaks for breastfeeding (sec. 195).

It reduced the period of leave of absence that a woman is entitled to request after a maternity leave (or to care for a sick child), without pay, from a minimum of six months and a maximum of one year to a minimum of three and a maximum of six months.

Similarly, it cut the period of protection of employment by reason of marriage from six months before and twelve months after the marriage to three and six months respectively, and it also introduced as a requirement to benefit from such protection the presentation of a certified notice to employers (sec. 197).

With respect to the workday, Law 21,297 granted employers power to establish, without prior authorization and even for reasons of economic convenience, a job rotation system based on work performed by teams (to which the limit of eight-hour workdays or forty-eight-hour workweeks or the reduction of work hours for night work did not apply) (secs. 214 and 219); it made it difficult to declare activities or workplaces health hazards (sec. 214); and it established that the prohibition of working during the weekly rest did not entail a reduction in the weekly total work hours (sec. 222).

On the subject of non-work-related accidents or illnesses, it eliminated the provision that established that a medical certificate issued by an authorized doctor was sufficient proof of the worker's inability to attend work, for the purpose of being entitled to receive compensation (sec. 226), as well as the precedence, to that end, of the certificate presented by the worker in cases in which there are differences between the worker's doctor and the employer's, and the employer does not appeal to the administrative authority to appoint an official doctor to decide on the matter (sec. 227). In contrast to the LCT, which established that the expiration of the term during which a job is reserved for reasons of illness (a term of one year, without pay, after the end of the paid sick leave) did not entail termination of the working relationship, Law 21,297 stipulated that upon such expiration, the decision by "either of the parties" (a euphemism for the employer) to terminate the relationship would not generate a compensation. In addition, it reduced the compensation that the employer was required to pay a worker with diminished working capacity upon not reinstating that worker following the end of his or her sick leave, an obligation that the LCT had set as severance pay plus the equivalent to one year of pay in those cases in which the employer had tasks that matched the residual capacity of the worker and failed to assign them to that worker, and as severance pay when it had none, bringing those compensations down to severance pay, in the first case, and half of severance pay, in the second (sec. 229).

At this point it should be noted that the disappearance and death of labor lawyer Carlos Alberto Moreno, who was kidnapped and killed in Tandil between April and May 1977, was basically caused by his role in successful court actions against the company Loma Negra in cases of occupational illnesses in which he represented workers. The recurring illness in these cases was silicosis, caused by overexposure to crystalline silica, which came to be known on the South American continent through the development of mining activities, in particular in the Andean region, under the brutal forced labor systems of *mita* and *yanaconazgo* used in mining. This is another clear example of the collaboration between business and the armed forces. Workers' demands in that company naturally decreased considerably as of that moment. The alternatives for the company were preventing illnesses by ensuring healthy working conditions in the workplace, indemnifying workers who brought successful suits against it, or persecuting anyone who protested. It chose the last, and perverse, alternative.

With respect to workers who had been entitled to time off for occupying elected positions at the national, provincial, or municipal level, it took away their right to enjoy job stability (that is, to be reinstated and not fired) during the year following the termination of their elected position, and the right to choose, in the event of a breach of that guarantee, between being reinstated, including the payment of wages until the effective reinstatement, or considering themselves dismissed and entitled, in addition to severance pay, to the equivalent of the wages they would have received during the period of stability. Such guarantees were replaced with the right to receive severance pay (secs. 232 and 233).

Regarding suspensions, the law eliminated the requirement that they be communicated with at least one business day notice (sec. 234); it repealed the provision that established that the lack or reduction of available work was excluded from the company's inherent risk and could not be claimed as fair grounds for suspension (sec. 236); it imposed as a requirement for receiving payment of suspension wages that the worker contest the suspension, even when the action taken by management did not comply with the corresponding legal requirements, in contrast to the LCT, which established that in such an event the worker was not required to contest the suspension (sec. 240).

With respect to the termination of the employment relationship:

- it reduced from three to two months the prior notice period for workers with a seniority of more than ten years (sec. 252);
- it eliminated the obligation of assessing with a restrictive criterion the employer's use of its disciplining powers during the term of prior notice (sec. 259);
- it admitted the validity of prior notice periods given while the worker involved was on leave or during periods of interruption of work, if such periods were to begin following the leave or interruption, a possibility not admitted under the LCT (sec. 260);
- it imposed on the worker the burden of notifying in writing the decision to terminate the employment contract for just cause, including a clear explanation of the motives on which such termination was grounded, in contrast to the LCT, which placed the burden solely on the employer (sec. 264);
- it eliminated the provision establishing that when invoking as grounds for dismissal the commission of criminal acts, the employer must back such grounds with a final court ruling (sec. 265);
- it added "normal and usual" as characteristics of the pay that is to be taken into account toward calculating severance pay (sec. 266);

- it eliminated the 50 percent increase for severance pay stipulated under special regulations (sec. 266);
- it eliminated the provision establishing that the company's inherent risk cannot be grounds for lack or reduction of work that would authorize dismissals with a 50 percent cut in severance pay (sec. 268);
- it eliminated the right to compensation in the event of dismissal for expiration of a short-term contract of less than one year (sec. 271);
- it eliminated the employer's obligation of giving prior notice to workers eligible for retirement as a prerequisite for demanding the initiation of the retirement process, and it eliminated the extension provided under the LCT as continuation of the employment relationship if the benefit was not granted within a year by no fault of the worker (sec. 273).

Law 21,297 also reduced the term for expiration of wage claims from four to two years, further prohibiting any extensions of this term under collective work agreements or individual contracts (sec. 278), and it eliminated certain grounds for suspension of the expiration (sec. 282).

With respect to the updating of the value of wage claims, it replaced the stipulations of the LCT, which established that they were to be adjusted according to the increase in the cost of living as of the moment each sum became due. It replaced that index with the industrial laborer wage index, and stipulated that it was to be applied as of the date in which the claim was brought (sec. 301).

CONCLUSIONS

As can be observed, the business sector had a special influence on the planning and implementation of the self-proclaimed Process of National Reorganization. Part of its "cut" were the unlawful benefits it obtained through the disciplining of the working class, its increased powers in the workplace, and the very substantial curtailment of rights that had been gained by the working class, both in economic terms and in their overall working conditions.

With the return of Peronism to the national government in 1973 the participation of wages in income distribution saw a strong recovery (the wage bill increased from 39 percent of the GDP in 1972 to 46.65 percent just two years later), which entailed a drop in surplus appropriation by companies. This process, however, was reversed as of 1976 with a strong transfer in favor of capital.[12]

As of the beginning of the last military dictatorship, a radical change can in fact be observed in the functional distribution of income – that is, the share of production

[12] J. M. Graña, "Distribución funcional del ingreso en la Argentina, 1935–2005," *Documento de trabajo del CEPED*, Universidad de Buenos Aires, December 2007.

appropriated by workers and by business. In 1976, the gross operating surplus reached 71 percent, with a hike of 16 percentage points in just one year. This increase was obtained at the expense of a drop in the participation of wages in production, which fell by the same percentage, as an inevitable consequence of the measures described in this chapter.[13]

Thus it may be concluded that, as of 1976, the leading beneficiaries of the brutal actions of the de facto government were companies, as they appropriated a large share of the total value of the country's production. The working class, instead, was relegated in this regressive income process. Under these conditions, organized labor was unable to put up a sufficiently strong opposition, as it saw itself divided and decimated by the kidnapping, murdering, and jailing of its members and by the paralyzing effect of state terror.

However, this regulatory analysis would not be complete if it failed to mention that what the civilian-military dictatorship could not eliminate was the fighting spirit of the working class, which – despite the human and material losses suffered – staged silent protests, first, such as the case of the "referendum decree" mentioned earlier, and, later, loud and massive expressions of resistance, such as the national strikes of April 27, 1979 and March 30, 1982. As is evidenced throughout this chapter, the regression and losses suffered by workers, both in gains and in rights, were great and many.

The recovery began in May 2003, and that tendency has continued and is currently maintained, but that does not mean that greater efforts are not needed, as there is still a long way to go before the long-sought goal of an equal, inclusive, and socially just society is achieved.

[13] Rapoport, "Mitos, etapas y crisis."

PART VI

Industrial and Agricultural Business Associations

Complicity and Benefits

16

Industrial Economic Power as Promoter and Beneficiary of Argentina's Refounding Project (1976–1983)

Martín Schorr

THE REFOUNDATIONAL NATURE OF THE MILITARY DICTATORSHIP AND THE SUPPORT OF ECONOMIC POWER

The March 24, 1976 coup d'état set in motion the most significant and dramatic economic and social restructuring in the history of Argentina. The dictatorial period resulted in the transition from an industrial society to one based on the financial valorization of capital.[1] The new model of accumulation was enabled by a change in the relation of forces between capital and labor, and by a reconfiguration within the sphere of capital, which produced a situation of acute inequality that would continue in the years following the dictatorship (at least until 2001–2002). At one end of the social structure are workers, who as a whole are at the lowest level of income participation since Peronism irrupted in Argentina's political life. At the other end is a small number of economic groups, large foreign corporations, and external debt creditors that, in the framework of a very intense process of concentration and centralization of capital, combine a growing participation in income with the capacity to subordinate the state apparatus, decisively and increasingly influencing the course of the economic and sociopolitical processes.

The import substitution model was not abandoned because it was exhausted. Proof of this is the fact that between 1964 and 1974 total GDP grew at an annual rate of about 5 percent in constant prices (in that same period, manufacturing GDP expanded at an average annual rate of nearly 7 percent), and that in 1975 exports of

I would like to thank Isabel Morayta for her invaluable collaboration and comments and Laura López Iglesias for her careful reading of an earlier version of this text and her observations. Any errors or omissions are solely my responsibility.

[1] See E. Basualdo, *Estudios de historia económica. Desde mediados del siglo XX a la actualidad* (Buenos Aires: Siglo XXI, 2006).

industrial products represented about 20 percent of total exports, compared to only 3 percent in 1960.

Similar to what happened in Chile under the genocidal regime of Augusto Pinochet, the dictatorship in Argentina sought to completely transform the complex economic and social structure built over long decades of industrial development (a process that, it should be noted, had not been free from conflict or limitations of various kinds).[2] Two of the leading goals of the military that took power by force in March 1976 and of the social bases that supported it were redefining the role of the state in the allocation of resources and drastically limiting the bargaining power that workers had in the framework of an accumulation regime in which exchange controls prevented capital flight, wage levels were not restricted by external competition, and unemployment levels remained low (in substantial terms, owing to the development and expansion of industry). In strategic terms, the intention was to radically and irreversibly alter the relation of forces arising from the presence of an industrial working class that was highly organized and politically and ideologically mobilized. In other words, the general aim was to modify the economic and structural foundations that had enabled the emergence of phenomena such as Peronism and sociopolitical processes such as the *Cordobazo*, *Rosariazo*, and *Tucumanazo* protest movements.[3]

The economic and political participation of workers was seen as a threat by local dominant sectors (Table 16.1), and that perceived threat made it possible for them to accept, advance, and celebrate the drastic program supported by

[2] Some of the most significant limitations were the decisive presence of foreign companies and the weakness of the national bourgeoisie, the tendency toward a predominance of a kind of frivolous or spurious protectionism instead of the so-called learning protectionism, the lag in the capital goods industry, and technological dependency. On these issues, see CONADE, "El desarrollo industrial en la Argentina: sustitución de importaciones, concentración económica y capital extranjero (1950–1970)," (Buenos Aires: mimeo, 1973); M. Diamand, *Doctrinas económicas, desarrollo e independencia* (Buenos Aires: Paidós, 1973); and F. Fajnzylber, *La industrialización trunca de América Latina* (Mexico: Nueva Imagen, 1983).

[3] In a pioneer study, Adolfo Canitrot characterizes the "political project of a higher order" of the military as follows: "The objective of the Armed Forces was social disciplining. Disciplining of all social relations but with a specific significance in the case of the working class: its political and institutional repositioning to put it in the subordinate place that is inherent to it in economic relations. Institutionally this disciplining goal requires the weakening of the collective and political organizations representing that class, achieved not only by legally regulating their capacities and activities, but also by way of an economic reform that eliminates the functional conditions that tend to promote their development." (A. Canitrot, *Teoría y práctica del liberalismo. Política antiinflacionaria y apertura económica en la Argentina*, 1976–1981 (Buenos Aires, CEDES, 1980), p. 6). In this sense, Martínez de Hoz himself highlighted: "The prospect of continuity that we enjoyed at the start of the program enabled us to privilege medium and long-term objectives over short-term goals." (Economy Minister, "Memoria 29/3/1976-29/3/1981," (Buenos Aires: mimeo, 1982), p. 42).

TABLE 16.1. *Positions adopted by the economic dominant sectors with respect to the socioeconomic and political situation in Argentina in the mid-1970s*

Position	Company	Economic group	Source
"A substantial change is effected as of March 24, 1976, when the Armed Forces, accurately interpreting the gravity of the situation, assumed the historical responsibility of taking power to put the country in order. Labor discipline is restored, subversion is combated with full intensity, and economic measures are adopted to meet external debt commitments and reduce inflation. Spending is limited and tax collection increases."	Acindar	Acindar	Letter for the Annual Report and Balance Sheet, no. 34 (1975–1976), June 1976
"Once the restraints that hinder progress have been broken and subversion has disappeared, Argentina will begin a swift takeoff, reaching in only a few years such levels of progress and welfare as will make it difficult to remember our recent past."	Acindar	Acindar	Letter for the Annual Report and Balance Sheet, no. 34 (1975–1976), June 1976
"Still fresh [in our minds] are the circumstances that left the Armed Forces no choice but to assume the responsibility of taking power and stopping the country from continuing in the downward spiral that was leading it inexorably into chaos and definite frustration."	Acindar	Acindar	Address by the president of the Buenos Aires Stock Exchange, July 1976
"The most salient feature of the past fiscal year has been the presence of highly critical political, economic, and social conditions. Briefly stated, we must consider them as two clearly different periods, separated by the events of March 24, 1976... The events of March 24 put an end to the situation of chaos, restoring the order necessary to achieve the Nation's economic, social, and political recovery."	Cía. Fabril Financiera	Celulosa Argentina	Annual Report and General Balance Sheet, June 1976

(*continued*)

TABLE 16.1. (*continued*)

Position	Company	Economic group	Source
"In our two previous annual reports, that is the two corresponding to the fiscal years that ended on March 31, 1974 and March 31, 1975, we expressed not only our concern but also our alarm at the prospects presented by the country's economic situation and that, of course, had a direct effect on our social development. The country had been pushed to extremes; which we described then as critical but that within a few months could only be defined as being framed in a general situation whose analysis and consequences were reaching unsustainable limits. Fortunately, in the final days of the social period that died last March 31, and, therefore, as we were embarking on a new annual stage of the Company, a major change took place in the political, economic, and social conditions of the Republic."	Garovaglio y Zorraquín	Garovaglio y Zorraquín	Annual Report and General Balance Sheet, March 1976
"Never before had the country seen such a serious crisis, aggravated by the inefficiency and lack of coordination, continuity, and authority of government action."	Dalmine-Siderca	Techint	Annual Report and General Balance Sheet, 1974–1975

Source: Prepared by the author based on the sources indicated.

the traditional exporting sector allied with big export-import commerce and the financial sector.[4]

The refounding project implemented by the military dictatorship to bring about that radical transformation of Argentine economy and society was imposed through the repressive disciplining of the masses. This is most vividly expressed by the 30,000 disappeared, the proliferation of concentration camps, the complicity of business in workplace repression (in the case of Acindar, Astarsa, Dalmine-Siderca, Ford, Ledesma, Mercedes Benz, and Saiar, among other companies), the control of trade unions by the government, the curtailment of long-standing labor gains, and the participation of top executives from many of the country's leading companies in strategic areas of the state (Table 16.2).

Considering the objectives pursued by the armed forces (in essence, the consolidation of a new project of social control built on radically different structural conditions) and the class fractions that formed its core base support, such a huge alteration of the model of capital accumulation in Argentina entailed, in the first place, attacking a socioeconomic structure established over the course of several decades in the framework of the various stages of the import substitution model. These stages had shaped an urban society with a complex and conflictive articulation of its social sectors. Second, because this socioeconomic structure was so solidly established, such a reconversion could not be achieved through a phase of economic expansion; it necessarily had to occur by way of a crisis that would succeed in marginalizing certain social sectors, redefining others, and enabling the rest to prevail. Third, the changes that were to be made to the basic pillars of import substitution industrialization, and the characteristics of the new accumulation model, had to be irreversible.

These efforts to structurally refound Argentine capitalism had to be based on a tight control of the state apparatus that would make it possible to move forward

4 With respect to the positions systematized in Table 16.1, Guillermo O'Donnell's insightful analysis is illustrative in that sense: "It is the emergence of behaviors or abstentions of subordinate classes that no longer conform, regularly and normally, to the reproduction of the basic social relations of a capitalist society. Rebelliousness, subversion, disorder, indiscipline of the labor force are terms that refer to situations that threaten the continuity of practices and attitudes of the subordinate classes and sectors that were previously taken for granted as 'natural.' … The depth of this questioning may be more or less intense; it may include anything from 'excessive' demands regarding working conditions to the seizing of production units or to discourses that question the social role of capitalists as owners and/ or of entrepreneurs as holders of the means of production. These situations – *that may be more or less immediately threatening to the existing 'order'* – entail at least two things: that ideological control has slackened and that the coercion (economic penalties or, simply, physical force) that should neutralize the resulting 'disorder' is failing. In other words, it indicates a state that is failing in effectively guaranteeing the existence and reproduction of fundamental social relations." G. O'Donnell, *El Estado burocrático autoritario. Triunfos, derrotas y crisis* (Buenos Aires: Editorial de Belgrano, 1982), pp. 51 and 52, emphasis added.

TABLE 16.2. *State participation of top executives from major companies, 1976–1981*

Name	Government position	Economic group
J. Martínez de Hoz	Economy minister	Acindar, Roberts, and Bracht
P. Terán Nougués	Vice president of the Central Bank	Garovaglio y Zorraquín
A. de Achával	Director of Banco Nación (government owned bank)	Garovaglio y Zorraquín
F. Soldati	Director of the Central Bank	Soldati
E. Oxenford	Director of YPF (government-owned oil and gas company)	Roberts
J. Gamboa	Vice president of Banade (National Development Bank)	Roberts
M. Braun Lasala	Undersecretary of institutional matters	Braun Menéndez
G. Meoli	Manager of Gas del Estado (gas utility company)	Astra
A. Plunkett	CEO of Gas del Estado	Astra
F. Puca Prota	Secretary of mining	National Lead
F. Nicholson	Undersecretary of planning	Ledesma
R. Podestá	Undersecretary of industrial development	Firpo
E. Ianetta	President of Banade	Banco Federal Argentino
G. Klein	Secretary of economic planning	Shaw and Renault
D. Brunella	Energy secretary	Renault and Ericsson
C. Etcheverrigaray	Vice president of Banco Nación	Camea

Source: Prepared by the author with information drawn from the directory of corporations *Guía de Sociedades Anónimas* (several numbers) and A. Castellani, *Estado, empresas y empresarios. La construcción de ámbitos privilegiados de acumulación entre 1966 y 1989* (Buenos Aires: Prometeo, 2009).

simultaneously in multiple (strongly interconnected) directions: restoring social domination through the disciplining of the working class, in particular, and of the smaller business segments (or those that were considered less internationally "efficient" by the advocates of monetarist orthodoxy, so widespread during those years); imposing a regressive redistribution of national income; redefining the way the state operated; modifying the production structure; and, in sum, reversing the dynamics of the import substitution model at the economic and social levels.

With such strategic objectives, it is not by chance that the domestic manufacturing sector shrank as dramatically as it did, so that in the years following the 1976 coup d'état more than 20,000 factories closed down and the gross industrial product

TABLE 16.3. *Evolution of total and industrial GDP, industrialization coefficient and employment, industrial wages, and industry gross profit margin, 1974–1983 (1974 baseline = 100 and percentages)*

	Total GDP		Industrial GDP		Industrial GDP / Total GDP	Employment	Industrial wages[a]	Gross profit margin[b]
	Absolute values	Per capita	Absolute values	Per capita				
1974	100.0	100.0	100.0	100	28.3	100.0	100.0	100.0
1975	99.4	97.6	97.4	95.7	27.8	103.8	96.6	96.2
1976	99.4	95.9	94.5	91.2	26.9	100.4	65.0	143.4
1977	105.7	100.2	101.9	96.5	27.3	94.3	64.1	163.6
1978	102.3	95.3	91.2	84.8	25.2	85.1	63.2	163.8
1979	109.5	100.1	100.2	91.6	25.9	83.3	72.2	169.6
1980	111.2	99.9	96.6	86.8	24.6	76.8	80.4	161.5
1981	103.7	91.5	81.4	71.8	22.2	67.2	72.2	172.7
1982	98.6	85.4	77.2	66.9	22.2	63.6	65.9	198.0
1983	101.5	86.3	85.1	72.4	23.9	65.7	82.7	166.4

[a] Average nominal wage deflated by the consumer price index.
[b] Average labor productivity / average real salary relation.
Source: Prepared by the author based on information from the National Institute of Statistics and Censuses (Instituto Nacional de Estadística y Censos, INDEC).

plummeted, as did the relative weight of the sector's activity in the country's economy as a whole, employment, and wages, in a scenario marked by considerable growth of gross capital returns (Table 16.3). Moreover, industry was displaced from its role as the guiding force and engine of the country's economic and social relations, and was no longer the economic activity with the highest rate of return. All of this was effected in parallel to the deployment of a brutal repressive strategy and through the implementation of different economic policies devised by organic intellectuals of the dominant sectors, such as the 1976 "attack on wages," the financial reform, and the "monetary approach to the balance of payment" (the *tablita*), which were combined with a far-reaching, albeit asymmetric, trade liberalization.

An analysis of the central aspects of the refounding project – the process of concentration and centralization of capital in industry and the accompanying redefinition of sectorial economic power – is provided later in this chapter and is based on the data in Table 16.3. The idea is to identify the limited core group of beneficiaries of the regressive restructure of the manufacturing sector implemented between 1976 and 1983.[5]

5 The following studies are suggested to complement the analysis and information provided here: D. Azpiazu, E. Basualdo, and M. Khavisse, *El nuevo poder económico en la Argentina de los años*

THE GROWING CONCENTRATION AND CENTRALIZATION OF CAPITAL AND THE REDEFINITION OF ECONOMIC POWER IN INDUSTRY

The evolution of industrial wages, employment, and gross operating margin illustrates the regressive nature of the acute deindustrialization experienced during the last dictatorship, but it does not show another of its distinctive features, equally linked to "the political project of a higher order" described by O'Donnell, namely the fact that a small group of national economic groups and foreign conglomerates, along with a few large transnational corporations,[6] far from suffering the impact of the crisis and the sector's restructure, achieved a privileged position. This contrasts with the critical course that a large part of the other business strata were forced to take.

Table 16.4 presents data of the leading census variables broken down according to the different concentration strata in the local manufacturing spectrum, between 1973 and 1984.

During those years – marked by a sharp sectorial regression – the branches of industry in which highly concentrated market structures predominated expanded their participation in total production: between the first and last censuses, these branches went from representing 47.2 percent of all production to almost 52 percent. In that same period, branches with medium concentration and those with low

ochenta. Edición definitiva (Buenos Aires: Siglo XXI, 2004); D. Azpiazu and B. Kosacoff, *La industria argentina: desarrollo y cambios estructurales* (Buenos Aires: CEAL, 1989); D. Azpiazu and M. Schorr, *Peronismo y dictadura. Textos inéditos de Oscar Braun* (Buenos Aires: Capital Intelectual, 2009), and *Hecho en Argentina. Industria y economía, 1976–2007* (Buenos Aires: Siglo XXI, 2010); A. Dorfman, *Cincuenta años de industrialización en la Argentina, 1930–1980* (Buenos Aires: Solar, 1983); A. Ferrer, *El devenir de una ilusión. La industria argentina: desde 1930 hasta nuestros días* (Buenos Aires: Sudamericana, 1989); J. Katz and B. Kosacoff, *El proceso de industrialización en la Argentina: evolución, retroceso y prospectiva* (Buenos Aires: CEPAL-CEAL, 1989); B. Kosacoff, *El proceso de industrialización en la Argentina en el período 1976–1983* (Buenos Aires: CEPAL, 1984); J. Schvarzer, *La política económica de Martínez de Hoz* (Buenos Aires: Hyspamérica, 1986); J. Sourrouille, *Política económica y procesos de desarrollo. La experiencia argentina reciente entre 1976 y 1981* (Buenos Aires: CEPAL, 1982); and J. Sourrouille and J. Lucángeli, "Apuntes para la historia reciente de la industria argentina," *Boletín Informativo Techint* no. 219, Buenos Aires, 1980. See also Chapter 5 in this book.

6 National economic groups and foreign conglomerates are business complexes formed by a large number of companies, which are coordinated by a group of executives common to all of them, have the same capital stock, and operate in a range of economic activities, not just in industry. Transnational companies, like their national counterparts (called local independent companies), limit their operations to a single sector. Thus, companies that belong to an economic conglomerate (whether national or foreign) operate according to a business strategy that necessarily takes into account the whole of Argentine economy, and not just a sector of activity, as is the case of the strategy of an industrial firm (national or foreign) that is not part of conglomerate-type business structures. Therefore, there are greater similarities in structure and behavior between national economic groups and foreign conglomerates than between the former and local independent companies, or between the latter and transnational corporations.

TABLE 16.4. *Distribution of branches, companies, employment, and production by level of concentration in Argentine industry, 1973–1984 (absolute values and percentages)*

	Number of branches		Companies		Employment		Production	
	1973	1984	1973	1984	1973	1984	1973	1984
Branches with high concentration[a]	92	94	11.0	10.9	33.6	31.4	47.2	51.8
Branches with medium concentration[b]	55	58	26.4	31.8	30.4	34.4	32.2	30.0
Branches with low concentration[c]	25	20	62.7	57.4	36.1	34.2	20.6	18.1
Total	172	172	100.0	100.0	100.0	100.0	100.0	100.0

[a] Branches in which the top eight companies account for more than 50 percent of total production.
[b] Branches in which the top eight companies account for 25 to 50 percent of total production.
[c] Branches in which the top eight companies account for less than 25 percent of total production.
Source: Prepared by the author based on data from D. Azpiazu, *La concentración en la industria argentina a mediados de los años noventa* (Buenos Aires: FLACSO-Eudeba, 1998), and ECLAC, "Cambios estructurales en la industria argentina. Análisis comparativo de los resultados de los censos industriales de 1974 y 1985," Buenos Aires Office, mimeo, 1988.

concentration (the ones that tend to form the production core of smaller companies) lost two percentage points in their contribution to aggregate production.

Behind the consolidation of a manufacturing structure with a high degree of oligopolization lies another phenomenon closely connected with the national refounding project implemented by the military genocides and their civilian allies: a major reconfiguration of industrial economic power. Table 16.5 shows the leading changes in the makeup of the top members of the industrial business sector between 1976 and 1983 (the 100 largest manufacturing companies by annual sales volumes).

During the period in question, industrial elite companies belonging to national or foreign economic groups significantly increased their relative participation in total sales: whereas in 1976 the two types of companies combined accounted for 40.6 percent of sales, in 1983 they represented 57.9 percent. The other side of this expansion was the contraction experienced by state-owned companies and foreign firms that were not part of economic conglomerates in the domestic market: the former reduced their weight in total sales by 11 percentage points, whereas the latter dropped by almost 7 percentage points.

The loss of participation by public companies is explained by the combination of a reduction in the number of companies in the group of top 100 companies of the sector and a significant transfer of surplus from the state to, primarily, private

TABLE 16.5. *Top members of the industrial business sector. Evolution of the number of companies and of the structure of sales percentages by type of property, 1976–1983 (absolute values, percentages, and percentage points)*

	1976		1983		Variation 1976–1983	
	Companies	Sales	Companies	Sales	Companies	Sales
State	13	34.3	6	23.4	−7	−11.1
EG	22	19.4	32	26.7	+10	+7.3
LIC	13	5.4	12	5.5	−1	0.1
TC	30	19.4	22	12.6	−8	−6.8
FC	21	21.2	26	31.2	+5	+10.0
Assoc.	1	0.3	2	0.7	+1	+0.4
Total	100	100.0	100	100.0	–	–

Key: State = companies owned by the Argentine state; EG = companies owned by a national economic group; LIC = local independent companies (not part of an economic group); TC = transnational corporations (not part of a foreign conglomerate); FC = companies owned by a foreign conglomerate; Assoc. = companies owned by an association of two or more firms.
Source: Prepared by the author based on information from the magazine *Prensa Económica*.

companies belonging to the leading local economic groups, as a result of the increase in physical volume and the drop in relative prices.[7] In the case of transnational corporations, several processes converge, most notably two:

(1) the drop in global sales owing to the crisis in the activities in which these companies had a significant relative weight (as in the case of several metalworking companies, in particular those in the automotive industry); and
(2) the repatriation of foreign capitals that occurred during those years as a result of the deterioration of manufacture (it should be noted that in contrast to foreign companies that became part of business holdings, these companies did not have a multi-sector insertion that would allow them to compensate, at least partially, the drop in the respective production levels in industry).[8]

7 Based on this observation, Azpiazu, Basualdo, and Khavisse conclude: "Several reasons can explain this disparity: there was a direct intention to damage state companies in order to benefit non-state activity, or the aim was to lower the growth rate of inflation by controlling the pressure placed on it by state company prices, combining this policy with an implicit subsidy to the large consumers of the goods, mostly intermediate goods, produced by the state." (D. Azpiazu, E. Basualdo, and M. Khavisse, *El nuevo poder económico*, p. 117).

8 The crisis that began in the early 1980s (see Table 16.3) caused a significant downsizing of industry linked to bankruptcies and suspension of activities in numerous companies, as well as mergers, transfers, and takeovers of companies and production units. This process also involved foreign companies, as

The leading factors that reveal the growing weight of conglomerate forms of ownership (independently of the origin of the capital) within the group of top economic players in manufacture (and, more generally, in the sector as a whole and in Argentine economy) include the following:

- the implementation by their owners of an integration and diversification strategy in line with the process of economic restructure underway, which, among other things, enabled them to participate in the activities that were more profitable during that period, in a stage characterized by significant fluctuations in relative prices (for example, in a form of speculation known as *bicicleta financiera*, or financial bicycle); the transferring of resources from companies with a better economic and financial situation to those with greater financial problems (as was the case of many industrial companies during the most critical moments of the deindustrialization process); and the accessing of differential levels of activity by conducting purchase and sale operations of inputs and/or products between related companies;
- a range of extraordinary benefits obtained from the state, such as the subsidies connected with the promotion of industry, the state procurement policy, the discretional handling of the relative prices of public companies, the peripheral privatizations, and, as of the beginning of the 1980s, the statization of the private external debt and the liquation of the internal debt, and the possibility of gaining increasing shares of the market in various branches through the intense centralization of capital effected in the period analyzed, and the retraction experienced by broad segments of business, especially the smaller and economically weaker companies, which, faced with the abrupt change at the macro- and meso-economic levels, were forced to engage in clearly "defensive" microeconomic behaviors (declaring bankruptcy, closing business, suspending production lines, ending manufacturing activities, and retreating to other economic sectors, etc.).

From then on, the large capitalists mentioned earlier would have enormous power in terms of defining and conditioning the course of the national economy, not only because they owned many of the leading industrial companies, but because they controlled conglomerates of firms that operated in a wide range of sectors of economic activity, thus giving them a decisive influence in the evolution of variables with ostensibly economic and social significance (price levels, relative

many of them, which were leaders in their respective manufacturing sectors, stopped operating in the country or were transferred to other national or foreign capitals (for example, General Motors and Citroën in the automotive industry, Olivetti in office equipment, Duranor in the petrochemical sector, and Sudamtex in the textile industry).

prices, external accounts, investment, fiscal equation, wage and distribution dynamics, etc.). As can be gathered from Table 16.6, a comparison of the *before* (1973) and *after* (1983) of the dictatorial period confirms that many national groups and foreign conglomerates that operated in manufacture increased the number of controlled and associated firms, in some cases considerably (most notably, Pérez Companc, Macri, Bridas, Garovaglio y Zorraquín, Soldati, Techint, Arcor, Alpargatas, Bagó, and Clarín).[9]

Through the evidence analyzed, however, it is not possible to grasp the full extent and depth of the processes of concentration and centralization of capital in the years of state terror. This is because, given the nature of the information used, it is impossible to compute a considerable portion of the surplus appropriated by this class fraction under the consolidation of a process of transition from a strategy of valorization of production based on industry and realized in the domestic market to a strategy structured around financial valorization and strongly oriented toward the foreign sector, from the viewpoint of both the current account and the capital account of the balance of payments.

In the words of Azpiazu, Basualdo, and Khavisse:

> If we analyze where the surplus appropriated by these capitals goes, we will see that a small part was channeled to new investments in production associated, in most cases, with the use of the benefits granted by the state. The bulk of it was channeled,

[9] With respect to the structural progress of these segments of economic power during the dictatorship, Acindar provides an illustrative example in this sense: "The 1980s emerge as one of the most significant decades in the history of Acindar. Despite its productive insertion in a particularly critical context, its oligopolistic consolidation and the internalization of great benefits have enabled it to access a privileged position among the country's top business players. The merger and acquisition of the Gurmendi group, concluded in March 1981, occupy a very prominent place given their implications for the configuration of the steel market. At the start of the decade, Acindar and the companies of the Gurmendi group (Santa Rosa and Genaro Grasso) concentrated a substantial share of the market of steel sheets, competing in some of its segments (non-flat steel with Gurmendi itself; special steels with Santa Rosa; seamed pipes with Genaro Grasso). Although Acindar was already relatively favored by the integration of its production process (Gurmendi acquired billet production from SOMISA), by increased levels of use of its installed capacity, and even by a greater and more diversified presence in the market, the acquisition of its leading competitor and the ensuing restructure of the new complex offered it – as it, in fact, turned out to be the case – almost limitless possibilities with respect to its hegemonic consolidation in the market.... Contemporaneously to its consolidation in the market of non-flat sheets, through acquisitions, the company faced a very difficult financial situation. In this sense, at the end of the fiscal year, on 6/30/1982, the company's external debt was in excess of US$500 million and its total indebtedness represented 1.5 times its net assets. Nonetheless, by then the company had applied for coverage under the exchange insurance regimes that had been established in the country in mid-1981 and that would lead, at the end of 1982, to the statization of private external debt in general, and Acindar's in particular. Likewise, the establishment in mid-1982 of a system of medium-term financing, at regulated – and negative – rates, enabled the firm to liquate most of its liabilities." D. Azpiazu and E. Basualdo, *La siderurgia argentina en el contexto del ajuste, las privatizaciones y el Mercosur* (Buenos Aires: IDEP/ATE, 1995), pp. 94 and 96.

TABLE 16.6. *Number of companies controlled by or associated with the leading national economic groups and foreign conglomerates operating in Argentine industry, 1973, 1983, and 1986–1987 (absolute values)*

Company	1973	1983	1986–1987
Bunge & Born	60	63	87
Pérez Companc	10	54	86
Techint	30	46	53
Bridas	4	43	52
Macri (formerly Fiat)	7	47	51
Garovaglio y Zorraquín	12	41	48
Arcor	5	20	34
Soldati (formerly Brown Boveri)	15	35	34
Corcemar	23	30	31
Werthein	20	29	28
Celulosa Argentina	14	23	23
Astra	18	21	22
Deutsch	8	13	22
Alpargatas	9	24	21
FV-Canteras Cerro Negro	4	19	19
Madanes (Fate-Aluar)	8	15	18
Huancayo-Constantini	2	18	18
Loma Negra (Fortabat)	16	16	16
Massuh	1	10	16
Ledesma	14	15	16
Nougués Hermanos	8	13	16
Intermendoza-Taurales	0	6	15
Laboratorios Bagó	2	14	14
Bagley	6	14	14
San Martín del Tabacal	4	14	14
Bonafide	11	13	14
Clarín	1	12	13
BGH	6	14	13
Grafex	8	14	12
Indupa (formerly Rhodia Richard)	1	9	11
Herman Zupan	3	9	11
Aceros Bragado	3	9	11
Astilleros Alianza	0	9	10
Canale	4	11	8
Noel	0	7	7
Atanor	4	8	0
Schcolnik	3	8	0
Total	344	766	878

Note: Although in the years of reference these groups had a strong presence in industry, it should be noted that, except for very few exceptions, they all had shares in companies that operated in other economic sectors.

Source: Prepared by the author based on M. Acevedo, E. Basualdo, and M. Khavisse, *¿Quién es quién? Los dueños del poder económico (Argentina, 1973–1987)* (Buenos Aires: Editora 12-Pensamiento Jurídico), 1990.

> essentially, to investments in the financial sector, in residential construction, and in other services and goods connected with high-income demand, as these sectors were not affected by the liberalization of the economy. Liberalization also fostered the transfer of surplus abroad, thus internationalizing the expanded reproduction of capital of these dominant fractions. These dynamics of accumulation closely integrated with the international financial market also provided a new indirect form of surplus appropriation: the transferring to the state of a large part of their significant external debt.[10]

During the dictatorship, then, there was a great redistribution of income, from wage-earners to non-wage-earners, operated through the drop in real wages, the deterioration of working conditions, and a savage increase in the rate of exploitation. However, this does not explain all of the changes registered, as among businesses there were sectors that were strongly affected by the socioeconomic crisis in general and the manufacturing crisis in particular (small- and medium-sized businesses), while others benefited (namely the oligopolistic firms, among which there were also significant ruptures that shaped a new industrial economic power). The oligopolistic capitals that controlled few companies and markets and had a scarce degree of integration and/or diversification tended to become less and less important in the sector as a whole, while a small number of large business groups increased their economic power and the control they had over a wide range of markets (not just manufacture). Consequently, the deindustrialization that Argentina suffered in this period cannot be seen as an anti-industrial process, but instead as a heterogeneous process with uneven impacts, as to a great extent the expansion of the new dominant fractions was the result of their maintaining or even increasing their already significant presence in manufacture.

In this respect, it should be highlighted that, based on the strategic objectives sought by the military, the organic intellectuals led by José Alfredo Martínez de Hoz, and the fractions of the dominant class that supported them both, not only was it decisive for the deindustrialization-centered economic restructure to occur under a crisis of considerable magnitude, a significant redefinition of business leaderships, and a drastic alteration of the capital-labor relationship, it was also vital, and for similar reasons, to reshape the structural profile of domestic industry.

From the perspective of these members and representatives of the local dominant sectors, this reshaping had to be effected because of the alleged "inefficiency" of numerous manufacturing branches with respect to the international market and because of the restrictions that, during the import substitution stage, the development of these branches had imposed on agricultural and cattle production and those related to the processing of raw materials. And, more broadly, this was

10 See Azpiazu, Basualdo, and Khavisse, *¿Quién es quién?*, p. 186.

necessary because of the social conditions and the type of political alliances forged by the existence of a dynamic manufacturing industry, which, despite its undeniable limitations and the degree of integration and diversification that characterized it, in the beginning of the 1970s had succeeded in laying down the structural bases to, among other significant matters, start easing the traditional "bottlenecks" of the external sector, with the ensuing benefits in terms of national autonomy.

In view of this characterization, the aim of Martínez de Hoz and his team was to harmonize financial speculation (taking advantage of the enormous liquidity that existed in the international market as a result of the oil shock of the beginning of the decade) with the expansion of the agricultural and cattle, fishery, energy, and mining sectors, as well as some industrial activities highly connected with the use of the abundant – and strongly concentrated in terms of ownership – domestic wealth of natural resources. All of this was done according to the principle of static comparative advantages, whereby each country should specialize in those goods whose production was less costly for them (it was argued, with no empirical basis, that exploiting these advantages "had done the country much good" during the agro-export model that had been in place from 1880 to 1930, approximately, and hence it followed that "history should be repeated").[11] In the words of the economy minister himself, economic liberalization – both trade and financial liberalization – would enable "not only competition but a greater specialization in efficiency and making the best of the advantages of the modern international division of labor."[12]

Thus, along with the considerable absolute and relative shrinkage of the sector, another of the critical legacies of the economic program of the military dictatorship was a marked re-primarization of manufacture and an ostensible "simplification of production" derived from the weakening and/or destruction of strategic focal centers of industry.

In this sense, while the widespread instability of industrial markets, favored by the intensity of the permanent changes in the structure of relative prices resulting from the

[11] The position expressed by the company Acindar in the *Prensa Económica* yearbook of 1979 is illustrative of this: "To modify the situation that existed [before the coup] it was necessary to change the direction that had been followed until then with such unfortunate results, and abandon the essentially redistributionist closed economy of import substitution, and move to an open economy that would enable Argentina to recover the relative position it had at other times in international commerce, far from the faded and almost humiliating place in the Third World troupe."

[12] Extract of a speech delivered by Martínez de Hoz at the opening ceremony of the First Conference on Industrial Modernization, held on November 17, 1980. On such interpretations of the theory of comparative advantages, Olivera aptly notes: "It is evident, then, that those who pass judgment on the inefficiency of our industries by simply comparing their real costs with those in other countries apply ... colonial commerce principles and not international commerce principles." J. Olivera, *Economía clásica actual* (Buenos Aires: Macchi, 1977), p. 77.

various political measures implemented, emerges as a common denominator of their development in the 1976–1983 period, the evidence available reveals:

(1) a marked retraction of several of the activities that had been the driving force of manufacturing growth during the different stages of the import substitution model, with the presence of a considerable number of small- and medium-sized companies (in various fields of production, including textile and garment, wood and furniture, metalworking in general, and capital goods); and
(2) a better relative performance of agro-industries and cellulose and paper, chemical products, nonmetallic minerals and basic metal processing sectors, where the economic groups that moved into the central position of the local economic power bloc had a very important share, and were at the same time the pivots of the process of expanded accumulation and reproduction of capital at the industrial level.

In other words, the industrial structure furthered specialized in branches located at the first stages of the manufacturing process, which produced commodities that were scarcely dynamic in the global market and were characterized by a high capital-labor ratio per output unit, by the predominance of greatly concentrated market structures (with a prominent role of companies associated with the *new economic power*), and by being closely connected to the production of raw materials and/or benefiting from the industrial promotion regimes implemented during this stage.

This process contrasts with what happened in many countries of the periphery, which during these years applied active and sustained policies of promotion and protection of industries considered by government authorities to be priority activities and of strategic importance; activities that, for the most part and not by chance, would become the most promising and dynamic "routes" of international commerce of manufactured goods in the coming years. Meanwhile in Argentina, sectors with enormous potential were undermined, sectors that moreover had a certain degree of development, which, although still incipient in some cases, was not negligible considering, among other things, their short "maturing history" and the dimensions of the domestic market (such as, for example, consumer and industrial electronics).

In this framework, the re-primarization of industry and the deindustrialization process effected during the emergence of the "financial valorization model" were the *initial kickoff* for Argentina's relative lag vis-à-vis developed countries and several of the countries of the periphery. This trend will be intensified under the democratic government that followed the dictatorship, accompanying the consolidation of globalization.[13]

[13] With regard to these issues, see H. Nochteff, "¿Del industrialismo al postindustrialismo? Las desigualdades entre economías. Observaciones preliminares," (2000) 172 *Realidad Económica*, Buenos Aires, pp. 11–31.

CONCLUSIONS

The military that took power by force in March 1976 and their civilian support bases set out to "solve" the problems inherent to the import substitution model or, in the words of Fernando Fajnzylber, opted to confront industrialization "by questioning its existence going back to bygone forms of international division of labor."[14] This, as part of a "political project of a higher order" that sought to drastically alter the structural foundations that under the import substitution scheme had enabled economic and industrial growth and its correlation in various political expressions of the popular sectors with a manifestly nonconformist and/or challenging tone toward capitalist relations of production.

In this context, in the early 1980s a clear "map" of winners and losers could be traced in manufacture, in terms of both sectors and economic players. This map was the result of the profound changes effected in Argentina's economy and society by, essentially, the various political (not just economic) measures imposed *through fire and sword* between 1976 and 1983.[15]

Thus, the main "legacies" that the nascent democracy would receive include:

- a new operating scheme for domestic capitalism that, founded as it was on a different insertion of the country in the international economy, would place the manufacturing sector in a very different place from what it had occupied in the mid-1970s;
- an acute process of deindustrialization and regressive restructuring of industry, having a correlation in a significant distancing of many manufacturing segments from the "international frontier" and the intensification of old problems (external restriction, technological dependency, etc.), which were taken to extreme levels;
- highly concentrated and centralized economic power, with a cycle of expanded accumulation and reproduction of increasingly diversified and

[14] See Fajnzylber, *La industrialización trunca*, p. 195.

[15] It was only in September 1980, on Industry Day and as the economic crisis was starting to impact some large companies, that critical voices against the economic policy and its effects on manufacture were heard from the Argentine Industrial Union (under control of the government) (J. Schvarzer, *Empresarios del pasado. La Unión Industrial Argentina* [Buenos Aires: Imago Mundi, 1991]). These critical opinions naturally did not include any mention of the scheme of winners and losers resulting from the drastic restructuring of manufacture underway. Up until that point, a "radio silence" had prevailed among big industry, with few exceptions. In this sense, in its Annual Report and General Balance Sheet of 1979–1980, Dalmine-Siderca, a company of the Techint economic group, one of the most favored by the dictatorship, observed, "Argentine industry faces artificially disadvantageous conditions with respect to foreign industry, which, if they were to continue – such as in the case of the exchange lag – , threaten to substantially reduce its profitability and compromise its financial position."

transnationalized capital (in industrial terms, very focused on the processing of natural resources), with a decisive structural capacity for conditioning economic and sociopolitical processes (veto power);

- a considerably more limited number of small- and medium-sized companies that are also enormously weakened in structural terms (which would greatly condition their "margins of action" from then on); and
- a working class submerged in unemployment, casualization of work, fragmentation, low wages, and a very reduced participation in national income.

In other words, these legacies represented the *success* of the refounding and social disciplining project that the military dictators and certain fractions of the dominant sectors of Argentina sought to implement when they took over the government in March 1976.

From this analysis, it can be concluded that these fractions not only supported the dictatorship politically, ideologically, and conceptually, they were also the sectors that most benefited economically from it. These are issues that will necessarily have to be considered when reflecting on the civilian component of the last dictatorship.

17

The Complicity of Agricultural Business Chambers

Mario Rapoport and Alfredo Zaiat

Three reflections are prompted by the overthrow of the democratic government on March 24, 1976 and the complicity of the leading agricultural institutions. First, it was a civilian-military coup in which these entities were actively involved. Second, the dictatorship that emerged from the coup was not something that materialized overnight. As Federico Pinedo, with his characteristic frankness, defined the fall of Hipólito Yrigoyen in the 1930s: "It was not lightning on a sunny day." It was the result of a long preparation that gradually corroded the government through the media and political opposition. Third, the slogan of the Argentine Rural Society (Sociedad Rural Argentina, SRA), "To cultivate the ground is to serve the nation," would be taken literally. The "nation" was the agriculture and cattle sector trampled by industrialization and populism. These two factors had jeopardized not only their interests but also – as they saw it – the interests of the whole of society, which they intended to "save" with the support of the military: on the one hand, to wipe out once and for all any kind of popular movements and their leadership; on the other, to re-primarize the economy.

The entities representing agriculture launched an active mobilization plan against the democratic government as early as the start of 1975. As they had announced in mid-1974, the SRA, the Rural Confederations of Argentina (Confederaciones Rurales Argentinas, CRA), and the Agricultural Inter-Cooperative Confederation Limited (Confederación Intercooperativa Agropecuaria Limitada, CONINAGRO) formed a Committee for Agricultural Action and called a twenty-four-hour lockout in the meat market for March 3, 1975. Their demands included the liberalization of the sector's prices, which were considered "political" prices. Two months later, the Argentine Agrarian Federation (Federación Agraria Argentina, FAA) and the CRA staged an agricultural strike on May 19, 20, and 21, which had a high degree of participation and led Economy Minister Alfredo Gómez Morales to stand down. Steep oil prices coupled with a fall in the terms of trade triggered a crisis of the balance of payments that, compounded with disputes with the labor movement, the acceleration of inflation, and, lastly, recession, precipitated the minister's resignation. He was replaced by Celestino Rodrigo.

At the traditional rural show held every year by the SRA, following the *Rodrigazo*, the president of the Rural Society, Celedonio Pereda, declared that the country was suffering a severe crisis as a result of the policies implemented by the Peronist government, and he called for the liberalization of the economy. From his point of view, Argentina was

> suffering a crisis that was economic, social, and political, but which also has deep moral roots. The country must not and cannot make any more mistakes. It cannot continue with these pitiful collectivist experiences that only lead us to general impoverishment. The economy must be set in motion through free enterprise, respecting property and individual incentives.[1]

For the representative body of large landholders, the economic policy of the Peronist government, which they saw as attacking free enterprise and generating low profitability, was

> an excellent breeding ground for the development of extremist ideas; there is evidence of subversive penetration among small and medium-sized producers, through bodies that constitute the political wings of extremism.[2]

The demand for increased profitability in the sector was associated with the "war against subversion" waged by the armed forces.

In September 1975, José Alfredo Martínez de Hoz presented the high military commands with an economic plan to be implemented in the event of their taking power, which he had been working on with his team over the previous three months.[3]

Celedonio Pereda, for his part, met with Antonio Cafiero to insist that the peso be devaluated to adjust the exchange lag with respect to domestic costs, and to demand a sharp turnabout in agricultural policy. These requests were made against a backdrop of active mobilization by the agricultural business associations, which had called on their members to suspend meat sales from September 19 to 29. In this context, the most active was the CRA, a third-tier entity that among other federations represented the Confederation of Rural Associations of Buenos Aires and La Pampa (Confederación de Asociaciones Rurales de Buenos Aires y La Pampa, CARBAP), with a more prominent role and an increasingly greater presence than the SRA (which had not participated actively in the September lockout) as the CRA had

1 SRA, *Memoria*, 1975.
2 Ibid., 1976.
3 See the testimony given by economist Jorge Gaggero in M. Rapoport and A. Zaiat, *Historia de la economía argentina del siglo XX* (Buenos Aires: Página/12, 2007), p. 586.

adopted a much tougher and more confrontational position toward the government. In an interview, Jorge Aguado, president of CARBAP, revealed the confederation's clearly coupist intentions:

> What we have in the country is not a coup d'état but a state of coup. And this situation stems from the government itself.... There are political elements that interfere in the national context. This is due primarily to the political participation of entities of a different nature, such as the CGT [General Confederation of Workers] and the CGE [General Economic Confederation], although I am not sure if the latter is as politically involved now as it was some time ago.[4]

The CRA came to fill a vacuum of representation in response to large rural landholders (especially from the humid Pampas region), who accused the SRA of answering to business interests, for which agriculture was only one of many investments.

The conflict in business intensified on October 24 when the CRA and the FAA staged an agricultural lockout that would last eighteen days, claiming that "no steps had been taken toward recognizing the right of the agricultural business associations to participate in the design of the country's economic policy."[5]

For Aguado, this measure by rural business associations was not only aimed at defending sectorial interests, as they also faced a risk of "destruction of the Argentine nationality and being." The pressure action reflected, in his opinion, the emergence of a "national spirit" that would confront "alien political and economic philosophies ... that promise happiness without work and at the expense of others."[6]

According to CARBAP, this destabilizing agitation was a way of building a prosperous future, as the "agitation we live today must lead to a civilized peace tomorrow and the time we devote now to this arid struggle waged by business associations in defense of the rights and interests of all will enable us to achieve, in the not so distant future, a thoroughly just and free reality."[7]

The head of CARBAP heralded what was about to come:

> It is the men who form part of the [state] institutions who must save them, so that they can in turn save the Republic, but if those men do not act according to the true national interest as members of the institutions, nobody can be surprised if both the government and the legislative, political, business or trade union associations disappear crushed under the weight of their own incompetence or uselessness.[8]

4 *El Cronista Comercial*, October 13, 1975.

5 See G. Sanz Cerbino, "Los golpistas. Las acciones de CARBAP, antes y después del golpe de 1976," paper presented at the conference Primeras Jornadas Internacionales de Investigación y Debate Político, Buenos Aires, 2008, pp. 8–9.

6 Ibid.

7 J. R. Aguado, *Cuatro años de acción gremial* (Buenos Aires: CARBAP, 1977), p. 216.

8 Ibid., p. 244.

On March 24, 1976, the coup d'état that established the bloodiest military dictatorship in the history of Argentina was staged. The leading business associations supported the overthrow of the government of María Estela "Isabel" Martínez de Perón. The rural business organizations were not placed under government control and welcomed the new de facto government, although with various degrees of intensity. The SRA greeted its arrival and looked forward to Argentina's reincorporation to the "greatness it was destined for." In its message of congratulations to the new president, Jorge Rafael Videla, the SRA offered to collaborate wherever it may be needed and recognized that Videla "and all other officers of the Army, Navy, and Air Force have taken on the difficult mission of turning Argentine decadence around."[9]

As soon as the dictatorial government had taken power, the SRA issued an unusual number of greeting letters to government officials, thus evidencing that among the authorities there was a great number of members of the association or connected with it.[10]

One of the most important of these letters was the one addressed to the minister of the economy and member of the SRA, Martínez de Hoz, who was described as "knowledgeable in all matters connected not only with the economy but also with agriculture, and the best guarantee that now more than ever the interests of the country will be thoroughly defended."[11]

Another welcoming letter was sent to the new agriculture and cattle secretary, Mario Antonio Cadenas Madariaga, a member of the SRA who was considered a "notable agricultural economist and also a producer, who will no doubt discharge his duties in the manner the country deserves and with great benefits for agriculture."[12]

Other members greeted by the SRA included Jorge Zorreguieta, undersecretary of agriculture, Raúl P. Salaberren, minister of the economy of the province Buenos Aires, and Juan M. Ocampo, president of the state bank Banco Nación. This active presence of the SRA in the government of the military dictatorship, the personal links of many top government officials with the directors of the agricultural business associations, and their common social and ideological background led the upper agrarian bourgeoisie to believe that their traditional demands would now be answered.

From his position at CARBAP, Jorge Aguado was also very optimistic in his reception of the new government and called on producers to offer it their collaboration.[13] He recognized that "the Argentine Armed Forces have assumed

[9] SRA, *Memoria*, 1976.

[10] See, M.L. Palomino, *Tradición y poder: la Sociedad Rural Argentina, 1955–1983* (Buenos Aires: CISEA-Gel, 1988), p. 154.

[11] SRA, *Memoria*, 1976.

[12] Ibid., 1976.

[13] See, Sanz Cerbino, "Los golpistas," p. 12.

their responsibility of taking power to prevent the continuation of a government that, through its incompetence and immorality, was plunging the country into a profound social, economic, and political crisis."[14]

CARBAP also contributed officers to fill executive positions in the military government, including its second vice president, Jorge Girardo, who was appointed minister of agrarian affairs for the province of Buenos Aires in 1976, and Jorge Aguado himself, who served as national minister of agriculture under the government of General Roberto Viola, and later, during the Leopoldo Galtieri and Reynaldo Bignone periods, as governor of the province of Buenos Aires.

It is not surprising, then, that as the right to strike was banned and trade unions and many business associations were placed under government control, the agricultural sector achieved almost all of its goals in terms of prices, trade, and taxes, and the bodies that represented the sector had a prominent participation in the decisions that affected it.[15]

The FAA, for its part, adopted a more moderate and defensive attitude with respect to the policies of the military dictatorship, as the government excluded cooperatives and the FAA from the design of the new agricultural policy. This was later made evident when these organizations were left out of the export quotas for some agricultural products, as well as by the persecution that some of its leaders would suffer.[16] The de facto government also imposed restrictions on the institutional operation of the FAA, through the Professional Associations Act (Law 21,356), which undermined its capacity to organize and mobilize in representation of the interests of its members.

This body, which was headed by Humberto Volando, advocated the idea of "land for those who work it" and viewed with concern the economic team's intention – later implemented – to amend the rural leasing and sharecropping law by reducing the legal term of lease agreements. With respect to the commercialization of production, while it recognized that its liberalization was meant to solve problems of the past, it also saw it as entailing serious risks of concentration by a small handful of national and international corporations. Consequently, it suggested that the government adopt a policy of "complementation of the state and the economic organizations representing producers, such as the cooperatives."[17]

Despite this distancing with respect to substantial aspects of the official policy, the FAA approved the price liberalization policy for agricultural products and

[14] Aguado, *Cuatro años*, p. 251.

[15] See H. Verbitsky, *La mano izquierda de Dios* (Buenos Aires: Sudamericana, 2010).

[16] See, J. A. Pierri, *Sector externo, política agraria y entidades del agro pampeano, 1960–1986: la Sociedad Rural Argentina y la Federación Agraria Argentina*, Master's thesis, FCE-UBA, Buenos Aires (2004), p. 127.

[17] FAA, LXIV Congreso Ordinario Anual de la FAA, 1976, p. 23.

maintained that "the already lowered export tariffs and the public commitment to permanently eliminate them encourages us to think that we are going in the right direction."[18] Neither did it spare compliments for the armed forces in its "war against subversion":

> A murderous terrorism has long been assailing the entire community of Argentina and implicating it in what has rightly been called a "dirty war." For several years now, the FAA has been using its forums to anathematize terrorism and alerting the rural community and public opinion of the dangers of indifference.... Our most emphatic repudiation of the anarchic violence that seeks to force upon us a world without God, without Nation, and without human dignity, and which by force we must combat. Our most sincere tribute to the forces of order that have offered up their lives for a higher ideal and continue to risk them every day.[19]

On April 2, 1976, Martínez de Hoz launched the economic plan of the military dictatorship, whose main goal was to restore the political and economic power of the upper agrarian bourgeoisie and the large economic and financial groups by undermining local industry and the domestic market, which constituted the support base from which the labor movement and the associated business community derived their strength. To do that, it had to raise the level of efficiency of the national economy by recovering the role of the market in the allocation of resources and limiting the participation of the state.

The increased efficiency would be accompanied by a focus on making the most of the comparative advantages of the country's production system, which would entail specializing in products with the greatest demand in foreign markets, such as agricultural commodities, and sacrificing all other industries.[20] The economic team believed that the results of this policy would be lower inflation and equilibrium in the balance of payments.

Agriculture occupied a predominant place in the strategy devised by Martínez de Hoz, who came from a traditional landed family and had addressed the problems of the sector in a book that contained a historical analysis and proposals for agricultural development. Thus, in his first speech he declared, "agricultural policy constitutes a fundamental chapter of our strategy, which aims to maximize the possibilities offered by the country in that area." In that way, shortly after taking office, the minister imposed a progressive reduction of export tariffs or fees (*retenciones*), which by 1978 would be completely eliminated, while the activity of the National Grain Board (Junta Nacional de Granos) was reduced to a minimum.[21]

18 Ibid., p. 24.
19 LXIV Congreso, pp. 28–29.
20 M. Rapoport, *Historia económica, política y social de la Argentina (1880–2003)* (Buenos Aires: Emecé, 2012, 5th ed.), p. 646.
21 Ibid., pp. 692–694.

Producers responded immediately, and production started to grow and continued growing almost uninterruptedly until 1983 (from 1975 to 1983 it grew by 42 percent), generating high profits. However, the agricultural sector was also touched by the evolution of key macroeconomic variables, the financialization of the economy, and the appreciation of the exchange rate. Even so, the greater volume produced and sold, along with the reduction in costs owing to the elimination of export tariffs and the deterioration of rural working conditions, enabled higher savings margins (with savings going from US$2.599 billion in 1972 to U$4.266 billion in 1978). Consequently, when, as of 1978, financial investments yielded much higher returns due to the revaluation and the rise in interest rates, investments in production registered a permanent contraction and agricultural surpluses began to be channeled massively to speculation.[22]

The SRA approved the criteria and objectives of the economic plan with the argument that boosting agricultural production would benefit the country in general. At the Annual Rural Show in Palermo, which was attended by dictator Videla, Celedonio Pereda described how the plan was in line with the liberal values of the institution:

> The economic program determines that the role of the State in the national economy is based on the principle of subsidiarity, that private enterprise is the true engine that moves all of the economy and that the State must only act in this field in a way that is complementary and subsidiary to the individual and intermediate social organizations. This is the same conception that is adopted by the social doctrine of the Church.[23]

Martínez de Hoz's program coincided with the SRA in its assessment of the origins of the economic crisis of that period. Such origins were to be found in the operation of the import substitution industrialization model, based – according to the SRA – on

> an overprotected industry, bulwarked by very high tariffs, which in many cases … enjoys the privilege of import bans on what it manufactures. This confinement, fear of competing, insecurity of business operators, which began as a response to the crisis of 1930, rested … on an economic philosophy that advocated autarchy at any price; anything produced in the country had to be supported for that condition alone, without questioning the cost of that substitution. … However, not everything could be substituted and some things had to be bought abroad: raw materials, equipment, technology, fuels, etc. Agriculture was not stimulated and it suffered a regression; industry was in no condition to export, and the country had to face recurring crises due to a lack of foreign currency.[24]

22 Data from the BCRA (Banco Central de la República Argentina) and the BAC (Banco de Análisis y Computación).

23 SRA, *Memoria*, 1977.

24 Ibid.

Its common interests with the government did not prevent the SRA from expressing its dissent on some measures that it considered moved away from the initial precepts of the economic program. The first demands in this sense had to do with the government's attempt to apply a land tax and the project to extend the VAT to agricultural production in 1978. Large agricultural producers and landowners opposed these tax increases but for very different reasons than those put forward by the FAA.

In the SRA's view, the state had not assumed its subsidiary role with respect to the economy and, instead, continued increasing public spending, expanding its spheres of participation, and in that way pressuring price levels. Instead of sticking to the program's objectives, the economic team was intent on putting greater tax pressure on agricultural business. For that reason, as a representative of large landholders, the association made its demands known to the military dictatorship, reminding it that:

> The government has made a major effort to guide the economy toward normal channels. Its achievements with respect to inflation are less significant than with respect to the foreign sector; unproductive public spending has not evolved favorably; the state's exaggerated interventionism has not been attacked with sufficient zeal.... The country must correct the distortions caused by thirty-five years of socialism.[25]

Despite having their sectorial interests affected, the SRA privileged the points it had in common with the military government in terms of program and ideological orientation. The association celebrated the measures adopted by the military junta that were in line with its anti-state liberal values, such as the elimination of price ceilings, export tariffs, multiple exchange rates, and the monopoly held by the National Grain Board, the abolition of export quotas, the reform of the meat law, the liberalization of the exchange and financial markets, the repealing of the rent law and the amendment of the lease law, the reduction of import tariffs, and the tendency to privatize companies.[26]

Similarly, Aguado celebrated the eradication of state commercialization monopolies and the elimination of price controls, and – while recognizing the need for certain corrections in economic policy – he expressed his optimism with respect to the path taken by the military government, and called on his organization's members to continue with their overall support of the Process of National Reorganization.[27]

Ideologically and politically, the military dictatorship had in the SRA one of its leading allies. On the first anniversary of the coup, the association published a paid ad in the press that read:

25 Ibid., 1978.
26 See Palomino, *Tradición y poder*, p. 165.
27 See, Sanz Cerbino, "Los golpistas," p. 12.

> A year ago today the country was grappling with the deepest crisis it has ever seen in its history. Corruption, lack of authority, misgovernment, and crime as political means were the leading features of that situation. In the economy, rampant inflation and fiscal chaos had become intolerable. We were at the brink of suspension of payments; in sum, the country was falling apart. At that point, we were all willing to do anything to have our life and property minimally guaranteed, to be able to breathe fresh air again. It was in such critical circumstances that the Armed Forces took the reins of the country with patriotic determination, to prevent it from collapsing completely. Their taking over the government was supported by all.... The unpatriotic and brutal guerrillas, to a large extent protected by previous authorities, have suffered harsh blows and are retreating fast. Now they attack the country from outside, through leftist press media, cynically abusing the term human rights, which they never respected.... We must dismantle the structure created by thirty-five years of slow but systematic socializing statization, which has ultimately shown its failure by impoverishing us all and by not bearing the fruits that some eager, confused, or mistaken sectors expected from its implementation. This process demands the support and sacrifice of all sectors, a sacrifice that must be made not only by business and labor, but in particular by the state, setting the example through budget realignment, which has already begun, the liquidation of state companies, and the downsizing of bureaucracy... Let us look back to March 24, 1976 and compare the situation we have today with the situation we had then, let us recall similar stages and we will see that past experiences indicate the inadvisability of demagogic attitudes, of prematurely granting greater political freedom, which can hamper or delay the country's effective recovery in every order. The Argentine Rural Society reiterates to producers and citizens in general its support for any action tending to complete the process that began on March 24, 1976, to thus attain the goals set out, which are ultimately the great objectives of the nation.[28]

The question of greater political freedom was an extremely important issue for the SRA, given the disputes that existed in early 1980 between the military faction dubbed *aperturistas* (favorable to a political opening) and the faction that was against holding elections to end the dictatorship. The SRA believed that, in order to discuss a transition to democracy, the armed forces first had to generate conditions that would ensure that there would be "no return to the ignominious past" that had required their intervention. For the association, the Process of National Reorganization was "an irreversible historical and political process," which could not admit any steps back, and whose historical mission lay in "reorganizing the Republic." The Process emerged from "a painful war" that had been imposed as "an absolute imperative, as the very Nation was at mortal risk."[29] The large landowners also believed that

[28] *La Nación* (Buenos Aires), March 24, 1977.

[29] SRA, *Memoria*, 1981.

the country could not go back to a traditional system of representation by the very political parties that had, in their opinion, been responsible for the crisis.

The persisting deterioration of the agricultural sector, and in particular the serious crisis faced by cattle-raising activities, reached acute levels and triggered criticisms from all of the sector's business entities. The SRA continued to see state intervention as the source of all problems and blamed the de facto government for not insisting

> enough on the need to reduce public spending and the state's participation in the economy. Neither do we see an emphatic attack on inflation. The advisability of giving the Central Bank full independence from political powers must be considered.[30]

In particular, the SRA attacked the new "attempt to control prices" and the slow progress in privatizing public assets that led the state to become heavily indebted and at the same time pressured local interest rates. It also expressed its discontent with what it claimed was a heavy tax burden and strong financial pressure, which resulted in insufficient margins for agricultural production. The SRA warned that any "departure" from the original philosophy behind the Process could awaken ghosts of the past, as "the enemy lost the battle in Argentina but is active around the world and looking to come back."[31]

Nonetheless, the SRA knew who defended its interests and clearly sided with them. When General Viola replaced Videla as head of the dictatorial government, in March 1981, Lorenzo Sigaut was appointed economy minister. Sigaut implemented measures to abandon the *tablita* exchange scheme, caused a sharp devaluation of the peso, reduced import tariffs slightly, and temporarily increased export tariffs.[32] The SRA expressed its confidence in the new administration and its capacity to mitigate the economic crisis, although it had some objections regarding the imposition of export tariffs:

> They are not part of our philosophy, but in the difficult moment that the country is going through, we accept them even though we do not agree on their advisability. To date, the ideas adopted in March 1976 have, unfortunately, not been implemented in the sense of reversing the statizing policy of the past decades.[33]

As of mid-1980, the CRA had been criticizing the official policy, as inflation was eroding the purchasing power of producers, while the financial costs of production increased and fiscal pressure intensified for the sector. For its part, the CONINAGRO

[30] Ibid., 1981.
[31] Ibid., 1981.
[32] See Rapoport, *Historia económica*, p. 672.
[33] SRA, *Memoria*, 1982.

leadership focused its criticism on the exchange policy and the overvaluation of the peso, which hampered agricultural production.

The most heated complaints, however, were raised by the FAA. In 1981, this body declared its opposition to the government:

> Five years have gone by, a much longer time than the constitutional government had, and, in economic terms, there are so few who can claim we have progressed that it is very difficult to find them. The economic system that governs us has failed utterly and the nation's productive apparatus stands in painful testimony to that failure.[34]

The FAA abandoned the discourse that questioned specific aspects of the economic policy for an open criticism of the overall model implemented by Martínez de Hoz, which it considered a revenge against small producers:

> It has been four years of an agricultural policy that condenses arbitrariness and resentment, because the voice of the real producers was ignored, and, instead, an apparatus of ongoing economic aggression was mounted, targeting former tenants, shareholders, and laborers who in past years had the unpardonable audacity of becoming small landholders. It is, without a doubt, the great revenge.[35]

At the end of 1980, the FAA and other entities that represented small- and medium-sized landholders gathered to form the National Business Call (Convocatoria Nacional Empresaria, CONAE), an organization with a position contrary to the economic policy of the government. The government accused its members of being "subversives, communists, and developmentalists," and the president of the FAA, Humberto Volando, was summoned by the ministry of the interior and warned about the actions of the body he represented.

The FAA continued with its criticism, attacking the tax policy and the new measures implemented by Sigaut. It denounced that, given the structure in place to commercialize agricultural production, the devaluations of the peso in 1981 had failed to improve the profitability of producers as the bulk of agricultural income was captured by the large intermediary companies. Consequently, the Federation called for the establishment of minimum prices that would ensure a decent income for producers.

Economic conditions were increasingly worse and the dictatorship was beginning to fall apart. The military junta tried to regain legitimacy by embarking on a war to recover the Malvinas/Falkland Islands. The SRA, forgetting its old ties to the British

34 Quoted in Pierri, *Sector externo*, pp. 132–133.
35 FAA, *Memorias*, 1981.

metropolis, issued a statement on April 2, 1982, the day the junta declared war on Great Britain, in which it stated:

> We are filled with patriotic satisfaction at the prospect of returning the Malvinas to the nation's territory, through the direct action of the Armed Forces … and we exhort producers to redouble their efforts, and thus lend their support to the action of the arms of the Nation, with sacrifice, generosity, and efficiency.[36]

The SRA lent the armed forces its facilities in Palermo to be used as a rations post, and the president of the association, Horacio Gutiérrez, traveled to the islands with an official party to attend the inauguration ceremony of the new military governor. Even as it supported the war, the SRA cynically continued to criticize the military government for its lack of "liberality" and the continued presence of the state in the economy.[37]

> There is a belief that the current situation (described as a "grave crisis") is the result of a free market policy adopted as of 1976. That is a mistake. Despite that sensation of freedom, controls were present. The import avalanche was not due to a genuine and real economic liberalization but to the lag in exchange parity caused by the Central Bank. The solution is in eliminating these controls.[38]

The reaction of the FAA to the Malvinas/Falklands war was the complete opposite of the SRA's, as the FAA viewed it as a desperate attempt by the government to recover internal support, calling on everyone "to forget the past and take each other by the hand. Exploiting our emotional spirit, it resorts to appealing to our feelings to cover, with silence and concealment, the very serious events that were happening up until only yesterday." Economically, they accused "Martínez de Hoz and his 'boys,' Alsogaray, Ricardo Zinn, Benegas Lynch, Alemann, and others," of seeking, through privatizations, to "do away with companies and bodies that are part of the nation's wealth," so that the FAA declared its complete disagreement with the economic policy of the military dictatorship. At the same time, it criticized the other agricultural business associations for their complacency with the military government: "Unfortunately, in the initial years of this last 'process' our organization was virtually alone in its criticism and struggles."[39]

The defeat in the Malvinas/Falklands war, then, paved the way for a process of transition toward the reestablishment of the system of democratic institutions. The SRA was confident that the new democratic government would enable the dismantling of the "statizing" policies, a dismantling that the military dictatorship

36 SRA, *Memoria*, 1982.

37 See Palomino, *Tradición y poder*, p. 167.

38 SRA, *Memoria*, 1982.

39 FAA, *Memorias*, 1984.

had not furthered. Paradoxically, while the dictatorship had failed to restore order, according to statements by the SRA, society had now reached the necessary maturity to take on such a task:

> It is necessary for us to detain our course and embark on the full recovery of our condition as a free society, reversing the statizing tendencies, so that we can position ourselves in the world as a civilized and progressive nation.... The future constitutional government must restore order.[40]

Or more exactly, "fix the disorder" left by the military dictatorship that many had sponsored. With its task completed, there was no longer any need for the dictatorship, but the neoliberal state had to continue with the liberalization of the economy, increasing the external debt, and selling the vast majority of the public assets that existed, which was what it would do in the 1990s. Thus, despite the fact that the convertibility would entail a new exchange appreciation, the authorities of the SRA did not protest much, as their members were busy with other financial businesses. It was only later, when a popular government tried to raise export tariffs, that the agricultural business associations reacted together in outrage to protect their huge agricultural profits, which they consider sacred. The slogan then became: "To grow soy is to serve the nation."

[40] SRA, *Memoria*, 1983.

PART VII

Illegal Appropriation of Companies

18

Organized Pillaging

Federico Delgado

The aim of this chapter is modest and of an exploratory nature. It seeks to give an account of the connections and patterns of behavior arising from several closed judicial proceedings[1] on *the particularist use of the state during the military dictatorship*. I use the term "commercialization of terror" here to describe how political power was used to do business under the general plan to reform society by fire and sword.[2] Or, more simply put: organized pillaging. In this chapter, I generally and briefly present some social groups – which are in some way related with economic activities – that provided ideological support to the regime and later occupied strategic government positions. This is followed by an account of the criminal features of an institutional dynamic that was repeated in cases in which business groups were dismantled.[3] The chapter closes with some conclusions.

Civilian complicity with the coup was investigated under court case No. 12,071/07.[4] The investigation failed, but the case provides evidence of the so-called Perriaux Group, a heterogeneous ensemble that succeeded in transforming – in symbolic terms – its own individual interests into general interests, and to position them in the institutions that embody the state. This group essentially blamed the country's problems on the import substitution policies applied in economic matters

[1] The information cited is drawn from old court files that, for the most part, are being used as evidence in criminal proceedings currently underway.

[2] On the importance of incorporating economic crimes committed during the authoritarian regimes into the agenda of transitional justice, see R. Carranza, "Plunder and Pain: Should Transitional Justice Engage with Corruption and Economic Crimes?" (2008) *International Journal of Transitional Justice*, 310–330.

[3] This description is limited to those cases for which information was available from federal courts of the city of Buenos Aires. Although more cases are known to exist, they are not included here as they could not be analyzed for this study. See a more extensive analysis in L. Filippini and A. Cavana, "Responsabilidad empresarial e terrorismo de Estado na Argentina" (2012) 6 *Revista Anistia Política e Justiga de Transigão*, 316–351.

[4] Brought in the Fourth Federal Court, Court Office No. 8 (Juzgado Federal no. 4, Secretaría no. 8).

and the redistributive policies applied in social matters. This judicial proceeding, then, provides useful information on the nature of the characters that operated as a sort of think tank of that time and who occupied important government positions after March 1976. These characters include Guillermo Walter Klein, Adolfo Diz, Alejandro Estrada, Manuel Solanet, Roberto Durrieu, Alberto Rodríguez Varela, Jaime Smart, and Raúl Salaberry, among others. The statization of Compañía Ítalo Argentina de Electricidad (CIAE), an electric power company, is perhaps the best example of the group's work, as in this case the ministry of the economy appears subordinated to the private interests of the officials in charge of the area.[5]

Another judicial proceeding that is connected with the above is the Comisión Nacional de Responsabilidad Patrimonial (CONAREPA) case.[6] Section 2(e) of the first document and section 2 of the second document (the *actas*) of the military junta that held de facto power as of 1976, dated June 18, 1976 and February 3, 1977, respectively, established a mechanism for identifying "the behavior of individuals responsible for damaging the higher interests of the Nation" and for "prohibiting individuals and legal persons from administrating and disposing of their property." Law 21,670 regulated the application of this measure, which – in broad terms – required individuals under suspicion to prove that their assets were legitimate. If they failed to prove the legitimacy of any assets, the procedure in place stipulated that such property was to be transferred to the state without compensation for the owner. A National Commission for Asset Responsibility (CONAREPA) was created under Decree 3245/77 as the implementation body, and given broad powers to investigate the makeup of assets of any individuals or legal persons considered suspects.

CONAREPA was a mask of sorts for identifying individuals who would be targeted by the particularist facet of the regime, which was translated into the economic exploitation of terror. Its distinctive feature was its arbitrariness. It became an iron cage in which government officials, acting in an impersonal manner and protected by the opacity derived from the cult of the file, decreed the civil death of anyone who fell under those nets and remained trapped in an eternal "during," as there was rarely a decision issued in CONAREPA cases declaring either the innocence or guilt of the suspect. CONAREPA thus needs to be approached as a concept. It was more than just a commission: it was a decisive element through which the state expressed its will. It holds the premises identified by Eduardo Basualdo in his tracking of the design and implementation of the model of financial valorization of capital resulting from the Process of National Reorganization.[7]

5 That subordination is revealed by an investigation conducted by Congress, which is included in the file of the above case.

6 Case 11,657, Juzgado Federal no. 3, Secretaría no. 6.

7 See E. Basualdo, *Sistema político y modelo de acumulación en la Argentina* (Buenos Aires: Atuel, 2011).

The prevailing tendency has been to reconstruct the last military dictatorship in the form of a pyramid, with a visible vertex and a monolithic state apparatus at the service of a blind will to inflict terror. This terror, however, had a purpose, a specific aim, whose motivations are recorded in the files of certain court cases. The worst of these has to do with cultural practices that are still intact, and which are examined more thoroughly in this chapter. The examples that follow help illustrate this.

On a certain occasion, a government officer asked his superiors for their opinion with respect to the continuity of Metropol Compañía Argentina de Seguros SA, an insurance company that was placed under the control of CONAREPA. His question arose from the contradiction between the company's solvency and the fact that it had been placed under government control. The officer was at a loss as to what to do. Finance Secretary Juan Alemann quickly responded that the measure adopted by the Executive entailed "very likely the company's liquidation."[8] In fact, "merely mentioning its connection with the 'Graiver' group will make it impossible for it to continue operating." In other cases, and supported by the legal bases on which it was grounded, CONAREPA took control of companies or declared through administrative decisions that their shares had lost their value and immediately issued new shares in the name of the state. The reason? Combating "subversion," the economic aspect of subversion. This is the excuse repeated in a large number of administrative decisions issued by this body.

It is there that the particularities of CONAREPA as a concept lie. But there were cases that reveal a commercialization of illegal repression that is somewhat more literal – that is, cases in which there was less institutional mediation and where individual motivation was more evident. Again, this can be illustrated by examples taken from the files of certain court cases, in which there are points in common that reveal the illegal dissolution of economic groups, resulting in benefits for people in some way related to the government coalition. These cases are, specifically: 8,405/10,[9] on the Chavanne group; 6073/03,[10] on the Oddone group; 3,260,[11] on the Defranco Fantín group; 12,649/2006/3,[12] on the Gutheim group; and 6,279/97/11,[13] on the Saiegh group. They all focused on a conglomerate of firms that operated in both industry and finance. The heads of these firms were all illegally deprived of their freedom, several companies were placed under control of court-appointed receivers by decision of a first instance federal criminal judge from Buenos Aires, and their business activities were abruptly suspended. In addition, in

8 These cases are taken from court documents added to cases that will be identified subsequently.
9 Brought in Juzgado Federal no. 3, Secretaría no. 6.
10 Brought in Juzgado Federal no. 12, Secretaría no. 24.
11 Ibid.
12 Brought in Juzgado Federal no. 5, Secretaría no. 10.
13 Ibid., Secretaría no. 9.

all of these cases the state intervened alternatively or jointly with the Federal Police of Argentina (Policía Federal Argentina, PFA), the Central Bank of the Republic of Argentina (Banco Central de la República Argentina, BCRA), and the National Securities Commission (Comisión Nacional de Valores, CNV).

The process was always basically the same: meetings were held in which the victim was pressured with regard to private matters but invoking the authority of the state. These were followed by the violent detention and illegal deprivation of freedom of the victim. Then came the judicialization of the case, which made it easy for the state to take control of the company in order to operate its business under a legal umbrella of sorts, in all cases under the broad criminal characterizations established under Law 20,840 on economic subversion.

In other words, a public policy – combating subversion – was invoked to conduct private business operations. If CONAREPA applied a brutal intervention policy cloaked in the impersonality of the administrative sphere, from a parallel but complementary perspective the Economic Subversion Act justified an even greater invasion. It should be noted that this law was passed in September 1974 and was amended during the dictatorship.[14] It was a national security law designed to punish acts that went against the constitutional program. It characterized as criminal offenses different acts of a political and economic nature. During the dictatorship, military courts were granted jurisdiction to hear cases brought for these offenses. The Graiver case was one of the most paradigmatic. If CONAREPA established itself as the administrative arm of the pillaging, Law 20,840 was the element that made it possible for judges to intervene. Going back to the path traced by the court case files examined, the circle was completed with the aura of legality that the judicial system provided.

- Reynaldo Defranco Fantín was a media entrepreneur. He published the magazines *Tía Vicenta* and *El Libro Gordo de Petete*. He also operated in the financial sector through the companies Casa Murillo and Boulogne SA. He had acquired 360,000 seconds of advertising space on Channel 13 for US$3.4 million. He bought them at the rate for black and white television with the intention of selling them at the color rate. When the army took control of the channel, Defranco Fantín requested that his contract be honored. While he was meeting with the intervention authorities, his companies were raided. The following day he was summoned to a mysterious office to pick up the documentation that had been taken in the raids. But this turned out to be a trap and he was taken into custody in July 1980[15] by order of the banking division of

[14] Under the dictatorship it was amended by laws 21,459/76 and 21,886/78, and later, under democracy, it was amended again by laws 23,077, 23,479, 23,974, and 24,286. It was finally repealed in 2002.

[15] It is still debated whether the detention took place before or after he was formally charged.

the federal police. The trigger was an anonymous tip reporting the existence of self-loans within the group. This gave way to case B 31,370, brought in the First Federal Court, Court Office No. 2 (Juzgado Federal no. 1, Secretaría no. 2), for the crime of economic subversion. Defranco Fantín was jailed for more than three years. The BCRA appointed intervention officials to take over the companies' administration and participated actively in the holding's subsequent bankruptcy proceedings in court. The judge appointed a receiver, who acted from mid-1980 to May 1988. After that, the case drifted aimlessly in the dense waters of the judicial system.

- Eduardo Saiegh was vice president and deputy director of Banco Latinoamericano SA and president of Inversai SA. He was on the verge of closing a major deal with the Crédit Lyonnais bank and had a significant share in the Austral airline, as well as strong business ties with Defranco Fantín. On October 25, 1980, the president of the BCRA ordered an inspection of Banco Latinoamericano, which was completed on January 16, 1981, when the group's executives applied to the monetary authority for self-liquidation of the bank, with the inclusion of Inversai. This self-liquidation benefited business operators connected with the BCRA. At the same time, an anonymous report filed on September 27, 1980 led to a court action that culminated on October 31 of that year with the arrest of Saiegh, who lost control of the group. The case also drifted aimlessly.
- Federico and Miguel Gutheim headed the Sadeco textile group. They were especially affected by the "particularist facet of the dictatorship." In October 1976 they received a complaint via telephone from the foreign commerce secretary regarding a contract-related conflict with Hong Kong companies, which had allegedly gotten in the way of a loan requested by Argentina. The news that the credit application had been denied was delivered to Economy Minister José Alfredo Martínez de Hoz himself while he was on an official mission in Hong Kong. On November 5, 1976, President Jorge Rafael Videla and Interior Minister Albano Harguindeguy ordered the arrest of the Gutheims, alleging that their business conduct was linked to the causes that had motivated the state of siege. They were held in custody under authority of the national Executive, without notifying a judge. The Gutheims were forced to renegotiate the contract from jail, under the surveillance of the federal police and with the involvement of government officials and executives of the Hong Kong firms. They were released only after an agreement was reached, on April 6, 1977.
- Luís Alberto Oddone controlled Banco Oddone SA and a group of associated firms. He was summoned by BCRA authorities in February 1980. He was pressured in connection with the emerging credit card business and received several accusations that amounted to administrative harassment, until on April

23, 1980 he was forced to request the banking authorities to take control of his own bank. The credit card business was left in the hands of an individual connected with the government's economic sector. At the same time, a court action was initiated on April 28, 1980, prompted by an anonymous tip received by the banking division of the federal police, alluding to self-loans, which resulted in an economic subversion proceeding. Oddone was arrested and released in 1982.[16]

- The Chavanne group was a way of accessing a coveted loot: the assets of the Graiver family, which owned Banco de Hurlingham and was linked to the Montoneros. The Chavannes had acquired this bank on December 17, 1976. In September 1977, the BCRA refused to authorized the transfer, and in June 1978, they sold their shares to Industrias Siderúrgicas Grassi, but the government took control and the members of the conglomerate were illegally detained and dispossessed. On September 13, 1978, a military investigation was initiated by order of the First Army Corps for violation of the Economic Subversion Act, based on reports from the BCRA and the CNV. Following the judicial intervention by the Third Federal Court, the previous arrests were legalized and new arrests were made. It all ended on February 11, 1986, when the Federal Court of Appeals (Cámara Federal) confirmed the nullity of the proceedings.

The evidence provided by these court case files allows us to build – with an almost heretic methodological license, of course – an ideal type, of the sort proposed by Weber, to define the organized pillaging as part of the criminal plan proved in the military junta trial, under case 13/84 of the Federal Court of the capital. The process, in short, involved national companies connected with financial activities, meetings between the companies' executives and government officials who pressured the former invoking the authority of the state, requirements made by the BCRA or the CNV that were formally valid but were motivated by individual interests, anonymous tips, illegal arrests, government control of company assets, and the judicial cover grounded on the Economic Subversion Act. This was the pattern and the dynamics.

A state involvement of such characteristics had several significant impacts on the victims and their rights. Without even considering the personal impacts, the criminal impact can be characterized as a first-order impact, which served to turn the illegal into legal through functional processes of pillaging. The second-order impact was the series of trials that followed, which were aimed at obtaining compensation for economic and criminal damages, and which were mired in eternal discussions and violated the right to access justice. In these specific cases, there are echoes of cultural practices of the dictatorship because, while the state recognizes its responsibility at

[16] In contrast to most of the others, this case was not lost in a judicial limbo and Oddone was found guilty of fraudulent administration. Nonetheless, the case in essence matches the rest.

the general level, bureaucratic resistances at the microlevel of the trials hamper the application of that general aim of taking responsibility.

There is, in effect, a gap between policy and administration. This means that, although this general policy is part of the acknowledgment of the crimes against humanity committed under the dictatorship,[17] this is not always observed by the middle levels of the branches of the state, which remain tied to secrecy practices, to the cult of the file, and to a functional formality that enables the rule of arbitrariness. This is one of the explanations for the pathological prolonging of actions for damages and criminal trials, in which there are still no decisions on the merits of the case.[18] There are obviously also fiscal implications involved, but the course of the court cases affected by the cult of the form clearly reveals that cultural aspect.

In sum, allowing for certain methodological licenses and a critical view of these old judicial cases, it is possible to identify a unique dynamic within the criminal plan that could be referred to as "commercialization of terror." It was exteriorized in the arbitrary classification of "economic subversion" with the aim of conducting private business operations invoking the general reform for which the dictatorship called. This criminal dynamic was cloaked in the universality of the law, understood as the ties that connect the general will embodied by the state with its citizens; it was crystallized in the confidentiality of the files, and operated in the administrative sphere through CONAREPA and in the judicial sphere through Law 20,840. These instruments made it possible to depersonalize the pillaging, because they shifted the process of colonization of subjectivity from the subject who tortured in a clandestine detention center and the moral rhetoric of the regime to the law diverted to serve private aims.

Lastly, this whole web of mediations that shielded the terror converged in the file. The file combined the regulatory horizons of combating economic subversion with the material interests of the civilian and military protagonists, who sought to obtain economic benefits for themselves. The files and the universality of the law have a rare capacity for enabling, in their name, the coexistence of the legal and the illegal. Everything goes in there and is distilled through a laborious process. That is where the key question lies, in that "during," in which such filtering of elements takes place, because in that interim the pillaging occurred and it was done in the name of the Economic Subversion Act or the moral premises behind CONAREPA. As economic relations were adjusted to the new accumulation model, shady business deals were also conducted.

17 A prominent case in this sense is Law 25,779, which declared the nullity of the Due Obedience and Full Stop Acts.

18 This exceeds the scope of this chapter, but the course of the administrative and judicial actions brought by the victims should be addressed in a specific study. It should be noted, merely as an example, that the bankruptcy declaration of the former Banco Oddone was made final in 2005.

The characteristics of this study do not allow for the development of a hypothesis of the specific relationship between the business pillaging and the economic policy of the dictatorship in terms of costs and benefits. Even with these limitations, it is a fact that the Copernican revolution effected in the country's economy as of March 1976 enabled those who designed part of the program and held high government positions to implement it to loot the assets of others, with the aim of either destroying them or misappropriating them. Some excuses repeated in the documents analyzed, such as the "higher interests of the nation" or the "threat to the way of life of Western Christian civilization," together with criminal law mechanisms such as Law 20,840 and moral repair devices such as CONAREPA, cloaked by the cult to formality typical of files, constitute a faithful record of a form of state being that combined a legal phase with an illegal phase and made it possible to confuse public and private interests.

Time played its part and the state shifted the opacity of state terrorism to public policies of acknowledgment and transformation of everything that happened during those periods. However, certain conducts remained and took hold in the logics of social action, namely the inertia that exudes arbitrariness and is palpable in the court actions brought by the victims after suffering the terror. This form of state being is a source of broad blame,[19] as opposed to narrow blame, which falls on individual subjects.

This distinction is a useful analytical tool, as broad blame indicates the institutional responsibility that supported that coexistence of a legal facade and an illegal reality. It is there, in the body of officials, where resistance lies and prevents the implementation of the state's acknowledgment of responsibility. Consequently, it is a field still to be studied.

[19] J. Malamud Goti, *What's Good and Bad about Blame and Victims* (Oregon: Lewis & Clark, 2005), or its version in Spanish: "Sobre lo bueno y lo malo de inculpar y de vernos como víctimas," *Nueva Doctrina Penal*, 2005-B, (Buenos Aires: Editores del Puerto, October 2005).

19

The National Securities Commission and the Assault on "Economic Subversion"

Alejandra Dandan

The intention of this chapter is to review a report issued in March 2013 by the Human Rights Office of the National Securities Commission (Comisión Nacional de Valores, CNV) under the title "Economy, Politics, and the Financial System," and highlight its main findings. Its authors, Celeste Perosino (anthropologist), Bruno Napoli (historian), and Walter Bosisio (sociologist), examine the role of the CNV during the dictatorship, a period in which this agency was used by the Economy Ministry as an operational tool to persecute a number of entrepreneurs and financiers accused of "economic subversion" in the framework of the dictatorship's combating of "armed organizations." This chapter describes the main aspects of that dynamic and highlights as one of the most valuable contributions of the report the fact that it reveals that even though the CNV persecuted certain sectors, its actions spurred the growth of others. Lastly, the report exposes another pattern that operated in the targeting of entrepreneurs, namely the "private robbery" conducted by other state agencies.[1]

Juan Alfredo Etchebarne was a member of the Azcuénaga Group, part of the core "organic intellectuals" of financial capital who held key positions in government

1 Oficina de Derechos Humanos, CNV, "Economía, política y sistema financiero," March 25, 2013. At time of writing, the report was still unpublished, and part of its conclusions were being updated. This chapter is based on the version completed in 2012. The authors of the report take responsibility for the information provided. This overview would not have been possible without the interviews conducted with the authors, their contributions in informal discussions, and their reading of the text. As a conclusion to the report, the authors published the book *La dictadura del capital financiero*, by Bruno Nápoli, Celeste Perosino, and Walter Bosisio, under the Peña Lillo Biblioteca Artillería del Pensamiento Collection (Buenos Aires: Ediciones Continente, 2014). In 2014, then head of the CNV Alejandro Vanoli was appointed president of the Central Bank of the Republic of Argentina (BCRA). In December 2014, he issued one of the first resolutions ordering the declassification of "all Board Minutes [of the BCRA], both regular and secret," for the years 1975–1985 as an "initial action toward implementing a human rights policy within the body and a first step toward acknowledging the role that the BCRA played during the civilian-military dictatorship." See *Página/12* (Buenos Aires), February 9, 2015.

as of the 1976 coup.[2] Etchebarne, a lawyer and a very close friend of José Alfredo Martínez de Hoz, took office on June 10, 1976 as president of the CNV, which had been placed under control of the ministry of the economy. The CNV had been created as the regulating body of the capital market in 1968 by the dictatorship of Juan Carlos Onganía. As is shown in this chapter, Etchebarne's intervention in the Azcuénaga Group and his relationship with Martínez de Hoz evidence the link between the policies implemented by the CNV after March 1976 and the broader project that sought the structural transformation of the country's economic model.[3]

As of 2010, the current heads of the CNV began receiving requests from different courts for reports on the involvement of its officials, including Etchebarne, in the kidnapping and dispossession of entrepreneurs and financiers during the dictatorship. Some of the victims placed Etchebarne in interrogations conducted in clandestine detention centers, and as the number of denunciations against these officials mounted and the body's files began to be examined, a much broader universe of involvement emerged. Consequently, the current CNV established a working team formed by an anthropologist, a historian, and a sociologist tasked with studying documentation from 1976 to 1983, and formalized an agreement with the National Secretariat of Human Rights.[4] The team worked for ten months, examining more than 500 board minutes and resolutions and interviewing direct victims to compare the data gathered.

On March 25, 2013, the CNV issued this report, presenting the preliminary findings of its investigation, which traced certain patterns of the period. These findings reveal that under Etchebarne the CNV functioned as an "intelligence agency," similar to spaces within the armed forces that operated as "information gathering places." One of the central points of the report is a description of an administrative machinery that operated with a double standard, by favoring or stimulating the growth of certain sectors while targeting others, including entrepreneurs, financiers, and stockbrokers, some of whom were kidnapped and in certain cases dispossessed of their property.

[2] In his notes for the presentation of the "Economía, política y sistema financiero" report of the CNV Human Rights Office, on March 25, 2013, Eduardo Basualdo elaborated on this idea, among others. He argued that the report reveals that there were members of the business community on both sides of repression. In a conversation with the author of this chapter, Basualdo also mentioned the existence of a logic that appears as a reflection of the struggle within "capital." On the Azcuénaga Group, the Perriaux Group, and the relationship with the positions they occupied during the dictatorship, see Vicente Muleiro, *1976. El golpe civil* (Buenos Aires: Planeta, 2012).

[3] The CNV is a state agency mandated with "guaranteeing the transparency of the securities market" and the "correct setting of prices," among other duties. Its scope of operation includes firms and companies listed in the stock exchange. It has a monitoring unit that oversees the market around the clock, controlling operations and with policing powers that allow it to inspect companies or financial firms. It can file reports and suspend trading.

[4] The authors of the report are members of the CNV's Human Rights Office.

Under the National Security Act (Law 20,840), the CNV framed its actions in the "fight against economic subversion." In its line of action, it coordinated tasks with the First Army Corps, the criminal and military justice systems, the banking division of the federal police and the Central Bank (BCRA), in a practice that combined "legal" and "clandestine" actions.[5]

According to the study's conclusions, this persecution reached its peak in 1978–1979, coinciding with a drop in the number of disappearances and unmarked burials of political and social activists.[6] This element led the authors to put forward the hypothesis that the "systematic attack on the business community" was a possible second stage in the evolution of repression: "The fact that the fight against 'subversion' was to a great extent completed meant that a repressive structure was left free to be used for other purposes."[7]

The report's data also show other dimensions of the relationship between these bodies and the policies of the repressive state. The logic under which the past CNV operated opened a door for a scenario populated by victims but also by beneficiaries. Its decisions favored some, as is shown in such cases as Acindar or Papel Prensa, and, at the same time, contributed to the physical and financial dismantling of other actors. These victims were part of a heterogeneous world – that is, they are "victims" who in some cases did not fit the more classic categories of political opponents. These factors therefore open the possibility of considering the existence of a struggle within capital.

In contrast to most analyses of the dictatorship's crimes, which embodied the economic dimension of the repression, the study of the CNV cases and the body's double standard does not point to the tension between capital and labor, but to an internal dispute within capital.[8] The victims are members of the business community who were labeled "economic subversives" by others in the heart of the financial system. Therefore, while there were some abductions motivated specifically by a political logic, as they targeted funds of armed groups, and cases that appear to respond to private interests, the more general map traced by the CNV report gives indications that suggest that the purpose of this persecution was the furthering of certain economic sectors. As Eduardo Basualdo argues, behind this process is a dimension of capital that operates upon itself to further a "monetarist policy that

5 CNV, "Economía," p. 117.

6 Ibid., p. 119.

7 Ibid., p. 120. From this perspective, the CNV appears to have had a specific kind of involvement, different from that of other bodies of the repressive state. The idea of it acting as an "intelligence agency" or as a "financial police" may distinguish it, in turn, from the way other commissions operated, such as CONAREPA, which Federico Delgado examines in Chapter 18 of this book and describes as an administrative police.

8 Drawn from a conversation between the author and Eduardo Basualdo.

interrupted industrialization to establish financial valorization as the core element of the restructure and defined the application of a new pattern of accumulation."[9] One of the leading conclusions of the report has to do precisely with that: it conceives the CNV as "head" of the civilian structure of illegal repression, together with the BCRA, which supported the replacement of the production model with the financial model that remained in place until 2001.

This chapter describes and analyzes the main points of the CNV report to recount how the body operated under the presidency of Etchebarne, who it targeted, and who it favored.

HEAD OF INTELLIGENCE

The financial world of the 1970s and 1980s was marked by the impact of the Financial Institutions Act. To give an idea of the effects of this law on the Buenos Aires financial sector, the report notes that prior to 1976 there were only thirteen exchange houses in all of Argentina, "that is, it was a very small market where everyone knew each other."[10] As of the appointment of Martínez de Hoz as minister of the economy, the dimensions of the market grew exponentially. New exchange houses emerged, such as Cambios Baires, linked to the minister,[11] and the number of private banks owned by domestic capital increased from 68 to 152 in only three years. New actors appeared on the scene: bankers, financiers, stockbrokers. The logic of the *tablita* exchange scheme and the financial bicycle produced a sharp change in a sector from which several of the victims emerged.[12]

On March 24, 1976, the ministry of the economy took control of the CNV. Shortly after, Etchebarne was appointed president, and René Garris was placed on the board of directors. Garris, a lawyer and notary who was also placed by victims in interrogations conducted at clandestine detention centers, served as the body's advisor until his retirement in 2001. These civilians were joined by members of the armed forces, although it was not until 1979 that all three arms were represented. The report sees this as coinciding with the period in which the CNV was most active in its persecution of business operators. It notes:

> It is noteworthy that this [the incorporation of the three forces] occurs in the peak year of CNV interventions and reporting of businesses and entrepreneurs.... This .... raises two hypotheses: (a) that the onslaught against certain business

9 Basualdo, in conversation with the author.

10 CNV, "Economía," p. 120. Among these, the report lists Velox, Cambios Norte, Cambios Koldovsky (whose owner was kidnapped twice), Alpe SA, Casa Piano, and Exprinter.

11 CNV, "Economía," p. 120.

12 Bruno Napoli, member of the CNV's Human Rights Office.

> groups was promoted by these representatives of the armed forces as part of the fight against "economic subversion"; or (b) that the civilian personnel of the CNV found sufficient support in the representatives of the armed forces in the board to be able to embark on these actions.[13]

The characterization of the board constitutes a concern that appears from the beginning of the report to highlight a continuity in the policy of the CNV, from its origins in 1968 to the coup. In this sense, the report notes that Etchebarne had already held the position of legal control manager at the CNV from 1969 to 1972. Therefore, it interprets the change in authorities in 1976 as a continuity. In contrast to what happened in other spheres of the state, the new civilian members of the board were no strangers to the institution but insiders, as the change entailed the promotion of mid-level CNV executives. Similarly, the officials who stepped down from the top managing positions did not leave the institution but were downgraded to lower-ranking positions.[14] Therefore, this modality, which underscores something that does not change but rather persists, fuels the concern with respect to the heart of the financial system, as stressed by the current president of the CNV, Alejandro Vanoli, in his presentation of the report in March 2013:

> Investigating civilian complicity during the dictatorship also entails projecting the precautions that we must take in the future, because the same lawyers, economists, and businesspersons who participated in this process continued holding the reins of power over the following years, conditioning democratic governments, which suffered the consequences through market coups.[15]

The most significant contribution of the report, however, is the outcome of the investigation of the agency's files. The actions of the CNV as head of the civilian structure are reconstructed through an extensive volume of supporting documents. The report combines fragments of board minutes with the analysis of cases and interviews. It shows Etchebarne and his team in the day-to-day running of the institution and traces the logic through which the authors conceive the hypothesis of the systematic nature of the attack on the business sector as of 1978–1979.

Most of the work of the CNV during this period focused on five cases: Banco de Hurlingham; Siderúrgicas Grassi; La Agrícola Cía. de Seguros; and the purchase and sale of stock of Celulosa and Canale, in addition to the Tucumán Stock Exchange. Certain elements are repeated in these five companies: they were all directly or indirectly connected with the purchase of Banco de Hurlingham of the Graiver family, a link that would lead to funds allegedly belonging to the

13 CNV, "Economía," pp. 24–25.
14 Interview with the report's authors.
15 *Página/12* (Buenos Aires), March 26, 2013.

Montoneros organization and managed by David Graiver until his death in August 1976. Moreover, the members of these companies were targeted under Law 20,840, on false charges of "economic subversion," they were kidnapped, and in some cases dispossessed of their property, starting in September 1978.

In presenting this series, the report notes:

> The investigation and monitoring of these cases throughout the dictatorial process is not something that happened by chance, as they are strongly linked to each other not only through business connections (money loans, work relations, etc.), but also through social and family connections.[16]

The investigation, in turn, traced

> a bureaucratic path, a course that has left its marks and, therefore, can be detected in the board minutes of the CNV. This path involved preliminary investigations, such as inspections, statements taken at the CNV, reports filed in court and identical reports filed in military courts. The filing of reports with the First Army Corps under the Economic Subversion Act led to the kidnapping of entrepreneurs and/or stockbrokers connected with the companies mentioned above, and, therefore, to human rights violations.[17]

Siderúrgicas Grassi is one of those cases and reveals the structure in motion. René Grassi participated in the Hurlingham purchase through Marcelo Chavanne, of the Chavanne Group, with whom he had joint business dealings. After Graiver's death, the bank entered a corporate succession process. In September 1976, it came under control of the BCRA and later the National Commission for Asset Responsibility (CONAREPA) confiscated its property and assets. In December, the Chavanne Group bought the bank from Graiver's widow. It signed a purchase agreement for US$600,000 with the promise of settling the balance when the Central Bank lifted its control. The BCRA placed more and more obstacles and ultimately rejected the Hurlingham transfer. When the term of the agreement with Graiver's widow was about to expire, Marcelo Chavanne asked René Grassi to take over the bank because he believed Grassi would receive no objections given that he had sufficient financial guarantees.

On September 12, 1978, Chavanne and Grassi signed an agreement. On September 13, Grassi placed an ad in the press announcing that Siderúrgicas Grassi had taken charge of Banco de Hurlingham. The kidnappings began that afternoon. First Grassi, Chavanne, and nine other people from both companies were kidnapped, and the abductions continued into November, reaching twenty-eight victims in all,

[16] CNV, "Economía," p. 50.
[17] Ibid.

who were held in the Remand Prison of the Campo de Mayo illegal repression circuit. When Marcelo Chavanne was released, the BCRA liquidated the bank.

The CNV report contains board documents that show how this body was involved in the case and how the persecution of these groups occurred. The board minutes indicate, for example, that in July 1978 there was a board meeting in which Etchebarne informed that "an investigation into the purchase of Alpargatas SA"[18] was underway and noted that, as that operation was "not progressing," he was going to take charge of it. After a number of searches, he found that two stockbrokers had participated as "strong buyers" in the Alpargatas deal and that two individuals connected with Siderúrgicas Grassi – Isidoro Carabassa and Juan Claudio Chavanne – were involved. In the days that followed, Etchebarne and Garris summoned Enrique García Mansilla, from the Hurlingham board, to CNV for "an inquiry."

When Mansilla reconstructed that meeting for the authors of the report, he explained that, as his father was a navy officer and formed part of the Azcuénaga Group, he considered Etchebarne an "acquaintance"; however, he described the behavior of the head of the CNV in that opportunity as "aggressive" and that he even "took out weapons." On August 30, 1978, Etchebarne ordered a thirty-day suspension of trading on the stock exchange for Siderúrgicas Grassi. He requested that it be put under control of the BCRA and filed criminal charges in court. On August 31, he reported the Chavanne Group for fraudulent administration, in violation of section 6 of the National Security Act (Law 20,840), on charges of "economic subversion" and fraud to the detriment of the interests of the national state, filing the report with the Rafael Sarmiento Federal Court (Juzgado Federal de Rafael Sarmiento). He filed an identical report with the First Army Corps and in Rosario.

The documents found by the investigative team show that in early September – only days before the kidnappings began – the chief of the First Army Corps, Guillermo Suárez Mason, already had in his power the accusation from the CNV. The report also reveals that, in September, Grassi knocked on every door of the navy commanders, appealing for help, but he was told that the accusations had come from all three arms. Lastly, the report provided important documentation that was presented as evidence in an investigation regarding this case that was conducted in parallel at the Third Federal Court (Juzgado Federal no. 3), under Judge Daniel Rafecas. From the court investigation it emerges that Suárez Mason formed a special "task force" to carry out the kidnappings.

The task force was headed by Colonel Roberto Leopoldo Roualdes, who in turn appointed Francisco D'Alessandri, a retired colonel, as chief of operations, and, Gendarmerie Commander Víctor Enrique Rei as one of its members. Among those kidnapped was a civilian intelligence agent, Raúl Antonio Guglielminetti.

[18] Ibid., pp. 55–66. What follows is a summary of the case provided in the report.

After the first eleven kidnappings in September, an additional thirteen people were kidnapped in October, including nine stockbrokers from the Hurlingham buying group, and four auditors in November.

On November 8, Roualdes requested four qualified experts from the Central Bank and four from the CNV to question the individuals who had been kidnapped. That document was incorporated into the file in the judicial case heard by Rafecas and, because of its evidentiary content, it is one of the most important pieces of evidence gathered in the report. Roualdes' request is contained in a radiogram (no. 063/78), which is signed by him:

> As a result of this command's investigative activities into economic crimes, I request the support and collaboration of the president [Juan A. Etchebarne] of this institution [CNV] with the contribution of 4 (four) of its most qualified experts.

The radiogram was classified as "restricted" and labeled "priority." According to the documentation, the CNV then responded by sending the experts Julio Spinoza, Horacio Muñoz, Carlos Berini, and Pedro García.[19] After these experts completed their "temporary duty," Etchebarne received a letter of congratulations for the "dedication, work ethic and sacrifice, the qualifications and the good judgment" of the professionals.[20]

On April 15, 2013, based on this evidence, Rafecas ordered Etchebarne's arrest for his involvement in the illegal deprivation of freedom and the kidnapping of twenty-eight people. In the analysis made by the court, it was held that the persecution of the Chavanne-Grassi Group was motivated by suspicions of alleged connections with funds of the Montoneros. The report suggests that same reading, but it also includes other alternatives for analysis that have still not been taken into account in the court case, and which could perhaps explain one of the more structural elements of that period: the CNV's double standard.

The investigative team devoted a section of the report to Acindar, the company connected with Martínez de Hoz. In that section, the investigators note that the firm appears several times in the CNV's board minutes. Etchebarne mentions it at a meeting early in his term. He acknowledges that he himself had "professional ties" to the company, for which he announced that he would refrain from participating in any matters connected with it. However, according to the report, this

[19] The sociologist Walter Bosisio, one of the members of the investigative team, draws attention to some bureaucratic aspects: "The Army asked for four experts to keep regular office hours in Campo de Mayo, and they discussed whether they would be paid a per diem or not. They didn't ask why they had to go; they just went and collaborated. The Army had twenty or thirty people, business owners, but it didn't know what to ask them. That was where the CNV came in, contributing experts, who were accountants and lawyers and who knew what each of these individuals had."

[20] CNV, "Economía," p. 76.

> was only observed [by him] in a few instances at the start of his term. … Not only did he not excuse himself from the board meetings – which he himself was presiding – when matters connected with this company were addressed, in some cases, such as … in Record 760, 12/12/1979, he participated directly to recall the importance of processing applications for authorizations for public share offerings.[21]

And he also "acted" to "ensure … the opening of a new plant that [would] spur growth." Lastly, the report adds another element: it sees the benefit granted to Acindar as a policy that could operate to the detriment of competing companies, such as Siderúrgicas Grassi, which was its main supplier of ferroalloys. This information is significant as it suggests a possible "rationality" in the body's dynamics, one of the structural reasons that the court case has failed to see thus far. In this sense, the report notes:

> Within the CNV, a connection can be detected between the executives … and their direct actions to benefit specific companies, such as Acindar, demolishing through state terror any direct business competition, including the competition that Industrias Siderúrgicas Grassi could have represented at the time.[22]

This last interpretation suggests, then, a double standard. The Papel Prensa case reveals a similar logic.

The report identifies Papel Prensa as another beneficiary of the CNV. It describes the body as having a "closer" relationship with the paper manufacturer than with the other companies. At the same time, it suggests that the "omission" of certain information in the CNV board minutes could be read as an attempt to "normalize" and, therefore, "legalize" the irregular transfer of the company.

> The fact that Papel Prensa SA's activities did not evidence any fractures in the CNV, despite the change of board of directors, is significant: it would entail the possibility of a forged, simulated normality in the face of the events that were unfolding, such as the kidnapping of the Graiver family and the irregular sale of company shares. … Just as there were faked clashes … there were also administrative acts that were made up in an attempt to furnish proof of a certain regularity to cover the irregular events that occurred with certain companies, their owners, and their employees.[23]

Evidence of this would be the absence of records on what was happening:

> The key in these cases was the omission of information, which can be seen in the case of Papel Prensa and the Graiver family, but also in … the investigations that the CNV and the First Army Corps conducted together, where, while these were

21 Ibid., pp. 114 and 109.
22 Ibid., p. 107.
23 Ibid., p. 54.

recorded in the CNV minutes, it was never specified what kind of investigation was being carried out. In this line, it may be argued that the dispossession of Papel Prensa SA from the Graivers is part of a greater persecution of the Graiver family and its economic group in general, which culminates in the kidnapping of many of them. Moreover, this persecution affected other people who had been connected with the Graivers or who had acquired part of their companies, as is the case with the kidnappings carried out in the framework of the Banco de Hurlingham investigation, the kidnapping of Fernando Combal (owner of Finsur SA), or the kidnapping of Pedro León Zabalía (owner of Cía. Financiera Río Paraná).[24]

MAPPING THE VICTIMS

The report sought to trace a "map" with a complete list of businesspersons kidnapped between 1976 and 1983, including both the cases in which the CNV was involved and those in which it was not. Preliminary figures show that there were 131 victims, eleven of which are still missing today. The list drawn up includes the names of the kidnapped, their companies, date of abduction, clandestine center where they were held, and repressive force involved. A first aspect that emerges from this map is a division into two periods: between 1976 and 1978, there were more kidnappings of individuals classified as "businesspersons," and in 1978–1983, there were more individuals classified as "financiers." The first period includes the more well-known cases, which are seen in general as part of the political persecution of armed organizations, because of the alleged economic ties to such groups. These are: Cerro Largo SA, in connection with the Chacras de Coria lands; Papel Prensa, owned by the Graiver Group, with sixteen people kidnapped; and Córdoba company Mackentor, with thirty-four individuals kidnapped. The second period corresponds to several cases analyzed specifically in the report. The kidnappings of members of the Grassi-Chavanne Group and cases such as that of Eduardo Saiegh, owner of Banco Latinoamericano, kidnapped along with members of his board and personnel, of the financiers Fernando Combal and Osvaldo Prisant, and of the banker David Koldobsky. Each of these groups evidences other logics, or complementary logics, as is shown later in this chapter, that operated in the financial system.[25]

[24] CNV, "Economía."

[25] Two groups stand out because of their repeated involvement in these cases. The first group, headed by Colonel Leopoldo Roualdes and formed by Francisco D'Alessandri, Raúl Guglielminetti, and Víctor Rei (Banco de Hurlingham), operated at Campo de Mayo. The other group was more active as of November 1978 and was formed by Rubén Bufano, Leonardo Sánchez Reisse, and Luis Alberto Martínez. As noted by the report's authors, many will later be involved in extortionate kidnappings under democratic governments.

Saiegh was kidnapped in October 1980 to dispossess him of Banco Latinoamericano, as with it he held, among other assets, the controlling shares of the Austral airline, which the dictatorship needed in order to close a statization deal. In this case, the BCRA had the same involvement as the CNV did in the Banco de Hurlingham case. Saiegh's kidnapping took place as he was about to sell his bank. He was taken to a branch of Banco Nación, in an operation commanded by the banking division of the federal police. When Saiegh recounts what happened, he notes that the bank and Austral shares theft occurred in the context of a much larger battle, in which the bank model he proposed questioned the aims of the "financial nation":

> It was a time of speculation and not of investment or production. There were no credits available for people to produce or expand. There was a need to have something [a bank] that loaned money. I had seen business banks in Europe: compact banks whose business was to receive deposits and loan them for economic growth. I felt and understood that it was the only way out of the financial system run by the "financial nation." My idea was [to create] a bank that would develop productive projects, instead of speculative ones. And while the Financial Institutions Act contemplated investment banks, they [the BCRA directors] didn't want them.[26]

Fernando Combal was kidnapped on May 8, 1979. He was a moneylender who could have easily been a guest on the television show hosted by Mirtha Legrand (a show featuring lunches with Argentine celebrities and personalities).[27] In addition to being the owner of the Finsur SA financial house, he had other businesses, including Carfina Compañía Financiera, Serfico SA, Cooperativa de Crédito Frutos y Pieles del País Ltda., Buselman SA, Raldeme SA, and Ahorroplan SA. He partnered up with Osvaldo Prisant and David Koldobsky to establish the company Holfinco SAFIyM. But he also owned Urbaires SA in association with Leandro Sánchez Reisse, a member of the 601 Battalion, and his wife, Mariana Bosch, both of whom were part of the group of kidnappers.

Combal had ties with Graiver. When the Mefina financial house closed in 1976, he brought many of its former employees to work at Finsur SA. This was mentioned by his son in an interview with the report's authors. He also said that his father had met Sánchez Reisse in his office located at 962 Santa Fe Avenue. Sánchez Reisse was the owner of Argenshow SA, established in 1976, and Combal owned Asesoría Turística SRL, a travel agency. The two "started meeting regularly after Sánchez Reisse went to the travel agency to purchase some tickets and, as he spoke with Combal, the possibility came up of financing a tour by the singer Paul Williams to Argentina. These meetings gave way to the establishment of Urbaires SA."[28]

26 *Página/12* (Buenos Aires), April 14, 2013.
27 Information from the authors.
28 CNV, "Economía," p. 94.

According to a member of the board, "at one point the company starts having problems because Sánchez Reisse brings in two new capitalists he had met at Bar 05 and who were known by the nicknames *Piripipí* and *El Japonés* (the repression agent Luis Alberto Martínez)," who was also a member of the kidnapping mob.

Koldobsky was kidnapped twice. The first time was in January 1979. Prisant was kidnapped on March 13, and Combal, who had been kidnapped for a day on May 8, was freed after payment of a ransom of almost US$1 million. His son stated that he was questioned about Finsur and the "little Graiver brothers." One of the kidnappers cautioned him to choose his friends more carefully, because, he said, a "little rat" had turned him in.[29] This case has similarities with others reconstructed in the report, such as the case of the Taub family, owner of Cambio Brasilia and Numismática Liberty, with a security system formed by military and police personnel.

Hence, each of the cases described presents a different form of involvement: the CNV in the Banco de Hurlingham kidnapping; the BCRA in the Banco Latinoamericano kidnapping; and the 601 Battalion partners in the Combal case. In other cases, the CNV acted after the kidnappings. The conclusions that can be drawn from these cases are still being drafted by the investigative team. Even so, in view of the general map of 131 entrepreneurs kidnapped between 1976 and 1983, the report proposes two theories toward understanding temporal connections and particularities. It notes:

> The kidnapping of entrepreneurs and financiers involved a repressive dynamic that is in some aspects specific and different from the kidnapping of individuals who were disappeared for political and social reasons.... The aim of these kidnappings was to identify the economic aspect of "subversion" in two ways:
>
> (1) searching for the money of organizations that were considered "guerrilla" or "subversive" ...
> (2) and searching for business operations that [supposedly] threatened Argentina's economy.[30]

The report later adds a third explanation: "robbery, that is, the kidnapping by 'private' initiative of businesspersons and financiers" as the "motive" or "excuse" for the actions.[31]

To prove the existence of the first group of cases, the report considers the testimonies of some businesspersons. According to Marcelo Augusto Chavanne (Chavanne-Grassi Group), "Etchebarne pushed to find the twenty million of

[29] Ibid., pp. 93–95.
[30] Ibid., pp. 118–119.
[31] Ibid., p. 121.

the Montoneros." Luis Taub (Cambio Brasilia and Numismática Liberty), for his part, said: "The kidnapping is motivated by an alleged handling of funds of the Uruguayan Tupamaros movement." The brothers Carlos and Alejandro Iaccarino, kidnapped during the first period, recounted: "When we were interrogated we were asked about our connections with the ERP" (Ejército Revolucionario del Pueblo, or People's Revolutionary Army).[32] To define the second group of cases, it considers, for example, Industrias Siderúrgicas Grassi, which could also fall under the first group.

By way of conclusions, the report proposes two readings. The first, more specific, analyzes how repression evolved from the first to the second moment, and emphasizes the excess workforce:

> It could be argued that the repressive apparatus, the task groups, shifted their attention from "subversion" (in the sense of militant, social, and other activists) to "economic subversion" as of 1978, as motive or excuse for the kidnapping of businesspersons and for dispossessing them of their property.[33]

It posits that

> The fact that the fight against "subversion" was to a great extent completed meant that a repressive structure, involving both repressive agents and spaces, was left free to be used for other purposes. This involves not only repressive tasks for combating "economic subversion" as the cause for the kidnappings, but also activities that use this "fight" as an excuse for carrying out "private initiative" kidnappings at the hands of certain gangs that were organized within the repressive structure.[34]

Toward the end, the report proposes a broader view, as it not only looks at the events from the logic of the victims, it also includes a general reading on the victim-beneficiary connection:

> Another explanatory factor for some of the kidnappings examined could thus be the generation of a change in the structure and makeup of the actors involved in the country's securities market, by kidnapping, eliminating, and dispossessing those who occupied an important place, to position new actors directly connected with the dictatorship. The fight against "economic subversion" reveals a great complexity that covers the implementation of an economic project that required displacing and dispossessing certain economic groups and robbing, that is, kidnapping businesspersons and financiers by "private" initiative. Moreover, explaining and understanding the kidnapping of businesspersons and other financial system operators during the last dictatorship entails investigating the web of relations

[32] Ibid., p. 119.
[33] Ibid., p. 120.
[34] Ibid.

> formed by victims and victimizers and which in that repressive context exposed the victims to the most violent state terrorism the country has ever suffered.[35]

The report's conclusion, the "map" that shows the targeting of businesspersons and their dispossession during the dictatorship or the "typology" of victims in each stage, reveals some of the forms of the intertwining of the financial and repressive systems during that period. It should be noted that the documents described in this chapter are not the only documents examined by the CNV investigative team. One example concerns the trial concluded on June 3, 2013 in the city of La Plata, in the case of the Iaccarino brothers, agricultural producers and construction contractors who were kidnapped, held in nine different clandestine detention centers, and forced to sign over their property to a financial group while still captive. The court found two policemen guilty of direct involvement in acts that it described as "abuses and severe treatment." A document found by the CNV team provided proof of the authorization granted by Banco Nación executives for the transfers "with knowledge of the situation," and it opened the door for investigating its directors.[36] Thus, the report contains this other form of evidence: the Iaccarino brothers case shows these documents contain the bureaucratic traces left by other financial bodies of the repressive state. The investigators have started analyzing Banco Nación resolutions and hope to be able to do the same with the BCRA. In sum, in the Iaccarino case, but also with respect to the Chavanne-Grassi group or Saiegh cases, the declassifying and examination of documents opens new channels for investigating civil responsibility in the dictatorship. But these documents do not merely offer the possibility of contributing to the finding of evidence in a case-by-case basis and to answer the demands for justice voiced by victims who have been waiting for more than three decades. Perhaps one of the more stimulating contributions emerges from the progressive reading of this material. That is, in the macroanalysis: these pieces, considered together, can show, through paper records and day-to-day operations, the process of structural economic replacement that took place in the country. In this sense, it would be important not only to focus again on those who were persecuted but also, and especially, on the beneficiaries. Because in the dimension of the "repressive state," which the justice system is beginning to view as a "macro-criminal state," formed by militaries but also by civilians with a comparable degree of responsibility (as noted in Chapter 13), this proposal for inquiry forces us to consider how each of the actors who benefited from the state, some of whom are identified in these pages, were connected with the repressive

[35] Ibid., p. 121.

[36] See "Socios civiles del secuestro y la extorsión," *Página/12*, June 2, 2013, and "Penas leves en el caso de los Iaccarino," *Página/12* (Buenos Aires), June 4, 2013.

state and with each other. In fact, in a case examined in this chapter, in July 2013, a court prosecuted the then CNV president with the understanding that "there was a clear persecution that targeted certain economic groups, which was carried out through the coordination of activities of military authorities and the National Securities Commission."[37]

[37] A. Dandan, "El jefe del grupo de tareas financiero," *Página/12*, July 17, 2013, available at www.pagina12.com.ar/diario/elpais/1-224677–2013-07-17.html.

20

The Papel Prensa Case: Notes for a Study

Andrea Gualde

THE CONTEXT OF THE TIMES

The transfer of the company Papel Prensa to the newspapers *La Nación*, *Clarín*, and *La Razón* in 1976 is the history of converging spurious interests. Understanding it necessarily entails discussing the plan for the extermination of dissidents along with the propaganda needs of the dictatorship, the strategic importance that newsprint had for printed media, and the advantages for the major newspapers of having a monopolistic control over this input.

The de facto government that came to power by force in 1976 operated in clandestine detention centers and in state and corporate offices, through direct actions or by way of sophisticated government and business procedures.

Analyzing what happened with the newsprint company Papel Prensa involves delving into a number of criminal conducts that precede the kidnapping of its owners, who were members of the so-called Graiver group, and which culminate in the crimes against humanity that targeted them, in an uninterrupted and indivisible continuum where the former appears as a condition of the latter.

March 24, 1976 marked the consolidation of a political model of state of exception – the terrorist state[1] – and an economic model of exclusion. The kidnapping, confinement in clandestine detention centers, mass torturing, and disappearance of individuals coexisted with practices that were less known during the stage of the first trials conducted immediately after the restoration of the constitutional order, but which were no less systematic or less planned. These practices consisted of the appropriation of assets and companies by military repressive agents with the

I would like to thank Adriana Alvarenga for her collaboration in providing material and reading the draft versions of this essay. Many of the ideas presented here were inspired by the work and writings of Eduardo Luis Duhalde, to whose memory I dedicate this contribution to a debate that he raised and enriched.

1 See E. L. Duhalde, *El Estado terrorista argentino* (Buenos Aires: Argos-Vergara, 1999).

involvement of civilians, from within and outside the genocidal state apparatus,[2] in complex complicity dynamics that are coming to light today as a result of the progress in the process of justice.

The appropriation of Papel Prensa is one such case, perhaps the most emblematic because of its impact on freedom of expression and how it contributed to the silencing of dissidents during those years, but, above all, because it facilitated the regime's propaganda efforts enormously.

To fulfill the goal of social disciplining, an authoritarian model was not enough; to achieve it, the state became a terrorist state, defined by Eduardo Luis Duhalde as an exceptional model based on absolute control of the government and the coercive apparatus of the state and on the disarticulation of political and civil society. The dissemination, legitimization, and acceptance of this model required and used publicity and propaganda.

After the March 24, 1976 coup, media activities were regulated under Communication No. 19, issued the very same day of the coup, which in practice completely suppressed freedom of expression and criminalized the dissemination of "subversive" activities. Prior censorship was institutionalized through a government office called "Free Prior Reading Service" (Servicio Gratuito de Lectura Previa).[3]

In that scenario, terror coexisted with the persecution of any journalists and press media that were less than unconditional supporters of the regime, in a campaign that involved the closing down, bombing, or raiding of such media outlets and left at least seventy-seven detained-disappeared or murdered journalists, with the complicity of big media, which aligned itself with the dictatorship and legitimized its actions on a daily basis.[4] It is in that context that the events leading up to the appropriation of Papel Prensa take place.

Studies that compile and analyze editorials and headlines from that time[5] expose a strategy for guiding relations between communicators and public opinion. Although

2 The legal debate on the applicability of the category of genocide to the Argentine case exceeds the scope of this study. The references made throughout the chapter to the genocide state are formulated based on the characterization by D. Feierstein, *El genocidio como práctica social. Entre el nazismo y la experiencia argentina* (Buenos Aires: FCE, 2007), and the rulings issued by the First Federal Oral Court of La Plata (Tribunal Oral Federal no. 1 de La Plata) in their description of the crimes punishable as committed "in the context of genocide."

3 See M. Borrelli, "Voces y silencios: la prensa argentina durante la dictadura militar (1976–1983)," (2011) 4(1) *Perspectivas de la comunicación*, Temuco, Chile, Universidad de la Frontera, pp. 24–41, available at http://publicacionescienciassociales.ufro.cl/index.php/perspectivas/article/viewFile/104/87 (accessed April 20, 2013).

4 See M. Malharro and D. Gijsberts, *La tipografía de plomo. Los grandes medios gráficos en la Argentina y su política editorial durante 1976–1983* (Buenos Aires: Ediciones de Periodismo y Comunicación, 2003), pp. 17–18.

5 See E. Blaustein and M. Zubieta, *Decíamos ayer. La prensa argentina bajo el Proceso* (Buenos Aires: Colihue, 1998); C. Díaz, *La cuenta regresiva. La construcción periodística del golpe de Estado de 1976* (Buenos Aires: La Crujía, 2002); and Malharro and Gijsberts, *La tipografía de plomo*.

all forms of media were important, the printed press played a decisive role. Four decades ago, there were no tools available for the production of news in the dynamic and instant way that technological advances have since made possible. Newspapers fed and informed the rest of the media and the circulation of information was thus less democratic and more monopolized, in a field where newsprint was a strategic input. In such a scenario, the appropriation of Papel Prensa marked a *before* and *after* in the role of the media. Its consequences are still being felt today, with a force that explains the importance of investigating it.

Some headlines from that period eloquently illustrate a continuum from the preparation of the coup to the open legitimization of the repressive actions of the state. On December 22, 1975, the newspaper *La Nación* declared in its editorial, "the phenomenon of decomposition has its epicenter in the government, because the Executive is vacant." This was only a few months before the newspaper *Clarín* heralded in the nascent dictatorship with a front page headline announcing "NEW GOVERNMENT," and the August 2, 1976 editorial in *La Nación* justified the dictatorship's conduct with respect to the media in the following terms:

> The Argentine press has accepted the need for the application of certain restrictions that are critical in the difficult times the Nation is going through. It accepts this because it is conscious that it too must make its contribution to the fight against subversion. In this sense, the national press has no problems with a government that pursues identical aims [as the press].

But just what were the aims pursued by the self-proclaimed "Argentine press" through these articles, headlines, and editorials, and what was, ultimately, its "contribution" to the "fight against subversion"? The military junta provides a blunt answer:

> The state of war imposes certain obligations on the press and on government authorities that go beyond a mere frontal opposition to the enemy. These obligations have to do, precisely, with the handling of information on the course of a battle underway, as it is of mutual interest to both parties to contribute to victory.[6]

Propaganda thus collaborated, dangerously, in the identification of the enemy.

A genocidal process does not just appear overnight and neither is it the product of a handful of deranged individuals and psychopaths.[7] It would be more comforting to think that and much easier in terms of preventing its repetition, but the history of the twentieth century proves otherwise. Genocides take many years to brew. The actual extermination – the most visible stage, that which stirs consciences – may last only a short time and it constitutes the culmination of a process. But that process inevitably

6 Malharro and Gijsberts, *La tipografía de plomo*, p. 62.

7 This idea draws on the study by J. Waller, *Becoming Evil. How Ordinary People Commit Genocide and Mass Killing* (New York: Oxford University Press, 2nd ed., 2007).

goes through other, less visible and more subtle stages, which is important to know and analyze.[8]

The genocide process experienced by Argentina between 1976 and 1983 was, according to Daniel Feierstein, a "reorganizing genocide." It was not by chance that it presented itself as a "Process of National Reorganization." The name refers to the refounding of the state under different rules, through the imposition of new forms of social relations.[9]

To establish these new relationships, it was necessary to construct a negative otherness, understood as the process that defines a social actor as a subject to be persecuted, singled out.[10] Once that enemy has been constructed through the distinction between "us" and the "others," the path is open for the second stage: the harassment, the passage from reflection to action.[11]

In both stages, the propaganda of a genocidal regime plays a key role. The election of the enemy is defined by the perpetrator, but the role of a complicit press and of propaganda is critical in the collective installation of that enemy, in the construction of the perception that it is necessary to adopt concrete measures to "order" the situation, and in the social legitimization of the actions undertaken. The Nuremberg judgments[12] and, decades later, the sentences handed down by the International Criminal Tribunal for Rwanda[13] set out the possibility of holding journalists and media owners criminally responsible if their behavior is proven to have contributed to the stereotyping and identification of the enemy in the context of a genocide.

In Argentina, the analyses of headlines, articles, and editorials that this chapter draws on reveal that the media helped shape the concepts of "subversion" and "subversive," and enabled the "fight against subversion," legitimizing it and painting it in a positive light. In the case of Papel Prensa, this contribution involved, as is shown in this chapter, associating the Graiver group with everything that was considered hostile to the regime, ultimately turning it into an enemy and, therefore, into a subject to be persecuted.

[8] This follows the classification by Gregory Stanton, who holds that genocide is a process that unfolds in eight stages: (1) classification, (2) symbolization, (3) dehumanization, (4) organization, (5) polarization, (6) preparation, (7) extermination, and (8) denial. See G. H. Stanton, "The 8 Stages of Genocide," originally presented as a briefing paper at the U.S. State Department in 1996, and available at http://genocidewatch.net/2013/03/14/the-8-stages-of-genocide/ (accessed April 20, 2013).

[9] Feierstein, *El genocidio*, pp. 104–110.

[10] Ibid., pp. 216–221.

[11] Ibid., pp. 221–226.

[12] Nuremberg International Military Tribunal, '*In re* Goering and Others,' judgment of October 1, 1946.

[13] See *Prosecutor v. Nahimana, Barayagwiza, and Ngeze*, Case ICTR 99-52-T, December 3, 2003 judgment.

THE APPROPRIATION

Putting these events in their proper dimension within this context requires a brief look at the history of the first Argentine paper manufacturer.[14]

The development of national industry based on import substitution, domestic consumption, and job creation (that is, the model plan of the first Peronism, which was continued during the developmentalist years), entered into an increasingly deeper crisis in the early 1970s. After the *Cordobazo* uprising, neo-developmentalism marked the course of the economy with specific initiatives for different areas of industry, including pulp and paper manufacture.[15]

As noted earlier, the printed press had a central importance in the media decades ago, and that centrality determined the strategic significance of its leading input. Newsprint was a very costly resource. As it had to be imported, it was shipped in generally from northern Europe by boat, subject to tariffs, and affected by the fluctuations of the recurring devaluations of Argentine economy.

In 1969, under the dictatorship of Juan Carlos Onganía, a Newsprint and Cellulose Production Fund (Fondo de Producción de Papel Prensa y Celulosa) was created with the aim of opening a call for bids for the construction of a newsprint production plant. The history of Papel Prensa is marked by that process, which wavered between producing newsprint domestically and importing it.

In the midst of those debates, in 1971 Papel Prensa SACIFyM was established, and in June 1972, during the de facto government of Alejandro Lanusse, following a failed international public bidding process, this company was authorized to operate by direct award.

Later, Papel Prensa was created as a corporation and its capital stock was issued. This capital was divided into Class A shares (26 percent, held by the founding group), Class B shares (25 percent, held by the state), Class C shares (20 percent, for newsprint users), Class D shares (10 percent, for the general public); and Class E shares (19 percent, for raw material suppliers).

This original makeup was modified a few years later with the incorporation of capital from the Graiver group, whose head acquired, in his own name or through third parties, Class A and Class C shares. Under the third presidency of Perón, David Graiver, who

[14] The analysis contained in this chapter is based entirely on the documentation furnished by the state as evidence in the private prosecution brought by the Human Rights Secretariat of the National Ministry of Justice and Human Rights ("Secretaría de Derechos Humanos s. denuncia") and published by that body: "Papel Prensa. Querella presentada por la Secretaría de Derechos Humanos con el patrocinio de la Procuración del Tesoro de la Nación en el Juzgado en lo Criminal y Correccional Federal n° 3 de la ciudad de La Plata," September 21, 2010.

[15] See D. Cecchini and J. Mancinelli, *Silencio por sangre*, available at sur.infonews.com/files/silencio_por_sangre.pdf (accessed April 20, 2013).

had ties with the economy minister, José Ber Gelbard, acquired the private shares of Papel Prensa through the firm Galería Da Vinci and the frontman Rafael Ianover. This was followed by a series of acquisitions, capital contributions, and transfers that are not detailed here as it is sufficient to say that at the time of his death under confusing circumstances David Graiver had complete control of the company.[16]

Sometime later, Graiver and his economic and family group began to be fingered by big media as "enemies of the nation." Amidst articles and editorials praising civilian and military repressors, fervently defending Martínez de Hoz's economic plan, and presenting the official story of the dirty war, the "Graiver case" became fixed in public opinion in connection with the alleged responsibility of the group in actions considered criminal by the dictatorial regime.

From the death of David Graiver and until November 1976, when the shares of Papel Prensa were transferred, *La Nación*, *La Razón*, and *Clarín* published an average of one article per week in an aggressive campaign to define in the media the need to investigate and criminalize the members of the group.[17] These articles alluded to Graiver's ties with the Montoneros and raised suspicions about the banks that the group owned abroad. These articles were also peppered with repeated references to the connection with Gelbard and the Jewish community. The allusions to the relationship with Gelbard were neither chance nor isolated mentions, as Gelbard, who was often associated with Graiver, had already been included in the institutional memorandums issued by the military junta and stripped of all his political rights, and there was an order for his arrest.

The constant negative references to the Graiver group intensified over the following months, with increasing pressure, until in the lead up to the transfer of Papel Prensa shares to the above newspapers, different people, through different means, made direct intimidations and threats.[18]

The testimonies gathered in the first investigation into this operation, conducted in 1985, all coincide in that the sellers in that operation had no intention of closing a business deal nor did they act on their own free will.[19] In his opinion rendered on February 29, 1988, National Administrative Investigations Prosecutor Ricardo Molinas found that the sellers did not choose the buyer and that there were no

16 Feierstein, *El genocidio*, chap. 3.

17 Feierstein, *El genocidio*, pp. 13–14.

18 See the testimonies given by Ship Captain R. Francisco Manrique, on November 2, 1977, and Miguel de Anchorena, on November 3, 1977, to the War Council, quoted in the private prosecution brought by the Human Rights Secretariat, "Secretaría de Derechos Humanos s. denuncia," pp. 94–95.

19 See the testimonies given by Isidoro Graiver, on November 6, 1985, and Lidia Papaleo, on November 7, 1985, to the National Prosecutor's Office for Administrative Investigations (Fiscalía Nacional de Investigaciones Administrativas, FNIA), quoted in the private prosecution brought by the Human Rights Secretariat, "Secretaría de Derechos Humanos s. denuncia," pp. 95–97.

negotiations to determine the price or the terms and conditions of the sales agreement.[20] From the file of that court action, it emerges that the sale to the newspapers was done against the will of the shareholders, who – nonetheless – had already been told, via different means, that they had to sell the company, but that they could not sell to foreign or Jewish capitals.[21] The sale, moreover, had to be authorized by the military junta as a precondition for the deal to be valid, and, in that sense, the Graivers were notified informally that the only deal that would be authorized would be a deal with the local newspapers.[22]

The second judicial investigation into these events, initiated in 2010 and still underway, is not limited to the irregularities already detected, but instead delves into different elements that could reveal the indivisibility between the illegal deprivation of freedom of the individuals connected with Papel Prensa and the illegal acts perpetrated in the transfer of shares, as indicated previously. This unity of action – that was the focus of a preliminary examination by judges and prosecutors – would enable the application of the legal consequences of the crimes against humanity suffered by the members of the Graiver group to all those actions.[23]

As a detailed description of the different circumstances that vitiated the transfer deal exceeds the scope of this chapter, only the most eloquent aspects are mentioned here.

As indicated, in the statements given in 1985 to the National Prosecutor's Office for Administrative Investigations (FNIA) the victims were unanimous in asserting that, at the time of the assignment, they were not given the chance to negotiate any of the terms and conditions of the sale. They did not even know the exact number of shares they were assigning, and only much later was an inventory made.[24]

Essential legal requirements were lacking. For example, the judge who was handling David Graiver's estate proceedings never signed off on the transfer of part of the stock capital (the Class C shares). With respect to another part of the capital stock (Class A shares), a number of successive transfers were made with individuals who had no power and in meetings of shareholders summoned irregularly,[25] notwithstanding which there is no official record of this in the National Securities Commission, a body that at the time was actively investigating other companies of the Graiver group and sending representatives to the shareholders' meetings.[26]

20 See the text of the private prosecution under the court file "Secretaría de Derechos Humanos s. denuncia," paragraph II(6), p. 177.

21 Text of the private prosecution "Secretaría de Derechos Humanos s. denuncia," pp. 97–98.

22 See the relevant section of the testimonies indicated in Note 19 in this chapter.

23 "Secretaría de Derechos Humanos s. denuncia," p. 206.

24 See the text of the private prosecution under the court file "Secretaría de Derechos Humanos s. denuncia," paragraph II(6), pp. 177–178.

25 "Secretaría de Derechos Humanos s. denuncia," pp. 119–124.

26 See the report issued by Coordinación de Políticas de Derechos Humanos, Verdad, Memoria y Justicia, *Informe de derechos humanos y sistema financiero* (Buenos Aires: Comisión Nacional de Valores, Ministerio de Economía y Finanzas Públicas, 2012), pp. 49–53.

Most surprising, however, is the identity of the buyer. The assignment of shares took place on November 2, 1976 in the offices of *La Nación*, and the buyer was Fapel SA (Fábrica Argentina de Papel para Diarios SA), a dummy company whose sole activity was the purchase of Papel Prensa SA. This company was formed by the directors of the three newspapers.

In only eight days, Fapel SA[27] assigned its shares to *Clarín*, *La Nación*, and *La Razón* with the same price conditions and the same form and mode of payment as the first sale.

This second transfer, just a week after the first, is illustrative of the irregularity of the deals: Fapel was merely an intermediary, who served the sole purpose of turning the newspapers into third parties purchasing in good faith. This intermediation was necessary for two reasons: to prevent any claims based on the fraudulent nature of the sale; and to put some distance between the newspapers and the Graiver group in the chain of transmissions. Otherwise, the enemy that was to be persecuted and dispossessed of its property because of its connections with the Montoneros would have appeared as the other party of an agreement with the newspapers, in a deal approved by the military junta.

In March and April 1977, David Graiver's entire family was kidnapped, along with some of his employees and close associates. From Jorge Rubinstein (David Graiver's right-hand man), who would die under torture, to individuals who were not as close or had no ties to him at all, such as Jorge Mazzola, Graiver's tailor, were held in clandestine detention centers in the circuit commanded by Ramón Camps, then chief of police of the Buenos Aires province.

An interesting fact that merits analysis is that the detention of Lidia Papaleo, Graiver's widow, occurs a few days after her last useful intervention in her husband's estate proceedings. On February 11, 1977, the official declaration of heirs had been issued, naming Graiver's parents, his only daughter (who was underage), and Lidia Papaleo, who on March 9, in representation of her daughter and as the administrator of the estate, had gone before the judge to request the approval of the sale of shares conducted in November.[28] This request – an unavoidable requirement that had to be met because there was a minor involved – could only be carried out once this process had been completed, for obvious reasons: it was only after the judicial declaration of heirs that Graiver's daughter became an heir and, thus, acquired the shares. Five days later, on March 14, Lidia Papaleo was kidnapped by military and security forces.

As a prior step to the liquidation of the group by the de facto government, its members – still detained illegally – were put under military jurisdiction, first, and,

[27] See Cecchini and Mancinelli, *Silencio por sangre*, chap. 3.

[28] See the text of the private prosecution under the court file "Secretaría de Derechos Humanos s. denuncia," paragraph II(4), p. 126.

then, under the Second Special Stable War Council (Consejo Especial de Guerra Estable no. 2), created under the military junta's Communication No. 33. This entailed a summary proceeding that carried the possibility of applying the death penalty.

The sequence of events in the pretrial preparations of that War Council is worthy of note as the dates provide interesting elements for investigating the relationship between the actions of the dictatorship and the directors of these newspapers.

The action is initiated on April 6, 1977, with the appointment of Brigade General Oscar B. Gallino, of the First Army Corps, as examining prosecutor. Even before he ordered the customary investigations in that illegitimate proceeding, on that same day, April 6, he was visited by the economy minister and the president of Banco Provincia de Buenos Aires. The following day, he received the representatives of the newspapers, whose reason for visiting him – as recorded in a letter signed by him and included on the second folio of the file – was "the acquisition of the package of the founding group of Papel Prensa SA." On April 9, Gallino met with the secretary of industry, Podestá – who had played a key role in the preliminary contacts between the newspapers and the Graivers, aimed at informing the latter that the junta wanted the company transferred only to the former[29] – and, again, with the newspapers' directors and advisors.[30] That is to say, then, that in just a dozen folios and seventy-two hours, those who ran the economy under the dictatorship and the newspaper directors who purchased Papel Prensa appeared in person to show their interest for a file opened to investigate the members of the Graiver Group, after these had gone through the clandestine torture center of Ramón Camps, and were still being held illegally on that date.

On April 16, the news of the arrest of fifteen members of that economic group ran on the front page of *Clarín*, and on April 20, the newspaper followed up this information under the headline: "Graiver Case: Revolutionary Justice Applied." It should be noted that, at the time, the fate of these individuals was unknown as they were still being held in absolutely clandestine conditions, and did not even appear as being detained under authority of the Executive, which was usually the situation of non-clandestine detainees who were not formally charged in court. This only happened on May 31, 1977, through Decree 1587.

In the time that goes from them being held in clandestine conditions and the "legalization" of their situation by decree, *La Nación*, *La Razón*, and *Clarín* ran an ad, on May 19, 1977, in which they made public that they had

[29] "Secretaría de Derechos Humanos s. denuncia," pp. 94–95 (testimony by Manrique, cited in note 18).
[30] "Secretaría de Derechos Humanos s. denuncia," pp. 131–132.

> acquired the Class "A" shares of Papel Prensa SA, prior consultation with and subsequent approval by the Junta of Commanders-in-Chief. This approval was later ratified by the affirmative vote of the state in the shareholders' meeting held on January 18, 1977, which approved the transfer of shares to the three newspapers.

In that ad, they declared that

> the three newspapers took steps to purchase the capital stock of Papel Prensa SA, prior consultation with the Junta of Commanders-in-Chief and the General Secretary of the Presidency of the Republic, and, then, once the approval at that top level was obtained, with the Minister of the Economy and the Secretary of State for Industrial Development. Having met with no objection whatsoever, the stock purchase agreements were executed on November 2, 1976. This purchase was made by Fapel SA, on behalf of the three newspapers, from Galería Da Vinci SA, Rafael Ianover, and the Estate of David Graiver.

The publication of this ad is significant as the newspapers themselves assimilate the first transfer made on April 2 – with Fapel SA – with the second one on April 8, in which they participate openly, with the Graivers now out of the picture.

On July 21, 1977, the military junta issues an institutional memorandum whereby all the companies of the Graiver group are prohibited and disabled by the National Commission for Asset Responsibility (Comisión Nacional de Responsabilidad Patrimonial, CONAREPA), an agency created by the dictatorship to investigate, with full powers, the assets of any individuals or legal persons persecuted by the regime. All the Graiver companies are affected except one: Papel Prensa, for the simple reason that the company was no longer part of the assets of the Graivers, but was instead owned by the newspapers.

In this sense, a peculiar piece of information provides more elements that support the arguments presented thus far: these deals ran countercurrent to the economic policies of the dictatorship. In a scheme that involved disarticulating the import substitution industrialization model and favoring concentrated capital and, in particular, financial-speculative and transnational capital,[31] the sale of Papel Prensa was explained by *Clarín* on November 11 – just three days after the illegitimate transfer from Fapel to the newspapers and a week after the initial deal with the Graivers – as "a weighty decision by the government of the Armed Forces in favor of import substitution."[32]

It must be noted that even at the height of the dictatorship there were voices that questioned these dealings. Most notably, such objections were raised by Ricardo

[31] See A. Pucciarelli (comp.), *Empresarios, tecnócratas y militares* (Buenos Aires: Siglo XXI, 2004), second part.

[32] See the text of the private prosecution under the court file "Secretaría de Derechos Humanos s. denuncia," p. 118.

Molinas. Even before he became the first investigator of these operations as head of the FNIA, as early as 1978, in a letter addressed to the Center for Legal and Social Studies (Centro de Estudios Legales y Sociales, CELS) Molinas examined them and warned of possible irregularities.[33] These same irregularities would lead him ten years later, now as government official, to bring the actions on which this chapter is to a great extent based. Particularly valuable are testimonies by individuals who were not even injured parties in the case, but which were gathered in that court file, as they corroborate the claims made by the Graivers.

Molinas issued his opinion in February 1988,[34] when the Due Obedience and Full Stop Acts were still in force. More than twenty years had to pass before his investigation and findings could be reexamined in the context of the opening up of a process of full justice for the victims of the crimes against humanity perpetrated by the military dictatorship.

TOWARD A CONCLUSIVE INVESTIGATION INTO THE FACTS

With impunity defeated and the crimes committed by the civilian-military dictatorship declared crimes against humanity and, as such, not subject to statutory limitation, trying such crimes without special judges or laws is a matter of state policy and a model for forging a relationship with the past that is unique in the world.

This process of justice is doubly valuable, as it impacts and repairs two dimensions: the individual dimension of the victims and the collective dimension. Genocidal processes damage the social fabric, and societies need to search for the truth in order to develop a useful memory of the recent past. Trials and judgments operate in that scheme as producers of meaning and truth. Today we know a lot more about our country's genocidal past than when the military junta trial took place. We have details about the specific repressive workings of each branch of the armed and security forces; about the joint actions and the collaboration among these forces and with the dictatorships of neighboring countries; we know more about the sexual crimes and the anti-Semitic crimes committed in the clandestine detention centers (the Graiver case is paradigmatic in that sense); and it has been judicially proven that the appropriation of children responded to a systematic plan.

In this context, the need to further the investigation of civilian participation in these crimes gains increasing importance. There is a reason why so much time has passed before this could happen. Taking on that challenge confronts us with our own weaknesses, at both the individual and social levels. It is unsettling to think that the perpetrators of the genocide are members and products of a society that

33 "Secretaría de Derechos Humanos s. denuncia," p. 177.

34 "Secretaría de Derechos Humanos s. denuncia," paragraph II(6), p. 177.

in part legitimized and justified them. But that disturbing feeling is more evident and greater with respect to civilians. First, because de facto powers do not lose their influence even after dictatorial regimes are overcome. And, at the same time, because the figure of "civilian perpetrator" is far from what society constructs as the material perpetrators of crimes against humanity. Civilian perpetrators do not fit the image of the torturers or murderers who perpetrate the crimes by their own hand. That figure questions us mercilessly as it comes closer to our own image. It is more real, less distant, less other.

At time of writing, the Argentine justice system was investigating these events in the private prosecution brought by the National Secretariat of Human Rights, on behalf of the national Executive. The judicial investigation – whose initiation has been delayed by petitions presented by the defense – will need to ponder, necessarily, the evidence provided and collected by the state on the events recounted here. This is a great opportunity for justice to unravel, through the Papel Prensa case, the complex webs connecting dictatorial and economic power, and to write an essential page in the history of the process of justice with respect to our recent past: the page on civilian participation, which will enable us, as a society, to take responsibility for our history.

PART VIII

A Range of Generous and Interested Supports

21

The Media: Unified Discourse and Business Deals under Cover of State Terrorism

Damián Loreti

A NEW LEGAL AND POLITICAL ORDER

"New Government," "Armed Forces Assume Power, President Detained," "Yesterday in Córdoba, a Day Like Any Other," "Everything in Order in the Federal Capital," "Calm Reigns at University," "Normal Day Nationwide": these were the headlines in the country's leading newspapers in March 1976, as media owners celebrated the start of the dictatorship. Perhaps the most vicious manifestation were the editorials in *La Nueva Provincia*, and in particular the one published on March 24, which stated that "Argentina is a Western Christian Nation" and listed as its enemies "the subversive apparatus, the third-worldist 'priesthood,' trade union corruption, the political parties, the usury by the 'economic right-wing,' and the left-leaning counterculture." "The enemy must be destroyed wherever he may be found, knowing that the second republic shall rise from redemptive blood," the editorial rallied with chaplain terminology, while suggesting employing an "order-restoring violence" that "makes no distinctions when it comes to using its clean force against opposing factions."

The institutional reflection of this position was found in statements by the Association of Argentine News Bodies (Asociación de Entidades Periodísticas Argentinas, ADEPA), which shortly after the coup expressed its satisfaction with "the change of style in relations between the government and the press."[1] In October 1976, ADEPA authorities told the Inter-American Press Association (IAPA) that freedom of expression in Argentina was "a reality."[2]

As these pages were being written, a trial involving the repression of trade unionists that culminated with the disappearance of two leaders of the Graphic Arts

1 A. Graham-Yooll, *The Press in Argentina, 1973–1978* (London: Writers and Scholars Educational Trust, 1979), p. 137.

2 E. Blaustein and M. Zubieta, *Decíamos ayer. La prensa argentina bajo el Proceso* (Buenos Aires: Colihue, 1998), p. 188.

Union (Sindicato de Artes Gráficas), Enrique Heinrich and Miguel Ángel Loyola, was beginning. Heinrich and Loyola had organized and participated in a strike by workers of the multimedia group led by *La Nueva Provincia*, which involved both television and written press workers and was prompted by the company's unilateral decision not to honor the collective bargaining agreement. At the same time, the Federal Oral Court of Bahía Blanca (Tribunal Oral Federal de Bahía Blanca) ordered that issues of the newspaper from that time be submitted as evidence in the first instance,[3] as in addition to publishing communiqués to cover up executions, the newspaper also ran photos that only the intelligence services could have. The judges ordered an investigation of the directors of the newspaper – which today is run by the torture apologist Vicente Massot – for possible "prosecutable offenses." Item 34 of the judgment requests an investigation of the owners of the newspaper for the murders of the former delegates Heinrich and Loyola, whose deaths the newspaper (mis)reported in a twenty-line piece when their bodies were found, and it never mentioned the incident again. The court called for an inquiry into possible crimes arising from those issues, which in turn led the Prosecution Unit formed by José Nebbia, Miguel Palazzani, and Antonio Castaño to request the indictment and detention of Vicente Massot and Mario Hipólito Gabrielli (case 158/12, "Diario 'La Nueva Provincia' s/ Inv. of Crimes against Humanity [denunciante T.O.C.F. de B.B.]"). The federal judge denied the request, and his decision was appealed by the Prosecution Unit. In the grounds for filing the appeal, the Prosecution Unit notes that what was involved was not a matter of freedom of expression but of participation in a different kind of criminal phenomenon, which entailed not relativizing the presentation of false clashes, the murder of the two press workers, the presence of two civilian intelligence officers and an officer of the prefecture "information" division, a rhetoric of hatred and incitement to eliminate a group of people who did not conform to the ideal "national being," the fiction of the "dirty war," the demonization of the "Other," and the call for extermination as the only solution, all of which – in the opinion of the Prosecutor's Office – arose from the pages of their editorials.

It is difficult to circumscribe to the 1976–1983 period the extremely serious impacts on freedom of expression, the relations between governments and media companies that made it possible to build a hegemonic discourse, and the persecution and silencing of dissident voices during a large part of the twentieth century in Argentina. But even though the kidnapping of journalists and social

[3] Judgment, Tribunal Oral Subrogante en lo Criminal Federal de Bahía Blanca, in the court case "Bayón, Juan Manuel y otros s. privación ilegal de la libertad agravada, reiterada, aplicación de tormentos reiterada, homicidio agravado, reiterado a Bombara, Daniel José y otros en área del Cuerpo Ejército V," Bahía Blanca, September 12, 2012.

activists, the torturing, the murders, the closing down of media outlets, and the systematic censorship did not begin on March 24, 1976, under the self-proclaimed Process of National Reorganization these practices took on a systematic nature and reached an unprecedented magnitude. To reach that level it was necessary to build a legal-bureaucratic web that sustained and gave legitimacy to this kind of action, conceived of as just another cog in the machine of state terrorism.

The platform that designed the leading public policies in the field of communications during those years found support in the complicity of some of the country's top press entrepreneurs, who were an essential ally in the cementing of the dictatorship's own legitimacy, the silencing of any denunciations connected with the grave human rights abuses that were being committed in the country, and the sustaining of the authority of the various dictatorial governments that, owing to disputes between factions in the armed forces, succeeded each other in power between 1976 and 1983.

The events that took place in the hours following the March 24 coup are key for understanding the system of political-business alliances and the (il)legal order that wiped out all constitutional guarantees and put in place a virtual state of siege in the media.

In the early hours of the day of the coup, the directors of the leading printed press media of Buenos Aires were called to the seat of the national government. There they were informed of how the "Free Prior Reading Service" (Servicio Gratuito de Lectura Previa) – a euphemism for the institutionalized censorship regime launched that very same day at the Casa Rosada presidential palace – would work. They were also given a new handbook that listed banned terminology and subjects. This kind of material was nothing new to the local media, as similar instructions had already been circulated the year before, but the Junta of Commanders-in-Chief wanted to make it clear that as of that moment the control would be absolute. However, the Free Prior Reading Service was not needed for long; just a month later it stopped functioning. The media companies that had not yet been placed under government control or shut down knew very well what could and could not be said, and made sure to enforce it in their newsrooms.[4]

On March 24, 1976, the junta released Communication No. 19, in which it announced that "any media outlet that reports, divulges, or spreads messages or images coming from or attributed to illicit associations or individuals or groups known to be engaged in subversive activities or terrorism will be punished with imprisonment for an indefinite term," and "anyone who through any means reports,

4 G. Postolski and S. Marino, "Relaciones peligrosas: los medios y la dictadura entre el control, la censura y los negocios," in G. Mastrini (ed.), *Mucho ruido, pocas leyes. Economía y políticas de comunicación en la Argentina (1920–2004)* (Buenos Aires: La Crujía), 2005, p. 162.

divulges, or spreads news, messages, or images with the purpose of disrupting, hindering, or discrediting the activities of the armed forces, the security forces, or the police will be punished with prison terms of up to 10 years."

At the same time, Decree-Law 21,272, known as the "law on penalties for those who commit acts of violence against military or security personnel," went into effect. This legal instrument took to an extreme the already restrictive laws on contempt, by stipulating that anyone who threatened, defamed, or in any way offended the dignity or decorum of military, security force, police, or national or provincial penitentiary personnel during the performance of their duties would be punished with up to ten years of prison time.

In line with the Statute of the Process of National Reorganization, which prohibited all political activity, Decree-Law 21,323 was also passed, stipulating in its section 1: "Anyone involved in political activities will be punished with one month to three years in prison." Section 3 of the law established that "the directors of any public media or information outlet that disseminates or spreads developments, messages, or images linked to the behaviors defined as criminal in section 1 will be punished with one month to one year in prison."

This was accompanied by a stiffening of the penalties stipulated in the Criminal Code for slander and libel, with the aim of punishing the use of public media channels by increasing the penalties for basic offenses and adding dissemination as an aggravating factor. Hence, sections 109 and 110, under which these offenses were traditionally classified, were changed to the following wording:

> Section 109. Anyone who falsely attributes to another the commission of a willful offense or willful criminal conduct, even if indeterminate, will be punished with six months to three years in prison and a fine of 20,000 to 500,000 pesos. The prison term will be of one to five years when the offense was committed in a manner that facilitated its dissemination.
>
> Section 110. Anyone who dishonors or discredits another will be punished with one month to one year in prison. If the offense was committed in a manner that facilitated its dissemination, the penalty will be six months to three years in prison and a fine of 10,000 to 300,000 pesos.

This legal superstructure was complemented with hundreds of provisions and administrative acts specifically focused on content control. That is, in addition to the universe of regulations and laws, numerous newspapers and other media were closed down by decree, there were ad hoc bans, and artists, plays, and other works were blacklisted.[5]

[5] H. Invernizzi and J. Gociol, *Un golpe a los libros. Represión a la cultura durante la última dictadura militar* (Buenos Aires: Eudeba, 2003).

The construction of this legal structure highlights the determination of the dictatorship and its civilian accomplices to generate a communicational and cultural platform favorable to their interests by monopolizing the public debate and reserving the greatest state violence for any expression of dissidence. Only the existence of business interests and complicities can explain that, in a context such as the one reviewed here, newspapers and a large number of media outlets – which can be described as traditional and veterans in the field – could claim that freedom of the press was "a reality."

Censorship and tight control over content, which run counter to the most basic principles that guarantee the exercise of freedom of expression in a democratic society, operated as fundamental tools that the civilian-military bloc managed at whim until the months following the defeat in the Malvinas/Falklands war, when the process of the recovery of democracy began. However, the censorship did not function in a centralized fashion or only through the direct action of representatives of the regime. Instead, it was a practice that impregnated the media outlets that survived state terrorism, based on a structure of cooperation with the regime determined by the business community. As Andrés Avellaneda states, the "provisions and decree-laws through which cultural control is translated are semantically intertwined and engender prescriptive practices that are gradually organized through contamination and by inclusion."[6]

ECONOMIC RELATIONS

In contrast to the support for illegal repression, whose discourse was adopted and constructed in a context of almost absolute complicity, the economic relationship between private commercial media and the dictatorship was plagued with tension. Nevertheless, as is seen in this chapter, some major deals can be identified, which by providing concrete financial advantages contributed to sustain the agreement between the government and the media. Most significant in this sense is the case of Papel Prensa, but other important elements are the continuity of permits and the exclusion of new actors in the area of broadcasting (which was the preserve of a handful of private stations), the exception from the general VAT scheme that entered into effect in October 1980, and the suspension as of March 24, 1976 of all labor rights, the improved benefits of the collective bargaining agreements, and trade union activity.[7]

6 A. Avellaneda, *Censura, autoritarismo y cultura: Argentina, 1960–1983* (Buenos Aires: CEAL, 1986). Also by Avellaneda, "El discurso de represión cultural (1960–1983)," available at comisionporlamemoria.net/bibliografia2012/ejes/cultura_avellaneda.pdf (accessed December 1, 2013).

7 Until the dictatorship and after decades of trade union activity, press workers had the highest wages, as a result of the 1975 joint committees.

The privileges enjoyed by business owners coexisted with a few interventionist and market control measures that contradicted the dictatorship's liberal script and that were resisted by some media outlets, particularly *La Nación*, which warned that some of the measures would hurt the interests of the rural elite.

In the sector, furthermore, there were serious differences over the implementation of the Papel Prensa project, the exclusion of print media from the broadcasting market, stipulated under section 45 of Decree-Law 22,285,[8] and the elimination of the 50-percent discounts provided for in the Journalist's Statute for state postal, telephone, and airline companies, which were not reinstated until 1990.

Although there is no data available on the amounts and the distribution of official advertising, the state was, by far, the main advertiser. This benefited, in the first place, advertising agencies (some of them multinationals like Burson-Marsteller or Young & Rubicam) and also, of course, the private media, in particular those closest to the regime. People still remember major campaigns that formed part of the dictatorship's propaganda machine, like the one broadcast during the Malvinas/Falklands war or another that extolled the advantages of buying imported goods, as well as ads based on the slogan *Los argentinos somos derechos y humanos* (literally, "We Argentines are honest and humane," playing on the term *derechos humanos*, or human rights, in the face of denunciations of human rights abuses).

In more general terms, with respect to support for the dictatorship's economic policies, it is a much more complex task to determine the positions taken by different newspapers. *Clarín* – still imbued with its developmentalist roots – maintained a position of relative distance and was even at moments critical of the policies of José Alfredo Martínez de Hoz, while *La Nación* often questioned the same measures but because it saw them as falling short. As Ricardo Sidicaro says,

> when it felt that what was being done on the economic front was insufficient, *La Nación* maintained its objections to the economy minister's performance. Certain statements by the business chambers prompted comments from it on the subject. The shrinking of the state, a promise that was deemed unfulfilled, was frequently addressed. When, in an effort to curb inflation, Minister Martínez de Hoz decided to control prices for 120 days, restricting the freedom businesses had to set prices, the newspaper made it clear it disagreed with that method, which was only acceptable in very specific circumstances. In its view, these were measures for a fictional economy; the real solution was to be found in the strict compliance with the original aims of the 1976 program.[9]

8 In the short term, this exclusion prevented Héctor Ricardo García from recovering Channel 11. It also kept the newspaper *Clarín* from accessing radio and television, although it did allow *La Nueva Provincia* to remain a multimedia group.

9 R. Sidicaro, *La política mirada desde arriba. Las ideas del diario La Nación, 1909–1989* (Buenos Aires: Sudamericana, 1993), p. 409.

THE IACHR MISSION

Some aspects of the news coverage of the 1979 mission of the Inter-American Commission on Human Rights (IACHR) are noteworthy. Still remembered today is Radio Rivadavia's coverage of Argentina's victory in the FIFA World Youth Championship, in which sports announcer José María Muñoz urged people celebrating in the streets to march to the venue of the IACHR meeting, by telling them: "Let's all go to Avenida de Mayo and show the gentlemen of the Human Rights Commission that Argentina has nothing to hide."

In its September 6, 1979 editorial, *La Nación* wrote:

> We also hope the members of the Commission will be capable of seeing the positive things that are happening in our country in terms of observance of human rights, such as the independence of a Judicial Branch that is not only concerned about enforcing general laws but also about subjecting the Executive Branch's actions to the criteria of reasonableness.

Clarín, for its part, highlighted the contrast between Argentines afflicted by low wages and high prices and the celebrations of the World Youth Championship, whose festive soccer fans at one point "merged, on Avenida de Mayo, with relatives of the disappeared who were lining up outside the OAS offices to file reports."[10] It also reported the irritation of journalists who felt harassed by the presence of strangers while they were interviewing members of the Commission.

Just as *Clarín* and *Crónica* devoted a great deal of space to covering the IACHR mission – although neither went as far as interviewing any of the thousands of relatives of disappeared persons lining up to give their testimony to the Commission – *La Nación* did not refrain from providing its own, albeit distant, coverage of the mission along with a list of 200 business chambers and other civil organizations that were preparing to place an ad bidding the Commission farewell. The title would be "We Argentines want to tell the world." Tell it what? That Argentina was at war and that the decision to enter that war was not made only by the armed forces.[11]

Around that time, the Atlántida publishing house magazine *Gente* stated, in its 373rd editorial comment, that "we Argentines will be facing a choice between two possible countries. The one that politicians and trade unionists – with rare exceptions – still want; and the one outlined by the Project for National Reorganization and firmly defended by President [Jorge Rafael] Videla in Rosario and praised by foreign politicians during their recent visits. It is up to us Argentines. The future is in our hands. The time has come to prepare ourselves and act."[12]

[10] *Clarín*, September 9, 1979, quoted in Blaustein and Zubieta, *Decíamos ayer*, p. 309.

[11] Blaustein and Zubieta, *Decíamos ayer*, p. 37.

[12] Ibid., p. 309.

Toward the end of 2012 the Federal Court of Appeals (Cámara Federal) summoned one of the heads of *Para Ti*, another Atlántida magazine, to testify regarding a fabricated report and interview with a mother of a disappeared individual. The story had been prepared when Thelma Jara de Cabezas was being held at the Escuela de Mecánica de la Armada (ESMA) clandestine detention center and was forced to participate in the notorious news report "Human Rights: Mother of a Dead Subversive Speaks Out."[13]

THE BROADCASTING ACT

Without a doubt, one of the most lasting legacies of the dictatorship with regard to the media was Decree-Law 22,285, signed into law by Videla in 1980. This law governed the fate of broadcasting media in Argentina – with more than a dozen substantial amendments after the return to democracy – until the passage of the Audiovisual Media Services Act (Law 26,522) in 2009. The spirit behind this policy of the military junta was fully in line with its economic discourse and the creation of a new system characterized by a new model of accumulation characterized by financial valorization, which began to be consolidated under state terrorism.[14]

Decree-Law 22,285 had a strong commercial bias – to the point that it discriminated against and prohibited the not-for-profit provision of broadcast services to individuals or legal persons – and a privatist slant as it relegated the state to a secondary role, allowing it to provide services only where there were no active private interests. These aspects coincided with the de facto government's own objectives of ideological control, which meant the law was also deeply authoritarian and antidemocratic. Under its articles the functioning of the media was subordinated to "national security" needs. By way of example, articles 7, 14, and 18, which remained in effect until the law was repealed in 2009, urged the media to "collaborate" with national security, contribute to "the strengthening of faith and hope in the fate of the Argentine nation," and publish any news involving "sordid, gruesome or repulsive events or episodes … decorously and prudently, keeping within the limits imposed by strict facts."

Nevertheless, the newspapers printed headlines like "Executive Enacts Broadcasting Act. Only Limits on Freedom of Information Will Be those Arising from the Constitution" (*La Nación*, September 16, 1980) and "Law 22,285 on Broadcasting Passed. Sixty-seven Radio and TV Stations to Be Privatized" (*Clarín*, September 16, 1980).

In short, at the same time that it established restrictions on content, the law guaranteed the continuity of all permits for twenty-five years as of 1982, while it

[13] *Para Ti*, September 10, 1979; see H. Verbitsky, *El silencio* (Buenos Aires: Sudamericana, 2005).

[14] See Chapter 5 in this book.

maintained, on one hand, a ban on noncommercial services – in terms in line with the restrictions placed on cooperative activities in the economy – and on the other, the "subsidiary" role of the state, which could only install media outlets in sites rejected by private companies or where they were not interested in participating in tenders.

The law was excessively centralist. Enforcement was left exclusively to the national Executive, excluding any representation of the provinces. Instead, it incorporated media owners in the main decision-making processes. Section 96 – also in effect until 2009 – established that the board of the Federal Broadcasting Committee (Comité Federal de Radiodifusión, COMFER) was to be formed by one commander-in-chief from each of the armed forces, one member of the Secretariat of Public Information, one member of the Secretariat of Communications, and two representatives of the associations of private broadcast license holders. Although this article was not repealed, after the return to democracy the agency was placed under control of an administrator appointed directly by the Executive.

The business community's official participation in the board was plagued by actions that ran counter to the freedom they claimed to defend. Artists, journalists, films, and songs were blacklisted and content was subjected to strict review through resolutions signed without exception by all COMFER board members. These resolutions were opened up to public scrutiny in 2009 and posted on the agency's Web site, and they carry the signatures of representatives of radio and television broadcasting companies until at least late 1982.

The dictatorship established that, in practice, the law would be implemented by means of a gradual process of privatization, which it called the National Broadcasting Plan (Plan Nacional de Radiodifusión, PLANARA)[15] and would extend until 1994. However, after the Malvinas/Falklands war and given the imminent arrival of a democratic government, the last de facto president, Reynaldo Bignone, issued a series of licenses to individuals and companies close to the military. Many of them were revoked by Raúl Alfonsín, but others remain in effect today. In 1984, by means of Decree 1151/84, Alfonsín dismantled PLANARA and suspended all calls for bids until a new broadcasting law entered into force. But, although the replacement of the dictatorship's law seemed imminent, another twenty-five years would have to go by before a new law was passed.

PAPEL PRENSA

On September 11, 1976 *Clarín* published the following front page story: "Import Substitution: Newspapers to Make their Own Newsprint."[16] The project to create

[15] Decree 286/81.
[16] On this case, see also Chapter 20 in this book.

a national company for newsprint production dated back to the late 1960s, when Argentina had the largest newspaper and magazine consumption in Latin America but imported nearly all the paper consumed in the country.[17] In 1969, the de facto government of General Juan Carlos Onganía ordered the creation of a "[f]und for the development of the production of newsprint and cellulose," for which all of the country's newspapers had to pay an import surtax of 10 percent with the aim of financing the construction of the plant. Going against the original project, which envisaged the participation of all newspaper publishers, the de facto government of General Alejandro Lanusse granted in 1972, through a direct award, 26 percent of the company's shares to a group headed by César Augusto Civita, the owner of the Abril publishing house, and a 25 percent interest was reserved for the state.

In 1973, as a result of pressure from then Economy Minister José Ber Gelbard, the shares in the hands of Civita went to another member of the original group, Luis Alberto Rey, who operated as frontman for businessman and banker David Graiver, who would later be accused by the military dictatorship of being one of the administrators of the funds of the Montoneros.[18]

After the March 24 coup d'état, the Junta of Commanders-in-Chief increasingly pressured the Graiver family, in particular as of the banker's death in a plane crash in Mexico in August of that year under circumstances that were never fully clarified. On November 2, 1976 the de facto military government forced Graiver's widow, Lidia Papaleo, to sign the preliminary sales promise for the shares to Fapel, a company formed by *Clarín*, *La Nación*, and *La Razón*, which paid US$8.3 million for Papel Prensa, three times less than the estimated value at the time. Ten years later, the company was valued at US$250 million.

In September 2010, the Executive, represented by the National Secretariat of Human Rights, filed a private prosecution against "the illegitimate dispossession of Papel Prensa SA from its owners," the members of the Graiver group,[19] and linked the representatives of the three newspapers to the crimes against humanity committed against the family. Whatever progress may be achieved in this case and whether or not the criminal responsibility of the representatives of the company

[17] O. Getino, *Las industrias culturales en la Argentina* (Buenos Aires: Colihue, 1995), p. 79.

[18] M. Borrelli, "'Una batalla ganada': el diario *Clarín* frente a la compra de Papel Prensa por parte de los diarios *La Nación*, *Clarín* y *La Razón* (1976–1978)," *Papeles de Trabajo*, electronic magazine of Instituto de Altos Estudios Sociales de la Universidad Nacional de General San Martín, year 2, no. 4, December 2008.

[19] The members include Graiver's widow Lidia Papaleo, her brother Osvaldo Papaleo, Isidoro Graiver and his wife Lidia Brodsky, Jorge Rubinstein (lawyer and David Graiver's right-hand man), Rafael Ianover (an employee of David Graiver), Juan Graiver and Eva Gitnacht (David's parents), Silvia Fanjul (employed by the Graiver family), and Lidia Gesualdi (secretary). They were all detained once ownership of the company was transferred. Most of them were tortured while they were detained and later "regularized," that is, placed at the disposal of the national Executive.

can be determined, one thing is clear, namely the fraudulent nature of the transfer of shares, which shortly after the return to democracy was denounced by former National Administrative Investigations Prosecutor Ricardo Molinas.[20]

In his February 29, 1988 opinion, after an extensive investigation initiated four years earlier, Molinas demonstrated that the company had been sold at an absurdly low price, with the Graiver family selling under pressure, and accused the state representatives in the company of breach of the duties of the civil servant. Four years later, the statute of limitations on the criminal action initiated with the prosecutor's opinion expired. Molinas himself called the Papel Prensa deal "one of the most serious cases of corruption in Argentine history."[21] As his prosecutor's office did not have jurisdiction, Molinas did not accuse the private businesses that benefited from the criminal conduct of the public officials involved.

As stated earlier, the takeover of the company triggered major divisions among newspaper editors. A few months later, after the deal was concluded by the three newspapers in partnership with the state, Papel Prensa launched an intense campaign aimed at legitimizing its origins and makeup, particularly in the eyes of other newspapers. Thus, a series of newspaper ads were published, justifying the tariff protection received by the company and highlighting once again how significant the enterprise was for "import substitution."

In the words of Sidicaro, "technical reasons were combined with ideological arguments that sounded paradoxical to those who recalled the objections set forth so frequently by *La Nación* with regard to the 'artificial' industries created under the umbrella of state protection."[22]

In a March 4, 1979 ad,[23] *La Nación* once again explicitly laid out the reasons that justified its participation in the project and the hike in tariffs on paper imports. The then secretary of finance of the military junta, Juan Alemann, questioned these statements and exposed the differences that divided the companies that participated in Papel Prensa and part of the government. Alemann argued that the protectionist demands of Papel Prensa were unacceptable and added: "I'd do great in business too if I did things that way; we all would."[24]

Papel Prensa responded with another ad in which it criticized Alemann for expressing an opinion on matters that fell outside the scope of his authority and

20 L. M. Lozano, "Libertad de expresión y derecho a la información: tensiones y desafíos en torno a la democratización de la palabra," in CELS, *Derechos humanos en Argentina. Informe 2011* (Buenos Aires: Siglo XXI, 2011), p. 290.

21 R. Molinas and F. Molinas, *Detrás del espejo. Quince años de despojo al patrimonio nacional* (Buenos Aires: Beas, 1993), quoted in Lozano, "Libertad de expresión," p. 290.

22 Sidicaro, *La política mirada desde arriba*, p. 418.

23 "Por qué *La Nación* participa en Papel Prensa," *La Nación*, March 4, 1979.

24 Statements to the Río Negro press and reproduced by the weekly *El Economista*, on March 30, 1979; quoted in Sidicaro, *La política mirada desde arriba*, p. 421.

asked whether he had made those statements as an individual or as the owner of a newspaper.[25] It did not take long for the finance secretary to publicly change his mind, which earned him such headlines in *La Prensa* as: "The Case of the Secretary Who Didn't Understand but Now Does."[26] The article claimed that Economy Minister Martínez de Hoz had ordered him not to criticize Papel Prensa.[27]

The explanations provided by the Papel Prensa partners did not satisfy the owners of the newspapers that had been left out of the business deal. The members of the editorial board of *La Prensa*, led by its editor, Máximo Gainza, launched a long series of public complaints about the price of paper, which would continue over the following three decades with different protagonists. In an editorial published on November 11, 1980, the newspaper, founded by José C. Paz, stated that while at that time newsprint cost US$345 to US$419 a ton, the price in Argentina was US$845 as a result of the tax burden aimed at favoring Papel Prensa.[28]

For their part, the editors Ovidio Lagos of the Rosario newspaper *La Capital* and Raúl Kraiselburd of the La Plata newspaper *El Día* complained to the IAPA, which took on itself the task of denouncing the danger that the existence of a company like Papel Prensa posed to print media and urged the government to eliminate all taxes on paper, in accordance with Argentine tradition. The response was immediate: at the same meeting, José Claudio Escribano, of *La Nación*, said that what was being discussed was actually a problem of interests rather than principles. He accused ADEPA of holding that same attitude and invited the IAPA to refrain from becoming involved in a conflict that had nothing to do with its purposes.[29]

The reference to ADEPA was no accident, as in December 1979 the institution's executive council had stated:

> In the Western world there is not a single example of economic integration comparable to what was achieved by the Papel Prensa SA company, formed and managed, essentially, by three metropolitan newspapers together with the key involvement of the state.... Conscious or not, if this process moves forward it will fatally lead to the suppression of freedom of the press. ... It is not difficult to imagine what an authoritarian government could achieve acting with all the means available to the state, through that concentration of power.[30]

25 "Solicitada Papel Prensa SA," *La Nación*, March 28, 1979.

26 *La Prensa*, March 21, 1980.

27 "Difundióse una nota del Dr. Juan Alemann," *La Nación*, March 27, 1980.

28 The *La Prensa* case merits a special analysis that goes beyond the scope of this book. Invited by the government to participate in the Papel Prensa initiative, it rejected the offer arguing that it had long-term commercial commitments with the Finnish company that supplied it with paper. Aligned with the dictatorship's repressive and economic policies, it was, however, one of the few newspapers that published ads by human rights organizations.

29 "Reparos a la posición de la SIP sobre la Argentina," *La Nación*, January 18, 1979, quoted in Sidicaro, *La política mirada desde arriba*, p. 429.

30 *La Nación*, December 18, 1979.

MALVINAS/FALKLANDS

True to the maxim attributed to U.S. Senator Hiram Johnson, who in 1917 said, "[t]he first casualty when war comes is truth," following the armed occupation of the Malvinas/Falkland Islands on April 2, 1982 and during the two and a half months that the conflict lasted, the local media reached peaks of misinformation and data manipulation that deepened the censorship put in place in earlier years. In the words of Horacio Verbitsky, the military junta directed the efforts to misinform its own people, even if in doing so it had to supply the enemy with valuable information. Its aim was to deceive not the British armed forces, but Argentine society, substituting words for the offensive actions that were not being played out in the battlefield. The media uniformly echoed the junta's version of events, blanket broadcasting from the first to the last day of the conflict, just as they had done during the dirty war over the previous decade, when the dictatorship believed it was a leading player in the third world war against communism.[31]

In addition to paradigmatic cases in print journalism, like that of *Gente* magazine, which zealously amplified the official versions, was the enormous symbolic weight that television had during the war. The public television network, ATC, with its *60 minutos* newscast anchored by Oscar Gómez Fuentes, became the official opinion-building space regarding the conflict. On April 2, the landing of troops was broadcast and, starting on April 12, Channel 7 provided live, on-location coverage of the war. The armed forces issued guidelines instructing television stations to broadcast only those messages and footage that would "not cause panic or undermine national unity." Throughout the conflict, the ratings of the channels increased steadily, peaking at 52.2 points, during the special fund-raising telethon, *24 horas por Malvinas* (24 Hours for the Malvinas) hosted by Lidia Satragno and Jorge Fontana.

In sum, during the armed conflict, the media was an essential ally of the dictatorship as it played a key role in furthering the regime's aim of disinformation. After the ceasefire, it also took it upon itself to begin the operation of enveloping the war and its martyrs in an aura of sacredness, avoiding any accounts by survivors, who were brought back at night to dark barracks, and blocking any reports of the human rights violations perpetrated on the battlefield. As Federico Lorenz notes:

> Criticism of the defeat in the islands, of the conduct of many of those who had led the war, spread simultaneously with the dissemination of reports of human rights abuses. It was then that such emblematic figures as Alfredo Astiz, a symbol of both illegal repression and ignominious defeat, were consolidated as icons and exposed

[31] H. Verbitsky, *Malvinas. La última batalla de la Tercera Guerra Mundial* (Buenos Aires: Legasa, 1984), p. 10.

> how there was not an armed forces that went to the Malvinas and an armed forces that was involved in the repression, but that they were one and the same.[32]

After the defeat, however, censorship and control were increasingly relaxed. New programs came on the air and actors who had previously been banned returned to television. Channel 9 started broadcasting the standalone series *Nosotros y los miedos*; Channel 13 aired *Compromiso*; and ATC broadcast *Situación límite*. Issues that until then had been absent from the small screen began to appear, and the media moved toward new formats and contents, coinciding with the return to democracy.

STATEMENTS, EDITORIALS, AND OTHER PARADIGMATIC EXPRESSIONS

In 1978, the IAPA sent Ignacio Lozano, the owner of *La Opinión*, a Spanish-language daily newspaper published in Los Angeles, California, and Edward Seaton, the editor-in-chief and publisher of the *Manhattan Mercury* in Kansas, on a mission to Argentina to investigate the extremely serious reports of violations of freedom of expression in the country. In their final report they said the editors of the main Argentine newspapers – *Clarín* and *La Nación* – had put national security above freedom of expression and had supported the de facto government's fight against guerrilla organizations. In that report, the IAPA observed with concern that the government had granted long-term loans to the newspapers for a paper factory, and expressed serious reservations about the project, as it posed a number of risks, not the least of which was the fact that it practically imposed a non-antagonistic position toward the government during the term of indebtedness.[33]

In that way, the report said, the owners of the leading newspapers that were still privately held in Argentina justified the censorship, declared themselves in agreement with the objectives and methods of the military dictatorship (in which they distinguished "hardline" and "moderate" positions), and cooperated with the de facto regime by refusing to report on forced disappearances. In exchange, they benefited from their partnership with the government in paper production.

On October 13, 1978, on the last session of the IAPA General Assembly, when the report was presented, the headline of *La Nación* was "Argentina Takes Firm Stance before the IAPA Assembly." The article reported that ADEPA had turned down the IAPA's Mergenthaler Award, granted collectively "[t]o Argentine journalists who died, were disappeared, or suffered imprisonment and persecution for defending

[32] F. Lorenz, "Lobos con piel de ovejas malvineras," in CELS, *Derechos humanos en Argentina. Informe 2012*, (Buenos Aires: Siglo XXI, 2012), p. 467.

[33] E. Seaton and I. Lozano, "Informe sobre la libertad de expresión en la Argentina," presented at the 34th IAPA Assembly, held in Miami on October 9–13, 1978 (a copy of the report is held by the author). The IAPA mission to Argentina was conducted on August 18–25, 1978.

freedom of the press." The Argentine delegation had proposed replacing that text with the following: "To Argentine journalists represented by the figure of Alberto Gainza Paz, who never wavered in his defense of the principles that sustain the IAPA." The proposed text was not accepted by the IAPA and no one removed the plaque, which was placed in the organization's headquarters.[34] Gainza Paz's merit apparently came from the October 5, 1977 publication of a paid ad by mothers and wives of disappeared persons.

In 1980, ADEPA paid tribute to its president in its first semester report and spoke of an improvement in the situation of freedom of the press in the government in ideological terms, but warned that this was not the case on the economic front. In particular, the complaint was over a 45 percent tax imposed on paper imports. What was not said was that it was linked to the Papel Prensa SA operation and "import substitution." It was not the first time ADEPA made such statements. A year earlier, in April 1979, the ADEPA board of directors had declared that in the period between September 1978 and April 1979 the government had taken a respectful stance toward Argentina's newspapers.

In June 1978, after the World Cup was held in the country, the Argentine Association of Advertising Agencies (Asociación Argentina de Agencias de Publicidad) published an institutional ad that amounted to a defense of the dictatorship and in which it stated that when Argentina really wanted something, it could achieve it, under the slogan "The real Argentina is also news." Curiously enough, this text was used as the title for an ad published by the Buenos Aires Stock Exchange, published in several languages on June 27, with the following footnote: "Support for the efforts to clarify Argentine reality."

This is not to deny the existence of different forms of resistance that enabled the circulation of information and artistic and cultural expressions, and which managed to break through the information blockade imposed by the dictatorship. Neither does it entail minimizing the role of the many media workers who, in situations of extreme risk, were able to carry out small heroic acts.

In this sense, along with underground efforts, like the Clandestine News Agency (Agencia de Noticias Clandestina, ANCLA) and *Cadena Informativa*, both of which were founded by Rodolfo Walsh and, after Walsh was kidnapped, were continued by Horacio Verbitsky, there were practices by some "legal" media outlets that dared to speak out against the repression and – within the scope of their possibilities – addressed the demands of families of the victims. Most notable among these were the *Buenos Aires Herald*, headed by Robert Cox until he had to leave the country in 1978; the Jewish community newspaper *Nueva Presencia*, whose editor was Herman

[34] H. Verbitsky, "Quién es quién," *Página/12* (Buenos Aires), March 6, 2005, available at www.pagina12.com.ar/diario/elpais/1-48103-2005-03-06.html (accessed February 8, 2013).

Schiller; and Radio Colonia, run from Uruguay by Ariel Delgado. In this scenario, the emergence of the magazine *Humor* in 1978 represented – despite its small circulation – a breath of fresh air in the midst of the news blackout.

The terrorist state, grounded on the concept of a period of exception, gave birth to a parallel legal framework that supported the operation of more than 340 clandestine detention centers across the country.[35] But that state system was only possible insofar as it was deeply rooted in society, permeating it and feeding off it.[36] Only in the context of that "rationally and centrally adopted repressive technology"[37] is it possible to think of the dictatorship's media policies, of which this chapter provides only a brief overview, with the inevitable risk of arbitrariness that any summary entails.

This is, thus, a contribution in memory of and tribute to the more than 100 disappeared media workers, those who were forced into exile, and those who, even in periods of democracy, have been persecuted, silenced, intimidated, and even killed.

35 A. Conte and E. Mignone, *Estrategia represiva de la dictadura militar: La doctrina del paralelismo global* (Buenos Aires: CELS, 1980).

36 P. Calveiro, *Poder y desaparición* (Buenos Aires: Colihue, 2004), p. 18.

37 Ibid.

22

The Price of the Church's Blessing

Horacio Verbitsky

Note

These pages contain no value judgments regarding the dogma or practices of the Roman Catholic Church and are only meant as an analysis of the Church's behavior in Argentina between 1976 and 1983 as a "sociological reality of a specific people in a specific world," according to the terms of its own Episcopal Conference. Its "theological reality of the mysteries of the faith,"[1] instead, is a matter that concerns only its faithful, who deserve my utmost respect.

The reasons for including the Catholic Church among the economic accomplices of the military dictatorship are not obvious.

In the first place because the Church is the community of believers who were among the many victims of dictatorial repression, the economic accomplice reference is only valid if it is circumscribed to the highest Episcopal authorities. In the criminal action for the murder of the priests Carlos de Dios Murias and Gabriel Longueville, the Federal Oral Court of La Rioja (Tribunal Oral de La Rioja) found that the Catholic Church "exhibited, in many of its authorities, silence toward, support for, and complicity with the dictatorial process."[2]

In the second place, there is the fact that, with the aim of furthering the ethereal common good, both catechism and papal encyclicals call for collaboration with any government that does not attack the institution of the Church. That "Social Doctrine of the Church," as it is called, allowed it to coexist without guilt with all sorts of dictatorships, even with the Nazi regime, which granted it great economic and social advantages, even though it meant persecuting many priests, as occurred in Argentina. A German priest and politician, very close to Pope Pius XII, based that alliance on the argument that "the authoritarian Church should

[1] Conferencia Episcopal Argentina (CEA), *Plan nacional de pastoral* (Buenos Aires, 1967), p. 14. See L. O. Liberti, *Monseñor Enrique Angelelli. Pastor que evangeliza promoviendo integralmente al hombre* (Buenos Aires: Guadalupe, 2005), p. 164.

[2] Tribunal Oral Federal de La Rioja, "Estrella, Luis Fernando y otros p. ss. aa. homicidio calificado reiterado, privación ilegítima de la libertad seguida de muerte y tormentos," judgment of December 7, 2012.

understand the authoritarian state better than others," and vice versa.[3] Or as the journalist and ideologue Mariano Grondona wrote in Buenos Aires, that alliance was grounded on "Argentina being Catholic and military."[4] This only changed with the end of those regimes. In his Christmas Eve message of 1944, Pius XII made his peace with the Saxon democracies,[5] and in 1981 the Argentine Episcopate resigned itself to democratic pluralism, through the document *Iglesia y comunidad nacional*.[6]

In the third place, the Church in Argentina also received enormous contributions from the state, both before 1976 and after 1983, as compensation for the property confiscated in 1822 during the short government of Bernardino Rivadavia. Which is why under Article 2 of the 1853 Constitution, still in force, "the federal government supports the Roman Apostolic Catholic religion."

This chapter, however, after reviewing the ideological affinity between the Catholic Church and the armed forces (which at its highest point had both institutions viewing each other as the pillars on which Argentine nationhood rested), giving a brief overview of the etiology of the state's assistance to the ecclesiastical institution, and quantifying those favors, determines the specific nature of the complicity between the Church and military hierarchies during the years of the terrorist state.

THE DOCTRINE OF EXTERMINATION

The doctrine of extermination was, in fact, instilled in the military by the Church. Antonio Caggiano and Adolfo Tortolo, who served consecutively as presidents of the Episcopal Conference, had also headed, at the same time, the Military Vicariate, which would later become a Diocese.[7] In the two decades prior to the coup, both Caggiano and Tortolo allowed the fundamentalist organization Ciudad Católica to speak to high-ranking officials of the three services in their own units and to preach to them that everything was permitted in the battle for God and the Nation.[8]

At Tortolo's request, the founder of the youth organization Tacuara, Alberto Ezcurra Uriburu, who had become a priest late in life, systematized the concepts that the military vicar is said to have used to defend torture before the Episcopate: the state should not set itself legal or moral limits, and anyone who denounced the disappearances was at

3 L. Kaas, "*Der Konkordatstyp des faschistichen italianen*," in J. Cornwell (ed.), *El Papa de Hitler. La verdadera historia de Pío XII* (Buenos Aires: Planeta, 2000), p. 150.

4 M. Grondona, "Iglesia, las relaciones cuidadosas," *Carta Política*, Buenos Aires, October 1976.

5 Archivo de la Secretaría de Culto (hereinafter, Culto), Box 7, 1944, RREE, Salidas.

6 Conferencia Episcopal Argentina (CEA), *Iglesia y comunidad nacional* (Buenos Aires: Oficina del Libro, CEA, 1981).

7 See all four volumes of H. Verbitsky, *Historia política de la Iglesia Católica en la Argentina* (Buenos Aires: Sudamericana, 2007, 2008, 2009, and 2010).

8 M. Ranalletti, "Du Mekong au Río de la Plata," PhD diss. (unpublished), under the direction of Professor Maurice Vaïce, Institute d'Études Politiques de Paris (2007).

the service of Marxism.[9] The general framework for these concepts was drawn from the papal encyclicals and the sixteenth-century Spanish scholastic thinker Francisco de Vitoria, who developed Saint Thomas's just war theology. In *De Jure Belli*, Vitoria argued that "supposing them also to have been guilty... there is nothing to prevent the killing of those who have surrendered or been captured in a just war" – that is, a war waged according to the principles of the Gospel and the Natural Order. Drawing on the bibliography of the French colonial army, Ezcurra says that in the so-called revolutionary war, "the university, the justice system, the means for psycho-political combat are just as much battlefronts as the bush or the mountains."[10]

The archbishop of Córdoba, Cardinal Raúl Francisco Primatesta, who was also vice president and later president of the Episcopate, anticipated that the cure would be harsh, "because God's left hand is paternal, but it can be heavy."[11] "Through the left" became the most common way of describing clandestine repression. The naval operations commander informed the top-ranking officers of all the units of the main navy base that prisoners were to be thrown from planes into the sea. He said this method had been approved by the Church hierarchy as a Christian form of death. When the officers came back disturbed from those flights, the chaplains comforted them with biblical parables about separating the wheat from the tares.[12] To justify the clandestine killings, high-ranking army and navy officers argued that the Vatican would not have authorized mass trials and executions.[13]

The heads of the Episcopate attended the presidential inauguration of Jorge Rafael Videla, and the bishops of each province accompanied the respective military governors as they swore by God and His Holy Gospels. Tortolo likened the military intervention with the resurrection of Christ[14] and said that violent action had to be taken "against subversion."[15] For Victorio Bonamín, Tortolo's military pro-vicar, the armed forces were "soldiers of the Gospel willing to sacrifice themselves by giving their lives for their brothers, following the example set by Christ."[16] The influence of the Church was so great that the dictatorship explained how it operated paraphrasing

9 *Mikael magazine* no. 27, Paraná, September–December 1981, pp. 125–126.

10 A. I. Ezcurra, *Moral cristiana y guerra antisubversiva, enseñanzas de un capellán castrense* (Buenos Aires: Santiago Apóstol, 2007).

11 Agencia Informativa Católica Argentina (AICA), "No podemos decir que fue un año fácil," *Boletín* no. 994, January 8, 1976, pp. 19–20.

12 Account by Captain Adolfo Scilingo. See H. Verbitsky, *The Flight* (The New Press: New York, 1996).

13 Testimony by Jacobo Timerman to the Buenos Aires Federal Court of Appeals (Cámara Federal de la Capital) under court case 13/84, May 2, 1985; explanation by former general Ramón Díaz Bessone. See M. M. Robin, *Escadrons de la mort. L'Ecole française* (Paris: La Découverte, 2004).

14 See AICA, *Boletín* no. 1009, April 2, 1976, p. 18.

15 "Lo dice monseñor Tortolo," *Gente*, April 8, 1976.

16 "Conceptos de Bonamín en Ejército," *La Nación* (Buenos Aires), May 11, 1976.

the Mystery of the Most Holy Trinity: "Three equal responsibilities for a common task, three military powers exercising the indivisible political power of the Nation, embodied in the Military Junta."[17]

FROM CONCEALMENT TO INVOLVEMENT

In May 1976, the Episcopal Assembly began its first meeting after the coup with a report from each bishop recounting the detentions of workers, the kidnappings, torturing, and murders that had occurred in their respective dioceses, including the persecution of priests and the harassment of two bishops who would die shortly after in alleged highway accidents. Nineteen bishops voted to make this atrocious news public, but thirty-eight voted against denouncing them.[18] These two-thirds decided to cover up the crimes and issue a commitment document.

In a pastoral letter entitled "Country and Common Good"[19] they declared that the state must "exercise its legitimate and necessary authority, even coercively" toward guaranteeing the "common good," to which individual good is subordinated. They did not explain where that alleged legitimacy came from. They sentenced that it was not time to demand the full enjoyment of human rights and asked for understanding for the military government, which could not act "with the chemical purity of times of peace." They condemned, instead, "the murder, preceded or not by kidnapping, of any individuals, whatever side they are on," thus positing an improbable equivalence. This set the tone for all collective documents issued by the Episcopate, with abstract exhortations to respect the dignity of the human person, explicit approval for the state's repressive methods, which the bishops were well aware of, and contempt for anyone who resisted.

In their next Plenary Assembly, in October 1976, the bishops prayed "for those who have the difficult mission of guaranteeing order in our dear Nation"[20] and, at the request of Videla, they received the minister of the economy, José Alfredo Martínez de Hoz. The minister spoke for two hours, stayed for dinner, and answered questions in an after-dinner session. He said he hoped to help those who lived in the greatest poverty, and the bishops wished him success.[21] At the insistence of the bishop of Quilmes, Jorge Novak, they also agreed to hear a group of workers accompanied by

17 Speech delivered by Air Force Chief of Staff Orlando Ramón Agosti on Air Force Day, August 10, 1976.

18 Asamblea Plenaria de la Conferencia Episcopal Argentina (APCEA), San Miguel, May 10–15, 1976, Archivo Devoto (AD), p. 29.

19 "País y bien común," Collective pastoral letter, May 15, 1976.

20 "Informe situación actual de la Iglesia Católica Apostólica Romana en la Argentina," Culto, Box 11, Binder 15, Document 3.

21 AICA, *Boletín* no. 1035, October 28, 1976, p. 2.

Catholic union leaders. But the workers were not received in the meeting hall or in the dining room. Instead they were received in the concierge's room, after dinner. Not everyone participated, only "those bishops who wanted to, nobody was forced to listen to them like we were with Martínez de Hoz, whom we had to listen to." Only twelve bishops stayed.[22] Similarly, they never let the Mothers of Plaza de Mayo past the entrance, even when it was raining heavily.[23]

A pastoral letter issued on May 7, 1977 under the title "Christian Reflections for the People of the Nation"[24] admitted the application of laws of exception and the sacrificing of individual rights. Nonetheless, it did say that "murdering the enemy, moral and physical torturing, and unlawful deprivation of freedom" could not be considered legal. It also spoke out against prolonged detentions without filing charges or allowing detainees to present a defense.[25]

These are the least ambiguous words pronounced by the Episcopate during the dictatorship, but they did not alter its behavior. On April 10, 1978, the heads of the Episcopate had lunch with Videla and inquired into the fate of detained-disappeared persons, including several priests. Videla's answer is reproduced in an informative note to the Vatican: "The most obvious thing to say would be that these [individuals] are already dead, it would be like tracing a line and saying these have disappeared and are no longer here." But that would prompt "a series of questions about where they are buried. In a mass grave? If so, who put them in that grave? A series of questions that the government cannot truthfully answer because of the consequences that would entail for certain people." Because they had to protect the kidnappers and murderers, that is. Primatesta explained that the Church was very careful about the words it used because it was well aware of "the damage they can cause the government."[26] The Church thus knew about the government's criminal methods and that it had the power to change them.

Antonio Plaza, the archbishop of La Plata, was the general chaplain of the police, with police chief rank. Individuals who were detained and disappeared, tortured, and subjected to mock executions in the Infantry Guard of La Plata came into contact with Plaza when he accompanied General Ramón Camps in his visits to

22 E. Mignone, L. Ripa, F. Mallimacci, O. Yorio, M. Fort, L. Zorzín, M. Colombo, and R. L. Brardinelli, "La Iglesia de Quilmes durante la dictadura militar, 1976–1983. Derechos humanos y la cuestión de los desaparecidos," Progress report, p. 133.

23 Interview with Nora Cortiñas, conducted by the author, April 14, 1995.

24 "Reflexión cristiana para el pueblo de la Patria," collective pastoral letter issued by the CEA, in *La Iglesia y los derechos humanos* (Buenos Aires: Oficina del Libro, CEA, 1984), pp. 33–36.

25 XXXV Asamblea Plenaria de la Conferencia Episcopal, May 2–7, 1977, draft versions of "Reflexión para el pueblo cristiano de la patria," its original title. CEA Archive (ACEA), document no. 17,315.

26 Comisión Ejecutiva de la CEA, report of the Commission's interview with the President of the Republic, April 10, 1978. ACEA, Folder 24-II, Document no. 10 949.

the ward, where prisoners were tied to beds with ropes and wires.[27] Plaza handed out medallions and celebrated mass for the hooded prisoners.[28]

–Do you know what's going on, Monsignor? – they asked him.
–I know perfectly well, and I'm very happy.[29]

The archbishop of Jujuy, José Miguel Medina, would tell political prisoners held at the Villa Gorriti prison not to bother telling him in confession about the abuses they were suffering because he agreed with what was happening to them, and suggested that they instead tell him something that could be of use to the military. When they informed him that some prisoners had been taken from their cells, he answered that they were in "a dirty war" and the prisoners had been executed.[30]

The priest Emilio Grasselli, general secretary of the Military Vicariate, had a very close relationship with Escuela de Mecánica de la Armada (ESMA) navy officers and carried a gun under his cassock. He told the relatives of a detained-disappeared individual that "out of the goodness of his heart, Videla" had devised a "rehabilitation program" because he did not want to "lose the intelligence of the subversives." But, he said, there was also another category of irredeemable cases:

– It's likely that [in those cases] some merciful soul will give them an injection and the irredeemable will fall into a permanent sleep.[31]

The U.S. government was aware of this program. "Individuals' attitudes toward family, religion and national objectives were 'strengthened' to replace their previous political-ideological personality support systems," U.S. Ambassador Raúl Castro wrote.[32] The head of intelligence of the ESMA task group claimed he spoke with Jesus: "If He says you have to die, I give you a *pentonaval* and up you go."[33]

Castro identified his sources as the French Embassy (whose colonial army devised the system) and the Catholic Church. His most frequent contact at the Church was the Vatican nuncio, Pío Laghi. The nuncio himself preached Saint Thomas's just

[27] E. Shaposnik, "La Plata. Camps y la Iglesia bancaban la tortura" (January 1984) *Caras y Caretas*.

[28] Horacio García, testimony given in the Truth Trial in the Federal Court of Appeals of La Plata (Cámara Federal de La Plata), September 5, 2001.

[29] Alberto Rubén Calvo, testimony given in the Truth Trial in the Federal Court of Appeals of La Plata, June 13, 2001.

[30] Ernesto Reynaldo Samán, testimony given to CONADEP, file no. 4841; Eulogia Cordero de Garnica, testimony to CONADEP, file no. 4859; Carlos Alberto Melián, testimony in court case 13/84 (the military junta trial), July 11, 1985.

[31] CONADEP, file no. 1560, Carlos Oscar Lorenzo, disappeared.

[32] Argentina Project, Buenos 00082 01 OF 02 042008Z. Rehabilitation programs for political prisoners. Navy Mechanical School rehabilitation program. AmEmbassy Buenos Aires to Secretary of State, Washington, DC, January 4, 1979.

[33] Testimony of Graciela Daleo to the Federal Court of Appeals, July 18, 1985, in case 13/84. This is a pun, transforming the narcotic pentothal in pentonaval (i.e., penthotal of the Navy).

war doctrine to the army troops, and he told them that "the law must be observed, but only as far as possible."[34] Laghi startled the human rights officer of the new U.S. administration, Patricia Derian, with his defense of the dictatorship: the country was getting back on its feet; the military staged the coup and applied harsh tactics because they were in fear of their lives, and the United States should not be "rubbing salt into the wounds" of the military, so as to avoid weakening "the moderate elements" that accompanied Videla, who was a "good Catholic."[35]

EDUCATION AND SOCIAL CONTROL

According to a bishop that presided over the Episcopate, even before the nation was born the Catholic Church had founded the first schools, institutes of learning, and universities where the soul of the nation was forged.[36] Education was conceived as a form of political domination and social control. With the liberal reforms of the last quarter of the nineteenth century, public secular education was established in 1884 under Law 1420. The secular cycle continued over the next six decades. On such an unusual day as December 31, 1943, the minister of public instruction of the military government that ruled the country at the time, Gustavo Martínez Zuviría (who under the alias Hugo Wast was also the author of anti-Semitic novels), issued a decree imposing Catholic education in all public schools in the country (Decree 18,411), and in 1947 this decree was passed into law. In an Inter-American Congress of Catholic Education, presided by Emilio F. Cárdenas, a large landholder and head of the organization Acción Católica, the Church demanded "the proportional distribution of the school budget."[37] It proposed that the total resources allocated by the state to education be divided by the number of school-age children, making that quotient the school voucher, and with each school receiving one voucher per student enrolled in that school.[38]

In the end, the Church did not succeed in having this formula implemented but, as of 1947, under the Teachers' Statute, state funds were used to subsidize the salaries of religious school teachers, who in only a few years were mostly priests

34 AICA, *Boletín* 1021, July 15, 1976, p. 6; "El nuncio habló a los soldados de Tucumán," *Vicariato Castrense* no. 51, August 1976, pp. 28–30.

35 Meeting between Laghi and Patricia Derian, as recounted in a memorandum drafted by the former undersecretary in 2005 upon request of the author, and a "Memorandum of Conversation" dated March 29, 1977, declassified in 2002 by the State Department.

36 "Carta del presidente del Episcopado, Adolfo Tortolo, al dictador Roberto Levingston del 11 de marzo de 1971," *AICA* no. 746, March 18, 1971.

37 "Efectuó otra reunión el segundo Congreso de Educación Católica," *La Prensa*, October 11, 1946.

38 See S. Bianchi, *Catolicismo y peronismo. Religión y política en la Argentina*, 1943–1955 (Tandil: Instituto de Estudios Histórico-Sociales Prof. Juan Carlos Grosso, 2001), p. 130.

(80 percent).[39] Thus, there was religious education in public schools and economic support from the state to private religious schools.

The constitutional reform of 1949 made the clash of legitimacies evident when the Church failed in its effort to replace the principle of popular sovereignty with the divine origin of power. The rupture became irreversible in 1954. In May 1955 religious education was eliminated from public schools and the tax exemptions for private religious schools were removed.[40] According to Perón, "with false and even simulated signatures," the state subsidy was being diverted to finance the Church,[41] which was already the brains and engine behind the conspiracy that would depose him in September of that year. The dictatorship that succeeded him in power paid the subsidies retroactively, restored tax exemptions,[42] and – a week before stepping down from the government – the dictatorial authorities signed over to the Church a property for it to rebuild the burnt Curia.[43] They also temporarily assigned the presidential residence located at number 1032 Suipacha street, purchased by General Agustín P. Justo and occupied by his successor, Roberto M. Ortiz, for use by the Buenos Aires Archbishopric while the Curia was being renovated.[44] The Marine Ministry gave the Military Vicariate a property to build the Stella Maris church.[45] This policy of donations would be intensified as of 1976.

In 1958, the Teachers' Statute brought the salary of private school teachers to the level of state schools[46] and the state subsidy to private schools was raised by decree, even for schools that charged their students tuition.[47] In 1964 another decree, which remained in force until 1991, established stricter objective conditions,[48] increasing the benefits granted to religious education.

To give an idea of the magnitude of this state contribution in current monetary values, in 2012 the Department of Worship paid salaries to 107 bishops and apostolic and/or diocese administrators, 481 border parish priests, and 1,143 seminarians for a total of $30.9 million pesos.[49] This sum pales in comparison with the funds channeled to religious schools, which are not covered by the constitutional provision that only refers to support for religious worship. In 2010, the nation, the provinces, and the city of Buenos Aires contributed $4.2 billion pesos to some 3,500

39 Law 13,047/47.
40 Laws 14,401/55 and 14,405/55.
41 J. D. Perón, *La fuerza es el derecho de las bestias* (Montevideo: Ediciones Cicerón, 1958), p. 67.
42 A. G. Correa, *Aramburu y los católicos* (Buenos Aires: n/d, 1963).
43 *Boletín Eclesiástico del Arzobispado de Buenos Aires* (BEABA), Year I, no. 6, June 1958, pp. 62–63.
44 Ibid., pp. 62–63.
45 Ibid., p. 71.
46 Law 14,473/58.
47 Decree 10,900/58.
48 Decree 15/64.
49 Source: Secretaría de Culto de la Nación.

Catholic education institutions.[50] Reconstructing these figures is not an easy task because religious education is not disaggregated as a specific item in the budget, as a result of efforts by the Roman Catholic Church, with the argument that it is public education under private management. If these sums are brought to 2013 values, the transfer of funds to Catholic education would be somewhere between $5.1 and $6.3 billion pesos (i.e., between US$880 million and US$1 billion), depending on whether the Consumer Price Index (CPI) of the National Statistics and Census Institute (INDEC) or the CPI/9 by province is used.

Education was a private reserve for the Catholic Church, which chose all the ministers of the sector that served during the dictatorship, including Pedro Bruera, who had the support of the navy; the leader of the Christian Association of Business Leaders (Asociación Cristiana de Dirigentes de Empresa, ACDE) Cayetano Licciardo, who had served as secretary of finance in the previous dictatorship; and Juan Llerena Amadeo, proposed to Videla by Cardinals Primatesta, Aramburu, and Pironio, in a dinner at the Argentine Embassy in Rome, on occasion of the Papal inauguration of John Paul I.[51] Llerena introduced Moral and Civic Instruction as a mandatory subject in public education, based on the social doctrine of the Church and natural law, so that non-Catholic students would learn about "the conviction of the majority of the population."[52]

CONTRIBUTIONS WITH AN AGENDA

Even though the sums allotted to religious education are huge, during the terrorist state years they did not suffer significant changes. There are, however, official documents that show that the secret transfers made to certain bishops, the tax exemptions, the payment of costly trips, and the assignment of real estate and other property were explicitly intended to secure the Church's support for the most despicable policies of the de facto government.

50 Ministerio Nacional de Educación, CGECSE/SsPE/SE, DINIECE, *Anuario Estadístico 2010*. In 2010, spending on education by provincial governments, the City of Buenos Aires, and the national Ministry of Education amounted to: $67,090,011,488 pesos.

Of that sum, 13.2 percent corresponded to allocations to private education: = $8,886,295,572 pesos (in 2010).

In 2010, there were 11,548 education institutions under private management. Considering the percentages available as of 2009, 67.3 percent of all private establishments were subsidized:

= 7,772 (estimated in 2010)

As of 2009, 47.3 percent of all subsidized private establishments were religious:

= 3,676 (estimated in 2010)

= $4,203,217,806 pesos in funds transferred to religious private education (estimated in 2010) (47.3 percent of $8,886,295,572 pesos).

51 "Roma Ida," in "Pases a retiro, ascensos y libertades," *Cabildo* no. 18, 2nd era, August-September 1978.

52 "Pluralismo y libertad de enseñanza," *Criterio* no. 1813, June 14, 1979.

Lieutenant Colonel José Luis Picciuolo, the Foreign Affairs Ministry officer in charge of liaising with the Church, sponsored trips by pro-regime bishops and clergymen to the Vatican to "inform the Holy Father of how greatly concerned the government is with respect to the defense of human rights."[53] The leading among these emissaries was Primatesta, who after signing the critical document of May 1977, traveled to Rome[54] to explain to the Pope that he should not take the document too literally, and neither should he heed the reports from congregations and priests.[55] He also "informed Paul VI of the involvement of priests in guerrilla groups" and "the magnitude of the challenge posed by subversion, critical for understanding how it was combated. The pope had a warm opinion of Videla."[56] Once back in Argentina, Primatesta reported on his efforts to the dictator.[57]

These cordial relations were grounded on brick-and-mortar foundations. In September 1978, sixteen bishoprics requested the assistance of the army to build, repair, install, renovate, and maintain the property of parishes, churches, seminars, schools, and other institutions.[58] Lieutenant Colonel Picciuolo also recommended providing monetary support for works by the diocesan bishops, facilitating their travels inside and outside the country, and rendering all types of services.[59] The embassy in the Vatican suggested that "representation expenses be allocated to Cardinal Pironio, taking into account that he is the only Argentine cardinal residing outside the country. The sum should be decent and not subject to accountability requirements."[60]

According to the Foreign Affairs Ministry, the cordial entente with the Church was also furthered by the purchasing of indulgences:

- "The trips by bishops to Rome (with payment of their airline tickets) have contributed to a change of image in Vatican circles."
- "A law granting life pensions to prelates retiring for health or age reasons, which provides them with decent living conditions in accordance with their position."

53 "Informe situación actual de la Iglesia Católica Apostólica Romana en la Argentina," Culto, Box 11, Binder 15, Document 3.

54 CEA, Secretariado General del Episcopado Argentino, *Resoluciones (mayo 1972-noviembre 1981)*, Buenos Aires, 1982, p. 29.

55 "El viaje a Roma de monseñor Primatesta," *La Nación* (Buenos Aires), May 24, 1977.

56 "Síntesis del cable originado por la SS, de fecha 31 de mayo de 1977, en el cual nuestra embajada informa sobre la situación actual con el Vaticano," Culto, Box 11, Binder 15, Document 3.

57 *Córdoba* newspaper, June 7, 1977.

58 "Requerimiento de apoyo de la Fuerza Aérea a la Iglesia Católica," Memo 212 sent on September 8, 1978 by the Worship Division of the Foreign Affairs Ministry to the Third Commander of Operations of the Army Chief of Staff, Culto, Box 12, Binder 16, Document 8.

59 "Informe de la situación actual," Culto.

60 Secret telegram no. 64, April 26, 1977, Culto, Box 9, Binder 2c. Arzobispado de Buenos Aires, Document 1, Murder of Pallottine fathers.

- "An increased budget that enables coverage of border and indigenous areas, Acción Católica Argentina, and Junta de Historia Eclesiástica Argentina, in addition to Exarcado Ucraniano and Rito Oriental."[61]

In 1977, Videla created a monthly pension for life, equivalent to 70 percent of the salary of a national first instance judge, to be paid to all archbishops and bishops upon their retirement for reasons of age or incapacity, and another pension equivalent to 60 percent for auxiliary bishops. This canonry was extended to 80 and 70 percent, respectively, two years later.[62] Only three of the seventy-six bishops turned it down.[63]

In 1980, a monthly allowance equivalent to a category 16 position in the national public administration was created by Law 22,162, to be paid to parish priests in border or other areas requiring development promotion, and Decree 1991 regulated the granting of transportation tickets to bishops, heads of religious orders and congregations, priests, clergymen, consecrated laypersons, catechists, and leaders of Church associations and movements. Trips within the country would only require authorization from the National Division of Worship; trips outside the country had to be approved by the Ministry of Foreign Affairs and Worship.

In the final hours of his illegitimate administration, on March 16, 1981, Videla also established a monthly life pension for priests who, at 65 years of age, had no retirement plan. This pension could be combined with other income, up to three minimum pensions. The brief dictator general Leopoldo Galtieri extended the monthly allowance to vicars capitular and apostolic administrators. In the fashion typical of the final days of a regime, the last dictator, General Benito Reynaldo Bignone, created an allowance equivalent to a category 10 position in the national public administration to support seminarians of all dioceses and religious orders.[64]

BREAKDOWN OF POSITIONS

The appointment as economy minister of the Christian democrat lawyer and businessman José Alfredo Martínez de Hoz is a strong indication of the Church's complicity with the dictatorship. As a director of the Christian Association of Business Leaders (ACDE), Martínez de Hoz had a direct connection with the Episcopate, which had established the association with the aim of evangelizing the world of business under the guidance of a priest. The ACDE edited the magazine

61 "Síntesis de la situación actual," Culto, Box 9, Binder 2c. Arzobispado de Buenos Aires, Document 1, Murder of Pallottine fathers.

62 "Laws" 21,540/77 and 21,950/79.

63 "Los cultos no católicos," *La Nación* (Buenos Aires), August 31, 1979.

64 "Laws" 22,430/81, 22,552/82, and 22,950/83.

Empresa. Its issue number 39, published in July–August 1975, already in the midst of a conspiracy, featured an article by Martínez de Hoz on private business and the state.

Under the team headed by Martínez de Hoz, another ACDE director joined the government: engineer Manuel Solanet Estrada, who served as director of the National Institute of Economic Planning from 1977 to 1981 and in 1981 was appointed finance secretary by the next-to-last dictator, Leopoldo Galtieri. His brother, Alberto Emilio Solanet Estrada, served as president of the Corporation of Catholic Lawyers and the Association of Lawyers for Justice and Concord, which views the trials as revenge against those responsible for the dictatorship and demands a new amnesty. Both organizations were created by the Church.

A significant case is that of Louis Flynn, who was president of the transnational corporation Cargill and advisor of the Episcopal Social Pastoral Commission and as such participated in political negotiations between government officials, politicians, and trade unionists.[65] As a rule, large cereal industry operators are active in the lay bodies of the Catholic Church. The president of the rural group of the ACDE, Pablo Hary, preceded Flynn in that role and Flynn was succeeded by soy producer Eduardo Serantes. This allowed the Episcopate to be finely in tune with that decisive sector of the country's economic and social power, which simultaneously deplores poverty and taxes.

Mario Amadeo, founder of the Federal Christian Democratic Union and one of Caggiano's leading collaborators, was appointed ambassador to the United Nations. He was behind the decree that declared the death of detained-disappeared persons. Rubén M. Blanco, the brother of a priest and vice president of the Catholic University of Argentina, was named ambassador to the Vatican. Catholic magazines, both liberal and fundamentalist, were a source of advisors and government officials for the different internal lines of the dictatorship.

Miguel Ángel Iribarne was the editor of the magazine *Verbo*, where he published a "Doctrine of the Restoration," in which he declared, "the war is religious, and to ignore that is to condemn ourselves to losing it."[66] The magazine's motto was "Training for Action" and Iribarne put it into practice when he joined the cabinet of Interior Minister General Albano Harguindeguy.[67] According to Catholic fundamentalism, the positions of the liberal magazine *Criterio* were influenced by the relationship of several of its contributors, such as Natalio Botana, Carlos Floria, and Rafael Braun Cantilo, with the political team of the presidency. Two

65 "Muchos hechos en pocos días," *La Nación* (Buenos Aires), October 9, 1981.

66 "Doctrina de la restauración (I)," *Verbo* no. 161, April 1976, pp. 5–17.

67 Ministerio del Interior, Resolution 28, January 8, 1980.

of them, Marcelo Montserrat and Fermín Fèvre, even had desks at government headquarters.[68] Floria was a member of the Justice and Peace Commission of the Episcopate and at the proposal of the bishop of Avellaneda, Antonio Quarracino, he counseled the army on national policy matters.[69] In 1978, he was named Interior Policy professor in the Sixteenth Higher Course on National Defense.[70]

In 1978, the priest Eduardo de la Serna was a student at the Catholic University. That same year he had Braun Cantilo as professor in the "Virtues" course, and he recalls that Cantilo never once mentioned social justice or human rights. A member of a powerful landed family that also owned Banco Galicia, "Raffy" Braun Cantilo was a personal friend of Jorge Zorreguieta, the undersecretary of agriculture under Martínez de Hoz, and was invited by his daughter Máxima to read a biblical message at her wedding to the Dutch protestant prince. This would later generate a heated discussion in the Netherlands, when the press revealed the *Criterio* editorials that had justified repression.

REAL ESTATE

After the reconstruction of the Curia building in Plaza de Mayo was completed in 1968, the archbishopric of Buenos Aires did not return the presidential residence of 1032 Suipacha Street, which was on 2,000 square meters of land, and instead established the headquarters of the Episcopal Conference there. Cardinals Raúl Primatesta and Juan Aramburu appealed to Videla to turn the temporary assignment into a final assignment, so they could build a large conference hall, offices, and an entranceway for vehicles.[71] Before stepping down, the dictator agreed to grant the assignment.[72] Today the Episcopate runs a parking lot and a modern hotel in that space.

The de facto military mayor of the Municipality of Buenos Aires, Brigadier Osvaldo Cacciatore, had assigned the use of the restored chapel on Bernardo Houssay plaza to the Archbishopric of Buenos Aires. This chapel had been part of the School of Literature of the University of Buenos Aires and had been demolished with the aim of driving thousands of students out of the city, as these students were believed to be amongst the most willing to mobilize for political issues.[73] Cacciatore

68 A. Padilla, "Caradurismo y amnesia deliberada," *Catapulta*, April 11, 2009, available at http://www.catapulta.com.ar/?s=Marcelo+Montserrat (accessed May 17, 2015).
69 Culto, Box 9, Binder 2c. Obispado de Avellaneda, Document 4, September 1978.
70 Ministerio de Defensa, Escuela de Defensa Nacional, *Curso Superior de Defensa Nacional*, 1978 program of studies.
71 Comisión Ejecutiva de la CEA, Folder 24-II, Documents 10,955, 10,956, and 10,957, July 1978, ACEA.
72 AICA, *Boletín* no. 1269/70, April 23, 1981, p. 20.
73 "Respuesta del Señor Cardenal Arzobispo," July 28, 1980, *BEABA* no. 209, July–December 1980.

also assigned a dozen very valuable lots to the Archbishopric for the construction of "worship facilities, housing for its ministers and auxiliary personnel, and facilities for education, cultural, social, and sports activities." These properties were located at Parque Almirante Brown, in sector C, facing Dellepiane Avenue and between Escalada Avenue and Saraza and Mozart streets; between Miralla, Balbastro, and Saraza streets, adjacent on its rear with the Cardenal Copello neighborhood; between Cazadores and Mendoza streets, Francisco Fernández de la Cruz Avenue, and the public highway, between fractions A and C of block 73-C corresponding to the General Savio neighborhood; between Álvarez Thomas and Dorrego avenues; a lot facing Santo Domingo Street in the Comandante Tomás Espora neighborhood; a lot facing General Paz Avenue, in the General San Martín neighborhood; a lot facing Mariano Acosta Street, in the Soldati neighborhood; between Lafuente and Balbastro avenues; a lot on land of the former penitentiary, and another on Rivadavia and Campichuelo.[74]

When the Sacratísimo Corazón de Jesús school requested that it be exempted from payment of its utility bills, and the state-owned water and sanitation company asked to see a balance sheet approved by the General Justice Inspection, the Archbishopric succeeded in having Videla and Martínez de Hoz issue a decree exempting all religious businesses devoted to worship activities plus all their "annexes or independent sectors" from payment of water and sanitation utilities.[75]

A MATTER OF RESPONSIBILITY

This active complicity with the terrorist state raises legal questions about the civil responsibility of the Church and the penal responsibility of its authorities. New developments in international law allow for the exploration of the possibility of legal action. In Argentina the priest Christian von Wernich has been sentenced to life in prison and actions have been brought against the priests Miguel Regueiro, Eugenio Zitelli, and José Eloy Mijalchyk, all of them military or police chaplains who attended torture sessions and/or pressured captives into giving information and/or were involved in illegal deprivations of freedom or in homicides. Bishop Justo Oscar Laguna was prosecuted for giving false testimony on the murder of his colleague Carlos Ponce de León. Charges were brought against Archbishop Plaza, accused of being present in clandestine detention centers, and against Cardinal Primatesta, accused of being involved in the kidnapping of children of detained-disappeared individuals, who had been taken by the task groups to the Casa Cuna orphanage

[74] AICA, *Boletín* no.1,324, May 6, 1982, p. 19.

[75] "Acerca de la reglamentación de la exención de Obras Sanitarias," *BEABA* no. 209, July–December 1980.

in Córdoba to be given in adoption to childless military couples. The three bishops died before their trials could move forward.

The archbishop of Buenos Aires, Cardinal Jorge Bergoglio – Pope Francis as of March 2013 – testified as witness in the kidnapping of two Jesuit priests, who have accused him of being the person who spread innuendo against them. The military chief of San Luis, Colonel Miguel Ángel Fernández Gez, who is serving a life sentence, accused Bishop Rodolfo Laise of having asked him to kidnap a priest who had left the priesthood to marry. But the court case is stalled because Laise is in Italy, under the protection of the Church.

Facilitating or contributing to the commission of crimes against humanity is expressly criminalized under international human rights conventions and instruments, without excluding non-state subjects from responsibility.[76] The International Criminal Tribunals for Rwanda and the Former Yugoslavia have applied this provision.[77] In addition, section 33 of the Argentine Civil Code gives the Catholic Church special status as public legal person with equal standing with the national state, the provincial governments, and the municipalities. This gives the actions of the Church a greater state character, which means the Church could be liable for the most serious consequences that apply to the actions of the state and/or its officials.

CONCLUSIONS

The political support provided by the Catholic Church hierarchy was instrumental for the success of the repressive plan implemented by the dictatorship, which acted invoking Western Christian values, in application of a counterrevolutionary war doctrine inspired by the theology of Saint Thomas Aquinas. The Episcopate kept silent even knowing in detail the criminal methods that were being used, including against bishops and priests, and collaborated in the concealment and fabrication of events. In exchange, it obtained benefits that went beyond ensuring the support

76 Convention against Torture and Other Cruel, Inhuman or Degrading Treatment or Punishment (Art. 4); International Convention on the Suppression and Punishment of the Crime of Apartheid (Art. 3(b)); Supplementary Convention on the Abolition of Slavery, the Slave Trade, and Institutions and Practices Similar to Slavery (Art. 6); Convention on the Prevention and Punishment of the Crime of Genocide (Art. 3(e)); Convention on Combating Bribery of Foreign Public Officials in International Business Transactions (Art. 1(2)); United Nations Convention against Transnational Organized Crime (Art. 5(1)(b)); International Convention for the Suppression of the Financing of Terrorism (Art. 2(5)(a)); International Convention for the Suppression of Terrorist Bombings (Art. 2(3)(a)); Protocol against the Smuggling of Migrants (Art. 6(1)(b)); Statute of the International Criminal Court (Art. 25(3)); and the Statutes of the International Tribunals for Rwanda (Art. 6) and for the Former Yugoslavia (Art. 7).

77 Akayesu case, September 2, 1998; Furundzija case, December 10, 1998; and Vasiljevic case, February 25, 2004.

of worship as prescribed under the national constitution: appointment of laymen close to the Episcopate to high government positions; tax exemptions for property not used for purposes of worship or education; airline tickets for traveling inside and outside the country; extraordinary stipends for certain dignitaries; monetary allowances or pensions for bishops, priests, and seminarians; real estate property in upscale areas, all of which constitute the economic aspect of an integral complicity.

23

The Hidden Italy Connection

Claudio Tognonato

It may perhaps not be necessary to explain why there is an entire chapter focusing on Italy in a book that deals with the relations between Argentine economy and society. That is because, despite the many kilometers that separate the two nations, there are deep ties between the two countries. Argentina is said to be the most Italian country in the world, apart from Italy, and they are believed to share both defects and virtues. Italy's presence in Argentina has been and still is decisive in all spheres of activity, and economic relations are no exception.

One of the arguments that underpin this book holds that the economy cannot be considered in isolation from either society or politics. It does not have an independent rationality that can remain autonomous as a natural law that operates relentlessly on society, because it is a human science. The father of liberalism, Adam Smith himself, did not teach economics, but ethics. At the University of Glasgow, Smith lectured on moral philosophy, and the work that first made him famous was *The Theory of Moral Sentiments*, published in 1759. There, among other issues he examined the rationality of economic agents based on the notion of sympathy. Economic laws must thus factor in the unpredictability of human actions.

Economy and society have always been present in the business exchanges and investments between Italy and Argentina, in a history formed by millions of small biographies. The economy represents an expression, a chapter in that history, which unfolded with profitable results, even under the 1976–1983 military dictatorship. This *normal continuity* in the context of gross violations of human, social, economic, and political rights committed in Argentina is the focus of this chapter.

The importance of its blood and cultural ties with Italy put Argentina in a privileged position with respect to other nations. For Italy, Argentina is not just another country: it is the country of emigration, the place where at least half of the population bears an Italian last name. What did Italy do during the dictatorship years? We could say it did little in terms of human rights, or worse, that it did business, or worse still, that it increased its economic relations. The *normal abnormality* was such in this period that it demands the establishment of a mixed parliamentary commission formed by both countries and mandated with studying the role played by Italy during that time and its responsibilities.

In contrast to similar experiences, such as the dictatorship imposed with the 1973 coup in neighboring Chile, the Argentine military dictatorship was always very concerned with its international image. It could even be said that that concern is its defining characteristic. On March 24, 1976, no tanks occupied the streets, the seat of government was not bombed, and the military did not regularly apply martial law or publicly arrest its opponents. Instead, the so-called task groups began a slow and persistent activity that sought to go unnoticed. The disappeared are the most emblematic consequence of that policy of concealment. The concern over the country's international image was such that, on several occasions, the regime hired public relations and communications firms, such as the U.S. company Burson-Marsteller, and global campaigns were conducted with the aim of improving the reputation of the military government and covering the atrocities that were being denounced.[1]

A few days after the coup, on March 30, 1976, the media announced that thirty-two countries had already recognized the new government. Among these were the United States, Britain, the Federal Republic of Germany, Italy, and the Vatican.[2] Later, in July 1976, the minister of the economy, José Alfredo Martínez de Hoz, traveled to Italy where he met with representatives of local industry and the financial sector at the offices of the AssoLombarda, the association that includes Milan, Lodi, Monza, and Brianza companies. What would have happened if the international community had condemned the junta? Sadly, we only know that that did not happen and that many years would go by in which kidnappings, torturing, and disappearances would occur on a daily basis, with a toll running into the many thousands. A long, complicit silence, both domestic and global, and even direct support for the dictatorial project were the elements that made it possible for the military junta to carry out its extermination plans with complete impunity.

P-2 IN ARGENTINA

Any analysis of Italy-Argentina relations during this period will repeatedly come across Propaganda Due (P-2), the Masonic lodge headed by Licio Gelli.[3] The height

1 See I. Guest, *Behind the Disappearances: Argentina's Dirty War Against Human Rights and the United Nations* (Philadelphia: University of Pennsylvania Press, 1990), p. 69.

2 See I. Moretti, *In Sudamerica* (Milan: Sperling & Kupfer Editori, 2000), p. 169.

3 The bulk of the documentation and information used for this chapter is the result of an international research study conducted under my coordination. Part of this material was published in C. Tognonato

of the activities of this secret lodge was the period stretching from 1973 to 1981, year in which it was outlawed by the Italian government. During those years, P-2 had an intense participation in private and public businesses between Italy and Argentina, with a clear interference in the political affairs of both countries.[4] The lodge tried to combine business and politics through different modalities and projects.

It is important to note from the start that Gelli was not merely an entrepreneur who brought together businesspersons and interests from the two countries, but an active international militant of the Italian Right and most probably an agent of the U.S. secret services.[5]

His relationship with Argentina was developed through Giancarlo Elia Valori. His brother, Leo Elia Valori, had been sent to Buenos Aires in 1948 by Enrico Mattei as representative of the oil company Ente Nazionale Idrocarburi (ENI). When Leo died, at a young age, Giancarlo moved to Argentina to take over his brother's business. There he met Arturo Frondizi, and through him he came into contact with Juan Domingo Perón, in Madrid. A close friendship was thus forged between Perón and Elia Valori, who would invite Perón and his wife Isabel to stay at his maternal home in Trastévere, Rome.

Several meetings were held between them until, in February 1973, at the Hotel Excelsior in Rome, which Licio Gelli used as headquarters, Elia Valori introduced Gelli to Perón. Also present at that meeting was José López Rega, who quickly found many points in common with Gelli. In his statement to the Commisione parlamentare d'indagine sulla P-2 (CpiP-2), Elia Valori – who Gelli ultimately expelled from P-2 – noted that on that occasion López Rega said to him laughing, "I've truly met the man of God."[6]

Still in Rome, before returning to Argentina on June 20, 1973, and through the mediation of Elia Valori and Gelli, Perón would find numerous Italian and Argentine businessmen interested in the new path that was emerging. Among these he met with Augusto Tibaldi, president of La Centrale and La Columbia (financial

(comp.), *Affari Nostri. Diritti umani e rapporti Italia-Argentina, 1976–1983* (Rome: Fandango Libri, 2012).

4 On March 17, 1981, Gelli managed to evade the police when Villa Wanda, his country house in Castiglion Fibocchi, was raided. In that raid, a list of members of the lodge was found. The names on this list are said to belong to second-tier members, or at least that there is another list with names that were not meant to be made public ever. There are a number of Argentines on the list, including José López Rega, Raúl Lastiri, Alberto Vignes, José María Villone, Emilio Eduardo Massera, Guillermo Suárez Mason, Carlos Alberto Corti, Juan Questa, Federico Lenci, César de la Vega, and Federico Barttfeld, among others.

5 There are confessions from Central Intelligence Agency (CIA) agents claiming that connection, but there is no conclusive proof.

6 The sessions of the Italian parliamentary commission that conducted an inquiry into P-2 (Commissione parlamentare d'inchiesta sulla P-2, CpiP-2) were held from December 9, 1981 to July 12, 1984. The final documentation contains 97,000 pages, gathered in 115 volumes. Most of the documentation on P-2 reproduced in these pages is taken from those records.

companies that were part of Roberto Calvi's Banco Ambrosiano group), and Agostino Rocca, president of Techint.

Before Perón returned to Argentina for good, Gelli held a celebration at Perón's Puerta de Hierro residence in Madrid to welcome the new ally to the P-2 lodge. A few days later, on June 28, 1973, the government issued Gelli an Argentine diplomatic passport (number 001 847). Under López Rega's sponsorship, Gelli was gaining increasing ground within the group of associates close to Perón, so much so that Perón awarded him the Order of the Liberator General San Martín on October 18. The irregularity of issuing a passport, and a diplomatic passport at that, to a foreign citizen was rectified when he was granted Argentine citizenship on September 13, 1974.

Licio Gelli was a key mover in the development of the continuity between democracy and state terrorism over the period that spans from 1974 to 1981. In addition to being issued a diplomatic passport,[7] on August 20, 1974, Gelli was hired by Foreign Affairs Minister Alberto Vignes – also a P-2 member – as officer in the Argentine embassy in Rome, and on September 2, Isabel Martínez de Perón promoted him to the position of "economic advisor in Italy." The military government would confirm Gelli in his post, where he remained until 1981 when the P-2 case exploded in Italy.[8] The lodge wielded a crosscutting power and could go seamlessly from advising Triple A groups to collaborating with Emilio Massera during the dictatorship.

AN ESOTERIC LINK

When this period in history is analyzed, the events that followed Héctor Cámpora's resignation as president of Argentina are often minimized. Raúl Lastiri, who succeeded Cámporas, was neither the national vice president nor the vice president of the Senate, either of whom should have taken office according to the order of presidential succession. It is often said that the reason Lastiri was chosen to succeed Cámpora was that he was López Rega's son-in-law, as if it were simply a matter of nepotism, ignoring the fact that he was also a member of the Masonic lodge. Seen from this perspective, some pieces on the board of Argentine history fade in

7 Licio Gelli actually had four diplomatic passports, issued on the following dates: June 28, 1973; November 7, 1977; July 29, 1978; and November 10, 1978. When he was arrested in Geneva, on September 13, 1982, he was carrying two fake Argentine passports. One of these passports, under the name Marco Bruno Ricci (passport number 2,148,876), had been forged at the ESMA.

8 Gelli's name does not appear in the files of the Argentine embassy in Rome, despite having had an office there for eight years. Neither is he in the Italian files that were consulted. Néstor Stancanelli and Raúl Guillermo Dejean, instead, are listed as economic advisors of that embassy.

importance while others emerge as defining, and, in this sense, the weight of P-2 in Argentina certainly gains a different significance.

It was not an alignment of the stars that caused the resignations of Cámpora and his vice president Vicente Solano Lima and the announcement by Senate vice president Alejandro Díaz Bialet on July 13 – a few hours after the resignations of the first two – that he was traveling to Brazil on an unexpected trip followed by a European tour. The esoteric link between Licio Gelli and López Rega had reached the highest levels of the state. Without calling too much attention to itself, the lodge quietly slipped into the presidency of the country. Before being sworn in as interim president, Lastiri had taken the secret oath in the P-2 lodge.

Licio Gelli was also connected with the June 20 clashes that broke out at Ezeiza between left-wing and right-wing Peronists who had gathered at the airport to welcome their leader. Perón's return was the last step in a campaign through which the lodge had insinuated itself into the leader's inner circle. According to Gelli, only Perón could prevent Argentina from going down a revolutionary path to socialism, as had happened in Chile with Allende. He was the only one who could improve the image of the discredited military and curb the popular support earned by the guerrillas. Owing to his fragile health, first, and his untimely death, later, Perón was unable to fulfill the role that the lodge had in mind for him. Gelli and López Rega thus opted for destabilization tactics, forming irregular armed groups, most notably the Triple A, to eliminate all forms of opposition through clandestine means.

After Perón's sudden death, López Rega gained even more ground and in a short time became the most powerful figure in the government. The P-2 lodge remained firmly represented in positions of power, and in 1975 López Rega succeeded in placing one of his men in the Ministry of the Economy: Celestino Rodrigo, known for his obscurantism, spiritualism, and astrology beliefs.

The process of wealth redistribution furthered since 1973 was hit hard by measures that caused a social earthquake: a 100 percent increase in public utility fees, currency devaluation, and a 180 percent rise in fuel prices. These measures triggered rampant inflation. Society seemed out of control. The country's destabilization was underway, the economy had burst, and drastic action was recommended to put things in order. It was at this point that the neoliberal program began to take shape. On the one hand, the actions of the Triple A death squads spread a climate of terror, using bombs, executions, and threats; on the other hand, unchecked inflation generated economic uncertainty. Elimination of adversaries and social exclusion and economic chaos and panic were two vital elements in pushing the country toward the implementation of "structural reforms."

Meanwhile, in Italy, the P-2 lodge also promoted "the tension strategy," a plan aimed at destabilizing the country with attacks, homicides, and terrorist acts. The goal was to generate fear over the growing support gained by the Communist Party and the possibility of a leftist government. The P-2 lodge developed a specific plan, *Il piano di Rinascita*,[9] in which it set out the steps to be taken to restore order in the country. All of this happened between 1975 and 1976, in the same period in which the Argentine military was drafting its Project for National Reorganization, and both processes evidenced two converging perspectives.

The maturity of Italy's political forces prevented a coup in that country, but for Argentina the solution was a new military government, longer and bloodier than any such government before it. When the situation reached a critical point, Gelli was able to get López Rega out of the country to Brazil, and from there to Spain, where, thanks to Manuel Fraga Iribarne's mediation, he continued on to Switzerland with false papers. In this way, Gelli was free of López Rega, allowing him, after the coup, to further his goals, now under the dictatorship.

COMMON PROJECTS

The presence of members of the lodge in both the deposed and the coup governments reveals the crosscutting nature of the project and the continuity in terms of policies. Whereas on appearance enemies, López Rega and Massera were united in Gelli's Masonic brotherhood project. The international financial institutions would come into play with a punctuality that speaks for itself: the day after the coup, on March 25, the International Monetary Fund granted Argentina a loan.

These international conditions that were favorable to the junta suffered a setback when Jimmy Carter became president of the United States and advised international financial institutions to refrain from granting any more loans to countries with a record of human rights violations. The P-2 lodge thrived as the military opened the door to private investments that, given the situation, could charge high interest rates. It was the golden era of the lodge. Banco Ambrosiano de América del Sur, founded by Roberto Calvi – one of the so-called "bankers of God," linked to the Vatican – and under P-2 control, opened its doors on January 1, 1980.[10] In Buenos Aires, the bank set up its headquarters on the ninth and eleventh floors of a building located at number 1136 Cerrito Street, where Admiral Massera had his office on the tenth floor. The position of vice chairman of the bank was assigned to one of Massera's men, a former navy officer by the name of Carlos Natal Coda.

Umberto Ortolani was another P-2 banker who, like Michele Sindona and Gelli, was willing to finance the fight against anything that could threaten

[9] The plan establishes the objectives, basis, and proposed actions for the short and long term. These documents reveal the clearly destabilizing nature of the P-2 political agenda.

[10] On June 18, 1982, Roberto Calvi's body was found hanging from Blackfriars Bridge in London. Although it was initially believed to be a suicide, it was later officially ruled a homicide. The case was never solved and is still one of the many mysteries in the annals of Italian history.

Western Christian civilization. According to statements by Sindona, gathered by the parliamentary commission, Ortolani and Gelli were interested in controlling the press and financing Argentina's military government.[11] Ortolani controlled three newspapers: *Il Corriere degli italiani* in Argentina *La Hora de Italia* in Uruguay, and *Il Giornale d'Italia* in Brazil. He also owned Banco Financiero Sudamericano (Bafisud) in Uruguay and Banco Continental in Argentina. In 1976, Gelli joined Bafisud as owner, thus consolidating P-2 hegemony in the financial sector. From that position of power, they launched an offensive and succeeded in controlling the Rizzoli publishing group and, through it, the leading Italian newspaper, *Corriere della Sera*.

Earlier, in 1970, the Rizzoli and Abril publishing houses had created the company Anesa. Abril was the leading publishing house in Argentina. César Civita, one of its founding members, had received threats from the Triple A and was forced to leave the country. After the coup, Civita thought he would be safe, but met with new threats and even an attempt on his life, which he survived unharmed. He then found out that the threats came from groups close to Massera and decided to leave Argentina again.

The pressures and fear of confiscation forced him to sign Abril over to the Crea publishing house. Crea, a company established solely with the purpose of carrying out this deal, was formed by Celulosa Argentina and Rizzoli. The agreement established a 51 percent interest for the Argentine company and a 49 percent interest for the Italian company, but a few months later Rizzoli decided to increase its capital. With a loan from Bafisud, it acquired a controlling interest in the company[12] and, with it, dozens of Argentine newspapers and magazines fell under the orbit of P-2. In *Corriere della Sera*, Piero Ottone would leave the position of editor to Franco Di Bella (another P-2 member). The Buenos Aires correspondent, Giangiacomo Foà, who had denounced the first disappearances along with the Italian consul, Enrico Calamai, was relocated to Brazil, and on the *Corriere* newspaper Argentina was pushed from the foreign policy pages to the sports section. Calamai himself would later leave the country, after having helped hundreds of people escape to safety.[13] The correspondence between Gelli and General Carlos Guillermo Suárez Mason, commander of the First Army Corps and a P-2 member, reveals Gelli's involvement in the preparations for the March 24 coup. These letters mention a meeting held on January 3, 1976, in the presidential residence of Olivos, between President Isabel

[11] Commissione parlamentare d'inchiesta sulla P-2 (CpiP-2), attached documentation, vol. III, t. VI, pp. 89 and ff.

[12] See E. Scarzanella, "L'editoria italiana in Argentina: la Rizzoli e il gruppo Crea," in C. Tognonato (comp.) *Affari Nostri*, p. 242.

[13] See E. Calamai, *Niente asilo politico* (Milan: Feltrinelli, 2006). On December 11, 2004, in Rome, the Argentine government awarded Calamai a medal for his actions during the military dictatorship.

Martínez de Perón and representatives of the three arms – Jorge R. Videla, Orlando R. Agosti, and Massera – in which Gelli appears to have participated as well. In a letter written after the coup, Gelli congratulated Suárez Mason for the great success of the uprising, which, he said, had been carried out "according to plan."

POLITICS AND BUSINESS

For years now, Italian society has been demanding the opening of files dealing with recent history. The law establishes that after thirty years the confidential classification of these files must be lifted, but government institutions ignore this provision. Italy's relations with Argentina during the dictatorship are victims of this policy of concealment. The reports and economic data that can be accessed in Italy on Argentina are limited to descriptive data, projections, and exchanges without any mention of the serious social situation of that country. After the demise of the de facto government, this period was referred to as a "dirty war" or deplored for its human rights violations, but when these were being committed, the leading economic groups, both public and private, made highly profitable deals.

Some aspects of Italy's official concerns can be glimpsed between the lines of certain reports of the Italian Trade Agency (Istituto del Commercio Estero, ICE).[14] In late 1979, the ICE bulletin described a general improvement in macroeconomic data and a reactivation of the domestic market. Assessing Argentina's prospects, it noted:

> While it is difficult to make projections, a better future can be expected from the continuity of the government, which having attained the goal of a certain degree of social peace can now apply itself with greater dedication to the country's economic problems and immense wealth.[15]

According to the ICE report, then, the "continuity" of the government guaranteed "social peace." But that government was a dictatorship and that peace was the peace of thousands of disappeared persons.

At a conference held in Rome in late 1980 on the subject "L'economia argentina oggi" (Argentine Economy Today), the institute's president, Luigi Deserti, highlighted the growing importance of Italy's relations with Argentina and the sharp increase in trade between the two countries, in particular in 1979 and early 1980.[16] For his part, Pasquale Pugliese, an officer of the Buenos Aires ICE, had no qualms about stating that "a steady growth [in that exchange] can be verified as of 1976."[17]

14 The ICE promotes and facilitates the internationalization of Italian companies around the world.

15 "Il punto sull'economia argentina nel '79," *ICE* no. 47, November 21, 1979, p. 1338.

16 In the first semester of 1980, Italian exports to Argentina grew by 45 percent. See *ICE* no. 51, December 17, 1980, p. 1415.

17 See the speech delivered by Pasquale Pugliese at the Buenos Aires headquarters, in *ICE* no. 1, 1981, p. 8.

The international strategy of P-2 was to use political relations to do business and to use business to further its political agenda. Political parties had been gutted and only survived in name, without content, like an empty shell. The lodge applied its strategy first under the democratic government and then under the dictatorship. It may be claimed that there is nothing political about economic interests and that they are not concerned with human rights abuses, that the market has no ideology and cannot be guided because it acts cyclically following its natural laws. Adam Smith's principles thus decontextualized become the bible of globalization.

In her final report, Christian democrat senator Tina Anselmi, president of the Commissione parlamentaria d'inchiesta sulla P-2, noted the enormous difficulty of investigating the international ties of the secret lodge. After gathering 115 volumes of documents and testimonies, the commission concluded that the network of connections that Licio Gelli had with Argentina must be the same or greater than that established in Italy, and therefore further investigations in that direction were recommended.

According to data from the Economic Commission for Latin America and the Caribbean (ECLAC), trade relations between Italy and Argentina during the initial years of the dictatorship increased visibly, peaking in 1980.[18] These data show that, out of all of Europe, Italy was the leading economic partner of the Argentine military government. As there are multiple elements that prove the importance of these relations, only a few illustrative cases are considered here.

According to statements by Elia Valori to the parliamentary commission, Massera traveled to Italy on October 24, 1977 and met with Prime Minister Giulio Andreotti. Both the trip and the agenda had been organized by Licio Gelli and the meeting was private, as Andreotti revealed in his memoir. The meeting was private because as the disappearances and human rights abuses in Argentina were being denounced by Italian media, a public meeting could have generated reactions or protests. Despite this, Andreotti had no problems accompanying Massera to the naval shipyards of Oto Melara to purchase weapons. The armed forces had decided to invest US$6 billion to modernize their equipment and neither P-2 nor Massera wanted to pass up the opportunity afforded by his trip. In the end, Massera did not go through with the purchase because he was met at the port of La Spezia by Italian trade unions who had been alerted to the presence of the dictator and had declared a strike in protest. Massera, offended, returned to Rome and decided against the purchase.

Some months later, with the aim of setting things right, Admiral Giovanni Torrisi (a P-2 member), chief of staff of the marine, traveled to Buenos Aires along with

18 ECLAC, *Banco de datos estadísticos de comercio exterior, División de estadísticas y proyecciones económicas* (Santiago de Chile: BADECEL).

Admiral Giovanni Ciccolo and General Carlo Foce (all members of the lodge) to sell high-precision electronic instruments, missiles, and radars manufactured by the company Selenia. The president of the company at the time, Michele Principe, also features in the P-2 lists.

Among the leading trade items between both countries were weapons. In 1980, Argentina was the world's largest buyer of Italian weapons. Considering the 1960–2000 period, weapon sales to Argentina from Italy remained steady on average, with some fluctuations but without peaking, except in 1980, when total sales were six times those of 1969, the second largest year in sales.[19]

The P-2 lodge was also involved in the deal for the purchase of French Exocet missiles. The military had requested Licio Gelli's mediation to purchase weapons. During the war, a delegation of the Argentine Socialist Party, led by Pasquale Ammirati, with the participation of Antonio and Franco Macri, met with then secretary of the Italian Socialist Party, Bettino Craxi, to ask him to intercede in lifting the European embargo. Thanks to Craxi's support, on May 17, 1982 the Italian government of Giovanni Spadolini decided to lift the embargo.[20] Because France maintained the embargo, the missiles could only be obtained through Italy, and the Argentine armed forces were willing to pay whatever sum was asked. The man in charge of the negotiations was Glauco Partel, a former U.S. marine officer, arms dealer, and Italian secret service agent. Argentina was represented in the deal by Navy Captain Carlos Alberto Corti (a P-2 member). Partel informed the British secret service and the deal fell through, but he maintained the charade until the last minute to prevent Argentina from seeking out other arms dealers.[21]

CONTRACTS AND HUMAN RIGHTS

Many arms and oil deals were conducted in triangulation with Banco Andino of Lima, another company owned by the Banco Ambrosiano group. The aim was to avoid leaving traces, as a bank linked to the Vatican could not be seen as trafficking arms. The money for financing the expansion of the Rizzoli group in Argentina was also channeled through the Banco Andino. Weapons, energy, and banks were the three strategic areas of P-2. General Suárez Mason, who was appointed to head Argentina's oil company Yacimientos Petrolíferos Fiscales (YPF), was in charge of

19 Stockholm International Peace Research Institute (SIPRI), data available at www.sipri.org (accessed February 26, 2010).

20 On May 24, Italy and Ireland cancelled the European embargo.

21 See C. Palermo, *Armi e droga. L'atto d'accusa del giudice Carlo Palermo* (Rome: Editori Riuniti, 1988). The false contracts signed by the parties are also filed under the P-2 parliamentary commission's records.

administering trade relations with Ente Nazionale Idrocarburi (ENI), a task that, as seen earlier, had previously been preformed by Giancarlo Elia Valori.

Being part of P-2 was an excellent letter of introduction for anyone wishing to do business with Argentina. That is how Lucien Sicouri, a member of the group and president of the Genoa-based Italimpianti, was awarded the contract for the construction of the Embalse Río Tercero nuclear plant, in the province of Córdoba. This agreement is particularly interesting for understanding the role of the lodge.

On December 20, 1973, a contract was signed by the consortium formed by the companies Atomic Energy of Canada Limited (AECL) and Italimpianti. Shortly after the works began, the military coup was staged and Gelli appeared as guarantor and mediator between the Italian company and the military. In this way, he assured both parties that the contract signed by José Ber Gelbard, the economy minister of the deposed government, would be the honored, and he gave military protection to the project.

In March 1981, the police raided Licio Gelli's villa and the P-2 case exploded in Italy. That same month, in Argentina, Martínez de Hoz and Videla stepped down from their posts. It may have been a simple coincidence, but – in any case – these events closed a cycle of national and international alliances and counter-positions. Massera was accused of having promoted Licio Gelli's appointment as economic advisor and of having issued him forged passports.

The Italian government did not do as much as it could have during the dictatorship. The news of what was happening in the country were featured in Italian newspapers, and the Radiotelevisione Italiana Spa (RAI), the official broadcasting company, illustrated what was already emerging as a brutal violation of human rights. However, economic interests prevailed. Argentine exiles in Italy were not granted asylum and for years they had to regularly renew their visas, like any tourist. There were also economic agreements, official visits, and a heavy silence on the part of the government. For anyone who called for solidarity with Argentina, even obtaining a parliamentary motion to denounce the situation or signatures for an open letter were huge feats. In this sense, there was one case that stood out, prompted by an international denunciation. The Comitato Antifascista contro la Repressione in Argentina (CAFRA), which gathered Argentine exiles, had filed a petition to denounce the situation in Argentina. It took months to raise the money to publish the petition as a paid ad and to gather the signatures of representative figures from politics, culture, and Italian institutions. One of the personalities who signed it was Giovanni Spadolini, in his capacity as secretary of the Republican Party. By the time the petition was published in the Argentine newspaper *Clarín*, Spadolini was prime minister and his signature was harshly criticized by the Argentine armed forces.

When the parliamentary commission received his testimony, he was asked if he had been aware of what was happening in Argentina while he was prime minister, and he answered: “Yes, I knew perfectly well what was happening, so much so that I had signed an international petition in defense of human rights in Argentina and because of that signature a major commercial operation of the Ansaldo company fell through.” Spadolini explained, moreover, that he believed the petition had actually been orchestrated by the secret service of some European country interested in foiling the Italian Ansaldo deal. In fact, the CAFRA petition had simply sought to denounce the disappearances.

This event is very representative because it synthesizes the position of Italian institutions, which were willing to denounce the human rights abuses, provided such denunciation did not interfere with business. This may not be surprising in the world of realpolitik, but if economic rationality is not limited, it is useless to talk about rights.

In Argentina, the armed forces imposed a bleak social calm, transforming the country into a huge “economic laboratory for neoliberalism.” Without strikes or trade unions or internal commissions, with the social variable out of the way, companies were free to increase their profit margins unchecked. The slightest protest could be reported as subversive and whoever furthered it would join the ranks of the thousands of disappeared.

In 2000, the first trials for disappeared Italian citizens reached the sentencing stage in Italy. While at that time it was impossible to hold such trials in Argentina, in Italy these trials were conducted correctly, duly, and timely. Although in Rome the accused military officers were judged and convicted, they remained free in Argentina. The verdicts could never be enforced because Italy did not issue any formal extradition requests.

At the same time, on August 6 of that year, Major Jorge Olivera, Suárez Mason’s defense attorney and a P-2 member, was arrested in the Fiumicino airport. Interpol had put out a warrant for his arrest as he was wanted by France for the disappearance of Marie Anne Erize, a French citizen. He was held in the Rome jail Regina Coeli, but a few weeks later he was released and immediately put on a flight back to Buenos Aires. The photocopy presented to an Italian court to obtain his release was clearly fake, but by the time the forgery was confirmed, Olivera was safe and sound, enjoying his freedom in Buenos Aires.

24

The Lawyers: From Repression to Neoliberalism

Horacio Verbitsky

It is to this government's economic policy that we must look for an explanation not only of its crimes but also of a greater atrocity that punishes millions of human beings with premeditated poverty. In a year you have cut the real wages of workers by 40%, reduced their participation in the national income to 30%, raised from six to eighteen the number of daily work hours required for a worker to pay the family basket, thus reviving forms of forced labor that are not found even in the last surviving strongholds of colonialism. By freezing wages with the butts of your rifles while prices surge at bayonet point, abolishing all forms of collective bargaining, prohibiting assemblies and internal commissions, extending workdays, hiking up unemployment to a record 9 percent and promising to increase it even further with 300,000 new layoffs, you have set back production relations to the beginning of the industrial era, and when workers have tried to protest you have labeled them subversives, with whole teams of delegates being kidnapped, in some cases turning up dead, in others not turning up at all. … Dictated by the International Monetary Fund based on a recipe applied indistinctly in Zaire or Chile, Uruguay or Indonesia, the only beneficiaries recognized by the economic policy of this Junta are the old cattle-raising oligarchy, the new speculative oligarchy, and a select group of international monopolies headed by ITT, Esso, the automobile companies, US Steel, and Siemens, to which Minister Martínez de Hoz and all his cabinet members are personally linked. A 722 percent increase in the prices of animal products in 1976 defines the scale of the oligarchic restoration undertaken by Martínez de Hoz, in line with the creed of the Rural Society as expressed by its president, Celedonio Pereda: "It boggles the mind how certain small but active groups keep insisting that food items should be cheap."

Rodolfo J. Walsh, Open Letter to the Military Junta, March 24, 1977

With very few exceptions, the Argentine lawyers who represent foreign companies in claims against the state before the arbitration panels of the World Bank, the Paris Chamber of Commerce, and the United Nations, either sit on the board or are members of the tiny and elitist Bar Association of the City of Buenos Aires (Colegio de Abogados de la Ciudad de Buenos Aires, CACBA) and the Forum for the Study of Judicial Administration (Foro de Estudios sobre la Administración de Justicia, FORES).[1] To this day, both organizations support impunity for the crimes of the terrorist state, the economic policy applied by that state, the repression of its social consequences, and the accessory role played by judicial, media, and business interests in covering up the crimes. They also defend the deregulation, liberalization, and transnationalization policies of neoliberalism and oppose any expansion of rights.

This is another way of establishing the identity of the social bloc that endorsed the civilian-military-business-ecclesiastic dictatorship in the 1970s and the adoption of the Washington Consensus policies in the 1990s. It also denotes the consistency between the policies developed in the two periods. None of these policies would have been possible without the dictatorship's prior destruction of the economic, social, and organizational foundations that in the two decades that preceded it had enabled a hegemonic tie between opposing alliances, as described by Guillermo O'Donnell, Juan Carlos Portantiero, and Eduardo Basualdo.

In fact, the prevalence of arbitral awards over national jurisdiction originated in one of the first decisions of the military junta, which amended section 1 of the Civil and Commercial Code of Procedure only a week after taking power. The original wording of this section prevented any action on property and financial matters "by foreign judges or arbitrators acting outside the country."[2] The amendment decree was signed by Economy Minister José Alfredo Martínez de Hoz. A few days later, the dictatorship created nine honorary commissions mandated with providing advice in pending trials involving large companies, which were for the most part transnational corporations.[3]

Martínez de Hoz declared that such actions should not be turned into "easy fodder for demagogy at the expense of the true and healthy interests of the country, which are above sectorial interests."[4] The Buenos Aires Bar Association was also a recruiting ground, then, for the civilians who contributed to these commissions, which had the mission of favoring the transnational corporations involved in litigations. Members of the CACBA were appointed as defense counsels in three such commissions: Alberto Rodríguez Galán, Alejandro Lastra, and Horacio García

[1] The source for all the data on the processes of the World Bank's International Center for Settlement of Investment Disputes (ICSID), the International Chamber of Commerce in Paris (ICC), and the United Nations Commission on International Trade Law (UNCITRAL) is the National Treasury Agency (Procuración del Tesoro de la Nación). The information on CACBA and FORES members was obtained from these bodies' own publications and registries.

[2] Decree-Law 21,305, April 30, 1976. Published in *Boletín Oficial*, November 6, 1976.

[3] Decree 223, April 27, 1976. Published in *Boletín Oficial*, May 3, 1976.

[4] "Comisiones de Asesoramiento," *La Nación* (Buenos Aires), May 14, 1976.

Belsunce. In addition, each commission had a colonel, a navy captain, and an air group captain, all of them with business expertise.

Until his appointment as minister of the economy, Martínez de Hoz had been president of the energy company Compañía Ítalo Argentina de Electricidad. Although he excused himself from taking part in the honorary advisory commissions,[5] he issued guidelines for them and directed their work, in which for ethical reasons he could not participate and which constitutes a historical model of predominance of sectorial interest over the national interest. Juan Carlos Casariego de Bel, an economy ministry official who claimed the Ítalo company was not worth more than US$8 million, disappeared on June 15, 1977, as he set out to meet with Martínez de Hoz's vice minister, Guillermo Walter Klein, and the state ended up paying US$400 million for the company.[6] After the dictatorship, a congressional investigating committee was formed to review this statization.

In 1984, as this committee was conducting a search in the law firm of Guillermo Walter Klein and Héctor Mairal, José Alfredo Martínez de Hoz (Jr.) and Mariano Grondona (Jr.) slipped out through the service door with two suitcases full of documents. Two hundred files were later recovered at a relative's home and enabled the reconstruction of capital flight operations conducted through that and other law firms, whereby money from Argentine nationals deposited in banks outside the country were considered loans that, once absorbed by the state, swelled the foreign debt that conditioned the post-dictatorship democracy.[7]

That first decree signed by Martínez de Hoz made it possible two decades later, at the height of neoliberalism, for President Carlos Menem to sign the Convention for the Settlement of Investment Disputes Between States and Nationals of Other States (ICSID Convention) in 1991. Congress then ratified fifty-six bilateral investment treaties (BITs), most notably with the United States, Spain, France, Great Britain, Germany, Italy, and the Netherlands, with the declared aim of protecting foreign investments from the risk of discriminatory treatment or denial of justice by the national state.

The relinquishing of sovereignty that these bilateral treaties entail prevents Argentina from setting targets in production, exports, domestic supplier integration, or reinvestment of utilities for any company from those countries that operates in Argentina. One of the many drafts prepared by Argentina's Foreign Affairs Ministry with proposals for the renegotiation of the BITs notes that Brazil has not signed any such treaties. Martínez de Hoz's son sits on the board of the CACBA, is the editor of

5 Decree 274, April 30, 1976. Published in *Boletín Oficial*, May 7, 1976.

6 "El ejecutor del plan económico de Videla," *Página/12* (Buenos Aires), March 26, 2008.

7 Congreso de la Nación, Cámara de Diputados, *El caso Ítalo. Informe y conclusiones de la Comisión Especial Investigadora*, Buenos Aires, 1985.

the association's magazine, and represents numerous companies before the ICSID. According to Martínez de Hoz, Jr., who has specialized in transnational arbitration, ICSID awards cannot be challenged in domestic courts, but they can be invoked as a defense in an action brought in the country.[8] This strict interpretation of the (inexistent) role of national judges in the control over arbitration awards is based on another de facto government decree, signed by dictator General Roberto Viola in 1981, the year after the Vienna Convention on the Law of Treaties entered into force, which no constitutional government has amended.[9] This decree does not honor the fact that the Argentine state, as a member of the Inter-American human rights system, must give priority to the observance of human rights over the enforcement of an award when there is a conflict between the two.[10]

When ratifying the American Convention on Human Rights in 1984, the Argentine government made a reservation that has been ignored by international arbitrators in cases arising from the economic crisis of the turn of the century. Pursuant to that reservation, still in force today,

> The Argentine Government establishes that questions relating to the Government's economic policy shall not be subject to review by an international tribunal. Neither shall anything that the national courts may determine to be matters of "public utility" and "social interest," nor anything they may understand to be "fair compensation," be considered reviewable.

In the Yaciretá case, an administrative litigation court found that national judges could have control over international arbitration proceedings in those cases in which a constitutional provision is affected. This sets a significant precedent, as because of a decision issued by an Argentine judge the International Chamber of Commerce in Paris suspended an arbitration that benefited an international consortium.[11] Human rights treaties, for their part, constitute applicable law in foreign investment matters and cannot be ignored by arbitrators.[12] The ICSID is also an inadmissibly opaque body in terms of accountability, publicity, participation,

8 V. Macchia and J. A. Martínez de Hoz, Jr., "La reciente doctrina de la Corte Suprema en los fallos Cartellone y Bear Services y los laudos del CIADI," *Revista del Colegio de Abogados de la Ciudad de Buenos Aires*, December 2005, pp. 59–62.

9 Decree 1042, August 18, 1981. Published in *Boletín Oficial*, August 27, 1981.

10 I/A Court HR, *Sawhoyamaxa Indigenous Community v. Paraguay*, 2006.

11 Juzgado Contencioso Administrativo Federal no. 3, ruling by Judge Ernesto Marinelli, "Entidad Nacional Yacyretá c. Eriday y otros," September 27, 2004.

12 See B. Simma, "Foreign Investment Arbitration: A Place for Human Rights?" (2011) 60(3) *International and Comparative Law Quarterly*, 573–596. And more broadly, Ú. Kriebaum (ed.), "Aligning Human Rights and Investment Protection," (2013) 10(1) *Transnational Dispute Management (TDM)*.

unification of jurisprudence, provisions on lack of independence, and conflicts of interests of its arbitrators.

THE BUENOS AIRES CITY BAR

The CACBA is the smallest body representing the legal profession, but it is also the most powerful, as it gathers the partners of the leading law firms, whose clients include major foreign corporations, in which those same lawyers have served as CEOs and/or sat on their boards. In April 1979, five members of the New York City Bar Association visited Argentina to investigate reports received from a number of Argentine colleagues, such as human rights campaigner Emilio Mignone. The mission was formed by former judges such as Marvin Frankel, Harold Healy Jr. of the prominent law firm Debevoise, Plimpton, Lyons & Gates, the former president of the association, Orville H. Schell, and the members Stephen Kass and Scott Greathead. These Wall Street lawyers put together a list of 190 Argentine colleagues detained during the state of siege, half of which were disappeared.

The mission found that "practicing law in Argentina today is not easy," and that labor or criminal lawyers run the risk of being disappeared if they defy official practices. Both the larger Buenos Aires Bar Association (Asociación de Abogados de Buenos Aires) and the Argentine Federation of Bar Associations (Federación Argentina de Colegios de Abogados, FACA) did all they could to obtain the release of some lawyers, and they "denounced specific acts of violence against the legal profession."

> [But] the group that could have made a difference is the Bar Association of the City of Buenos Aires, the leading organization of the local legal profession. Its president and steering committee cordially received us and listened with respect to our points of view. The representatives of the Bar declared that, as a matter of doctrine, it agreed that all citizens, even "subversives," had the right to know the charges against them, to have a prompt and fair trial with the assistance of a defense counsel, and to receive humane treatment in jail. However, they told us that the observance of such details would have to wait until a firmer victory over the terrorists had been secured, after which a gradual reinstatement of the rule of law would be feasible.

To explicitly convey that opinion, they gave their visitors a copy of an August 22, 1978 declaration, in which CACBA commended the armed forces for having restored order "in a technically irreproachable way," and stated that "in the war there are wounded, dead, and disappeared on both sides, the side of the subversives and the side of the liberators." The visitors concluded that CACBA's leading concern was "left-wing terrorism," against which they considered "the dirty war a deplorable but necessary and justified response."

FORES

The New York City Bar delegation also met with "a vigorous and active group of young lawyers members of FORES." For them too, "the horrors of the 'dirty war' were, if not justifiable in theory, they were at the very least necessary" and, in any case, less important than judicial reforms. "What most shocked us was how a significant number of our colleagues apparently consented to the current state of unlawfulness." However important the administrative reform of the justice system may be, "it does not justify ignoring the substantial problems listed in this report," the Wall Street lawyers concluded.[13]

FORES is a lobbying group formed in October 1976 to, in its own words, "respond to the anti-Argentina campaign" in line with "the spirit that guides the Process of National Reorganization," as the dictatorship chose to be known.[14] One of its founding members was Jaime Lamont Smart, who as interior minister of Buenos Aires organized the Conferences on Judicial Reform summoned by FORES in 1977 and 1978, presided by Generals Albano Harguindeguy, Manuel Ibérico Saint-Jean, and Oscar Alfredo Saint-Jean, and sponsored by the steel company Acindar and the U.S. embassy.

In 2012, Smart was sentenced to life in prison on fifty-seven counts of kidnapping and one count of homicide. His accusers included the sons of editor Jacobo Timerman, Héctor and Javier Timerman. There are also investigations still underway concerning the former president of the CACBA and lawyer of the newspaper *La Nación*, Roberto Durrieu,[15] and the justice minister under dictator Jorge Videla, Alberto Rodríguez Varela. They both served as general attorneys in the province of Buenos Aires during Timerman's illegal deprivation of freedom and the torture he suffered.

For the CACBA, these investigations are a "political persecution" based "on vengeance and inequity."[16]

[13] The Association of the Bar of the City of New York, *Report of the Mission of Lawyers to Argentina, April 1–7, 1979*, May 22, 1979.

[14] FORES, *Declaración de principios*, 1976, public deed no. 796, and *Conclusiones de la Segunda Conferencia sobre Reforma Judicial*, Mar del Plata, October 12–15, 1978, p. 224. See N. Baruch Bertocchi, *La cara civil de los golpes de Estado* (Buenos Aires: Galerna, 1988), pp. 133, 165–166, 202. The FORES and Bar quotes for which no source is indicated are all taken from this book.

[15] H. Verbitsky, "De eso no se hablaba," *Página/12* (Buenos Aires), September 23, 2007.

[16] CACBA, "El CACBA ante la detención de funcionarios civiles del gobierno militar," May 7, 2008, *La Hoja on-line* no. 125, October 2009, available at www.colabogados.org.ar/la-hoja/declaracion.php?id=65 (accessed May 18, 2015).

At the 1978 Conference on Judicial Reform, FORES president Horacio Lynch declared that "a war has been won" and that in the development of the military junta's political plan lawyers "must make an essential contribution to the men of arms." In 1979, FORES informed the Inter-American Commission on Human Rights that the justice system in Argentina "had never been more independent," and the president of the CACBA, Manuel V. Ordóñez, said the human rights situation was much worse in the United States than it was in Argentina.[17] When they testified in the military junta trial, in 1985 Ordóñez and fellow CACBA officer Ernesto O'Farrell defended again the actions deployed against "terrorist aggression."[18]

Placing itself to the right even of the dictatorship, FORES questioned the "Final Document" with which the last military junta tried to justify the method of forced disappearance of persons, because the text failed to analyze "the reasons for abandoning legal forms of repression."[19] In a book that justified the illegal repression methods used, FORES stated that when an armed group "snatches a young man from his home and guns him down," the responsibility is of "the teachers who poison their [those young men's] minds." It found the report of the committee set up by President Raul Alfonsín to investigate the fate of the disappeared (CONADEP) ideological, incomplete, and deficient, because it did not explain the phenomenon of subversive violence and presented the victims as "innocent persons."[20] Lynch went as far as praising South Africa's apartheid justice system in the magazine of the CACBA.

The positions of both bodies regarding the present are consistent with their positions during the dictatorship. In February 2003, the City of Buenos Aires Bar (at the time headed by Durrieu) demanded that the government apply a "heavy hand" to deal with the roadblocks of "those calling themselves *piquetero* groups," who according to the CACBA were guilty of "the crime of sedition."[21] In 2008, however, it supported the agricultural business chambers, which in addition to blocking roads, threatened to cut distribution and leave the cities without agricultural products. In a statement signed by its president and secretary, Enrique del Carril and Héctor Huici, it called the export tariffs applied by the government "arbitrary measures," as

[17] "Sobre derechos humanos y el futuro democrático habló Ordóñez," *Convicción*, September 16, 1979.

[18] H. Verbitsky, "Nueve acusados pero una sociedad enferma," *El Periodista de Buenos Aires* no. 34, May 3–9, 1985, pp. 7–8.

[19] "Declaración de FORES. Critica el documento de la Junta sobre la subversión," *La Nación* (Buenos Aires), May 19, 1983.

[20] FORES, *Definitivamente … Nunca más (La otra cara del informe de la CONADEP)* (Buenos Aires: FORES, 1985); and "Severa crítica al informe de la CONADEP," *Clarín* (Buenos Aires), April 4, 1985. See Baruch Bertocchi, *La cara civil*, pp. 127–128, 149.

[21] "Reclamo del Colegio de Abogados," *La Nación* (Buenos Aires), February 27, 2003.

they expressed "the hegemonic tendency of the central government," and it urged legislators to vote against the government, regardless of their "party loyalties."[22]

Huici is a partner in the law firm M. & M. Bomchil Abogados,[23] which represents companies in actions brought against Argentina in the ICSID, namely CMS Gas Transmission, which obtained a favorable award for US$133 million, and Enron, which obtained US$106 million in an award that was later annulled. Rabbi and right-wing legislator Sergio Bergman,[24] who was invited by the CACBA to a camaraderie lunch, rewrote the lyrics of the national anthem substituting "Security" for "Liberty," criticized the use of Central Bank reserves to service the public debt instead of turning to voluntary credit markets, and exhorted "the opposition to .. promptly recover the democratic and republican form of government."[25] In addition, the CACBA considered that the detention of José Alfredo Martínez de Hoz on charges of instigating the illegal deprivation of freedom of businessmen Federico and Miguel Ernesto Gutheim during the dictatorship constituted a "repression system based on revenge."[26] It also condemned same-sex marriage,[27] and the Supreme Court ruling that ratified that all terminations of pregnancies resulting from rape are considered non-punishable abortions.[28]

FORES's positions on this subject are inspired by the Corporation of Catholic Lawyers, which responds to the *longa manus* of the Episcopate. In 2010, this corporation created an Association of Lawyers for Justice and Concord (Asociación de Abogados por la Justicia y la Concordia), which operates as a pressure group against the trials for crimes against humanity. Conceived to attract liberal sectors without appearing too ecclesiastic, the new association is formed by FORES and CACBA leaders, including its presidents Enrique V. del Carril and Eugenio Aramburu, the editor of the CACBA magazine and member of FORES's National and Transnational Arbitration Committee, José Alfredo Martínez de Hoz, Jr., lawyers of large transnational corporations, former government officials who served during

[22] CACBA, "El CACBA ante el conflicto entre el campo y el gobierno nacional," March 28 2008. Public statements by the Bar Association of the City of Buenos Aires, *Revista del Colegio de Abogados de la Ciudad de Buenos Aires*, 2008, pp. 97–104, available at www.colabogados.org.ar/larevista/articulo.php?id=76&pag=97 (accessed May 18, 2015).

[23] M. & M. Bomchil Abogados, "Abogados," available at www.bomchil.com/cv.aspx?AbogadoID=463 (accessed May 18, 2015).

[24] "155° Almuerzo de Confraternidad. Rabino Sergio Bergman," *La Hoja on-line* no. 112, June 2007.

[25] CACBA, "Repudiable medida de gobierno que acentúa la declinación institucional," March 2, 2010, available at www.colabogados.org.ar/posicion/declaracion.php?id=110 (accessed May 18, 2015).

[26] CACBA, "Connotaciones del caso Martínez de Hoz," May 7, 2010, available at www.colabogados.org.ar/posicion/declaracion.php?id=115 (accessed May 18, 2015).

[27] CACBA, "Matrimonio civil: ante la reforma legal en curso," May 6, 2010, available at www.colabogados.org.ar/posicion/declaracion.php?id=114 (accessed May 18, 2015).

[28] CACBA, "Errónea decisión de la Corte," March 22, 2012, available at www.colabogados.org.ar/posicion/declaracion.php?id=142.

the dictatorship, participants in the armed uprisings against the constitutional governments, and relatives of individuals arrested for the crimes whose prosecution they contest.

THE PARTNERS OF FOREIGN CAPITAL

The actions brought by businesses against Argentina total some US$17.167 billion in damages,[29] plus interest for the years since the 2002 devaluation. Calculating the interest is complicated because each contract establishes different conditions, but applying the Libor rate it would amount to US$4.375 billion.

There are already rulings against Argentina totaling US$1.495 billion, plus interest.[30] Two arbitration awards rendered in favor of Enron and Sempra, were later annulled and Siemens desisted from receiving the damages granted on another award, with which the awards pending total US$1.043 billion. Other proceedings have been suspended through settlements between the parties, which are negotiating new contracts; some cases were awarded in favor of the country; and in several cases, the proceedings are still underway and are at different stages (decision on jurisdiction, determination of damages, reconstitution of the panel, annulment of the action).

ICSID arbitrators understand that BITs entail a complete relinquishing of sovereignty. A recent award even ruled that the BIT in question had been breached by a press conference in which a prime minister criticized the inefficient administration of the potable water supply service provided by the private investor.[31]

The facts indicate that the system of international arbitration is dominated by a small club of lawyers with strong ties to law firms in the northern hemisphere, and with a structural bias toward benefiting claimant investors[32] from developed countries.[33]

29 The total amount of US$17,167,313,006.47 includes amounts in pesos, euros, and pounds converted to dollars. In some actions, the amount claimed is stated as "undetermined," so that the final amount is greater. In the actions in which the amount claimed fluctuates between two sums, "depending on the method adopted for calculating damages" (Enron, Propyme, Pan American), the average of the two sums is considered.

30 This includes the conversion of sums in pesos. The total is US$1,495,102,835.03.

31 ICSID, *Biwater Gauff v. Tanzania*, award rendered on July 24, 2008.

32 See the report by P. Eberhardt and C. Olivet, "How Law Firms, Arbitrators and Financiers are Fuelling an Investment Arbitration Boom," Corporate Europe Observatory and the Transnational Institute, Amsterdam-Brussels, 2012.

33 G. Van Harten, "Pro-Investor or Pro-State Bias in Investment-Treaty Arbitration? Forthcoming Study Gives Cause for Concern," International Institute for Sustainable Development, Winnipeg, April 2012, available at www.iisd.org/itn/2012/04/13/pro-investor-or-pro-state-bias-in-investment-treaty-arbitration-forthcoming-study-gives-cause-for-concern/ (accessed May 18, 2015).

Argentina has suffered this biased system of dispute resolution. Even though, with the aim of overcoming the economic catastrophe of 2001, the government adopted general emergency measures that affected both national and foreign investors alike, the ICSID considered that, in almost all the cases brought before it, Argentina had discriminated against foreign investors. The ICSID did not take into account the state of necessity arising from the national emergency. Decades before, to come out of severe crises, the developed countries implemented norms that benefited the general interest and affected individual property rights, without generating massive compensations for investors. The same is happening now with the global economic crisis. Nobody even thinks of challenging the United States for the measures it took during the 2009–2012 crisis to save U.S. automobile companies without benefiting their Japanese counterparts.

Eduardo Roca, an honorary CACBA member and former ambassador to the United States under the de facto government of General Juan Carlos Onganía, boasted at a conference that in 1966 he had recommended the ousting of elected President Arturo Illia. Roca claimed that under Onganía, Argentina was "truly governed by the rule of law."[34] Three decades later Roca participated as an expert witness for Banco Santander Río in its claim against Argentina in the International Chamber of Commerce. That bank is a donor for special projects implemented by FORES.

Another honorary member of the CACBA, Eduardo Aguirre Obarrio, defense minister under the de facto presidency of General Alejandro Lanusse in 1972, was charged for the Trelew massacre (that the CACBA calls "alleged homicide"),[35] but he died in September 2011, before he could be tried. Aguirre Obarrio was introduced as expert witness by TSA Spectrum in a claim brought before the ICSID for US$510 million.

Lawyers from the Pérez Alati, Grondona (h), Benites, Arntsen & Martínez de Hoz (h) law firm,[36] a CACBA sponsor, claimed a total of US$5.198 billion in different proceedings for the companies Wintershall (German oil company), MASA and MEDA (both owned by ExxonMobil), El Paso Energy and Pan American (oil, gas, electricity), the U.S. reinsurance company RGA, the shareholders of Aguas Provinciales de Santa Fe and of the former Aguas Argentinas Suez and Vivendi (France), AGBAR and Interagua (Spain), and the British company AWG, as well as an additional US$1.3 billion on behalf of the group of 75,000 Italian bondholders grouped in a mass claim known as "Matilde Abaclat" (formerly "Giovanna Beccara").

34 Quoted in Baruch Bertocchi, *La cara civil*, pp. 112–116.

35 CACBA, "El CACBA frente a los sucesos de Trelew," March 17, 2008, *La Hoja on-line* n° 125, October 2009, available at www.colabogados.org.ar/la-hoja/declaracion.php?id=62 (accessed May 18., 2015).

36 PAGBAM Abogados, "Socios," available at www.pagbam.com.ar/?modulo=abogados&cat=0. (Aaccessed May 18, 2015).

The law firm that Rodolfo Barra shares with CACBA member Luis María Fernández Cronenbold represents the interests of two groups of Italian bondholders in claims brought before the ICSID for 21 million euros and US$1.7 million, respectively ("Giovanni Alemanni" and "Giordano Alpi"). As the author of the legal doctrine of intangibility of compensation for the individual co-contractor, Barra was the organic intellectual of the "contractor nation" that under the dictatorship favored and justified the depletion of the state by large economic groups, invoking the guarantees of equality before public burdens and of sanctity of property rights, established under articles 16 and 17 of the national constitution. Accepted by the Supreme Court, the new doctrine reduced the risks for contractors to an absolute minimum just as the oligopolization of large public works was starting, with an annual rate of inflation of more than 100 percent. Barra forgot that, having been a Supreme Court justice, he is morally inhibited from litigating against the national state.[37]

Mairal & O'Farrell, a law firm that sponsors the CACBA and a FORES donor, represents nine claimants against Argentina (Sempra Energy, El Paso, DaimlerChrysler Services, Impregilo, HOCHTIEF, Siemens, CMS Gas Transmission, Matilde Abaclat, and British Gas Group). Francisco Macías, a partner in the same law firm, represents the BC Group in a claim before UNCITRAL.

The former secretary of the Supreme Court of Justice, Guido Tawil, is one of the representatives of the law firm M. & M. Bomchil Abogados, which participates in some of the largest cases in terms of claims: Siemens (US$550 million); Enron (US$546 million); Azurix (US$566 million); CMS Gas Transmission (US$243.6 million); and Camuzzi Internacional, which controls several electric energy distributors and carriers (US$215 million). Tawil, Máximo Luis Bomchil, and Máximo José Bomchil sat on CACBA committees and are lecturers at FORES. Another partner at that firm is Rafael Mariano Manovil, who is a lawyer in the Siemens case and appeared as an expert witness in the URBASER and Aguas de Bilbao cases.

Ricardo Ernesto Barreiro Deymonnaz, former senior associate at Estudio Allende & Brea and current partner at Rattagan, Macchiavello, Arocena & Peña Robirosa, represents EDF International SA and Electricidad Argentina SA (in a claim for US$833 million plus interest) and EDF International SA, Saur International SA, and León Participaciones Argentinas SA (US$255.5 million plus interest). The senior partners in both law firms (Teodosio César Brea and Gabriel Ricardo Macchiavello) are CACBA members, and the Estudio Allende & Brea law firm is a sponsor and donor of both CACBA and FORES.

37 "Duras críticas contra Bossert," *Diario Judicial*, February 16, 2006, available at www.diariojudicial.com.ar/contenidos/2006/02/17/noticia_0003.html (accessed May 18, 2015).

Valeria Anabela Dentoni, of Bruchou, Fernández Madero & Lombardi (a firm that is part of the Pro Bono Work Commission of the CACBA and is a donor and sponsor of FORES), represents Teinver, Transporte de Cercanías SA, and Autobuses Urbanos del Sur, who claim US$1.036 billion. Another lawyer who represents these companies is Horacio Fargosi, a CACBA member. Sergio Le Pera, also a member of the CACBA, brought a claim for US$335 million on behalf of the bankrupt paper company Papel del Tucumán. Ignacio Colombres Garmendia, a member of FORES's National and Transnational Arbitration Committee, obtained a favorable award for Compañía de Aguas del Aconquija and Vivendi Universal for US$105 million plus compound interest.

Also prominent on the list of litigators against the Argentine state are Emilio Cárdenas and Juan Carlos Cassagne, CACBA and FORES members, officers, benefactors, and lecturers. When they were partners, they brought a claim before the United Nations Commission on International Trade Law (UNCITRAL) for US$600 million on behalf of Bank of Nova Scotia. Cassagne was legal director of the Economy Ministry during the first months of the dictatorship and later collaborated with Barra and Roberto Dromi (who had been mayor of Mendoza during the dictatorship) in designing the privatizations of the 1990s.[38] One of Cassagne's partners today is his son Ezequiel, and another is Máximo Fonrouge,[39] current CACBA president. Fonrouge and another member of the law firm, Patricio García Moritán, brought a claim for US$149 million on behalf of Asset Recovery Trust SA. Ezequiel Cassagne participated as counsel and his father as expert witness in the claim brought by National Grid PLC before UNCITRAL, in which Argentina was ordered to pay US$53.6 million plus interest and lawyers' fees. María Agustina Fanelli Evans, of the O'Farrell law firm, also worked in that case. Uriel O'Farrell is a member of the International Institutional Relations Commission of the CACBA and a FORES lecturer. Julio César Durand, a member of the CACBA represents Spanish and French water companies that are claiming US$265 million before the ICSID and US$1.6 billion before UNCITRAL.

CACBA member Ángel Alberto Bartolomé Bianchi is counsel or expert witness for companies that claim more than US$2 billion from the Argentine state. Diego Bunge, a member of both bodies, was presented as expert witness by Continental Casualty Company, which had brought a claim for US$69 million and obtained US$2.8 million. The counsel in that claim was Roberto Alejandro Fortunati, whose law firm merged with Bécar Varela's firm, a CACBA and FORES sponsor. Leandro Héctor Cáceres, a partner in the Brons & Salas law firm, a CACBA benefactor,

[38] "Dromi pisa el acelerador," *Página/12* (Buenos Aires), August 30, 1989.

[39] Cassagne Abogados, "Los abogados," available at www.cassagne.com.ar/equipo.asp?tipo=socio (accessed May 18, 2015).

was not as fortunate: he represented Metalpar and Buen Aire SA, which claimed US$18 million, but the award was favorable to Argentina.

For both the CACBA and FORES that past time was the best. From the start of Néstor Kirchner's presidency, they opposed every one of his initiatives in economic, justice, security, and human rights matters. FORES challenged the appointments of successive General Attorneys Esteban Righi (arguing that the 1973 amnesty law and the dissolution of the Federal Criminal Court that he approved as Interior Minister "destroyed the legal means for combating terrorism, thus contributing to the subsequent illegal repression"), Alejandra Gils Carbó (for her bad relationship with the Federal Court for Civil and Commercial Matters)[40] and of Justices of the Supreme Court Raúl Zaffaroni (because he "focuses his attention on the rights of the accused") and Carmen Argibay (for her position on abortion),[41] In March 2007, FORES accused the Executive of threatening and pressuring judges and jeopardizing judicial independence.[42] In 2009, the CACBA declared that the Judiciary Council's investigation into the Court of Cassation for delaying repression cases harmed the independence of the Judicial Branch.[43] In 2012, the CACBA alerted that "the Republic is being trampled" by the "flagrant pressure campaign" carried out by the government against the judges involved in the dispute with Grupo Clarín,[44] and that "fear will soon overtake the country,"[45] which for the CACBA is circumscribed to the financial district (the "City") of Buenos Aires.

[40] *La Nación*, August 7, 2012.

[41] FORES, "¿Es Zaffaroni el juez que la sociedad argentina necesita?," *Boletín FORES*, July 2003, available at www.foresjusticia.org.ar/boletines/2003/JULIO.htm (accessed May 18, 2015); "FORES ante las postulaciones de los Dres. Esteban Righi, Carmen Argibay y Elena Highton," *Boletín FORES*, April 2004, available at www.foresjusticia.org.ar/boletines/2004/Abril.htm (accessed May 18, 2015).

[42] FORES, "Se está asfixiando al Poder Judicial," *Gacetillas*, March 29, 2007, available at www.foresjusticia.org.ar/noticia_detalle.asp?IdNoticia=118&IdTipoNoticia=1&TipoGacetilla=G (accessed May 18, 2015).

[43] CACBA, "La independencia del Poder Judicial una vez más agraviada," March 3, 2009, *La Hoja on-line* no. 125, October 2009, available at www.colabogados.org.ar/la-hoja/declaracion.php?id=87 (accessed May 18, 2015).

[44] CACBA, "El avasallamiento de la República, una instancia cada vez más próxima," October 31, 2012, available at www.colabogados.org.ar/posicion/declaracion.php?id=159 (accessed May 18, 2015).

[45] CACBA, "Declaración pública," September 7, 2012, available at www.colabogados.org.ar/posicion/declaracion.php?id=155 (accessed May 18, 2015).

Conclusion

Outstanding Debts to Settle: Work Agenda

Horacio Verbitsky and Juan Pablo Bohoslavsky

Having enhanced our knowledge and understanding of the role played by the economic accomplices of the dictatorship, the next step is the full attainment of the goals of transitional justice (truth, justice, memory, reparations, and institutional reforms). This requires adapting the current tools of transitional justice (or designing new ones if necessary) to incorporate economic complicity into its universe.

This final chapter proposes a number of instruments for discussion that serve that general objective, and looks at the possible political and economic effects that could arise from their implementation. The proposed measures are classified here according to the goals of transitional justice, but these categories are for illustrative purposes only and are not meant to rigidly compartmentalize such measures, as most of them serve more than one of those goals.

Holding the economic accomplices effectively accountable fulfills a mandate of international law whereby those who contribute to the perpetration of the most heinous crimes must be punished. As examined throughout this book, making economic accomplices accountable also entails establishing stricter rules for economic agents operating in the country today, toward guaranteeing that such events will not be repeated in the future, thus consequently reshaping national economy. This could involve a risk in terms of sovereignty, namely the setting of the country's economic agenda by international law – or by those who determine it. However, the approach proposed here tends to minimize that risk: the measures to be adopted to make the accountability of accomplices operative must be conceived, debated, designed, and implemented within the country with a broader sense of participation, inclusion, and transparency.

The views and conclusions presented in this chapter are solely those of the authors and are in no way intended to reflect those of the institutions with which they are affiliated.

IN SEARCH OF THE TRUTH

Although the Argentine state has implemented initiatives for investigating economic complicity, these have only covered certain sectors. The Papel Prensa investigation was limited to that case;[1] the Special Unit for Investigating Economically Motivated Crimes Against Humanity, created by the National Secretariat of Human Rights,[2] only addresses cases of dispossession of property of dictatorship victims; and the Office for the Coordination of Human Rights, Memory, Truth, and Justice Policies, established within the National Securities Commission,[3] focuses exclusively on the role of that institution and its officers during the 1976–1983 period.

Establishing a new National Truth Commission could contribute to the process of truth and memory in terms of economic complicity by integrally investigating and officially and publicly exposing the most salient aspects and the consequences of the economic, monetary, industrial, trade, and financial policies adopted during that period, and identifying companies and businesspersons and their possible contributions through the provision of goods or services, and their factual connections to the continuation of the regime and to the human rights abuses committed. Lastly, it could recommend the corresponding measures to be adopted.

The proposed commission would actually present *a* truth. Even agreeing on the facts and on the maximum importance of democratic values, the interpretation of those facts can vary depending on the analytical perspectives and the relations of forces. The official report issued by such a commission must not, therefore, entail the construction of a single and centralized system of knowledge of the facts, nor signify an end to the investigations, but instead it must be meant as a contribution to a collective and ongoing search for the truth, into which civil society, NGOs, academia, business, and political parties can bring their views, information, and even their interests.

It is worth stressing, then, that the commission should take on a single task, as its agenda would move away from the typical work connected with physical integrity and human rights violations to concentrate on more complex actions and relations, such as those involved in economic complicity. Such commission would face at least three types of challenges:

(1) Having the powers and instruments necessary to carry out its investigative mandate;

[1] Secretaría de Comercio Interior, resolution 126/2010.

[2] Unidad Especial de Investigación de los Delitos de Lesa Humanidad con Motivación Económica, Secretaría de Derechos Humanos, created by Decree 3216/2010.

[3] Oficina de Coordinación de Políticas de Derechos Humanos, Memoria, Verdad y Justicia, Comisión Nacional de Valores, created by Resolution 594/11.

(2) Overcoming the pressure from power groups who might oppose its establishment and/or work; and
(3) Finding ways to move forward once the investigative stage is completed.[4]

The commission should have access to and be able to process a very large volume of economic and political information, for which a solid, independent, and interdisciplinary body of professionals is required, along with administrative support appropriate for a task of such magnitude. It should also be given the power to resort to the justice system if any individuals, institutions, or companies arbitrarily refuse to respond to its requests.

The design, adoption, and work of the commission should be guided by the aim of enabling the greatest possible participation. It should be created by a law passed by the national Congress and be given a mandate, makeup, powers, and timetable of activities that are both flexible and realistic from a political point of view.

Finally, the inclusion of and coordination with other state bodies and agencies (fiscal, parliamentary, etc.) is crucial for attaining the objectives set and effectively implementing the recommendations of the commission.

More than three decades ago, in 1977, Professor Antonio Cassese was appointed Special Rapporteur by the United Nations Commission on Human Rights with the mandate of assessing the connection between the financial aid received by the Pinochet regime at the time and the human rights abuses suffered by the Chilean people. In his more than 260-page report, Cassese developed a sophisticated methodology for integrally measuring the impact of financial aid on the situation of human rights.[5] The work of the commission could benefit from that scientific development.

Given that the economic dimension of state terrorism in Argentina presented a clear redistributive component, tax secrecy could be lifted[6] with the aim of assessing whether the state's economic policy deliberately benefited certain social and economic groups inside and outside the country, and how it benefited them, and if those same groups provided political support to the government in return for the benefits they received (purchasing of loyalties). This measure could also be useful

4 These considerations were initially developed for the case of Brazil and were limited to financial accomplices, in J. P. Bohoslavsky and M. Torelly, "Financial Complicity: The Brazilian Dictatorship Under The 'Macroscope,'" in D. Sharp (ed.), *Justice and Economic Violence in Transition* (New York: Springer Publications, 2014), pp. 233–262.

5 A. Cassese, "Study of the Impact of Foreign Economic Aid and Assistance on Respect for Human Rights in Chile," vols. I-IV, 1978 (E/CN.4/Sub.2/412), available at http://business-humanrights.org/en/corporate-complicity-and-finance-as-a-killing-agent-the-relevance-of-the-chilean-case-full-text-requires-subscription-0#c56126 (accessed November 10, 2014).

6 This is not a novel proposal in Argentina's legal universe. The Financial Information Unit (Unidad de Información Financiera) has the power to lift bank secrecy when investigating "suspicious operations" (Law 25,246/2000, sec. 14(1)).

in terms of not forgetting or concealing the participation and support of national groups that benefited from the regime.

The criminal trials already held and those that are still underway offer another window for obtaining more details on economic accomplices. These trials could provide material information on how the crimes investigated were supported and facilitated by a web of economic complicities, to help complete the puzzle of the narrative and promote a broader scope of justice in the country. In that way, the criminal trials against perpetrators of violent crimes could leverage more comprehensive accountability processes, as by evidencing the role of economic accomplices – who may or may not be defendants in such trials – they would force the development and application of proper mechanisms for channeling that economic dimension in a transitional justice perspective.

As progress in the efforts to further the accountability of economic accomplices has been fragmented, and many of the developments have been scattered and unconnected with each other, there should be a repository of documentation and information on cases and court actions connected with the issue, so that victims, academics, government officials, and interested parties can access systematized data easily and free of charge.

PROMOTING JUSTICE

Several chapters have presented the legal arguments that would make it possible to bring legal action against those considered accomplices. In this aspect, Argentine law is in line with international human rights standards. Similarly, the effects of the passage of time on the possibility of bringing action, both in civil and in criminal courts, was also examined and it was concluded that the possibility is still open.

Thus, in extreme cases, criminally prosecuting accomplices (who can be considered instigators, collaborators, accessories, etc.) and obtaining a conviction is a possibility that is still available. Civil actions for damages can also be brought against accomplices, potentially generating a concrete dissuasive effect on economic agents. Even if seeking economic accountability in court were not in order, there would still be the possibility of bringing an action with the exclusive aim of learning the truth about economic contributions and how they helped in the consolidation of the regime,[7] as knowing the truth is a goal in its own right.

7 UN Commission on Human Rights, "Study on the Right to the Truth Report of the Office of the United Nations High Commissioner for Human Rights," UN Doc. E/CN.4/2006/91, February 8, 2006.

As can be seen, the role played by judges is key in terms of furthering justice with respect to accomplices, as well as in terms of generating proper dissuasive signals for the future.

FORGING MEMORY

The commission could recommend changes in the curricula of contemporary history courses with the aim of incorporating the economic dimension of state terrorism. Cultural projects could also be implemented, with public and/or private funding, to show and remember the role of economic accomplices in the context of the dictatorship.[8] Museums and other public spaces could add information on the subject, as is currently the case with the permanent exhibit of the External Debt Museum in Buenos Aires.[9]

Another instrument could be the placement of plaques and other commemorative elements placed in physical spots that witnessed the disappearance of workers (factories and company premises). Also in the business associations (chambers) that were involved as accomplices.

As workers and their representatives were the leading victims targeted by repression, and given the fact that in many cases this was due to the complicity of their employers, and that part of the top authorities of the labor movement were also complicit in these crimes, first-, second-, and third-tier labor organizations could conduct projects for studying, systematizing, disseminating, and remembering these events and facts.

COMPENSATING DAMAGES

Considering that the compensations granted to victims by the state were standardized and limited, it would still be possible, in theory, to bring civil actions for damages against accomplices, depending, of course, on the circumstances of each case. Business operators who were divested of their properties and have received no compensation could also bring actions for the crimes committed against them. While state compensations in these cases could be subject to the same limitations noted earlier, the accomplices and beneficiaries of such theft operations should pay compensation in the same measure as the economic damage caused.

Another form of reparation for the victims is the issuing of public apologies by the companies – and/or the chambers that represent them – who were guilty of

8 An example of this is the Cinema for Truth project implemented by Instituto Cultura em Movimento and supported by the Amnesty Commission of the Ministry of Justice of Brazil, which screens movies and promotes debates in universities, including the 2009 documentary *Cidadão Boilisen* on the role of private companies in the financing of the crimes of the Bandeirantes Operation in São Paulo.

9 Museo de la Deuda Externa Argentina, organized by Universidad de Buenos Aires. For further information on the museum see: www.museodeladeuda.com.ar (accessed November 10, 2014).

complicity, including by acknowledging the facts and assuming their responsibility in them.[10]

Apologies may seem, prima facie, a meaningless measure and, therefore, may be easily accepted by companies. Without prejudice to the personal compensation that such apologies may mean for the victims, the acknowledgment of illegal behaviors in the past could entail legal consequences in terms of responsibilities.

INSTITUTIONAL REFORMS FOR NON-REPETITION

Reforms at the regulatory level can be introduced to deter future complicit economic behaviors. This could be done, for example, by incorporating rules into the Civil Code that stipulate the nullity of monetary obligations contracted by the state during an authoritarian period, provided certain objective characteristics are present and without requiring additional evidence in terms of the subjective element (objective responsibility).

The statutory limitation of civil actions derived from serious human rights violations – that is, the denial of compensation to those same victims by reason of the passage of time – can entail damaging the right to adequate compensation, promoting impunity, and preventing access to reparatory justice. For these reasons, the relevant sections of the Civil Code should be amended to reduce the obstacles that stand in the way of accessing justice when it comes to bringing claims against perpetrators of crimes against humanity and/or their economic accomplices.[11]

It can also be established that any companies that contributed to the regime cannot operate in the country and/or contract with the state. This measure is aimed at generating a dissuasive effect: being an economic accomplice of authoritarian governments would mean risking the possibility of doing business in the country and/or with the state.

The issue of responsibility for economic complicity also underscores the importance of putting in place programs for conducting background checks to prevent accomplices in human rights violations from occupying public positions.[12]

10 Article 22(e), Basic Principles and Guidelines on the Right to a Remedy and Reparation for Victims of Gross Violations of International Human Rights Law and Serious Violations to International Humanitarian Law, December 16, 2005, United Nations General Assembly resolution, UN Doc. A/RES/60/147.

11 See, for example, the proposal for non-applicability of statutory limitations to civil actions arising from crimes against humanity presented by Centro de Estudios Legales y Sociales (CELS) to the Bicameral Commission for the Reform, Updating, and Unification of the National Civil and Commercial Code, dated August 22, 2012.

12 See A. Maye-Rieckh and P. de Greiff, *Justice as Prevention: Vetting Public Employees in Transitional Societies* (New York: Social Science Research Council, 2007).

As Argentina has signed dozens of bilateral investment treaties that are still in force, incorporating such a clause in these treaties[13] would serve as a warning that investments that strengthen a criminal regime and facilitate human rights violations will not be protected by those same treaties. This is in line with the Constitution reformed in 1994, which established in its Article 36 that anyone who commits an act of force against the institutional order and the democratic system shall be banned for life from public office and be ineligible for pardon and commutation of sentence, and shall be civilly and criminally responsible for their participation in actions that shall not be subject to statutory limitations.

REALPOLITIK: RESPONSIBILITY FOR COMPLICITY AND ECONOMIC POLICY

Would the country's economy grind to a halt if any or all of the measures proposed here were incorporated into Argentina's political agenda and later implemented? To address this question we need to analyze the object of these measures and how they would affect each complicit company, in particular, and the functioning of the economic system, in general.

The measures aimed at learning all the facts and completing the historical puzzle do not, in principle, have direct economic consequences for the accomplices. In this sense, while it is reasonable to expect resistance to these initiatives from those implicated, such resistance will be grounded on a desire to keep the truth of the heinous acts of the past from being known, and in the current context this can hardly be translated into political or economic arguments that can be justified or aspire to universality.

In contrast, the measures with a financial impact in the short term (such as compensations) or in the medium term (institutional reforms) will probably be met with open objections from those affected and their allies. If holding economic accomplices accountable and reforming the regulatory framework touches the nerve of the privileges and the socioeconomic tensions that contribute to explain the motives for the 1976 coup, and which have persisted for decades, the opposition to such measures will possibly be colored by economic policy arguments aimed at spreading and generalizing the fears of the accomplices so that they are internalized by all other market operators as fears of their own. As explained later in this Conclusion, for that reason the definition of the object, scope, and sequence of the transitional measures that affect economic accomplices needs to be pondered with the utmost scientific and political rigor.

[13] B. Choudhury, "Exception Provisions as a Gateway to Incorporating Human Rights Issues into International Investment Agreements" (2010–2011) 49 *Columbia Journal of Transnational Law*, 670.

Complicit companies that operate in markets in which the political stains of the past can have corrosive effects on their current profit and loss accounts may show an interest in accepting – and even furthering – policies aimed at their effective reconciliation with the victims, the state, their clients, and public opinion.[14] Starting in 1995, and over several years, the banks that contributed to the government of Nazi Germany suffered a very damaging public campaign in the United States for their complicity with that regime and for resisting the claims for compensation. That public pressure was decisive and forced the banks to accept a billionaire reparation agreement in favor of the victims.[15] Thus, the coordinated economic behavior of consumers and users, based on moral reproaches aimed at companies for their past conduct, can contribute to hold economic accomplices accountable.

At a more general level, as transitional justice mechanisms promote and strengthen the rule of law, with obvious positive implications in terms of development (predictability, stability, responsibility, etc.),[16] the opportunity costs that furthering such an agenda could entail would be offset by that institutional, and presumably economic, spillover effect.

From a perspective limited to the analysis of consequences, in deciding the content, scope, and sequence of the transitional measures to be implemented, a complex assessment must be undertaken, including considerations regarding the foundations of the country's economy, the degree of dependency with respect to the possible accomplices, the perception of the rule of law by other investors, the opportunities that an accountability scenario would open for business, the mutually beneficial effect between economic development and justice, and the way in which transitional measures influence each other.

The latest quantitative studies have shown two simultaneous tendencies.[17] First, that the scope of transitional justice measures is proportional to the economic growth and development of the countries in question. Second, that the probability of implementing such measures increases as time goes by.[18] Considering the performance

[14] M. Rulli and J. Justo, *Guía de derechos humanos para empresas. Proteger, Respetar y Remediar: Todos Ganamos*, guide issued by Red Argentina Pacto Mundial, United Nations Development Programme, Buenos Aires, 2012.

[15] S. Eizenstat, *Imperfect Justice: Looted Assets, Slave Labor, and the Unfinished Business of World War II* (Cambridge, MA: Perseus Books Group, 2003); B. Neuborne, "Holocaust Reparations Litigation: Lessons for the Slavery Reparations Movement" (2003) 58 *New York University Annual Survey of American Law*, p. 615.

[16] J. Alexander, "A Scoping Study of Transitional Justice and Poverty Reduction," Department for International Development (DFID), London, 2003.

[17] T. Olsen and others, "At What Cost? The Political Economy of Transitional Justice" (2010) 6(1) *Taiwan Journal of Democracy*, 165–184.

[18] In contrast to what had happened in past decades, the Buenos Aires stock market index (Merval) increased by 1 percent on June 15, 2005, a day after the Supreme Court of Justice confirmed the nullity of the Due Obedience and Full Stop Acts. See T. Olsen and others, "Taking Stock: Transitional Justice and Market Effects in Latin America" (2011) 10(4) *Journal of Human Rights*, 521–543.

of the Argentine economy in the past ten years and the time that has passed since the restoration of democracy, the prospects for the agenda proposed here are promising.

Another factor that influences the will and decision to hold the economic accomplices of the dictatorship accountable lies in a greater and better understanding of the role played by such actors during that period. This book aims to contribute in that direction.

Index

For EU product safety concerns, contact us at Calle de José Abascal, 56–1°, 28003 Madrid, Spain or eugpsr@cambridge.org.

www.ingramcontent.com/pod-product-compliance
Lightning Source LLC
LaVergne TN
LVHW011531200926
848484LV00001B/224
* 9 7 8 1 1 0 7 1 1 4 1 9 7 *